Infrastructure

Space

Edited by
Ilka & Andreas Ruby

Including a Visual Atlas
Compiled by Something Fantastic

Ruby Press

Freeways are the cathedrals of our times.
—David Byrne, *True Stories*, 1986

Is infrastructure but the plumbing and wiring of the human environment, or is it the true lifeblood of the spaces we inhabit? Infrastructural systems facilitate the flow of anything from people and goods to resources and information. While engineered to perform an array of specific tasks, such networks also determine the structure of buildings, cities, and metropolitan regions, if not of entire nations and the planet itself. Yet these vast service armatures tend to be pushed to the background, remaining out of sight as long as they function, as the common observation goes. They are the products of generic protocols often applied irrespective of contextual specificities and eventual environmental consequences. Ubiquitous and anonymous, they have become so ingrained in our lives as to steer the habits of collective behavior. Infrastructure, in this sense, could be considered a conduit of conduct, an underlying logic of space that perpetuates unchecked conventions of production and consumption.

Since infrastructure is the embodiment of long-term investments, its impact in determining the organization of flows extends well into the future, for developed and developing countries alike. Whereas the former are confronted with the need to maintain and renew highways, electrical grids, sewage systems, and the like, the latter are scrambling to meet the needs of their own expanding populations. In both cases, massive investments for retrofitting or for new infrastructure are key to sustaining the human habitat. Faced with the challenges of unsustainable practices on a world scale, infrastructure must be seen as key to reorienting our ways of inhabiting the globe. It must, therefore, be regarded as more than a mere servant to utility; it must become responsive to cultural and contextual distinctions, and be reclaimed as a truly public resource.

To make these broad objectives achievable in the first place, infrastructural systems—whether centralized or decentralized— must be viewed as more than a technical issue, and treated equally as a social issue in scope and design and a common good in an ecology of interrelationships vital to furthering life. This is to say, infrastructure development and renewal is a powerful but greatly underutilized agent for making and altering space. With this opportunity in mind, the roles of infrastructure will have to be expanded and renegotiated up front as both a technical *and* social matter of concern for all, claimed not only as the means for achieving more resilient forms of development, but moreover as a right to a sustainable way of life. Having moved to the front of the stage as a social, economic, and political imperative, forms of physical infrastructure will also have to be considered in terms of their civic value and aesthetic impact if they are really to be "the cathedrals of our times."

Infrastructure for whom, to what end, by whom, where, and how?

Contents

Infrastructure as Thing

Document:
Africa's Infrastructural Appetite
Carlos Lopes

Infrastructure as Network

Infrastructure as Agency

Infrastructure Takes Command: Coming out of the Background

Marc Angélil and Cary Siress

Desire is part of the infrastructure[1]
—Gilles Deleuze and Félix Guattari

In the mid-1950s, a young Jean-Luc Godard—years before Godard became Godard—traveled to a remote spot high in the Swiss Alps to join crews working on the construction of one of Switzerland's largest infrastructural projects, the Grande Dixence hydroelectric dam. Godard became ever more engrossed day by day with the epic scale of the task at hand. After having been transferred to a less demanding job on site as a switchboard operator, he soon came upon the idea to document the dam's construction, which provided the material for his debut film, shot with a borrowed 35-millimeter camera. The short documentary, entitled *Opération béton,* was based on the two-page script "La Campagne du béton" that had been hastily written by a companion also working on the dam, whose felicitous turn of phrase translates as 'The Campaign of Concrete' or 'The Concrete Countryside.' The double entendre —implying both military-like logistics and an engineered transformation of the Swiss landscape—says much about the role of concrete

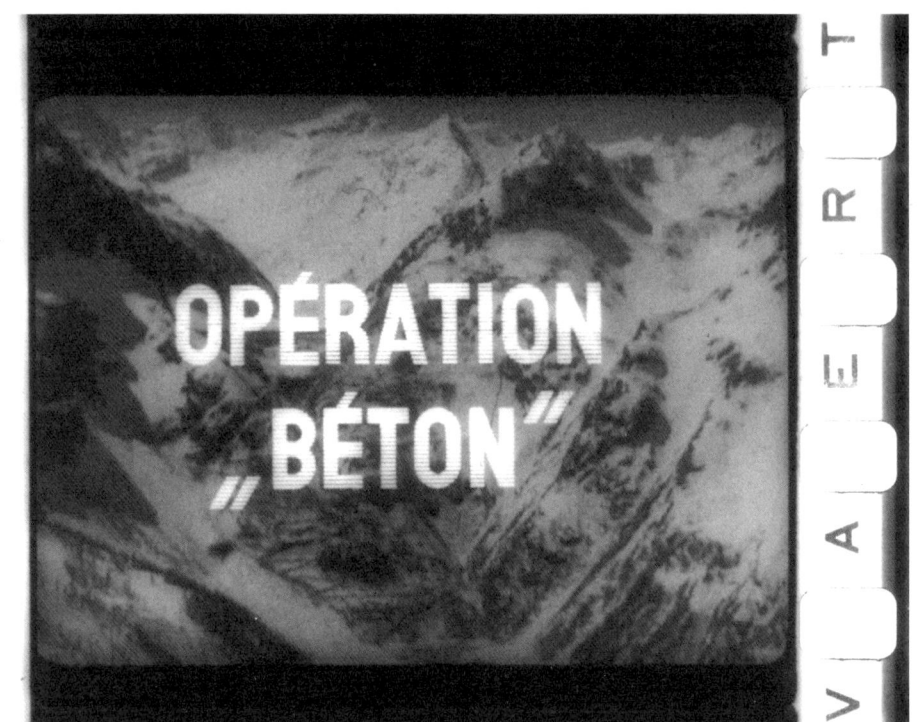

Fig. 1: Title shot of *Opération béton,* 1954-55, documentary by
Jean-Luc Godard filmed on the construction site of the Grande
Dixence hydroelectric dam in the Swiss Alps; original script by
Jean-Pierre Laubscher entitled 'La Campagne du béton' dated
October 17, 1954 and translated as 'the campaign of concrete'
or 'the concrete countryside'; cinematography by Adrién Porchet;
released in 1958.

in facilitating the urbanization of the small Alpine country in the ensuing decades, a process led primarily via the construction of such grand infrastructural projects as the Grande Dixence.

Opération béton begins with a scene showing the imposing mountain range of the Alps, followed by a quick cut to the dam underway, a montage meant to put the man-made feat on par with works of nature as if confirming—in an almost Freudian way—that "where nature was, there infrastructure shall be."[2] And so we find ourselves "at an altitude of 2,500 meters where a thousand men are fabricating a wall of concrete as high as the Eiffel Tower."[3] So begins the opening lines of Godard's upbeat foray into the production of what, in effect, induces the sensation of an engineered sublime, the qualities of which the filmmaker narrates strictly through numbers: so many tons of earth moved, so many cubic meters of concrete, and so many linear meters of steel reinforcement, all collected in an industry-inspired litany of figures that presumably left audiences of the time 'breathless,'; the dam required some six million cubic meters of concrete for its completion.[4] This deference to man's domination of nature apparently paid off, for Godard convinced the dam's construction company to buy the movie for a "sufficiently large sum to bankroll himself for the next two years" and with it, fund his next film.[5] Some Godard aficionados even claim that this fortuitous turn early on in his professional life furnished that thematic repertoire for which the auteur would later become known in the film industry: "labor, capital, nationalism, and the machine-like systems that surround humanity."[6]

Curiously enough, these themes, as significant as they were in his time and continue to be today, never really surface in the rather objective survey of *Opération béton*, as if Godard was blinded by the ostensibly neutral, technical aesthetic of infrastructure and saw the Grande Dixence only in terms of technology and engineering.[7] What he seems to have overlooked in the process of filming is the discretionary political power that was needed to assemble sufficient funding as well as a substantial workforce to carry out such an operation, not to mention the social and environmental impact of reformatting the Alps to become an energy-generating landscape. With this oversight, however unwitting it might have been, he failed to see the dam as one specific concretization of more diffuse "discourses, institutions, architectural forms, regulatory decisions, laws, administrative measures, scientific statements, as well as philanthropic propositions" that in tandem determine what is taken for granted and considered indisputable.[8] For the dam itself, a product of these diffuse forces, stabilized their relations in such a way as to frame the entire undertaking in the irrefutable terms of a daring public works project put to the service of a nation, as well as of the then-burgeoning European electricity grid.

Do we not to a certain extent also share Godard's nearsighted fascination with infrastructure today? Mention the word 'infrastructure,' and more than likely the first thing that routinely comes to mind is a huge dam, a large freeway, a giant power station, or the like, all just out there somewhere, simply there because they are there. Other than the occasional ribbon-cutting ceremony or inconvenient disruption, infrastructure seldom sustains mindful attention, manifesting instead the stuff of an unremarked substrate simply servicing the basic basics of everyday life, thus remaining largely inconspicuous by being always at hand and available without question. Were one to assign a color to infrastructure, it would probably be gray, as Godard would later point out in a short video from 1981 portraying the city of Lausanne in a reduced palette of blue for the lake, green for the mountains, and gray for everything in between.[9] Paradoxically, infrastructure could be said to command by virtue of its anonymity. To suggest that infrastructure might constitute the discreet conduit of conduct by determining "the gestures, behaviors, opinions, and discourses of living beings" would certainly help explain why all those services upon which our way of life depends appear as a given.[10]

What would it bring to pry into this tacit dimension so central to our identities and habits alike, to get to the rather colorless bottom of things, so to speak? Architectural historian Sigfried Giedion took just this task to hand by researching the human impact of industrialization in the nineteenth and early twentieth century, work published in 1948 as *Mechanization Takes Command: A Contribution to an Anonymous History.*[11] Rather than approach the built environment through the conventional lens of progressive, heroic episodes of technology and architecture, Giedion probes the often unspecified social and material underside of the industrialized world. Through the mirror of overlooked fragments of industrial history with an emphasis on conventional domestic life, he looks specifically at how this mechanized legacy, as unassuming as it might appear, fundamentally shaped modern orthodox dispositions. By showing how standardized everyday practices are integral to modernization, the idealized unity usually imputed via masterpieces of the architectural canon falls away. In their place, Giedion discloses a mosaic of practices that, for example, led to the conception of the assembly line, the creation of the factory worker, the automation of production processes, the introduction of mechanical comfort, and the mechanics of food production, in order to offer glimpses into how such modest practices "accumulate into forces acting upon whoever moves within the orbit of our civilization."[12]

One could argue that the scenes shown in *Mechanization Takes Command* function as a veritable 'mirror stage' for architecture and engineering, presenting both disciplines with the brute realities undergirding their idealized projections. Psychoanalyst Jacques Lacan suggested that human identity and behavior is carried by the misrecognition that arises in infancy when a child mistakes its mirror image for a unified and ideal figure, whose illusory wholeness stands in contradiction to the fragmented conditions of lived reality. By revealing an apparatus of quantifications, automations, standardizations, and other such transformative agents, it is as if Gie-

Fig. 2: Scene from the film *Pierrot le fou*, 1965, showing
a highway fragment stranded in the French countryside
with a mast for overhead high-voltage electricity lines
in the background; directed by Jean-Luc Godard;
cinematography by Raoul Coutard; produced by
Georges de Beauregard; starring Jean-Paul Belmondo
and Anna Karina.

dion entered the psyche of modern culture. He basically laid bear the forces of a 'technological unconscious' that, as infrastructural substrate, bends bodies, things, and environments around a bundle of supposedly guaranteed relationships that appear as a given.[13] In sum, Giedion presents "not the ideal, unified, and singular picture of modern society, but a fractured and exposed underside of the systems and processes producing that society."[14]

Coming back to Godard, his later movies would become more pointed in their depiction of contemporary life, with infrastructure itself taking on a role as actor in framing the adverse conditions experienced. Take, for example, the shot in *Pierrot le fou* from 1965 showing a defunct fragment of a highway overpass stranded in a field from which somehow a car has fallen to be engulfed in flames below. We are no longer in that sublime Alpine landscape featured a decade earlier, but rather find ourselves somewhere out there in a peri-urban region of France that, although remote, is clearly plugged into an infrastructural network via high-voltage electricity lines running overhead. Despite this allusion to a sense of connectivity—in this case to the power grid itself—audiences are left not so much breathless as they are clueless as to how all of these elements hang together. In effect, we come upon a random moment of encounters that do not seem to follow a coherent story line, the connective logic thereof being just as fugitive as are the characters themselves. Other Godard films of the same period such as *Alphaville* from 1964, *2 ou 3 choses que je sais d'elle* from 1967, or *Week-end* from 1967, likewise implicate infrastructure as an agent in steering the course of lives in their respective stories—the omnipotent computer in *Alphaville*, the subway connecting or separating the *banlieue* from the center of Paris in *2 ou 3 choses que je sais d'elle*, and the road as the scene of a major car crash in *Week-end*. Such works put forth a critical stance vis-à-vis an unquestioned faith in the ubiquitous signs of progress of a technologically advanced society, showing instead how society is shot through with precarious conditions of its own making that undermine the image of a perfectly functioning world. In resonance with Giedion's earlier excavation of anonymous histories of mechanization, Godard's film-ic forays into a later stage of technological dependencies and their social ramifications would seem to have put audiences of his time before a mirror of their shared condition. In so doing, he enacted through such works what could be termed an 'infrastructural mirror stage,' revealing stubborn gaps between narratives of 'progress' that were supposed to suffice as the world's unifying plot and the ever more schizophrenic realities inhabited and produced. In place of a full-body assumed to be simply there and working, Godard presented a *mélange* of part-experiences and fragmentary circum-stances of built and lived spaces alike, hinting at a 'de-organ-ized' state where an 'organ-ized' one had been assumed.[15]

Having tapped into the infrastructural nerve of modern society, Godard began to use his art form as a proactive political tool to raise public awareness about how 'machine-like systems' have woven themselves into the fabric of everyday life to become in-distinguishable from it. In the late 1970s, he explored ways to use television as a medium for raising critical questions about its role in shaping society. The short video *Faut pas rêver*, for example, broad-cast on French Public Television in 1977, shows a thoroughly do-mestic scene with a girl sitting at a kitchen table distractedly talking to her mother while watching TV on a set situated somewhere off-screen. The video suddenly shifts from this ordinary household scene to a text that appears line by line on a screen assumed to be that of the television. The text reads: "when the left is in power, will television still have so little connection to people?" In only two shots, Godard essentially enters the medium that enters the space of every home in order to reveal the ideological functioning of TV, allowing us to see what we usually miss when caught up in this or that show, namely, an infrastructurally-induced passivity. By turning the tables on TV, what Godard seems to ask is how we can get

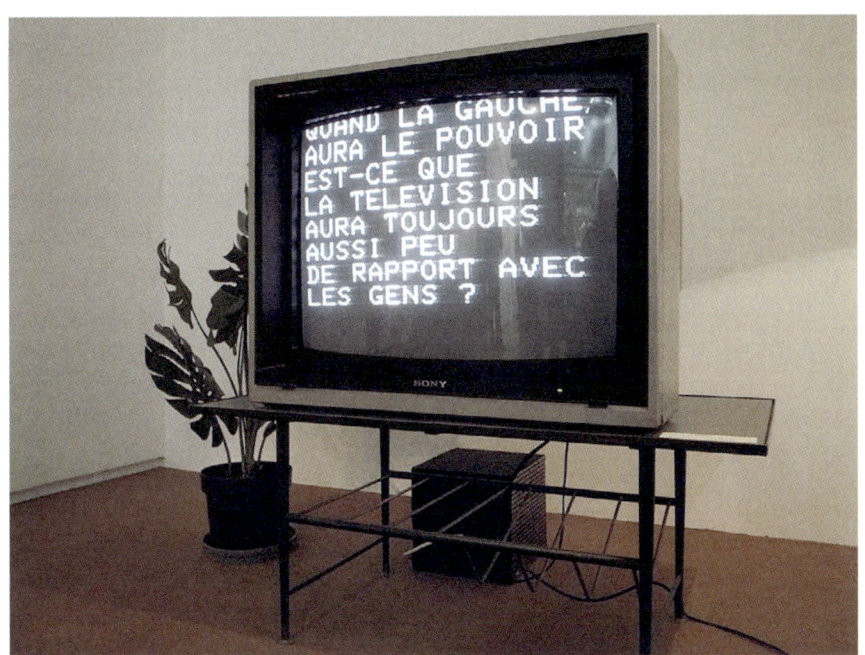

Fig. 3: Installation at the Musée National d'Art Moderne, Centre
Pompidou in Paris, 2012, with a television set showing the video
film *Faut pas rêver*, which was created by Jean-Luc Godard and
Anne-Marie Miéville in 1977 for French Public Television.

infrastructure to do more than just servicing a generally compliant society, suggesting that there is significantly more that infrastructure can really do.

With the work of Godard and Giedion in mind, we might consider what it would mean to bring infrastructure to the fore of collective consciousness today by acknowledging it as the structure of society that shapes our every way of doing things, be it for better or worse. Should we ever take it upon ourselves to ask what infrastructure can really do, we would have to recognize it, if not desire it, as something potentially more than just a mute provider of those taken-for-granted services upon which we depend. Perhaps then we would be better positioned to fathom how to reframe and reconfigure infrastructure as a common project to serve humanity as a whole. For this is ultimately what is at stake. To deploy an expanded infrastructural logic more proactively and put it to work as a public work, however, would mean that infrastructure, by definition and design, would have to go beyond its current techno-logical mandate, usually specified in particular problem-solving terms alone. Put directly, what else can infrastructure do? Insofar as this question bears on how to harness as-of-yet untapped agencies of what remains in large part a mere background substrate, and given the urgency of tackling those pressing predicaments that are becoming increasingly collective by default, then the technical mandate of solving problems will have to be augmented with more inclusive political, economic, social, environmental, and even aesthetic responsibilities. But before this can happen, it is incumbent upon us to open up new channels for cooperation and to engender a shared desire for a common project of world-making rather than one of world-draining, if infrastructure is to truly take command.

Admittedly a tall order, it is to these ends that the work assembled in this publication is committed. The subject matter of the various essays were debated at a forum entitled *Infrastructure Space* that was held in Detroit from April 7–9, 2016, and organized by the LafargeHolcim Foundation for Sustainable Construction. The conference was structured according to interrelated scales of infrastructure, with the workshops concerning the building/architectural scale moderated by Georges Teyssot and Laurent Stalder, those pertaining to the urban/metropolitan scale moderated by Jason Young and Jesse LeCavalier, those addressing the regional/territorial scale moderated by Kathy Velikov and Geoffrey Thün, and those covering the global/planetary scale moderated by Neil Brenner and Christian Schmid. In sum, the sessions took the lead in probing that gray anatomy of infrastructure space itself. As for the infrastructure of this book, its contents are arranged not so much according to predefined scalar categories as they are in consonance with thematic threads that surfaced during the event and follow-up discussions, moving—not unlike the above-mentioned phases of Godard's work—from infrastructure conceived as 'thing' to infrastructure as 'networked' system to infrastructure as 'agency'.

The essays are periodically interspersed by an 'atlas' of examples —prepared by Elena Schütz, Leonard Streich, and Julian Schubert from Something Fantastic—that playfully aims to read infrastructure through the lens of architecture.

We would like to express our deepest appreciation to Edi Schwarz and Sarah Nichols from the LafargeHolcim Foundation in Zurich who provided insight and expertise that greatly assisted the publication, Ilka Ruby, Andreas Ruby, and Fiona Shipwright from Ruby Press, as well as to Something Fantastic in Berlin who designed, edited, and produced the book. Sincere gratitude is extended to all participants whose work has contributed to bringing infrastructure out of the background.

1. Gilles Deleuze and Félix Guattari, *Anti-Oedipus: Capitalism and Schizophrenia*, trans. Robert Hurley, Mark Seem, and Helen R. Lane (London: Anthlone Press, 1984), 104; originally published as *L'Anti-Oedipe: Capitalisme et schizophrénie*, 1972.

2. Peter Sloterdijk, *Sphären* series. *Plurale Sphärologie: Band III: Schäume* (Frankfurt am Main: Suhrkamp Verlag, 2004), 554; translation by the authors. The orininal quote reads: "Wo Natur war, soll Infrastruktur werden." For the English translation, see Peter Sloterdijk, *Foams: Spheres Volume III: Plural Spherology*, trans. Wieland Hoban (New York: Semiotext(e), 2016). Sloterdijk is alluding to Sigmund Freud's well-known claim "Where id was, there ego shall be." See Sigmund Freud, New Introductory Lectures on Psychoanalysis 1933, in *The Standard Edition of the Complete Psychological Works of Sigmund Freud*, ed. and trans. James Strachey (London: The Hogarth Press, 1953-1974), vol. 12, 80.

3. *Opération béton* produced by Jean-Luc Godard from 1954-1955, based on a script by Jean-Pierre Laubscher and shot by Adrien Porchet. The documentary film was released in 1958 by Actua Films. The opening line reads: "A 2'500m d'altitude, dans le val des Dix, un millier d'hommes dresse un mur de béton aussi haut que la tour Eiffel: le barrage de la 'GRANDE-DIXENCE'." The following line reads: "Le froid rendant impossible le bétonnage, la 'campagne du béton' tient le chantier en haleine dès la belle saison et se déroule comme une opération militaire."

4. R. James Breiding, *Swiss Made: The Untold Story Behind Switzerland's Success* (London: Profile Books, 2012), 298. See also Marc Angélil and Cary Siress, "Operation Switzerland: How to Build a Clockwork Nation," in trans: *Architecture and Politics*, vol. 18 (March 2011): 64–75.

5. Colin MacCabe, *Godard: A Portrait of the Artist at Seventy* (New York: Farrar, Straus and Giroux, 2003), 84.

6. Richard Brody, *Everything is Cinema: The Working Life of Jean-Luc Godard.* (New York: Henry Holt, 2008), 33.

7. The interpretation of infrastructure in Godard's early documentary builds on exchanges with Sarah Nichols and her analysis of the film in her lecture "Opération Béton" at ETH Zurich on September 28, 2015.

8. Michel Foucault, "The Confession of the Flesh," interview held in 1977 and published in Michel Foucault, *Power/Knowledge: Selected Interviews and Other Writings 1972-1977*, ed. Colin Gordon, trans. Colin Gordon, Leo Marshall, John Mepham, and Kate Soper (New York: Pantheon Books, 1980), 194.

9. Jean-Luc Godard, *Lettre à Freddy Buache*, short video film of approximately 11 minutes, 1981; cinematography by Jean-Bernard Menoud. Godard was hired to make a documentary celebrating the 500th anniversary of the city of Lausanne. The film is essentially Godard's videotaped refusal to accept the assignment to make a promotional film as requested by city officials. The authors would like to express their gratitude to François Charbonnet for calling attention to this particular work.

10. Giorgio Agamben, *"What is an Apparatus?," in What is an Apparutus? and*

Other Essays, trans. David Kishik and Stefan Pedatella (Stanford: Stanford University Press, 2009), 14; originally published as "Que cose un dispositivo?", 2006.

11. Sigfried Giedion, Mechanization Takes Command: A Contribution to an Anonymous History (New York: Oxford University Press, 1948).

12. Ibid., 3.

13. Nigel Thrift, "Remembering the Technological Unconscious by Foregrounding Knowledges of Position," Environment and Planning D: Society and Space, vol. 22 (February 2004): 175–190.

14. Mirjana Lozanovska, "Thought and Feeling in Giedion's Mechanization Takes Command," in Proceedings of the Society of Architectural Historians, Australia and New Zealand 30, Open, eds. Alexandra Brown and Andrew Leach (Gold Coast, Queenland: SAHANZ, 2013), 889.

15. It is as if during this phase of his work in the late 1960s Godard was anticipating what Gilles Deleuze and Félix Guattari would call 'body without organs' or 'corps sans organes'. According to them, every actual body has a limited set of properties, yet is also extended via a "virtual dimension of potential traits, connections, affects, movements, and so forth." This collection of potentials is what they term a 'body without organs'. See Gilles Deleuze and Félix Guattari, Anti-Oedipus: Capitalism and Schizophrenia, trans. Robert Hurley, Mark Seem, and Helen R. Lane (Minneapolis: University of Minnesota Press, 1983), 9; originally published as L'Anti-Oedipe, in 1972. While Deleuze and Guattari were critical of the paralyzing modes of 'organ-ization' of modern society, they held out hope for ways to break out of culturally established conventions by tapping into this "collection of potentials." Concurrently, Godard was critical of the malfunctioning of modern society despite its common portrayal as being advanced yet he perhaps missed opportunities to reconsider other more nuanced functions of modern infrastructure than those for which it was designed, and to probe its "potential traits, connections, affects, movements, and so forth."

Document:

The following is the transcript of a dialogue between Cary Siress and François Charbonnet that took place on July 14, 2016. The discussion focuses on the lecture Charbonnet delivered at the 5th International Forum of the LafargeHolcim Foundation for Sustainable Construction in Detroit on April 9, 2016. In the lecture, he presented design probes from his team's ongoing exploration of plausible common ground between architecture and infrastructure. The composite structures that result are novel in this respect, bred as they are from the crossing of building practices that, by convention, most often operate in mutual isolation. Charbonnet's resourceful experimentation offers an overdue wake-up call to what should already be self-evident; namely, that while these practices still seem worlds apart, they are both working in and on the same world. By cross-pollinating discrete modes of material production, he calls attention to their untapped spatial potential when coupled and offers a vision for prolific mergers that might not only alter the profiles of design and construction industries, but the space of architecture and the space of infrastructure as well.

Shades of Gray and a Green Thumb
with Out-of-the-Blue Couplings

François Charbonnet and Cary Siress

Cary Siress (CS): I would like to open this dialogue with a reference to the short video by Jean-Luc Godard—*Lettre à Freddy Buache,* from 1981—that you used as an opening to your lecture at the "Infrastructure Space" conference in Detroit. Having been invited to make a film celebrating the 500th anniversary of Lausanne, Godard refused to comply with the host authorities to provide what was to be essentially a splashy commercial promotion of their city. Instead, he took the liberty to portray Lausanne with only the abridged palette of blue for the lake, green for the foliage of the hills, and gray for everything in between. One could say that Godard's Lausanne presents the "*oh là lame*" rather than the "*oh là là*" of the fabricated environment as originally desired by the film's sponsors, and, by this means, underscores the perennial tension between works of nature and works of man. Moreover, he wryly implicates both architecture and engineering as patron disciplines in the ongoing construction of a monotonous 'gray zone' in which buildings and infrastructure become indistinguishable, as so much colorless matter of our daily surroundings.

Notwithstanding Godard's rather drab assessment of our constructed world, your lecture seems full of hope in suggesting that architects and engineers still have much to learn from each other, especially if they would join forces in exploring timely interfaces of architecture and infrastructure. Your design research unearths an underexplored gray zone between them and, just as provocatively, your work demonstrates that the space of architecture and the space of infrastructure can be amplified through ingenious, out-of-the-blue couplings of spatial production. On the basis of this admittedly sketchy appraisal of your position, and via a somewhat rhetorical dialectic, what might constitute the gray zone between architecture and infrastructure, and why do you think that infrastructure is still usually relegated to the background of collective awareness?

François Charbonnet (FC): I am not certain how we would define what you call a gray zone between architecture and infrastructure, but our interest in infrastructure as architects, which might be contradictory to what one would normally expect from our discipline, is that infrastructure's range is truly transversal. It entangles engineering, architectural, social, technological, economic, and political issues into an amalgamated hyper-structure of material matters that concern us all. Much like the premise that the *oikos*, or economy, has overtaken the civic body of the polis, infrastructure cuts across the variegated fabric of man-made and natural systems to form an operational weave of our world. This transversal influence and impact is lacking in architecture, which is perhaps a problematic issue that must be confronted by architects. What is significant to us with respect to the so-called gray zone of architecture and infrastructure is that the latter is more intimately linked to quantifiable parameters. In distinction to architecture, infrastructure is driven by determinate necessities, by its verifiable performance, and not how it looks when performing. Considering that infrastructure stands on the evidently firmer grounds of objective specification, it takes on credibility as a general matter of fact. This stands in stark contrast to what is commonly perceived as an idiosyncratic matter of style in architecture's representative formal expressions, or is often seen as a personal matter of interest of this or that architect in responding to the contextually defined requirements for architecture. In the end, we are particularly drawn to infrastructure space insofar as it can be promoted, defended, and articulated more convincingly to a much larger constituency of spe-

III

cialists and laypeople on the shared evaluative basis of concretely measurable actions.

As to why infrastructure still remains to a large degree "backgrounded" in collective awareness, as you put it, I would reiterate that this apparently muted standing is due to infrastructure's transversality and matter-of-fact givenness. Infrastructure is so ingrained in our way of life that it is essentially everywhere. It is omnipresent and intrinsic to almost everything we do, making it therefore difficult to single out as a discrete artifact with distinct attributes at any given moment or location. It is simply there, practically unrepresentable in and of itself, which is both fascinating and alarming. It is for this very reason that architects—and perhaps engineers—tend to underestimate what infrastructure could really do for architecture in enhancing the performance and reach of situated design practices.

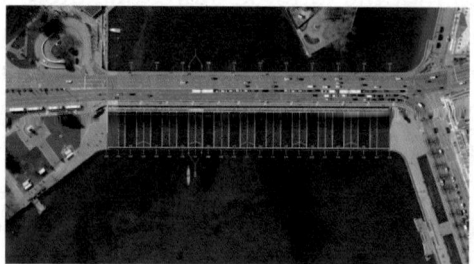

Fig. 1: Design proposal by Made In for the Mont Blanc Bridge in Geneva, 2012, diagram of flow patterns on and along the bridge structure.

CS: In one part of your lecture, you presented your project for the Geneva lakeshore, with the "gray line" of the Mont Blanc Bridge supplemented by a giant, retractable public promenade and event tarmac. The rotating cylinder that functions as a large pivotal hinge for this surface also creates a waterfall in the heart of the city to produce electricity and modulate both wind flows and traffic noise, while also providing pedestrians and commuters with a periodic attractor that is as much a work of architecture as it is of infrastructure—or, for that matter, as much a part of the cityscape as it is of the natural landscape. You use this almost whimsical, yet by no means less exhilarating design proposition, to make the serious claim that the common understanding of infrastructure—the underlying base that supports a social system and its signifying superstructure above—must be amplified by what you call a "multiplication of imperatives" to better explore other capacities of infrastructure that outperform its current status quo purposes. You also suggest that the very hierarchy according to which infrastructure is situated at the bottom of the signifying chain must be "inverted" if we are to devise more proactive roles for infrastructure that are as political and social as they are economic and aesthetic. With such bold claims you seem to imply that we have not sufficiently given untapped agencies of infrastructure their due. What is more, we have not yet brought them to bear on the more noted agencies of the built environments that we inhabit, nor have we fully considered infrastructure as a vital representative of a more extensive field of uses and users. Relative to your own body of work, what can infrastructure do for architecture, which alone is typically supposed to represent in built form, and, inversely, what can architecture do for infrastructure, which alone is usually supposed to perform as a built service conduit?

FC: As for the issues of multiplying imperatives for infrastructure or inverting the given hierarchies that tend to demote it to a subordinate rank of service functions, we can ask ourselves why infrastructure has become such a widely relevant notion today. In the nineteenth and early twentieth centuries, infrastructure was a very precise and delimited entity as that which, literally, subsided *below* the societal "structure," a "pre-work" that served that structure itself in undergirding situated domains of national (re)production. In our time of flexible labor and ubiquitous channels of control and surveillance, infrastructure has assumed the more prevalent and diffuse role of facilitating a spectacle-based and service-based global economy. Attentive to the underlying systemic shifts that have accompanied such broad changes in social and spatial organization during the past decades, we critically track, for example, the successive shifts in the role of base "infrastructure," from delivery to *monitoring*; in the role of social "structure," from supporting to *staging*; and in the role of ideological "superstructure," from signifying to *advertising*. We investigate how the amplified functions of infrastructure today might play out in building design, given that there is now hardly a form of architecture that is not somehow conscripted as a platform for monitoring, staging, or advertising. With this said, we are convinced that our field is already implicated in a performative or infrastructural "turn," whether fully recognized or not. Concerning what one branch of design and construction can do for the other, we assert that architecture can stage infrastructure and make it participate at the level of the highly visible, collectivizing "image." This would go a long way in bringing infrastructure out of the ranks of subservient provider and into the foreground as a proactive agent of influence and change. Conversely, infrastructure could contribute much-needed quantifiable degrees of agency to architecture by regrounding the more stationed, representative functions of built form in a diffuse, operative web of services, signals, stimuli, and sensations. With this said, however, I am convinced that infrastructure has largely determined the nature of the world in which architecture must now perform by raising the measurable and the quantifiable to the status of an all-pervasive standard for any design practice. If, for example, an engineer says that you need this much cable or that much volume of shaft, who is the architect to say that such quantities are unacceptable to a specific design proposition? On what basis can said architect argue against the irrefutable factuality of such requirements, on conceptual, charismatic, or creative grounds? None of these rationales are really convincing today.

Fig. 2: Upstream view of retractable tarmac that augments the functions of the existing bridge with a transformable public promenade.

CS: To some, this might sound like the confessions of a devout pragmatist …

FC: On the contrary! The still-underexplored opportunity for architects in these everyday confrontations with what is most often viewed as the gray monotony of pragmatic demands is the staging of calculable data in new performance-derived spatial ensembles. These stagings would involve much more than merely embodying an enigmatic concept in representative form or expressing the personal flair of a designer-author. The more challenging, if not enticing work entails making the pragmatic logics of constructing things exceed their specified parameters and function beyond just solving a quantified problem at hand. Sure, engineers are master problem solvers, but architects have mastered the skill of questioning given problems themselves and, in so doing, have crafted innovative research methodologies, not to mention novel modes of designing. What is just as undisputable is that the range of demands and necessities encountered in these parallel fields remains quite distinct and are often contradictory. So, there are differences between architects and engineers that do make a difference, just as there are distinctions that do count between architecture and infrastructure. Nevertheless, both disciplines, as well as both realms of spatial production, can only profit from more concerted efforts in the design community at large to pool specialized strengths and put them to work in exploratory joint ventures that might indeed break new ground in transforming those very processes by which we construct our world.

CS: Quoting Gilles Deleuze and Félix Guattari's book *A Thousand Plateaus*, you addressed Edmund Husserl's notion of "proto-geometry" in another part of your lecture. This term alludes to a now distant stock of "anexact yet rigorous" shapes—i.e., almost smooth surfaces, fairly rough edges, reasonably even planes, or nearly straight lines—that emerged from ancient human observations about the particular formal properties of things that made them useful for certain tasks. It is the cumulative knowledge gained through such primordial acts of shape sorting that, according to Husserl, established the conditions of possibility for an abstracted geometry of pure and exact forms. What seems to catch the attention of Deleuze and Guattari is the fleeting or "nomadic" sense of the exactness of proto-geometry, whose forms are no less precise in their hazy, unclean, or muted profiles because they are expressive of real but often transient desires associated with human existence. More to the point, geometry as we know it grew out of concrete trials of testing what was tangibly at hand with regard to its possible conduct as an artifact, as something *made*, rather than from some secret principle of the perfect circle, square, or triangle as reconciled, through some veiled means, in an equally idealized figure of the human body. We may well have to reasonably "freeze" the fluxes of the world through geometric form to appreciate the shape of things at any given moment, but the particular challenge for architects and engineers now is how to loosen their blinkered perspective. To do so, the cramped confines of our geometric order of things will have to be markedly relaxed to allow for more elastic modes of producing space and more adaptive means of making material form matter for larger constituencies. Can you elaborate on how the notion of proto-geometry plays out in your work, and are you advocating "anexact yet rigorous" practices of design and a proto-geometric logic of space-making?

FC: This particular quote is significant for me because it resonates with our experience when presenting the competition entry for the Museum of Fine Arts in Lausanne, or Musée cantonal des Beaux-Arts (MCBA), to a panel of jurors. Intuitively, we already had a hunch that the specific images we used to articulate the hybrid architectural and infrastructural "build" of this project could jeopardize our prospect of winning the commission, insofar as the links between the images or the rationale for their selection were not necessarily obvious at first glance. Still, for us at least, the hazy logic of our presentation afforded a constructive ambiguity that left its reading open. We showed, for example, the Uffizi Gallery in Florence and the Carson Pirie Scott building in Chicago side by side, next to photographs of the giant vaulted roof of the Galerie des Machines in Paris alongside a panorama of the Alps in Lausanne, and juxtaposed with an aerial view of the aircraft carrier USS *Ronald Reagan* at sea. These images were all interlaced with the requisite architectural plans and sections for our museum proposal, which incorporates the amalgamated logics of these man-made and geological formations and sets them into new aggregate relations. Since these highly charged images of existing things were conscientiously extracted from history and the origins of most are quite distant from us in time (and space), they tended to override the trivialities of taste that so often prevail in juried competitions, whether voiced or not. So the issue of whether a juror "liked" or "disliked" the Uffizi, the Galerie—or the Alps, for that matter—never came up.

With this visual collection, we were aiming to stimulate a collective memory of significant forms and their performance-based logics through multiple cues. We were also trying to prompt panel members to *interpret* these specific images and their possible supplementary readings relative to new demands in a contemporary setting, and not just *look* at them unresponsively with passing interest. The jurors had to actively become part of those images—that is, by projecting themselves into each one of them—which thus subtly challenged their designated roles as detached spectators. I should admit that there was a violent reaction to our presentation. Ironically, the jurors were expressly nervous for the very reason that we used real projects or existing natural elements such as those cited above to articulate our design position rather than opting for renderings of a prospective, unbuilt project through what is often called "augmented reality," whatever that really means. More than likely, juries tend to favor such hypothetical renderings due to their mediating power in turning nearly any design proposition into an instant product or icon that can be immediately evaluated at face value.

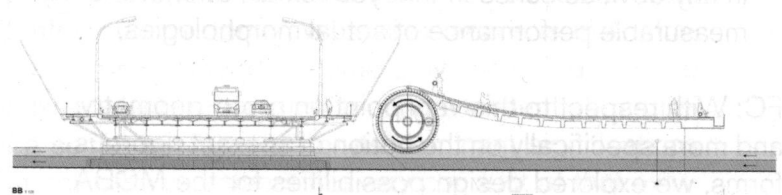

Fig. 3: Sectional drawing of the Mont Blanc Bridge and retractable event-surface whose large rotating cylinder produces hydroelectric power while also modulating noise from passing traffic as well as wind flows across the river.

what the offspring of these copulations might be, but it would be a welcome acknowledgment if one were to think that the work of our team is indicative of what such prospective crossings might yield.

If we seriously consider Teyssot's conjecture, and reflect on what cross-fertilizations of architecture and infrastructure might possibly engender, then we have to think about what it would mean to couple the logics of something as omnipresent as infrastructure with the logics of something like architecture, which is more locally bound to situated programmatic necessities. And this would require first and foremost a sober account of the true standing of architecture and infrastructure today. We as architects might very well still like to think of infrastructure as that gray subsystem of services operating below the more colorful spectrum of design pursuits that catch all the attention. Yet we might reconsider which form of material and spatial production is actually more opportunely poised to respond to the world's ever-proliferating needs.

To close with a suggestive caricature of the orthodox disposition of an architect with regard to our discipline, it is as if architecture would constitute some buoyant hot-air balloon whose eye-catching envelope is weighted down and constantly being tugged on by the infrastructure of the burner and gondola for the user-passengers below. But in our time, the inverse would seem to be a more accurate portrayal of our shared condition, with infrastructure itself as the inflated balloon that, in perpetual flight, pulls along with it the basket of architecture underneath. And where such an infrastructural turn will take us all, architects and engineers included, is still—pun intended—up in the air.

Scales of Infrastructure

Architectural, Metropolitan, Territorial, Planetary

Laurent Stalder and Carlotta Darò, Jesse LeCavalier and Jason Young,
Kathy Velikov and Geoffrey Thün, Neil Brenner and Christian Schmid

Eight Points on Infrastructure and Architecture

Laurent Stalder and Carlotta Darò

Hardly any other area of the built environment has had such a paradoxical existence as the field of infrastructure. While few other means have inscribed themselves so deeply into architecture, becoming part of our daily lives and vocabulary, infrastructure remains, in effect, an invisible presence. It's only when the system breaks down, or the connection is lost, that we become aware of it, and then usually in a negative sense. This lack of awareness seems all the more surprising given that over the last 200 years infrastructure has widely undermined the traditional conception of architecture as an enclosed space.

Indeed, the far-reaching transformation of architecture in the recent past is less the result of formal innovations such as the international style or postmodernism than a new set of fields of expertise (for instance, in hygiene), processes (for instance, in electrification or access to water), and agents (such as building, machine, or sanitation engineers) that allow the regulation of the environment, or the surroundings of buildings, through a series of new apparatuses, devices, or appliances. This expertise would bring with it a comprehensive reorganization of architecture and urban planning, and large-scale reallocations among the various practitioners. These changes, which are in the broadest sense political, have generally been linked to the development of infrastructure.

But how have these new practices changed our relationship to space? In what ways have they altered our understanding of architecture? Lastly, and most fundamentally, what does infrastructure mean in relation to architecture?

1. Infrastructure is a modern neologism. It originated with the French railways in the late nineteenth century to describe the earthworks necessary for the laying of rail tracks. Only in the postwar years did its definition expand to take in airports, oil pipelines, fuel storage tanks, and various communications and air defense systems, before it finally acquired its current social and economic meaning. With this final expansion of meaning, the term belatedly—only very recently—entered architecture, implying at the same time a division between a superstructure and an infrastructure.

2. In architecture, infrastructure does not refer to the substructure that carries a superstructure—that would be a foundation—but rather to those technical systems that are designed to optimize the use of the space and make it permeable to people, goods, media, and energy. Infrastructure does therefore not support a building, but rather its use and ever-changing conditions in time.

3. Infrastructure refers to requirements that are linked to the performance of architecture. In the first instance, this means only the individual pieces of equipment that provide for the smooth running of a building, such as the heating or ventilation systems that enhance comfort, the telephone lines that improve communication, or the water supply that ensures sanitation. These requirements have led not only to a precise regulation of the various flows (of water, electricity, people) into and out of the house, but also,

27

increasingly, to a programming of the space itself—the bathroom, kitchen, laundry room, etc. Infrastructure is thus not only a physical component or a system, but both at once.

4. What characterizes the technical object is the close monitoring of its efficiency—its many infrastructural operations (heating, cooling, ventilation, communications) all being subject to constant evaluation and optimization. Therefore, what characterizes infra-structure is the fact that the various functions of architecture—isolating, load bearing, moving, circulating, etc.—are laid out in such a manner as to render the different dimensions of existence explicit. Correspondingly, it is possible to conceive these functions individually, but also to give them form, or alter, improve on, or reject them.

5. This transformation far more comprehensively reflects the modernist attempt to objectivize the means and instruments of architecture by differentiations: between served and servant spa-ces, between load-bearing and supported elements, between ornament and structure, or indeed between infrastructure and architecture. This division finds its expression, bureaucratically, in the proliferation of safety, energy, and fire regulations and norms, but also in the increasing specialization of architectural education.

6. To speak about infrastructure therefore implies making a fun-damental distinction between different types of elements within a building. In this process, the design of infrastructure, with its sophisticated technologies, is often separated from the realm of architectural design, since it is thought to concern only isolated, specific functions of architecture, for which responsibility can only be delegated to a specialist in that field.

7. But in reality the opposite is true. Technology does not only concern specific, isolated aspects of architecture to which particular functions can be assigned, in the manner of household appliances or kitchen and bathroom fittings. Technology, in its broadest sense, is—and always has been—also the precondition of architecture. From this perspective, infrastructure is no longer to be seen as a product of modernity's civilizing march, but rather must be understood in a much broader cultural and historical context, as a technology or tool used to provide for human needs or alleviate scarcities.

8. In its etymological sense, technology means artistry. It denotes the capacity, using the means of a given time and place, to not only find a concrete solution for a problem, but also to give it a meaning. In this way it helps to reassert, as shared experience, the aesthetic dimension of life. For what technology is doing is not only representing a new reality, but helping us to decipher that reality.

The Metropolitan Relational Matrix

Jesse LeCavalier and Jason Young

The more immediately apparent infrastructures of roads, bridges, and conduits tend to carry with them perceptions of permanence and weight. More nimble forms are entangled with these sunken infrastructures, which are political as much as they are digital and physical. Through these intersections, infrastructure—perhaps imagined as a precondition for development—becomes a far more involved agent in urban transformation. Rather than mere technical provision or a stable background, infrastructure produces its own space characterized by intersecting and overlapping adjacent systems. This "infrastructure space" includes obscured configurations of things like communication networks, regulatory structures, and exchange protocols that shape the forms, exper-ience, and knowledge of the urban, often in habitual and less evident ways. These hidden conditions provoke new mobilities and also afford opportunities for new collectivities and economies to emerge. In the same sense, to speak of cities as finite, hard entities is to risk estranging the nimble, networked, political, and digital aspects of infrastructure from conceptions of urbanism. It may be more inclusive to think through the metropolitan as a relational matrix that exceeds the stubborn, heavy, and stable identities that frequently define inquiries into cities. In this context, the metropolitan might be defined by, and thus understood through, the formations found at the intersection of the city's hard permanence and its soft latencies.

Infrastructure space exists between other spaces, providing switches and couplings that link diverse systems. These links between scales and systems are inclusive by nature but, conversely, are also defined by how and what they exclude. Infrastructure space often lacks visibility, as it remains in the background while supporting one's experience of urbanism. Certain events, however, can pressurize infrastructure space and suddenly render it visible, thus making its effects palpable through direct experience. These moments of radical visibility underscore the constant conditioning infrastructure space provides. In this sense, infrastructure is less about providing the necessary services for a society to function, and more about the process of naturalizing decisions about resource provision.

In most cases, interventions at the scale of infrastructure can be mobilized because of a perceived urgency. But the speed with which these transformations are enacted is dramatically exceeded by the efforts that would be necessary to undo them. Thus, infrastructure is commonly thought of as the most permanent and enduring of our civic investments. Yet, despite the prevailing sense that infrastructure is a long-lasting commitment, the temporal dimension of infrastructure space, like the politics of its visibility, is inherently contested. If conventional conceptions of "infrastructure" invoke permanence and durability through time, infrastructure space asks us to reconsider why we would invest in permanent solutions for situations that will likely prove to be only temporary problems. The stable sense of time and its innate linearity is unsettled by the latency and expectation brought on by a culture of speed and acceleration. Infrastructure space harbors dormancies that can be called to use temporarily, animated and enlivened for short durations, but nonetheless persistent within the network of linkages and switching mechanisms. As contemporary metropolitan citizens expand the ways in which they render themselves public, they ultimately produce infrastructures that are more nimble and can anticipate more variable futures.

With an expanding cognition of contemporary media systems, we know that a click of a mouse in one location can mean the construction of a new data center in another. These dependencies are distant and externalized, making the consequences of parti-cipation within infrastructural systems difficult to discern. Even if, by design, the presence of infrastructure can be elusive, its networks can be mapped and measured, and its effects can be studied in order to understand what they do and how they do it. The metropolitan is one such infrastructural adjacency that loosely connects countless systems, often to provide resources to support its inhabitants. While the expansiveness of infrastructural systems resists tidy containment, the metropolitan scale serves as a useful conceptual boundary for sampling and examining infrastructural specimens. As a way of designating collectivity, the metropolitan also provides opportunities to develop participatory models that seek to imagine scenarios beyond the immediately local or temporal context.

Infrastructure works at different levels to shape the forms, experiences, and knowledge of the city, just as the very stability of this category is under pressure. Indeed, it is increasingly pos-sible, perhaps even necessary, to think of urbanism beyond or even without the city. Such conceptual and physical mobilities are enabled and prevented by infrastructures, both physically and immaterially. However, it is very possible that the soft metropolitan infrastructures might become incredibly powerful in an expanded context for their ability to persist, to exist beyond ownership, to flare up and then retreat: dormant but always awaiting activation. Underpinned as it is by physical systems, infrastructure space becomes a crucial site of engagement and contestation in the struggle to create open and just forms of urbanism. Infrastructure—soft and hard, nimble and rooted, temporary and enduring—becomes both project and platform for imagining and cultivating collective metropolitan futures.

The Production of Territory

Kathy Velikov and Geoffrey Thün

Infrastructure, whose contemporary meanings, associations, and applications vary broadly, is a modern term that has been associated from early on with the production of territory. First having appeared in the English language by the early twentieth century in reference to the civil engineering works of the French railroads, the term was appropriated by NATO in the 1950s to refer to their multinational program of defensive installations implemented in Europe, and included not only physical installations (highways, bridges, railroads, airports, and military bases), but also facilities for communications, power, irrigation, and flood control, as well as warehousing, storage depots, fuel supplies, and the funding frameworks to enable these installations.[1] Thus, infrastructure is not only a modern term (temporally speaking), it is also a modern concept, referring not to any singular object or thing, but rather to an instrumentally designed, interrelated, heterogeneous system, or, to use the term coined by Michel Foucault, an *apparatus*. Moreover, it is inherently associated with geopolitics and with the production of territory.

Critical geographer Stuart Elden has pointed out that the etymology of the term "territory" comes not only from the Latin word for earth, *terre*, but also from *terrere*, meaning "to frighten."[2] Territory is therefore inherently associated with acts of violence in the establishment and maintenance of boundaries: with inclusion and exclusion.[3] Further, territory is not an object, but rather is akin to Henri Lefebvre's conception of space and the urban; it is more accordingly understood as an outcome, or as a process that inscribes social relations upon a terrain. Territory is continually produced and reproduced through political technologies, through technologies of management and control, and through conflicts and contestations.[4] Infrastructure operates as one of the primary technologies of the territorial process, actively structuring and restructuring the geo- and biopolitical relations between groups of humans, and between humans and the environment.

Tracing the etymologies of infrastructure and territory becomes productive in considering a number of things that are at stake with regard to contemporary territorial infrastructures. This is especially critical since societies across the globe now need to rethink and redesign infrastructural systems within the contexts of scarcity, security, and risk, relative to the ambitions of becoming low carbon.

There is a necessity for designers, planners, and policy-makers to be able to think and recognize the extent and calculus of infrastructure's apparatus—and to be able to account for the agency and relations of its material properties, its institutional and governmental actors, and its circulatory flows and codes. Infrastructure is not a stable thing, but transforms over time. Infrastructures tend to increase in complexity and scope as cities and societies grow; they are continually augmented with new technologies, retrofitted with more precise capacities, extended to meet expanding needs, recoded through new legal parameters, institutional practices, or financial formulas, and appropriated by new institutional, governmental, and community actors. These transformations often happen piecemeal and in incremental ways, reshaping the systems from within. In many cases, contemporary bureaucracies compartmentalize elements of infrastructural systems into separate silos of governance and funding, belying the cooperation and coordination needed to purposefully transform urban infrastructures. Therefore, infrastructure studies requires practicing a kind of forensic analytics in order to excavate, expose, and comprehend the apparatus—be it with regard to border, fuel, water, logistics, or defensive infrastructures.

The recognition of the infrastructural apparatus is, ultimately, empowering for the design and redesign of infrastructure. It instrumentalizes the design, implementation, and operation of new infrastructures, such as those for renewable energies, through the framework of their socio-technical assemblages. This also enables the transformation of infrastructural systems through their own internal logics, codes, and processes so that, incrementally, less violent relations can eventually be produced between human inhabitations and lands, waters, atmospheres, and other species.

It is important to develop an understanding of the agency of infrastructure in the production of territory not only through its material properties, but also through the relations of violence intrinsic to the control of space, and through its symbolic dimensions, such as social identity. Here, we speak not only of societal violence—such as when border infrastructures control sovereign territory, or when resource territories are inscribed onto indigenous lands, or the violence enacted upon communities when they are excluded from access to civic infrastructures—but also the relations of violence between the natural world and ourselves, which encompass everything from environmental degradation to "natural disasters" such as floods, hurricanes, or earthquakes. If we can frame terms such as sustainability or resilience through their functions of relationships, then the agential capabilities of infrastructural systems can be approached more productively.

1. H. William Batt, "Infrastructure: Etymology and Import," *Journal Professional Issues in Engineering* 110, no. 1 (1984): 1.
2. Stuart Elden, *Terror and Territory: The Spatial Extent of Sovereignty* (Minneapolis: University of Minnesota Press, 2009), xxix.
3. Ibid., xxx.
4. Stuart Elden, *The Birth of Territory* (Chicago: University of Chicago Press, 2013), 16–17.

Planetary Urbanization

Neil Brenner and Christian Schmid

During the last several decades, the field of urban studies has been animated by an extraordinary outpouring of new ideas regarding the role of cities, urbanism, and urbanization processes in ongoing global transformations. Yet, despite these advances, the field continues to be grounded upon a mapping of human settlement space that was more plausible in the early twentieth century than it is today.

The early twentieth century was a period in which large-scale industrial city regions were being consolidated in conjunction with major demographic, socioeconomic, and environmental shifts in the erstwhile "countryside." Consequently, the field of twentieth-century urban studies defined its agendas through a series of geographical contrasts. As debates raged regarding how best to define the specificity of urban life, the latter was universally demarcated in opposition to a purportedly nonurban zone, generally classified as "rural." The bulk of twentieth-century urban studies rested on the assumption that cities represented a particular *type* of territory that was qualitatively specific, and thus different from the putatively nonurban spaces that lay beyond their boundaries. The demarcations separating urban, suburban, and rural zones were recognized as having shifted historically, but the spaces themselves were assumed to remain discreet, distinct, and universal.

During the last thirty years, however, the form of urbanization has been radically reconfigured. Aside from the dramatic spatial and demographic expansion of major megacity regions, which have been widely noted, recent decades have also witnessed several equally far-reaching implosions and explosions of the urban at all spatial scales. These include:

The creation of new scales of urbanization. Extensively urbanized interdependencies are being consolidated within extremely large, poly-nucleated metropolitan regions to create sprawling urban galaxies that stretch far beyond any single metropolitan region, and often traverse multiple national boundaries.

The blurring and rearticulation of urban territories. Urbanization processes are being regionalized and reterritorialized. Former central functions, such as shopping facilities, corporate headquarters, multimodal logistics hubs, research institutions, and cultural venues—as well as spectacular architectural forms, dense settlement patterns, and other major infrastructural arrangements—are being dispersed outward from historic city cores into erstwhile suburbanized spaces and hinterlands, among expansive catchments of small- and medium-sized towns, and along major transportation corridors such as superhighways and rail lines.

The disintegration of the hinterland. The erstwhile hinterlands of major metropolitan regions and national territories are being reconfigured as they are operationalized, infrastructuralized, and enclosed—whether as back-office and warehousing locations, global sweatshops, agro-industrial land-use systems, data-storage facilities, energy-generation grids, resource-extraction zones, fuel depots, waste-disposal areas, recreational areas, or corridors of connectivity—to facilitate the metabolism of industrial urbanization and its associated planetary urban networks.

The end of the wilderness. Erstwhile "wilderness" spaces are being transformed and often degraded through the cumulative socio-eco-logical consequences of unfettered worldwide urbanization, or are otherwise being converted into bio-enclaves offering "ecosystem services" to offset destructive environmental impacts generated elsewhere. In this way, oceans, alpine regions, the equatorial rain forests, major deserts, the arctic and polar zones, and even the earth's atmosphere itself are being more tightly intermeshed with the rhythms of planetary urbanization at every geographical scale.

Under contemporary conditions, therefore, the category of the "city" has become thoroughly problematic as a basis for understanding the patterns and pathways of urbanization. Correspondingly, it is no longer plausible to rely upon the inherited urban/rural distinction to characterize the variegated differences between dense agglom-erations and less densely settled zones. And most importantly, the urban can no longer be understood as a particular "type" of settle-ment space, whether defined as a city, a metropolis, a metropolitan region, a megalopolis, or otherwise. While the process of agglom-eration remains essential to the production of this new worldwide topography, political-economic spaces can no longer be treated as if they were composed of discrete, distinct, bounded, univer-sal types of settlement. In short, the creatively destructive forward motion of planetary urbanization has deconstructed the core me-ta-geographical assumptions that have long underpinned the entire field of urban theory and research.

Four decades ago, Henri Lefebvre already put forward the radical hypothesis of the complete urbanization of society, a transforma-tion that required, he argued, a radical epistemological shift from the analysis of - to the investigation of processes of urbanization.[1] However, a systematic application of this fundamental thesis has yet to be undertaken. Perhaps, in the early twenty-first century, the moment is ripe for such an undertaking. In our view, the epistemological foundations of urban studies today must be fundamentally transformed.[2] We need new theoretical categories through which to decipher emergent socio-spatial, infrastructural, and ecological transformations. A new conceptual lexicon must also be created for identifying the wide variety of urbanization processes that are currently reshaping the planet. Lastly, we require adventurous methodological strategies to facilitate the empirical investigation and visualization of these processes. Whether or not a distinct field of "urban" studies can (and should) persist amid such intellectual tumult is a question that remains to be explored.

1. Henri Lefebvre, *The Urban Revolution*, trans. Robert Bononno (Minneapolis: University of Minnesota Press, 2003).
2. Neil Brenner and Christian Schmid, "Towards a New Epistemology of the Urban," *CITY* 19, nos. 2–3 (2015): 151–82; and Neil Brenner, ed., *Implosions/Explosions: Towards a Study of Planetary Urbanization* (Berlin: Jovis, 2014).

A Visual Atlas

Part 1

Compiled by Something Fantastic

Fig. 2: Server center in Detroit, USA

Fig. 1: Water reservoir in Olinda near Recife, Brazil Architect Luis Nunes used *cobogós*, decorative elements for ventilation and lighting, in this 1934 industrial façade.

Fig. 3: Garage in Marburg, Germany

Fig. 5: Wind catchers on the roofs
of houses in Chupanagh, Iran

Fig. 4: Wakefern Food Corp.
distribution center in Port Elisabeth, USA

Fig. 6: Picote Dam
on the Douro river, Portugal

Fig. 8: Transonic Wind Tunnel at the
Langley Research Center in Hampton, USA
NASA uses artificially produced wind
to measure airflow and aerodynamic forces
on aircraft and spacecraft.

Fig. 7: Gotthard Base Tunnel in Sedrun,
Switzerland

Fig. 9: External hallways of the SESC
Pompeia in São Paulo, Brazil
The stacked gyms of Lina Bo Bardi's
community center from 1977 are connected
to a vertical access tower by irregular,
branched bridges.

Fig. 10: Elevated highway in
Berlin, Germany

Fig. 11: Ganter Bridge in Valais, Switzerland
Reinfoced concrete bridge along the Simplon pass designed by Christian Menn
and completed in 1980.

Conical

Fig. 13: Grand Central Water Tower, Midrand, near Johannesburg, South Africa

Fig. 12: Grain silo in Hidalgo, Mexico

Fig. 14: Open pit diamond mine in Mirny, Russia
In the 1960s, about 10 million carats of diamonds were mined from this pit each year.

Fig. 15: Ice House near Abarquh, Iran
Since the seventeenth century BC these walls, wells and
domes have stored ice all year round.

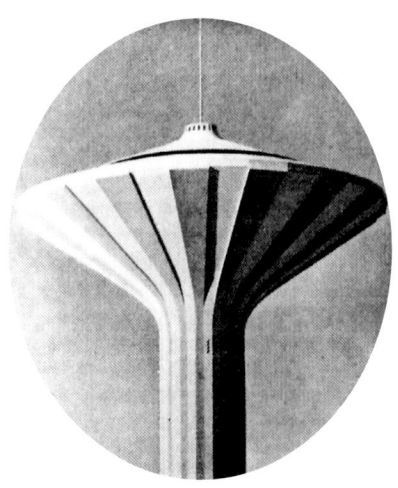

Fig. 16: Water tower in Örebro, Sweden

Fig. 17: Hydroelectric dam control room in Ferrara, Switzerland
Simulated day light deep inside the Swiss Alps.

Fig. 18: Galeries Royales Saint-Hubert
shopping arcade in Brussels, Belgium

Fig. 19: Public square in Andalusia, Spain
A textile canopy frames and shades
a large, outdoor urban space.

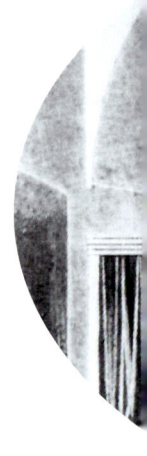

Fig.20: Brick bridge at Great Haywood Junction, England
Constructed as a roving bridge in 1772, ramps allow horses
to change canal side when towing a boat.

Fig.21: Stone bridge in Cevennes, France
This bridge was built in 2011, after the original one was
destroyed by a flood. In the course of a research project, all
resources used were documented and taken in to acount.

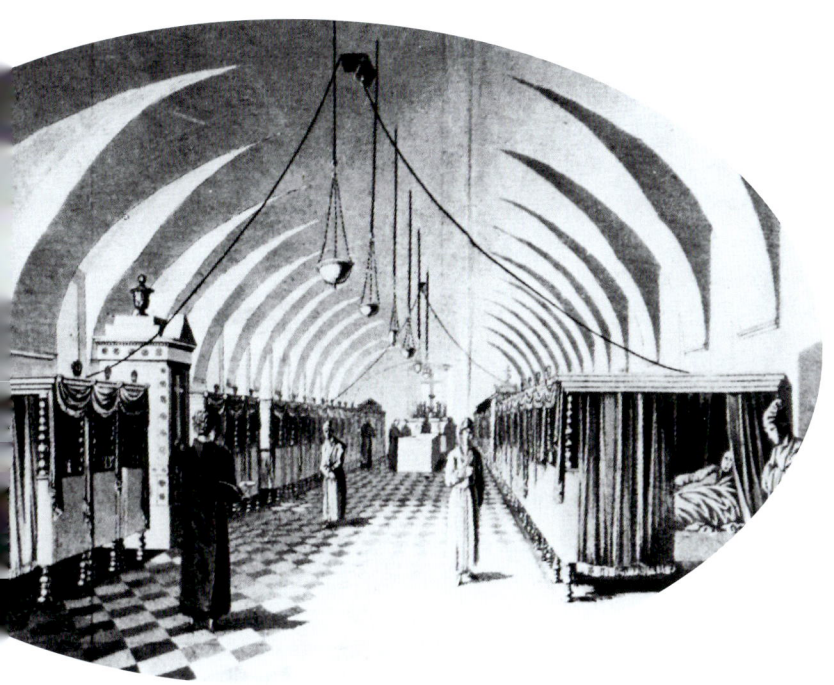

Fig. 22: Hospital dormitory
opened in 1820, in Prague,
Czech Republic

Fig. 23: Overpass used by wildlife
in Banff National Park, Canada

Cylinders

Fig. 24: Gasometer in Berlin, Germany
Gas was stored in the expandable bell
inside the steel frame structure.

Fig. 25: Installment of a concrete tube
Pier Luigi Nervi designed cantilevers on
either side, to allow the tubes to hang freely
after being mounted, adapting to
changing moments.

Fig. 26: Centre Georges Pompidou in Paris, France

Fig. 27: Cooling tower in Schmehausen, Germany
The world's first cable-net cooling tower,
built in 1974.

Fig. 28: Boston Naval Ship Yard dry dock in Boston, USA

Fig. 29: Step well at Mahadeva Temple in Karnataka, India
This traditional Indian well type also serves as a place for social gatherings and religious ceremonies providing relief from daytime heat.

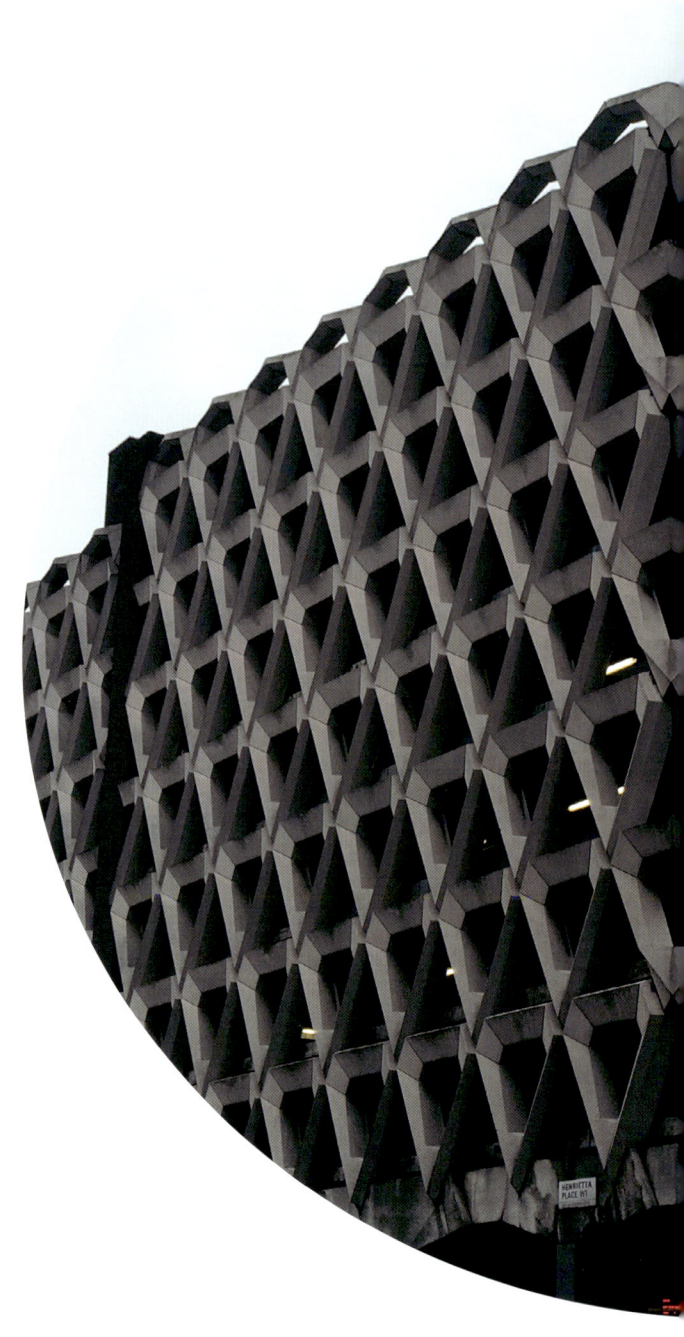

Fig. 30: Welbeck Street car park in London, UK
This façade made of prefabricated concrete elements was
designed by Michael Blampied and Partners in 1970.

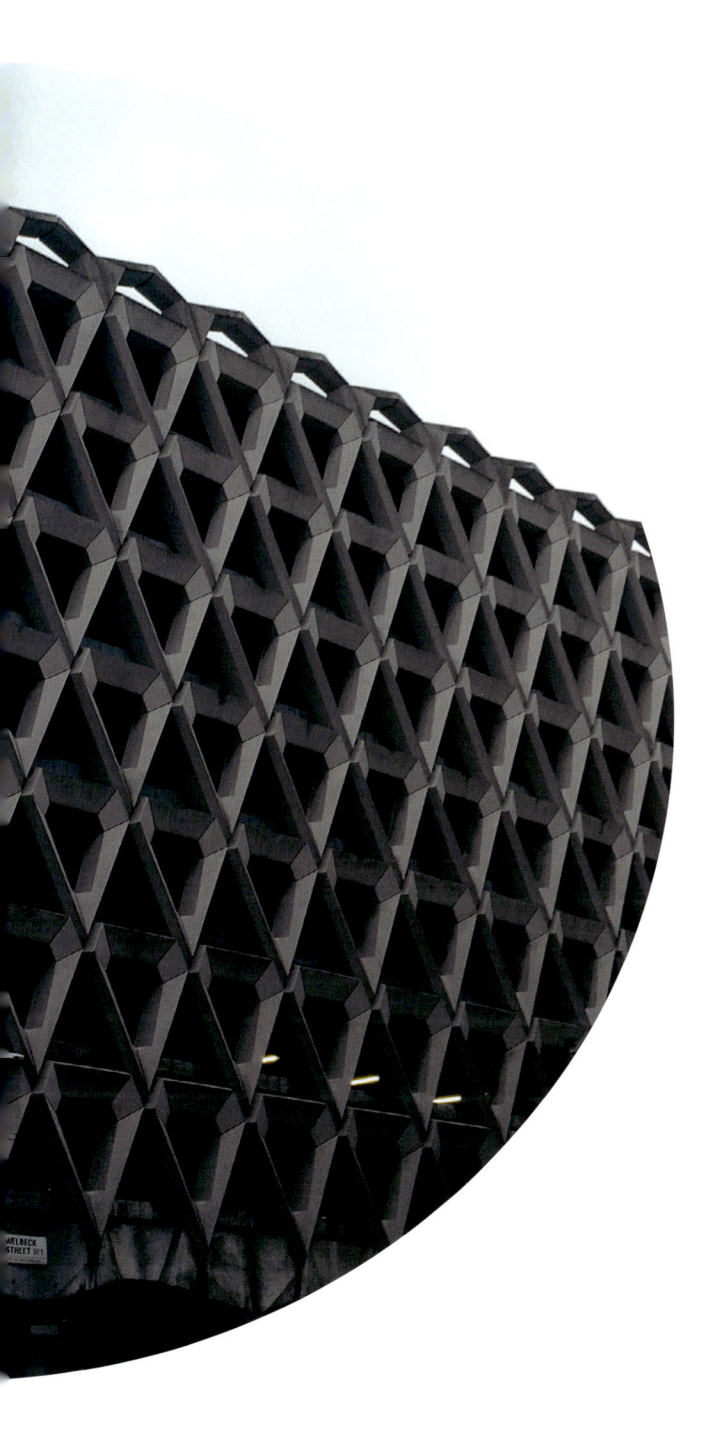

Carved

Fig. 31: Tunnel underneath
a waterfall in Wyssebach,
Switzerland

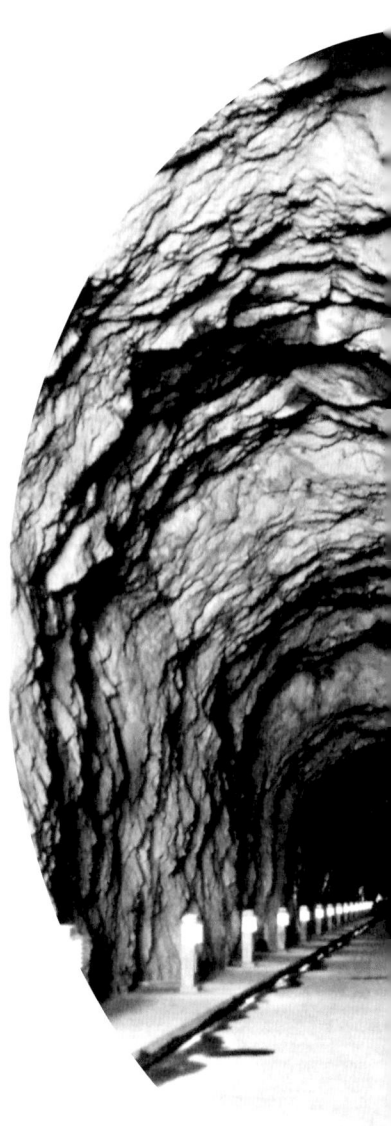

Fig. 32: Radens Power Station
in Isère, France

Fig. 33: Window in Arcos de la a Frontera, Spain
The wall's concave carving allows for
a longer view down the street.

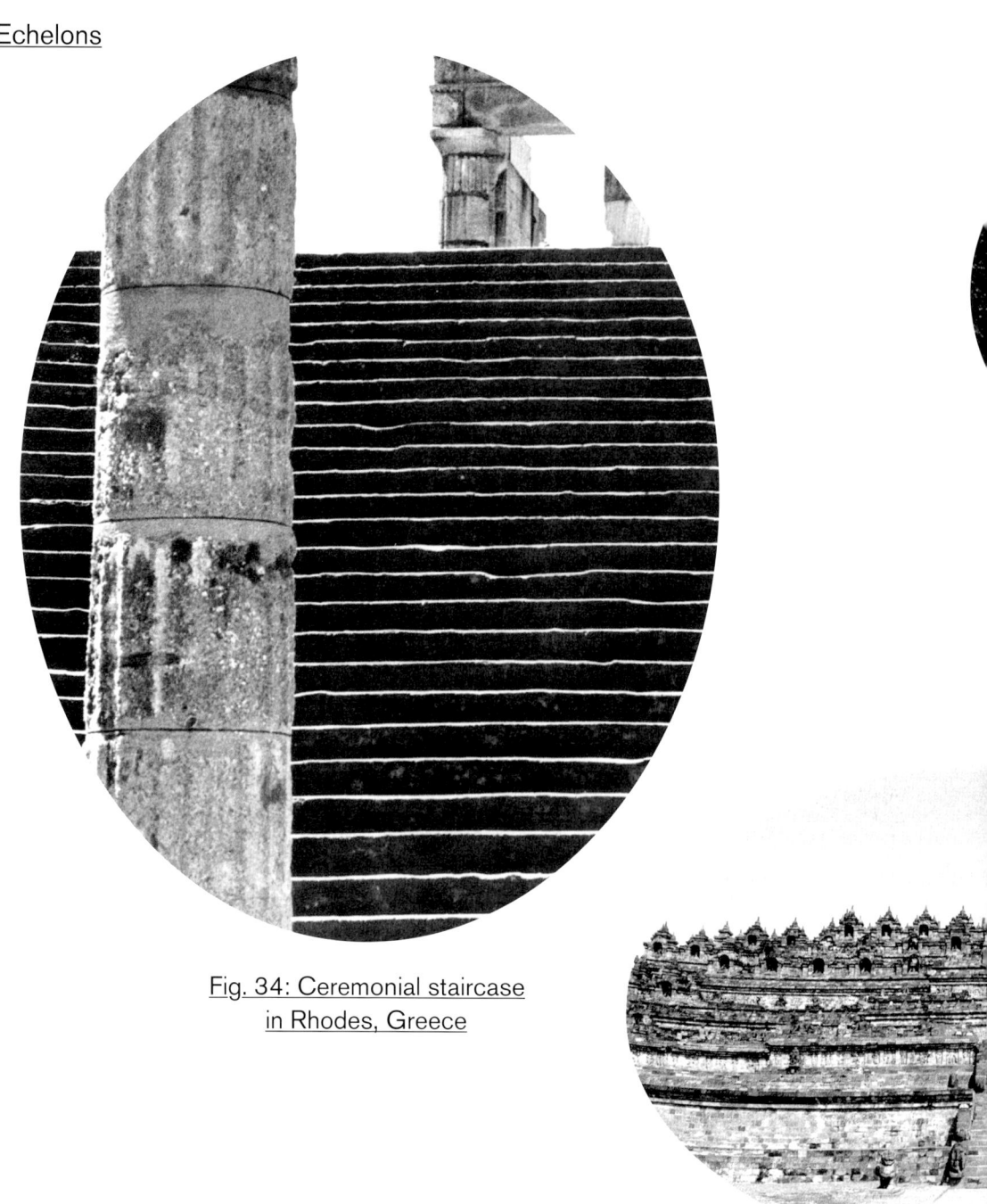

Fig. 34: Ceremonial staircase
in Rhodes, Greece

Fig. 35: Borobodur Temple in Magelang
on the island of Java, Indonesia Pilgrims begin at
the base of the monument and follow a path around each
level that slowly ascends to the top.

Fig. 36: Lemon pergola by Lake Garda, Italy
During the colder months the multistory
structure is converted into a greenhouse.

Fig. 37: The Koromo River flowing below
Tennōji Temple in Tokyo, Japan

Fig. 38: Highways and pedestrian
walkways in Detroit, USA

Fig. 39: Smithsonian Subway station in Washington DC, USA

Fig. 40: Central Station in Reims, France

Fig. 41: Sandö Bridge in Kramfors, Sweden

Fig. 42: Central de Abastos in Mexico City, Mexico
Sprawling across a 3,270,000m² site with 11 km of passageways,
this wholesale market connects the producers, wholesalers, and retailers
of the entire country, and even has its own postcode.

Fig. 43: Ponte degli Scalzi in Venice, Italy
The horizontal thrust weighing on this daringly flat stone arch construction
is transferred into the banks of the Grand Canal via wooden pillars.

Document:

The following work is taken from Atelier Bow-Wow co-founder Yoshiharu Tsukamoto's book *Windowscape: Window Behaviorology*, the central ideas of which he presented at the 5th International Forum of the LafargeHolcim Foundation for Sustainable Construction in Detroit in April 2016. Tsukamoto proposes that we have become dulled to the capacity of windows to function as much more than just standardized, mass-produced or extraneous, decorative elements. Instead he advocates taking a "behaviorology" approach to engender an *expanded* concept of the window as the sum of all of the various behaviors that accrue around the physical object itself. As partial openings in enclosures, windows function as a form of *dis*-closure, allowing for exchanges between interior and exterior. As a result, the window constitutes a crucial piece of infrastructure— both social and architectural—at the center of an entire ecosystem of numerous, differently behaving elements and interactions that allow humans to better perceive the world around them.

Windowscape

Yoshiharu Tsukamoto

I

Hawa Mahal: Jaipur, India

The windows on the east side of the Hawa Mahal (The Palace of Winds) feature a lower arch-shaped aperture that can be closed off using two rectangular timber elements that open inwards. The upper part of the window is covered by a stone panel punctured by small vents. This stone filter does more than just block radiant heat from entering the adjacent courtyard; as it flows into the building, the warm air from the outside travels through the small vents, each of which slope upwards towards the interior. The air is then cooled within the shaded interior of the vent, finally seeping out as an almost-imperceptible breeze.

III

IV

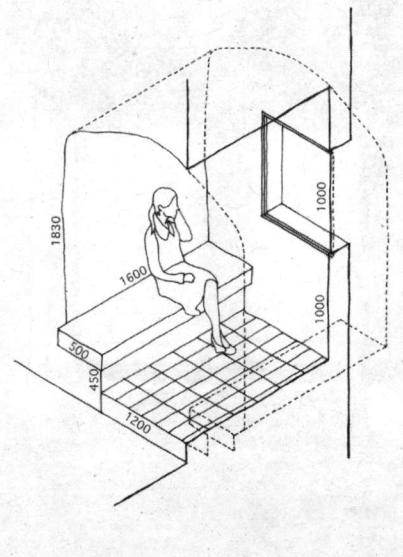

Kula Lotrščak: Zagreb, Croatia

This structure was first constructed as a lookout tower
in the thirteenth century, near one of the gates of the old
town wall. Light entering from outside pools in the alcove
created by the tower's thick walls, into which
benches have been built.

V

VI

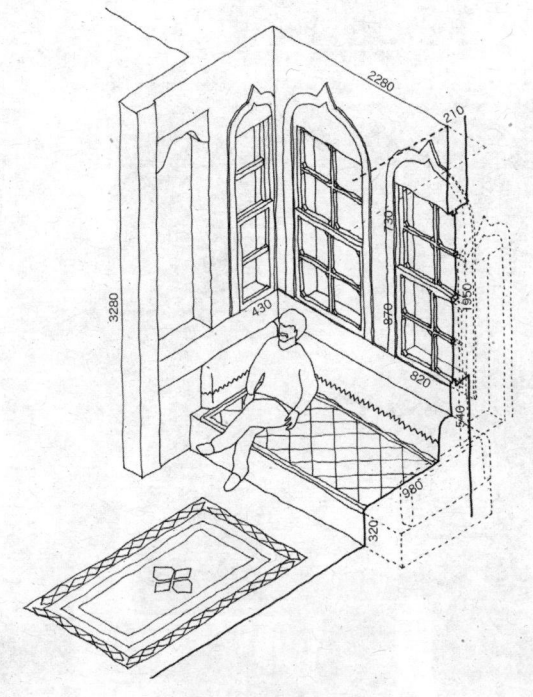

Mumtazia Preserved House: Safranbolu, Turkey

This is typical residence in Safranbolu, Turkey dating from
the nineteenth century. Sitters using the sofa nestled into
the space created by the oriel window forfeit the view
outside, instead feeling the warmth of the sun on their backs
as they look into the room.

VIII

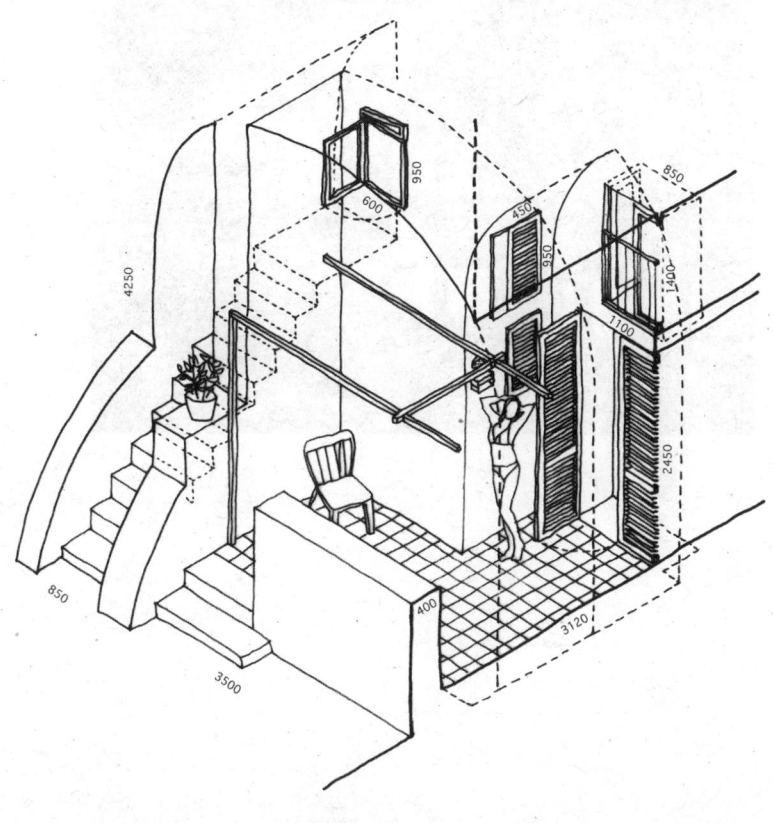

Marina di Chiaiolella: Procida, Italy

This residence is located in in the village of Chiaiolella on
the Italian island of Procida. A large archway built into the
façade envelops a partially exposed space with a shower,
a window belonging to the apartment behind it, and a
staircase leading to the apartment upstairs.

IX

X

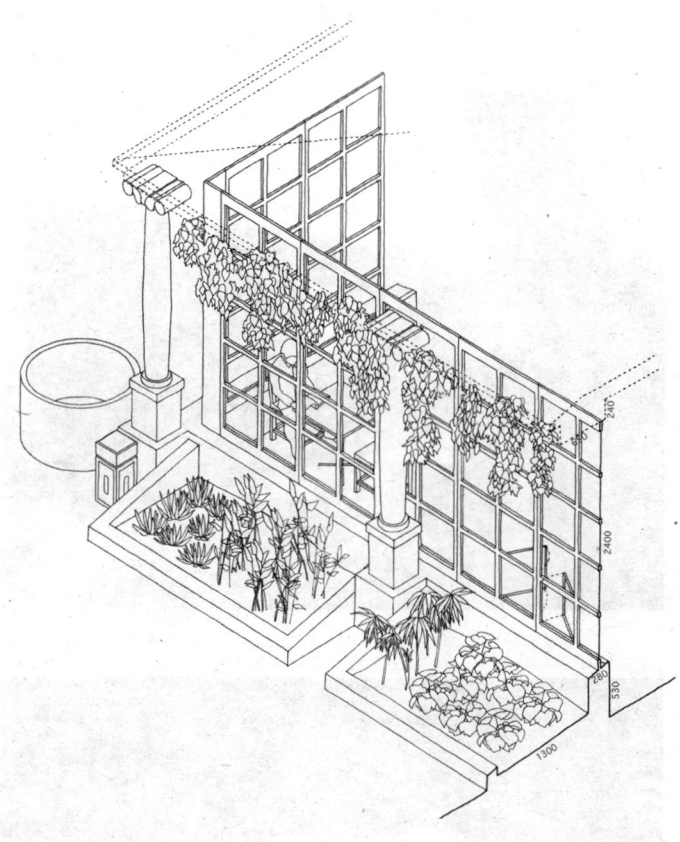

Plečnik House: Ljubljana, Slovenia

This is the sunroom of the residence where Slovenian architect Jože Plečnik's and members of his family lived. Fronted by columns topped with decorative capitals, the sunroom's windows cover three walls and are subdivided into small units by steel muntins, allowing a number of the units to be opened inwards for ventilation. Trellises hosting vines and planters have been installed above and below the windows, respectively. By concentrating greenery at the point where the interior meets the exterior, the boundary between the two is made ambiguous.

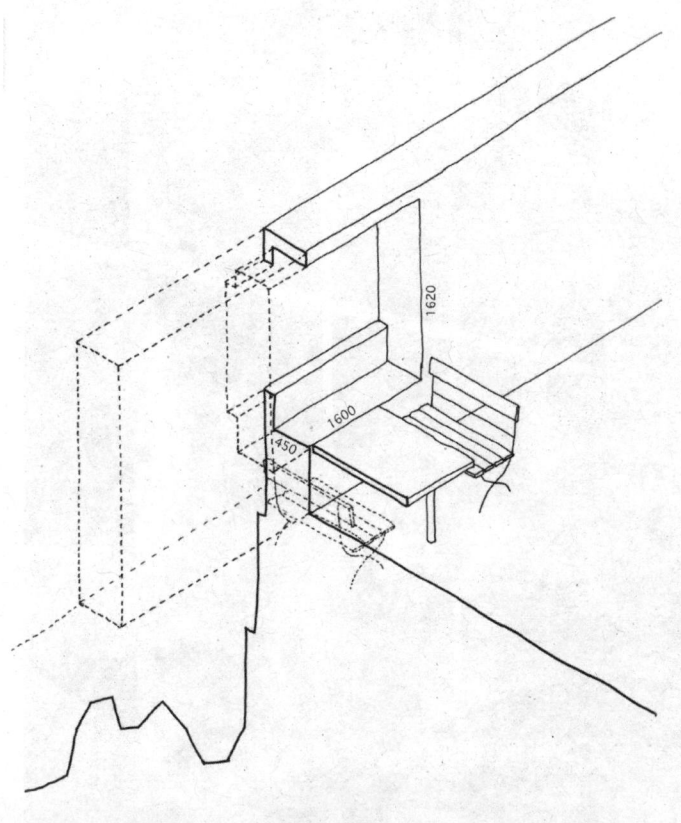

1620

1600

1450

Villa Le Lac Garden: Vevey, Switzerland

This garden belongs to the house Le Corbusier designed
for his mother. A window has been opened up in the
concrete wall facing the lake and a table attached. Guests
who sit here are shaded by the large Paulownia tree and
enjoy a view across Lake Geneva. The resulting intimate
mood of the space is more commonly associated with an
indoor rather than a garden setting.

XIV

Millowners' Association Building: Ahmedabad, India

Le Corbusier designed this building, which functions as an office and public hall. Its windows are connected to brise-soleils that protrude at an oblique angle to block out the western sun. These brise-soleils, the vegetation behind them, and the fixed, glass surfaces further back form a multi-layered boundary between interior and the exterior. Small windows for ventilation have been installed in the wooden mullions between the windowpanes. Some of the panes have since been replaced by built-in air conditioning systems.

XV

Infrastructure as Thing

Essays, Part 1

Julia King, Michael Dear, Rahul Mehrotra and Felipe Vera,
Salmaan Craig, Charlotte Malterre-Barthes,
Miho Mazereeuw and Claudia Bode, Milica Topalović

Incremental Infrastructure: Politics, Legality, Development, and Engagement in Delhi

Julia King

In the absence of infrastructure provision by the state, marginal communities are forced to find alternate solutions for basic needs, either as individuals or together. Taking the case of a sanitation project in Savda Ghevra, New Delhi, Julia King considers the relationship between collective incremental development and civic life.

In 2003, New Delhi, the capital of India, won the bid to host the 2010 Commonwealth Games, triggering the largest slum[1] clearance scheme the city had seen for decades. Although the figure is much debated, it is estimated that one million people were displaced from inner-city slum settlements.[2] Many of these ended up in resettlement colonies like Savda Ghevra. Savda Ghevra provides what can be best described as a marginal civic experience. Water arrives by tanker, which means that residents, mostly women, have to wait to collect it and then carry it to their homes. The resettlement of Savda Ghevra did not involve the construction of new housing; instead, residents were

simply relocated to partially serviced blocks of plots. Under this scheme, each family develops their plot based on the means and resources available to them, resulting in an urban formation that is the accumulation of multiple individual decisions.

Fig. 1: Women collecting water from a DJB tanker Piped water networks have not been planned for or built in the area which is predominantly reliant on water tankers.

The plots (18 or 12.5 square meters) are too small to be developed in any meaningful or extensive manner. Added to this is the fact that general health is compromised by the lack of sanitation and the site is so far from the city center that getting to and from places of employment is difficult and costly. The plots are arranged in a linear fashion and have neighboring properties on three sides. The result is an urbanity underpinned by a plan of regularity, in contrast to the spontaneous development traditionally associated with illegal slums. Despite this formal planning, the site has not developed in a consistent manner—in part because the infrastructure supplied by the government remains unbuilt or incomplete, but largely because the relocated families have mainly built their homes incrementally and on their own. The sanitation project in Savda Ghevra presents a case study of infrastructure as politics, *de facto* legality, driving development, and finally a process of engagement and participation.

The planning of Savda Ghevra by the Municipal Corporation of Delhi (MCD) included only nine community toilet complexes, a sum that is insufficient to meet the needs of a growing population. Assuming that all the existing latrine seats in the complexes are usable, the ratio of seats to female inhabitants is 1:250—well under any recommended level. During interviews, many residents complained of the prohibitive costs of the few functioning complexes; the result is that 88 percent of the population defecate in the open.[3] Women particularly suffer from having no accessible safe toilet. To protect their modesty, they often wait until nightfall to defecate in the open—but waiting is also the cause of widespread gastric disorders. What emerged in response to these conditions was a sanitation project born of a coalition of active community members, a local nongovernmental organization known as the Centre for Urban and Regional Excellence (CURE), and the author acting as architectural designer. The project explores the possibility of developing infrastructure—in this case, sanitation—and asking: Would it be possible to use

incrementalism to develop a collectively shared commitment to a common problem, beyond the level of the individual house? The proposed intervention was a community-based sanitation system connecting individual (household) toilets to a shared septic tank and up-flow filter that forms a Decentralized Wastewater Treatment System (DEWAT), which treats mostly black water but can handle gray water as well.

Fig. 2: Variation of houses found in Savda Ghevra The assortment of house types represents the variegated architectural aspirations and ability of the residents.

The technology of DEWAT can be feasibly built, managed, and maintained by the community, and is capable of adapting to the rapid, haphazard changes that happen on the urban fringe as a consequence of a lack of planning and infrastructure. The project posed a key question: Would the outcome establish a principle that a collective commitment and incremental techniques could "build" a town? Instead of demanding—and

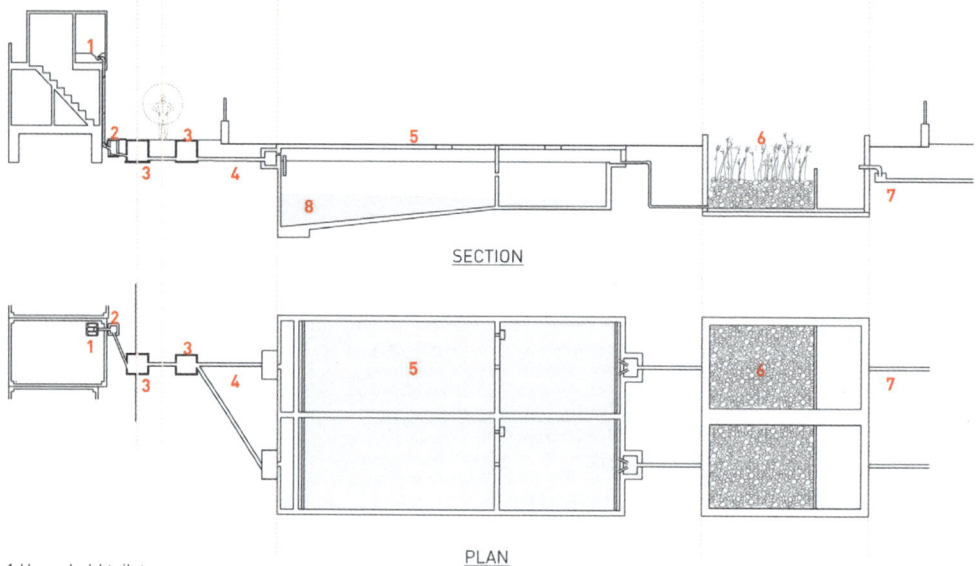

SECTION

PLAN

1 Household toilet
2 Toilet connects to household chamber
3 Which in turn connects to Manhole (multiple per lane)
4 Common sewer pipe
5 Two chamber septic tank (primary treatment)
6 Up-flow filter (secondary treatment)
7 Outlet for water for re-use
8 Sludge

Fig. 3: Diagrammatic representation of sanitation model
The effluent runs from households via small diameter sewers to
a large septic tank. In the septic tank the effluent mostly settles
to form 'sludge' at the bottom of the tank and a thin 'scum' layer
floats to the top. This process is called sedimentation.

then waiting for—what are often inadequate (and certainly expensive) "services" from the city or state, the project proposed that there could be an important point early on in the resettlement of a colony ideally suited to the building of the primary connective tissue or infrastructure through collaboration. By delivering the part of the process that the community cannot do themselves—sewerage—an open system for what they can do was created at the household level, encouraging and building upon current incremental growth patterns.

The infrastructure was completed in January 2014. As of 2015, 116 households were connected and at least fifty more had signed up (and paid a membership fee) for the scheme. Ongoing work is focused on helping poorer households upgrade their homes through the addition of toilets, thereby allowing them to connect to the system. On the back of the shared management of the project, a formal organization emerged in the form of a Residents' Welfare Association (RWA), the first of its kind in a slum resettlement colony in Delhi.

Infrastructure as Politics

The Savda Ghevra project highlighted the lack of adequate sanitation and began a relatively significant program of capital investment in a decentralized sewerage treatment system. Parallel to these infrastructural improvements, the process created a neighborhood dialogue in which residents, involved in the "politics of shit,"[4] can go from being a victimized population to one that can instead stake a claim and become politically active in urban life. This is most apparent in the all-women operation and maintenance team responsible for the long-term management of the project, which is also the first port of call for residents who wish to connect to the system. But it is also evidenced by the establishment of the RWA. Both are examples of what Arjun Appadurai calls "deep democracy"[5]: efforts among the urban poor to mobilize and mediate between the extremes of world-class city aspirations.

The RWA was, at the time of conception, the first of its kind in a slum resettlement colony in Delhi. RWAs are typically associated with groups of upper- and middle-class private-property owners. Geographer and professor Dr. Asher Ghertner has extensively explored how inner-city upper-class RWAs were some of the many drivers in the push to eradicate slums in the first place, leading to the eventual creation of settlements like Savda Ghevra.[6] RWAs are institutionalized spaces that facilitate and mediate relations between the neighborhood residents and government (municipal) authorities. In order to participate in the city, the residents of Savda Ghevra managed to create consensus and agency, at first via CURE and afterward through institutions like the RWA—a process that is ongoing at the time of writing. It is therefore critical to recognize the importance of partnering with the NGO CURE in facilitating a parallel structure of political representation.

Fig. 4: Community consultation
Long-term engagement occurred through repeated interactions in large design workshops and smaller meetings, often held in the park.

The RWA exists alongside a cast of usual suspects—political parties, representatives, workers—all of which usually negotiating with municipal bureaucracies in marginalized spaces. They might not be totally absent, but they are hardly involved. The sanitation project acts as a kind of infrastructure in itself, producing political agency. An aggregate of individuals is often the opposite of "community." Yet, an intermediate level of politics that can be produced by a temple, hair salon, or sanitation system is an important process that deserves more acknowledgment.

Infrastructure as *De Facto* Legality

The practicalities of enacting the sanitation project made clear that infrastructure, for the residents, implies state presence. This was embodied in a letter of permission that was printed, laminated, and then displayed in a public place. The document, issued by the Government of New Delhi via the Delhi Urban Shelter Improvement Board (DUSIB), approved, in "the public interest," the construction of the sanitation project, which it named Community Septic Tank (CST). The significance of this should not be overlooked, as such permissions are notoriously hard to secure and often take years to be granted. A sewer connection is arguably the best proxy for legality in cities like Delhi, which have mostly evolved outside the master-planning process.

A whole housing economy also emerged, triggered when the permission was initially received and unprecedented since completion. While some of the housing changes may have happened without the arrival of sanitation infrastructure, it has nevertheless played a role. In 2011, before the project started, the tallest buildings to be found in "A" block (where the project was constructed) were three stories, and ninety percent of the housing stock was single story. Today (based on surveys carried out by the author in February 2016) the tallest buildings are four-and-a-half stories; and structures of two to three stories represent 34 percent of the housing stock. The housing economy is in part prompted by a desire of residents to have an in-house toilet, but also results from the confidence of this *de facto* tenure.

The hypothesis is that consolidation

Fig. 5: Incremental accumulation
Since the arrival of sanitation, houses have grown much larger and been predominantly developed by small-scale developers.

of houses not only creates a unified collective presence and voice, it also engenders, the *pucca* (well-built) physicality of the community. This enables the community to apply more pressure on the municipality to deliver better services while also decreasing the likelihood of demolition. It can be argued that all cities grow incrementally; what I am interested in here is a particular kind of incrementalism defined by this process of consolidation. Consolidation means more than a process of densification. Consolidation requires the individual to reconcile him- or herself as a part of a whole, where collective improvements are greater than the sum of individual ones. The process of consolidation is the collective creation of a "town" through improving houses and developing infrastructure, which involves several stages, advancing from the house to the neighborhood and, eventually, to the city. A "town" is made by the addition of shops as well as through the diversity of tenure supported by infrastructure (water, sanitation, and electricity), which in turn signals the advent of civic decorum. During the early stages of the sanitation project we already saw the emergence of political representation at a local level, which in turn reflects increased participation and recognition at the city scale. Consolidation of a settlement into a participating increment of the host city is not a purely bottom-up process, nor a simple aggregate of improved individual dwellings to which institutions are attached; rather, it's a process of city and settlement growing *together*.

However, consolidation also threatens the original slum dwellers' ability to exist in Savda Ghevra. Asher Ghertner makes a compelling case that multiplicity of tenure is what keeps such spaces from being outside of the property market.[7] There is an investment in keeping something not quite capitalized, maintaining its status as being not quite part of the market so

that capital—speculators—cannot enter. But in Savda they have entered. Land value has risen by 500 percent in the catchment area of the sewage project and value has risen even for those plots that haven't been connected to the system. In the two years since completion, many of the original residents who formed the operation and maintenance team back in 2013, as well as the RWA, have cashed in and sold their plots, allegedly moving back to the inner-city slums that have started to emerge following a change in government. This push-and-pull effect of gentrification has again made the community very vulnerable and raises critical questions that must be addressed when infrastructure is constructed.

Infrastructure Driving Development

If consolidation is a claim for permanence, the processes of sedimentation and accretion (to use material metaphors) describe this change. (Fig. 6) shows the incremental process of consolidation represented as a spectrum of stages of the growth of homes (taken from 2013 figures). The principal conclusion that can be drawn here is that there is a potential limit for the effective use of resident-led, incremental methods of addition and of improved engagement with opportunities provided by the city—in this case, sanitation infrastructural improvements. The research suggests that there is a "sweet spot" where sharing and incrementalism can be most effective in driving infrastructural improvements. At the poorer end

							Savda Ghevra	Kalyanpuri / Dakshinpuri
							←	→
TYPE	kuccha	semi-pucca	semi-pucca	pucca (1)	pucca (1.5)	pucca (2)	pucca (2.5)	pucca (3)	pucca (3.5)
AREA	12.5 sq m	12.5 sq m	12.5 sq m	12.5 sq m	19 sq m	25 sq m	30 sq m	75 sq m	87 sq m
COST (INR) (GRB)	5000-8000 60-95	25000 - 35000 300 – 400	100000 - 130000 1000 - 1400	150000 - 160000 1600 - 1800	160000 - 180000 1800 - 2000	190000 - 250000 2000 - 3000	≈ 350000 ≈ 250000	≈ 40000 ≈ 4500	≈ 45000 ≈ 5000

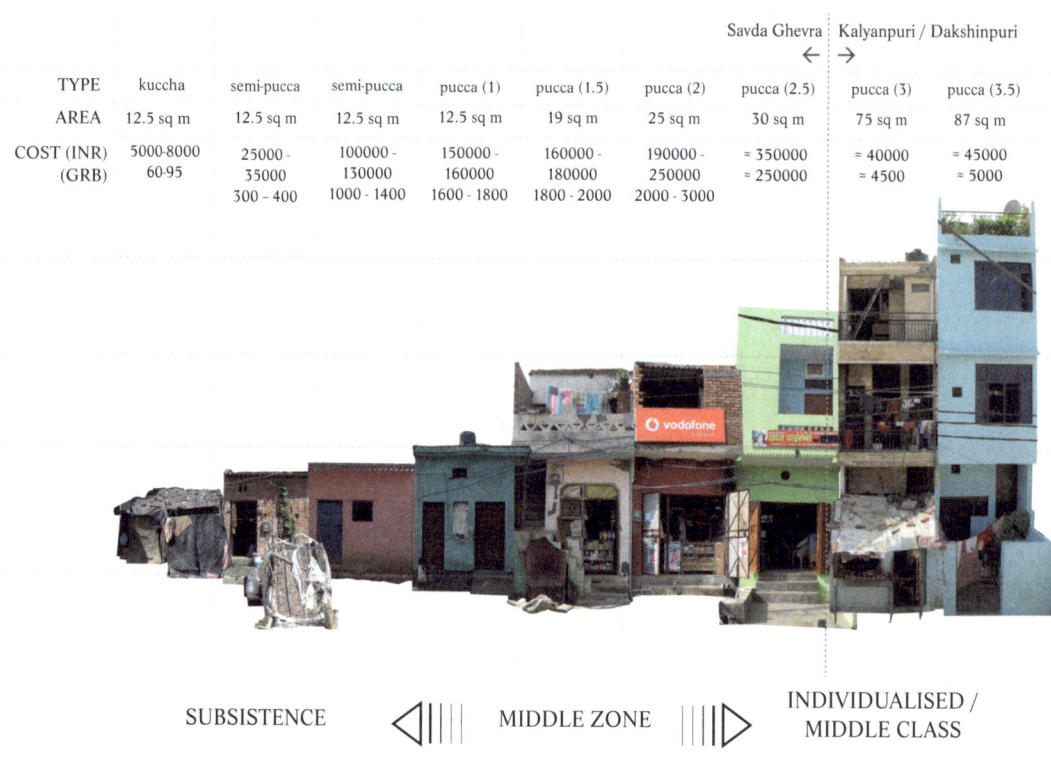

SUBSISTENCE ◁|||| MIDDLE ZONE ||||▷ INDIVIDUALISED / MIDDLE CLASS

Fig. 6: The middle of the spectrum This middle zone appears to be where incremental development is most effective in driving change.

of the spectrum, *kuccha* (shack-like) dwellings are usually too basic to form a foundation for improvements and their residents are too impoverished to get engaged. At the other end of the spectrum, when a house reaches two stories, improvements and additions tend to be carried out by a contractor, indicating an inherent limit to resident-led incrementalism. The middle of the spectrum, dominated by single-story pucca structures, is the ideal housing stage at which to deploy the sharing and incremental approach as a development strategy.

Incrementalism and shared improvement work prevailed—from a state of basic subsistence to one of collaboration and conviviality, followed by individualization. This middle zone, or sweet spot, fostered a condition where the commitment to a common good overrode individualized behavior. Those families who had already built individual household cesspit tanks recognized the benefit of collective action and were the first to sign up to connect to the shared infrastructure. This collective action, which at first appeared to be subject to a purely social arrangement organized within the family or as part of a network based on ethnicity, gender, and religious ties, inevitably acquired a political dimension. This was particularly the case as conflicts developed, either within the settlement itself or between the settlement and the civic authorities. The sweet spot is where residents have the means to produce community infrastructures but not the middle-class values that transcend them. If this is a continuum, then how do we reconcile the "politics of shit" with class ascendance? What are the ways of being in the city that do not have bourgeois citizenship as their final subject?

Infrastructure as Engagement and Participation

Of the three hundred households within the catchment area of the sanitation project, just over a third are connected (as of 2016); more are joining, but it is a slow process. As is often argued, however, such a speed is critical in engendering less powerful citizens to engage with and build the world—their world.[8] However, unlike rural settings, where a slower pace of change is easily accommodated, urban settings tend to have much more dynamic land markets. Infrastructure and people can arrive quickly, often creating flows that conflict with the slowness and high social investment required by community-led improvements to infrastructure. Furthermore—and specifically in the case of Savda Ghevra, where only half of the "A" block was included in the pilot project due to limited funding—change can foster jealousies in adjacent un-serviced sites. In 2016 there have been two reported cases of vandalism, which has resulted in CURE having to monitor the project more closely than originally anticipated. While the material motivation of the project is undoubtedly noble—to provide basic infrastructure to a peripheral, marginalized space—it raises significant concerns. The arrival of infrastructure in Savda Ghevra accelerated a process of material change parallel to the displacement of many of the original residents. It is difficult to ascertain why so many have left, but a concern remains: the arrival of sanitation marginalized the more vulnerable segments of the population.

The inability of the project to sustain itself without the presence of CURE also raises questions. First, in the continued absence of the state, does such a project—at best—take pressure off government, or—at worst—does it produce and legitimatize an internal infrastructure for second-class urban residents? While the provision of sanitation and the benefits of community processes are clearly valuable, the absence of the state and resulting reliance on local NGOs exposes the institutional capacity required to sustain such processes. Secondly, maintenance requires not only technical expertise, but also social brokerage skills, which most members of the community simply do not have the time to develop without a corresponding source of income. As such, how can a purely public infrastructure be sustained without putting a burden on the community's social capital, time, or monetary resources? Maintenance is not the only issue: the sunk costs of infrastructure are high, and they require further social costs to sustain themselves in community-led contexts.

How can this be reconciled with the role of the infrastructure designer? Is it possible to "design out" the negative effects?; in other words, is it possible for design to "lock in" equity?

Concluding Remarks

The urban topography of Delhi is delineated by various epochs of India's past, from the Mughal period (1526–1707) through British colonial rule (1858–1947) to post-Independence (from 1948 on). In this sense, Delhi, like all cities, has grown incrementally. As large cities become more populous, their centers become progressively gentrified, pushing to the periphery the people who cannot afford to live or work there (and their activities). Urban culture thus dissipates into a topography of "serviced well-being" in which the potential for civic participation by the poor becomes either ever-receding, or a matter of establishing local towns within the comparatively thin peripheral area. The term "incremental," as used here, can be best described as "civic." There is a relationship between the topography of the city (its structure of differentiation) and the quality of civic life, where civic life is understood to empower or disempower people politically, through conflict, negotiation, accommodation, or collaboration. In other words, in the incremental city there is the capacity to see oneself involved with, committed to, and in solidarity with one's place or town. For this to happen, "place" needs to be visible within the city, providing a scale within which people can orient themselves and commit. Here, we arrive at one of the key elements of the concept of incrementalism: its architecture. Its construction and substance are both vehicles for structuring difference, allowing for "place" or "town" to emerge as the setting for the civic.

The shared practice of incremental infrastructure is necessarily embedded in the practices and production of place-making. Particularly in contested and marginalized city spaces, the architect must evolve from the endeavor of the lone genius to one of a collaborative maker. Architecture, in this way, is understood as a tool for engagement and dialogue, empowering communities to contribute to shaping their city. Thus the role of the architect goes beyond that of design to encompass a whole range of skills, from finance, political lobbying, fundraising, community liaison, and the traditional skills of design development and project delivery. This approach to architecture emphasizes the process as opposed to the final product; negotiating permissions is as important as technical detailing. In this sense, incrementalism is both a strategy for developing marginalized neighborhoods and a response to contemporary urban design obsessed with the aesthetic of the physical final product. City-making projects under the guise of regeneration are often manifested through large-scale, hierarchical, inflexible, high-capital, and centralized processes. Such methods often fail to grasp the complex and rich dynamics that define cities; the obsession with form tends to gloss over political, economic, and social experiences. As such, an architectural practice operating at the intersection of the built environment and sociopolitical and economical processes enables a rich framework from which urban spaces can be assessed, and incremental interventions, despite all the challenges, put into practice for positive urban change.

1. The term 'slum' (full of pejorative connotations), in this text, refers to what is locally called jhuggi-jhompri (J.J. for short) which are settlements characterized by precarious living and housing clusters. Officially, for planners and the judiciary, 'slums' are illegally occupied land and so referred to as squatter settlements. 'Slum areas' designated under the Slum Improvement and Clearance Areas Act of 1956 under Section 3 are eligible for benefits despite being seen as illegal (DUSIB, 2013).
2. L. Batra, "Out of Sight, Out of Mind," in *Finding Delhi: Loss and Renewal in the Megacity*, ed. B. Chaturvedi (New Delhi: Viking Penguin, 2010), ch. 2.
3. CURE (Centre for Urban and Regional Excellence), "Sanjha Prayas: Bhagidari with the Poor; Socio-economic Study Report—Savda Ghevra Resettlement Colony," *CURE Independent Report*, [New Delhi, CURE] (ca. 2010): 11.
4. Arjun Appadurai, "Deep Democracy: Urban Governmentality and the Horizon of Politics," *Environment & Urbanization* 13, no. 2 (2001): 37.
5. Ibid., 25.
6. Asher Ghertner, "The Nuisance of Slums: Environmental Law and the Production of Slum Illegality in India," in *Urban Navigation: Politics, Space and the City in South Asia*, ed. Jonathan S. Anjaria and Colin McFarlane (New Delhi: Routledge, 2011), 23.
7. Asher Ghertner, *Rule by Aesthetics: World-Class City Making in Delhi* (New York, NY: Oxford University Press, 2015).
8. Nabeel Hamdi, *Small Change: About the Art of Practice and the Limits of Planning in Cities* (London: Earthscan, 2004).

Occupation and In-Between Zones: US-Mexico Border, 1848–Present

Michael Dear

Is a border a barrier or a connective membrane? Michael Dear considers the space along the US-Mexico border as a 'third nation' overtaken by a ballooning security apparatus and calls for restoration of the land and communities affected by the infrastructure of occupation.

In 2002, I began traveling the entire length of the US-Mexico border, on both sides, from Tijuana/San Diego on the Pacific Ocean, to Matamoros/Brownsville on the Gulf of Mexico: a total of 4,000 miles. What began as an opportunistic journey of discovery was rapidly overtaken by current events. I had the good and bad fortune to begin just before the United States undertook sealing and fortifying its southern boundary, and so became an unintentional witness to the border's closure. As time passed, I became less focused on the customary trinity of borderland obsessions (drugs, immigration, national security), and more absorbed with the lives of border communities that exist between the two nations. I realized that these in-between spaces form a "third nation," not *separating* Mexico from the United States, but instead acting as a *connective membrane.*[1]

Third-nation citizens on both sides readily assert that they have more in common with each other than with their host nations. The in-between zone is not a sovereign nation-state, but it contains many of the elements that warrant the appellation "nation," such as a shared identity, common history, joint traditions, and shared lives. Yet there is much more to the third nation than a cognitive awareness.

Fig. 1: Boundary spike between Nogales, Arizona, and Nogales, State of Sonora. In the late nineteenth century, boundary spikes driven into the ground were often the only visible "infrastructure of occupation" marking the separation between the US and Mexico.

Both sides are also deeply connected through trade, family, leisure, shopping, culture, education, and legal obligation. Border-dwellers' lives are interwoven through these everyday connections, and buttressed by myriad formal and informal institutional arrangements. Such a third-nation perspective radically alters the way we perceive infrastructure, risk, and territory in the US-MX borderlands.

Creating the Border: A Brief History

On February 2, 1848, the Treaty of Peace, Friendship, Limits, and Settlement was signed at Guadalupe Hidalgo, terminating the Mexican-American War. The so-called Treaty of Guadalupe Hidalgo required the designation of a "boundary line with due precision, upon authoritative maps, and to establish upon the ground landmarks which shall show the limits of both republics."

Fig. 2: A marble monument near Tijuana marks the first point established by the boundary survey following the 1848 treaty. This photograph was taken at the end of the nineteenth century after the original monument was renovated and fenced to prevent vandalism, and renumbered as monument 258. (source: Blanco, 1901).

The subsequent surveys took six years to complete, ending in 1855. Only 52 markers were erected along the 2,000-mile boundary, mostly on the land-based section. Seven of these were made of marble, weighing about five tons apiece; other markers were piles of stones.

Fig. 3: Ancient boundary monument number XVI was a simple pile of stones. (source: Blanco, 1901).

Fig. 4: Monument number 185; the monuments erected during the second boundary survey at the end of the nineteenth century were iron columns. (source: Blanco, 1901).

During the late nineteenth century, disputes over the exact location of the boundary line proliferated as the population and settlements expanded. A new joint commission began work in 1892 to resurvey the land boundary, locate and rebuild the old monuments, and install additional markers as necessary. The resurvey took two years, and increased the number of boundary monuments to 258 (currently there are 276 official monuments jointly maintained by both nations, and almost 500 smaller "markers").

Fig. 5: Border fencing from the era of 1990s Operation Gatekeeper, near Campo, CA.

For most of the twentieth century, the international boundary line between Mexico and the United States remained loosely marked and casually observed. Outside the cities, the divide was often left unmarked. In 1924, as a result of increasingly chaotic crossing conditions, the US Border Patrol was inaugurated: the first agency with direct authority to police the line. By 1945, in another border "first," the rising rate of undocumented crossings into California caused a chain-link fence to be erected for five miles on either side of the All-American Canal near Calexico, using materials that had been recycled from a former World War II internment camp.

For the remainder of the twentieth century, the volume of undocumented crossings into the United States

continued to grow, largely due to US demand for workers combined with economic hardship in Mexico. In the mid-1990s, the United States undertook more concerted efforts to build border fences at cities such as Tijuana and Ciudad Juárez. These were constructed from steel plates that had originally served as temporary landing strips for aircraft during the Vietnam War—the panels turned upright to construct the fence. Subsequently, the numbers of undocumented did not diminish, but more people turned to remote desert and mountainous regions to cross the line, and the number of migrant deaths increased rapidly.

The Secure Border Initiative: Infrastructures of Occupation

After 9/11, the Bush administration created the Department of Homeland Security (DHS) to ensure operational control over the nation's borders. The centerpiece of DHS operations was the 2005 Secure Border Initiative (SBI), engaging the Coast Guard, Border Patrol (USBP), and Immigration and Customs Enforcement (ICE) agencies. DHS activities also impacted some functions of agencies with no direct responsibility for immigration, such as the caseloads of the Department of Justice, and the widespread suspension of environmental protection laws.

The DHS outsourced many of its obligations to states and municipalities, thereby co-opting local law enforcement into national security protocols. ICE contracted with multiple private corporations (such as the Corrections Corporation of America and Boeing) for the construction of physical and virtual fences, the provision of security training and services, private detention facilities, and deportations.

<u>Fig. 6:</u> The post-9/11 fence at San Luis Río Colorado, AZ. The locked box contains boundary monument 201.

After his election in 2008, President Obama continued the policies of his predecessor. First, a strategy of "prevention through deterrence" assumed that a concentration of resources (e.g. for walls, policing, and surveillance) would deter unauthorized crossers; and second, "enforcement with consequences" would discourage border transgressions by imposing tougher penalties for offenders. By 2012, the Obama administration was spending nearly $18 billion annually on a suite of "enforcement first" strategies, making it the nation's premier immigration policy.

Today, much of the US-MX borderland resembles a military zone of occupation. The DHS presence is announced most directly in fences and walls, surveillance towers, official ports of entry, and border-patrol stations. However, the detritus of occupation is also manifest in dams, stadium lighting, diverted drainage channels, landfills, airborne surveillance, custom-built access roads, staging areas, parking facilities, internal checkpoints, endless vehicular patrols, heavily armed foot patrols, large-scale earth removal, warehousing, acres of trash, drones, and the ubiquitous signage of prohibition. Border residents in Arizona refer to this occupied zone as a "police state."

SBI Performance Outcomes

A comprehensive accounting of SBI program outcomes is unlikely ever to be achieved, given the diffuse nature of the DHS efforts and absence of fully representative data sources. For instance, while the federal government collects information on many immigration measures, none explicitly measures the most significant SBI indicators; namely, the volume of undocumented border crossings, and the extent to which the border is in fact "secure."[2]

In 2006, just as the SBI was beginning to gain traction, RAND security expert Jack Riley testified before the House of Representatives that the United States had "woefully underinvested" in developing a comprehensive border security strategy. While the nation was developing numerous security programs, "the impacts and cost-effectiveness of virtually all of these initiatives are poorly understood." Eight years later, when SBI interventions were fully operational, Riley lamented that his assessment remained essentially unchanged.[3] On the best available evidence, the following is my estimate of an aggregated account of SBI outcomes to date: By January 2013, DHS contractors had installed a total of 651 miles of fencing along the border: 352 miles to stop pedestrians, and 299 miles to block vehicles. This total was only two miles short of the distance identified by the USBP as "appropriate" for barrier construction (some land is simply too steep, and fencing water boundaries is impractical). During the most frenzied period of construction (2006–9), the extent of fencing grew from 150 to 600 miles. After that, the rate of construction quickly declined, and few extra miles were added.

In order to complete fortification, congressional appropriations (which included money for surveillance technology) increased from $25 million in 1996 to $298 million in 2006, and peaked at $1.5 billion in 2007. Since then, expenditures on these "tactical infrastructure appropriations" steadily dropped, to $324 million in 2013. The number of border patrol agents along the boundary more than doubled after 2000, to over 20,000 personnel, with growth concentrated in Tucson and El Paso, the sectors of major undocumented crossing activity. Immigration enforcement actions resulted in almost 421,000 migrant apprehensions in

2013, the lowest level since the early 1970s. Almost two-thirds of these apprehensions were made by the USBP, and the remainder by ICE officials acting in the US interior.

In the five years up to 2014, there were two million deportations from the United States, the highest level ever recorded. In 2013 alone, a historic high of 438,000 people were removed. Two-thirds of all deportations originated from the border region, the rest from the interior. Later, when Obama stepped in to slow deportation rates by executive order, lawsuits by several states delayed their implementation.

Fig. 7: Multimillion-dollar canyon landfill, with new fencing and access roads on top, Smuggler's Gulch, near Tijuana.

Between 2005 and 2011, as the number of apprehensions fell and deportations reached record levels, the outflow of Mexicans from the United States began to exceed the inflow. The unauthorized migrant population living in the United States fell from an estimated 12.4 million in 2007 to 11.1 million in 2011. DHS enforcement actions likely contributed to these trends, but many other factors were influential, including rising deaths and injuries incurred by border-crossers; their increased exposure to personal violence, such as kidnapping for ransom; and the spiraling costs of assisted border passages. In addition, declining job opportunities in the United States caused by economic recession were slowing the "pull" factor of migration into the country, just as improvements in the Mexican economy were reducing the "push" factors encouraging Mexicans to migrate. What no one is able to demonstrate conclusively is the specific contribution of any single variable toward the decline of the undocumented population in the United States since the SBI began.[4]

The Border-Industrial Complex

Consciously or not, since 2005 the SBI has caused the creation of a vast border security apparatus. I refer to this as a "border-industrial complex" (BIC), deliberately invoking President Eisenhower's 1961 warning of the emergent military-industrial complex in the United States. Some observers may be heartened by this consolidated national-security apparatus. However, as BIC influence penetrates ever more deeply into the territory and fabric of the United States, complaints about overreach and abuse are emerging.

The USBP has authority to operate within a 100-mile zone inside the nation's borders, including its water boundaries—a territory encompassing two-thirds of the US population.

Its agents possess stop-and-search capacities that exceed those of local law enforcement. Journalist Todd Miller claims that the entire country has been transformed into a "virtual border zone" under the authority of a "border patrol nation."[5]

Fig. 8: Mobile surveillance tower and Border Patrol vehicle, Algodones Dunes, CA.

An increased belligerence toward law-abiding citizens has become characteristic of border policing. The USBP is often accused of excessive force, including situations that resulted in death. A culture of impunity is also part of citizens' rebuke. In 2014, new guidelines were issued to ensure greater restraint by USBP agents. ICE officials have also been accused of exceeding their authority. In 2013, revised guidelines were issued governing its conduct during raids on private homes in search of undocumented migrants.

As the numbers of migrant apprehensions increased, ICE's detention system expanded into a far-flung network consisting of more than 500 county jails, for-profit prisons, and federal jails, where detainees were held prior to deportation. According to Tom Barry, these centers represent a new mode of incarceration: "the speculative public-private prison, publicly owned by local governments, privately operated by corporations, publicly financed by tax-exempt bonds, and located in depressed communities."[6] Immigrant advocates reserve their harshest complaints against these privatized, for-profit jails under contract with ICE. They are often under-regulated and non-accountable, whith detainees sequestered in unsafe conditions without representation or adequate medical care, and transferred unnecessarily within the detention system, making it more difficult for them to maintain contact with legal counsel and families. Excessive use of solitary confinement in detention centers is an especially contested practice currently undergoing review.

Fig. 9: Holtville Cemetery, CA, containing many unmarked graves of migrants who died attempting to cross into the United States.

And in what is the greatest irony, migrants held in detention centers often work in kitchens and laundry rooms, for which they usually get paid $1 per day. Such coercive use of detained migrant labor makes the federal government—which prohibits hiring illegal workers—the largest single employer of undocumented migrants in the country.

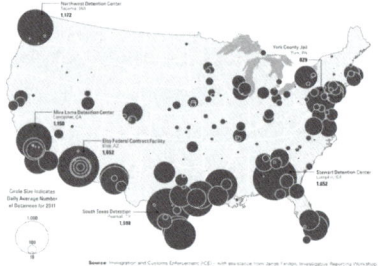

Fig. 10: Location of private detention centers in the United States, 2011.

Opposition to DHS practices emanate from across the political spectrum, and, cumulatively, they have begun to effect changes. Most dramatic was the termination of the Secure Communities (SC) program, a benchmark policy in both the Bush and Obama administrations. Marketed as a program to identify and deport serious criminals among the undocumented population, SC suffered in two ways: from "bait and switch" tactics (i.e., the program was justified as described, but implemented differently) and "mission drift" (a conscious or unconscious deviation from original program intentions). Either way, roughly three-quarters of those deported under SC had no criminal record, only convictions related to minor offenses. In 2015, DHS conceded that SC had failed to meet its stated goal of making communities more secure, and terminated the program.

Third Nation

I have revisited many places along the border many times since I began exploring in 2002. Today, the raucous efforts toward fortification have slowed down, replaced on both sides by busy efforts to open new ports of entry in the wall, or expand the capacity of existing ports.

Most memorably, I returned to El Paso Ciudad Juárez, where the river boundary meets the land boundary at monument number 1. Accustomed by now to the walls' shadows, I was taken aback to discover that there was no border fence at this critically important juncture in the boundary line. Instead, the border is marked only by a shallow earthen berm with a modest sign atop it, announcing the international border. The ambience during my visit that day was relaxed. I chatted amiably with people on the other side, exchanging courtesies in Spanish and English. Things were as they should be. Of course, I knew from past experience that someone, somewhere was observing our behavior, but such surveillance may be the price of security without walls.

In the three decades since the 1986 Immigration Reform and Control Act was passed, the United States has spent over $187 billion on immigration control and border security.

The unlamented 2013 Senate proposal for immigration reform included provisions for $40 billion more to be spent on another 700 miles of walls, and a doubling of USBP agents to 40,000. (The trade publication *Homeland Security Today* described the bill as a "treasure trove" for contractors in the border security business.) We may forever lack a comprehensive cost-benefit analysis for the SBI program, but sufficient evidence exists already to suggest that many such emphases have little or no justification based in evidence.

What do the citizens of the borderland third nation want? In a nutshell, they want to get their lives back; to manage their own destinies without interference from outsiders; and to act urgently to help themselves. In my many conversations, they are clear about their preferences:

End the occupation. Border communities deeply resent the pervasive presence of agents of the "police state," especially in the US interior. Justifying the presence of immigration-enforcement agencies, judging their performance, and curtailing abusive practices are integral to any program evaluation calculus.

Take down the wall. The DHS long ago backed away from the claim that the fortifications have sealed the border, instead asserting that they were intended solely to slow down migrants who would then be apprehended by conventional USBP agents. Where other means of adequate surveillance and security are, or can be made available, the well-being of the third nation outweighs the profitability of the border-industrial complex.

Restore the land. The occupied zones near the line often resemble sites of military occupation or natural disaster. The cost of cleaning up this mess should be charged to past and present contractors, and be incorporated into borderland risk assessment and infrastructure planning.

Fig. 11: Monument number 1 between El Paso and Ciudad Juárez, noteworthy for the absence of fences or walls. From the left, panel 1 shows the Casa de Adobe, the restored headquarters of Mexican Revolution leader Francisco Madero; panel 2, a bust of Madero; panel 3, a berm topped with a sign marking the international boundary; and panel 4, the ancient monument.

Invest in Economic Health and Community Development

The prosperity and well-being of third-nation communities on both sides are vital to our binational economies. Every dollar spent on risk infrastructure

along the border should be measured alongside the opportunities foregone.

1. Complete references and citations for this essay are available in Michael Dear, *Why Walls Won't Work: Repairing the US-Mexico Divide* (New York: Oxford University Press, 2015), ch. 1, 7, 11. Quick access to many of my arguments and sources is available at: http://blogs.berkeley.edu/2015/09/16/dousing-the-flames-of-immigration-rhetoric-with-facts/; http://blogs.berkeley.edu/2015/10/06/beware-of-the-growing-us-mexico-border-industrial-complex/; http://blogs.berkeley.edu/2015/11/04/an-eight-point-plan-to-repair-the-u-s-mexico-border/.
2. Henry H. Willis, Joel B. Predd, Paul K. Davis, and Wayne P. Brown, "Measuring the Effectiveness of Border Security between Ports-of-Entry," (RAND Technical Report, 2010, RAND Corp., Santa Monica, CA).
3. Jack K. Riley, "Strategic Planning for Border Security" (testimony before the Committee on Science, Space, and Technology, Subcommittee on Research and Technology, Subcommittee on Oversight, United States House of Representatives, July 31, 2014), 2.
4. A concise discussion of this issue is provided by Lisa Seghetti, "Border Security: Immigration Enforcement between Ports of Entry" (Washington DC: Congressional Research Service 7-5700, December 31, 2014.) http://trac.syr.edu/immigration/library/P10204.pdf
5. Todd Miller, *Border Patrol Nation* (San Francisco: City Lights Books, 2014), 211.
6. Tom Barry, *Border Wars* (Cambridge: MIT Press, 2011), 6–7.

Image Sources:

Jacobo Blanco, *Vistas de los monumentos a lo largo de la línea divisoria entre México y los Estados Unidos de El Paso al Pacífico,* 1901.

Fig. 11: Artwork by Dreamline Cartography.

The Ephemeral Metropolis: The Kumbh Mela and Other Temporary Cities

Rahul Mehrotra and Felipe Vera

What if we conceived of the city not as a centralized spectacle that is constantly accumulating and instead thought of it as being a kinetic entity, always in flux? Rahul Mehrotra and Felipe Vera explain their notion of "ephemeral urbanism" and what we can learn from the elastic, adaptable infrastructure of the temporary city of Kumbh Mela in Allahabad, India.

Looking at the contemporary landscape of cities, one could argue that today's urbanism seems to be suspended in a constant negotiation between two contrasting conditions. The first derives from the assumption that development is about accumulation. This generates a common anxiety that then invests capital into cities, producing what can be called a "hyper-city." In this traditional context, architecture and urban design emerge as an almost purely material exercise, often disconnected from the social implications of urbanism. Architecture, as the basic unit of urbanism, seems to be obsessed with the idea of the city as the centralizing spectacle driven by the inherent impatience of capital. Currently this is the most predominant disciplinary focus—and it extends to infrastructure. After all, the very notion of "sustainability" literally translates to the idea of perpetuating the current state of things. To "sustain" suggests the ability to maintain.

The second condition in debates about urbanism is derived from the idea that there is a more elastic, and thus weaker, expression of the urban, referred to as a "kinetic city."[1] This completely different observation of urbanity considers the city in a state of constant flux. This continuous, kinetic quality is characterized by physical transformations that shift the very fabric of the typical notions of accumulation and its relationship to development. Furthermore, the kinetic city cannot be understood as a two-dimensional entity. Instead, it is a multifaceted, three-dimensional conglomeration of incremental development, perceived as if in motion.

In a way, the kinetic city is home to an emergent population that is excluded from normative transnational networks of commerce and civil interaction. This is not to say that the kinetic city is merely for the impoverished. Rather, it is a temporal articulation and occupation of space, creating a richer sensibility of spatial reasoning that includes formerly unimagined uses in dense urban space. Therefore, as the proposed alternative conceptualization for elasticity in urbanism, the kinetic-city approach attempts to describe a surrogate city without using

Fig. 1: One of the biggest temporary settlements the world has ever seen springs into live every twelve years to accompany the Kumbh Mela festival in Allahabad, India.

the binary of the formal and informal, which does not accurately describe the intertwined physical, economic, and cultural conditions.

Understanding how to operate in a kinetic city is specific to certain contexts of rapid growth and is in a state of perpetual flux. Therefore, in an attempt to embrace more extreme conditions, to make this reading resonate more broadly and productively, the notion of the kinetic city could be expanded from "kinetic" to "ephemeral," and from "city" to the more encompassing term "urbanism." By reformulating the categories, the new focus would potentially shift from the notion of the kinetic city as a means to describe some specific local conditions to the notion of ephemeral urbanism. This reformulation offers a more accurate acknowledgment of the temporary nature that is expressed when describing a city as kinetic. It becomes a conceptual instrument that encompasses a range of alternative forms of urbanism across more diverse geographies. For example, it offers an approach to urbanism where density is not the overriding criteria and conditions within and outside the boundaries of the city are simultaneously negotiated to build more meaningful, productive, and inclusive urban expressions.

Expanding the realm enables the possibility to assemble evidence and move toward a more open urbanism. It calls to mind the question recently posed by urban scholars Peter Bishop and Lesley Williams: "Given overwhelming evidence that cities are a complex overlay of buildings and activities that are, in one way or another, temporary, why have urbanists been so focused on permanence?"[2]

Richard Sennett answers this question when he describes "open" as meaning "incomplete, errant, antagonistic, and non-linear."[3] However, these connotations do not consider that the study of "ephemeral landscapes" presents us with conditions that are unfinished. The idea is that incomplete constructions are based on specific conditions with open templates yet to be developed, transformed, and materialized. Despite these implications, the growing attention that environmental and ecological issues have gained in urban discourses, articulated through the concerns surrounding the recent emergence of landscape as a model for urbanism, demonstrate the need to evolve more nuanced discussions on the nature of the city. Ideally these discussions will clarify the limited representation of the urban condition. The physical structure of cities around the world is evolving, morphing, mutating, and becoming more malleable, more fluid, and more open to change than the technology and social institutions from which they are generated.

The Kumbh Mela as an Extreme Example of Ephemeral Urbanism

The Kumbh Mela festival is held in Allahabad, India. In 2013, more than 100 million people from all walks of life came to bathe in the confluence of the Ganges and Yamuna Rivers during the 55 days of the festival (January 14 to March 10). This would be a marvel of civic planning and logistics even if the festival was held in Allahabad itself, but it is not. Instead, in just eight weeks from mid November to early January, leading up to the festival, a *nagri* (temporary city) springs up on the riverbanks, on an otherwise uninhabited floodplain that was under water only a month before the start of construction. On the most important days of the 2013 festival, attendance reached an estimated twenty million people, so this temporary city had to provide not only lodging and provisions, but an entire infrastructure complete with roads, bridges, sanitation, power grid, hospitals, seven train stations, and a police force of over 12,000. In the three weeks after the festival ended, the entire city was disassembled and the plain returned to the rivers, which would flood it again a month later.

sheer numbers of people, the Kumbh Mela deploys its own roads, pontoon bridges, cotton tents serving as residences and venues for spiritual meetings, and social infrastructure, such as hospitals and vaccination clinics—all replicating the functions of an actual city. The pop-up settlement for the Kumbh Mela, a Hindu religious festival held every twelve years, seamlessly serves three million people who gather for the full 55 days, and an additional flux of ten to twenty million people who come for 24-hour cycles on the six main bathing dates.

Fig. 3: Sanitation infrastructure on site at the Kumbh Mela.

Fig. 2: The main way to the Sangam, the confluence of the Ganges and Yamuna Rivers.

The case of the Kumbh Mela is the most extreme construction and biggest manifestation of an infra-light paradigm. One of the biggest public gatherings in the world in terms of

This temporary city, and its infrastructure, is extremely elastic. It is constantly adapting to radical fluctuations in the number of people it hosts and to the monsoon's effect on the amount of water that moves through the shifting rivers. The vacant space, especially along the riverbanks of the Ganges, transforms dramatically with the drastic expansion of the river's surface during the monsoon season. From May until late October, the whole plain is inundated, leaving less than eight weeks in between the waters receding and the deployment of this ephemeral megacity. This short timeframe creates many design and planning challenges for the construction and administration of the Kumbh Mela. Unlike a more permanent city, where the construction of the physical environment happens as an aggregation of relatively permanent parts that progressively materialize the space, the Kumbh Mela takes form like a choreographic process of temporal urbanization, happening in coordination with environmental dynamics. It comprises five stages: 1) planning, 2) construction, 3) assembly, 4) operation and disassembly, and 5) deconstruction. These stages are directly linked to the makeshift context and timings determined by the presence of the monsoon in the region. Large fluctuations of people and the shifting of the river make the Kumbh Mela site an unpredictable environment for addressing even the most basic design challenges. Issues of social inclusion, urban diversity, and even expressions of democracy arise under the framework of neutralizing grids of roads that differ in structure, module, and geometry—organizing a seemingly endless texture of materials such as textiles, plastic, and plywood.

Fig. 4: Looking over the temporary city towards the Sangam.

The origins of the grid as the fundamental physical planning device can be traced to mid-nineteenth-century British colonialism. In the case of the Kumbh Mela, the planning process starts with a grid that serves as a framework for the administrators of the festival to allocate spaces and structure the organization of different facilities. The final form of the city is the result of a progressive resolution of uncertainties ranging from the geology of the riverbed to speculations on the numbers of people anticipated to visit on major bathing days. As more information is available, the city's master plan evolves progressively while adjusting to the grid's geometry. The final geometry of this grid gets adapted to the morphology of the floodplain, which is only revealed once the river has actually receded. By the time the Ganges retreats, the administrator or *Mela Adhikari* (the commissioner for the city) must have transformed this complex spatial and political landscape into a simple grid that, in the case of the 2013 festival, divides the space into fourteen self-sufficient sectors, upon which the infrastructure is deployed. These sectors are the spatial translation of an administrative structure. Each of these sectors is conceived as an independent and almost self-sufficient unit. Although sectors aim to work independently, different sectors accomplish different functions within the ephemeral city as a whole. This subdivision is represented on a map that captures the spatial parcelization of the sectors and camps. The areas contained by the grid differ in

structure, module, and geometry. Unlike other temporary settlements, the basic grain of the Kumbh Mela is not the repetition of a unique structure, like a tent, but the definition of bigger open areas—the units of the camps. These camps are given to religious communities without preconceived internal regulation. This grants authority to each community to organize their space creatively, in ways that express their individual identities, resulting in the emergence of various forms of spatial organization. The resulting network of roads, bridges, and shelters, as well as social infrastructures—such as temporary hospitals, markets, police stations, and social centers—replicates the functions of a permanent city.

Fig. 5: View from one the temporary pontoon (floating) bridges installed over the Ganges during the Kumbh Mela.

The Kumbh Mela of 2001 comprised eleven sectors, while the 2013 edition had fourteen. The different parts of the camps are built using bamboo, fabric, corrugated metal sheets, or plastic sheets, the same materials with which slums or tempo-

Fig. 6: The infrastructure that serves the pop-up city is as complex as that found in its more permanent counterparts, but its temporary nature lends it the advantage of adaptability.

rary buildings in urban India are built traditionally. More permanent areas, like hospitals, are built in plywood. The government invests what is necessary to flatten the sandy ground on the banks of the Ganges and on the Yamuna, which is where the tents and an array of temporary structures will be located. These sectors are connected by other elements that facilitate mobility. One that is especially present in the imagination of the ephemeral city is the floating bridge—one of the most used layers of infrastructure. The function of these pontoon bridges is to provide accessibility to and from camps, and to help bridge the edges of the Ganges river; seventeen were built in the latest version of the Kumbh in order to interconnect different areas within it, articulating the network of projected roadways.

The grid is initially inscribed onto the sandy riverbed via a ceremony carried out by priests of the different *Akharas*, or sects, that occupy and sanctify the land. This grid finds its physical manifestation in the form of diverse layers of infrastructure, such as water, electricity, sewage, roads, and bridges. Not unlike the grids of more permanent cities like Chandigarh or New York City, these administrative and infrastructural lines contain neutral spaces where diverse residential, commercial, and cultural activities can evolve. The seventeen pontoon bridges, built to supplement the existing bridges, are core components of the physical infrastructure. While bridges in conventional cities tend to be limited to specific points, the large

number of these floating bridges ties the grid across the two sides of the river like a continuous seam—with virtually every road spanning the river via a bridge. While the existing infrastructure, such as bridges, roads, railway lines, train stations, and power lines, are heavy, rigid constructions that support continuous use over time, the Kumbh Mela's specific infrastructure is soft and adapts dynamically to the current flow of people, water, and energy. The limited number of necessary pieces works to maximize the potential for reconfiguration and future use beyond the Kumbh Mela. Many of the more durable and complex components are stored or reincorporated into regional construction to serve other festivals or disaster relief in other parts of the state, resulting in a seamless feedback of material flow. Other elements are disassembled and recycled, while softer organic materials, such as thatch or bamboo, are left in the ground to be reabsorbed by the agricultural fields, or to be washed away in the next monsoon.

Without having seen images of the Kumbh Mela one could hardly believe that a complex city of such scale could be set up, even using all the technology and discipline that we currently possess. However, the lack of technological specificity and reversibility as a pre-defined constraint, on account of the specific expiry date for the city, is where the robustness of its construction lies. It is designed to be easily dismantled; this is what makes the process of planning and design run so smoothly. Hence, one of the

Fig. 7: The pontoon bridges are temporary constructions that serves as infrastructure for the thousands of pedestrians who cross the river during the Kumbh Mela.

most valuable lessons offered by the Kumbh Mela is the implementation of infra-light tactics to build a whole city that does not aim to be permanent. We should focus our attention on the temporary solutions for temporary problems. The alignment between the temporality of the problem and that of the solution is something we could— and should—incorporate as a mode of operation for the cities we reshape and create.

While the word "infrastructure" usually brings to mind heavy and corporeal constructions, smart processes of incremental aggregation can reach the scale of significant interventions by presenting a soft or even extremely light infrastructure. The roads of the Kumbh, for instance, instead of being paved, are constructed from steel plates that can be carried by local people without any heavy machinery. The unspecific and adjustable technology used for connecting pieces of infrastructure grants them the possibility of being reintroduced into the regional economies of construction once the festival is over. On account of the ease with which this infrastructure can be dismantled there is a prompt and effective recycling of the material that is used to construct the city. The paraphernalia that are not reused are usually made out of reabsorbable material, such as thatch or bamboo, which get incorporated into the site or merged with the natural terrain through organic decomposition.

Fig. 8: The flood plain in the evening, with the pontoon bridges visible in the background.

Once the festival is over, the whole city is disassembled as quick as it was deployed, reversing the constructive operation and disaggregating the city into its basic components. By March everything is dismantled and taken back to storage, or sold to construction sites in the region. Finally, in July the river floods over the traces of the city, until October, when the river again reaches its lowest levels, and the site is exposed again to be used for agriculture. It will be a productive site for twelve years, until a new version of the ephemeral megacity will be built again to sit lightly on the sandy banks of the Ganges for a few weeks.

At the Kumbh Mela there is a sense of openness that manifests at different scales and stages, from the scale of the construction detail to the scale of the master plan, as well as from the scale of its macro-planning to its later deconstruction. However, perhaps the most powerful aspect of the Kumbh Mela city is that its robustness and resilience are first conceived of as an open work, as a text written in dialogue with its users. The pragmatism of the officials who plan the festival is complemented by the use and appropriation of the site and materials by devotees and saints. The fluid openness that defines the urban fabric of the Kumbh Mela is based on an implicit contract of confidence and a common religious purpose. Again, the ephemeral city of the Kumbh, unlike the closed city, is resilient exactly because, in Sennett's words, it "is a bottom-up place; it belongs to the people." Challenging current trends, as an extreme case of design and planning with uncertainty, the Kumbh Mela shows us how improvisation and incompleteness can become fundamental in the construction of strength and unity.

In the camps, highly heterogeneous structures are organized around combinatory systems that rely on very few building strategies. Each of the few building techniques implemented at the Kumbh are based on the repetition and recombination of a basic module with a simple connection, generating a wide range of enclosures, from small tents to complex structures that give expression to diverse social institutions such as theaters, monuments, temples, and hospitals. All of them are constructed out of the same elements—

bamboo used as a framework and connected to laminar materials such as corrugated metal and fabric.

The process of construction and re-construction, as well as formation and reabsorption into the various ecologies and geographies of the region, serves the Kumbh Mela, as well as the whole regional economy. This open condition of planning, urban design, space occupation, and constructability could also be applied to other non-permanent settlements such as refugee camps or disaster relief efforts, as well as to future urban design and redesign projects.

While recently there have been efforts to incorporate the unspecific into architectonic projects, a willingness to embrace randomness, incompletion, and incrementality in design at the urban scale could be quite beneficial. The aspiration of almost absolute control, brought on by the empowerment of new technologies, has started to be challenged by some practical and conceptual efforts to accept incompletion and incrementality as more effective strategies than the certainties and entropy of digital modeling—which is a form of the absolute! Therefore, in the same way that urban designers have learned from the experiences of incremental social housing, we can also extract lessons with respect to how openness and adaptability could be introduced into the metropolitan scale from the city of the Kumbh Mela.

Perhaps design can anticipate diverse temporalities into its images for the future. In single buildings, as in master plans, embracing change as an active dimension in spatial production is something that architects and planners need to consider more fully. Change is everywhere. Whether perceptibly or imperceptibly, different materials fade at different paces and geographies change at different speeds. The modulation of change through design processes allows for the production of flexible, elastic, and weak structures at all scales—where the transitory is privileged, if not dealt with on equal terms as the absolute! Moving forward, we can learn from the city of the Kumbh Mela to deal better with the ephemeral nature of the built environment; developing a more intelligent management of change is an essential element in the imagination of the urban.

1. Rahul Mehrotra, "Negotiating the Static and Kinetic Cities: The Emergent Urbanism of Mumbai," in *Other Cities, Other Worlds: Urban Imaginaries in a Globalizing Age*, ed. Andreas Huyssen (Durham, NC: Duke University Press, 2008).
2. Peter Bishop and Lesley Williams, *The Temporary City* (New York: Routledge, 2010), 10.
3. Richard Sennett, "The Open City," working paper, accessed February 9, 2016, http://www.richardsennett.com/site/senn/UploadedResources/The%20Open%20City.pdf.

Mass and Material Architecture: How to Unplug from HVAC Infrastructure

Salmaan Craig

Even as climates become more extreme, interior temperatures remain constant through the use of HVAC (heating, ventilation, and air conditioning) systems that exacerbate the very conditions they are meant to control. Focusing on cooling, Salmaan Craig argues for a dual approach: broadening the definition of thermal comfort and designing architectural solutions suitable for bulk use.

Blunted Sensorium

At the dawn of twentieth century, during the era of electrification, demand for artificial light far outstripped any energy savings from improved light-bulbs.[1] The same is happening today with artificial cold. Globally, energy for cooling is set to exceed energy for heating by 2060.[2] The "cold crunch" is on the horizon, and more efficient versions of the same buildings won't buck the trend.[3]

Before thinking of alternative designs, we must question our expectations for thermal comfort. Our Paleolithic tolerances have narrowed alongside the evolution of air-conditioning technology.[4] The story is documented in thermal-comfort standards written by air-conditioning engineers (who were invariably white, male, and conservatively clothed).[5]

For the major part of the twentieth century, engineers' attention was focused on reliably changing the state of the air-vapor mix.[6] This was complex enough; the subtlety of human physiology and psychology was secondary and intractable. They worked on refining a definition for a universal range of thermal conditions. The more people, activities, climates, and buildings this applied to, the better. The implicit goal was to nullify thermal sensation. The simplest way to control complexity, after all, is to avoid it entirely.

The designation of thermal "comfort" implies some recognition or anticipation of contrast. It's that mild endorphin reward released on a favorable change, or at the prospect of a favorable change. Marketeers in America's golden age of cinema knew this well; when air-conditioning was rare in homes, offices, and cars, and the thought of escaping to a cold movie theater was genuinely enticing.[7]

Today it is quite possible to move from home to car to office to mall without having to experience the outdoors. In the absence of contrast, thermal "comfort" begins to lose its meaning. Thermal "monotony," "neutrality," or "indifference" is more apt.[8] Or perhaps thermal "non-sense."

In the history of technology, the sleepwalk into luxury traps is a well-trodden path.[9] Luxuries tend to become necessities and to spawn new obligations. Once people get used to a certain luxury, they take it for granted. Then they begin to count on it. Finally, they reach a point where they can't live without it.

How does the dulling of thermal sensibility affect us? It's hardly a hot topic of research. One old military study shows that while each of us have broadly the same number of sweat glands, the total that grow to be fully operational depends on how much heat stress we experience in youth.[10] This effect is the same as a person that has strong bones today because while growing up she spent more time running and jumping than sitting and watching television.

Breathing Buildings

New thermal-comfort standards acknowledge important subtleties in thermal sensation, such as our automatic adaptation to seasonal changes.[11] This hard-fought revision has loosened the shackles significantly. A wider target comfort range, and a closer overlap with exterior temperatures, means that air-conditioning can stay switched off for longer. Design teams can now seriously consider natural ventilation.

It is hard to overstate the importance of this revision. The target comfort range is the starting point or closing door to all conversations on passive design. Not efficiency add-ons and afterthoughts, such as hi-tech glazing or new insulation materials, but bold, effective architectural designs, centered on natural ventilation. An overly conservative comfort range can give design teams the false impression that natural ventilation is possible for only a small proportion of hours in the year. Little wonder that connections to the exterior—atria, chimneys, buffer zones, and plenums—often appear frivolous.

One of the major challenges of natural ventilation is the unpredictable frequency, direction, and strength of wind. In the last decade, however, significant progress has been made in understanding a more reliable driving force. Buoyancy ventilation is natural ventilation too, but it does not rely on the wind—it is powered by the waste heat from occupants, computers, and other internal heat gains. The greater the internal gains, and the taller the room, chimney, or atrium, the greater the driving pressure difference. Out flows warm stale air from the top; in flows fresh cool air from below. Unlike wind-driven ventilation, the fresh air is pulled in, not pushed.

Much of the theoretical work has come from a lineage of researchers with connections to a group at Cambridge University.[12] The findings have been summarized into simple mathematical models so that engineers can size openings and stacks relative to the internal heat loads, and thereby deliver a reliable stream of fresh air and sustain a comfortable interior temperature.[13]

With wind-driven ventilation, there is often a mismatch between occupancy and the availability of the breeze. Not so with buoyancy ventilation. As occupancy rises, so does the driving force. With sensible space planning, buoyancy ventilation is viable when the exterior is as cool as 10°C/50°F. Plenums, buffer zones, transition spaces, common areas, or winter gardens can preheat the fresh air before it enters the occupied space proper.

In hot climates, when the interior must be cooler than the exterior, downdraft buoyancy ventilation is a theoretical possibility. Chilled ceilings cool the space and the flow reverses. Energy is needed to cool the water in the pipes embedded in the soffit, but tepid water is sufficient because of the large cooling surface area. And there is no need for ductwork. While untested, this arrangement could be of importance in hot, dry, polluted cities where the air higher up is cleaner.

The influence of the Cambridge group is starting to show. Some designers are starting to realize that buoyancy ventilation makes natural ventilation a more feasible prospect. For instance, a trend can be seen in the buildings of Foster+Partners. The practice's Commerzbank Headquarters, completed in 1997 in Frankfurt, was branded as the world's first ecological office tower. A series of staggered winter gardens meant openable windows could be placed near most occupants, giving free access to side ventilation. 30 St Mary Axe in London, designed for Swiss Re and completed in 2004, had spiraling mini-atria, each stacked six stories high, enclosed by an aerodynamic form, giving occupants access to wind-driven or buoyancy ventilation, depending on conditions. It was a complex arrangement and its performance is unknown. The Apple Campus in Cupertino, currently under construction, is designed around the simpler principles of buoyancy ventilation. The Bloomberg HQ in London, also under construction, is another deep-plan office designed to run on buoyancy ventilation for the major part of the year.

Fig. 1: New office headquarters —with no HVAC infrastructure whatsoever—designed by and for Medellín's urban planning department, *Empresa de Desarrollo Urbano* (EDU).

For the first time we can contemplate high-density offices free of HVAC (heating, ventilation, and air-conditioning) infrastructure. At the time of writing, I am consulting on the design of a mid-rise office tower in Medellín, Colombia, a climate so perfect for natural ventilation that they call it *la eterna primavera*. There is little wind, however, so we are applying a new model to design the building so that it is controlled by buoyancy

Fig. 2: The exterior shading screen is made from prefabricated Glass-fibre Reinforced Concrete (GRC). A single-glazed facade will be fitted behind the screen, on the interior side. The lack of HVAC infrastructure means double or triple glazing is unnecessary.

ventilation, powered by internal gains, with a boost in the afternoon from a west-facing solar chimney.[15] There is also exposed thermal mass to reduce the radiant temperature, and the effect of mass on stack pressure has been accounted for. The idea is that every person will receive the same twenty liters of fresh air per second, and experience the same range of operative temperatures.

On each floor, 28 people will share a space of 100 square meters, but no HVAC infrastructure will be installed. The new headquarters is for the

Urban Planning Department (EDU) of Medellín, which is willing to see it as an experiment in robust, buoyancy-centered design, not only for its architects but for the wider research community too. We plan to monitor the behavior of the building and the response of occupants live on the Internet. The performance of simple measures will be under the spotlight. For instance, the windows will be manually operable, with graphics on the glazing indicating by how much that window should be opened depending on the occupancy on that

Fig. 3: Buildings can be ventilated naturally and reliably in the absence of wind by exploiting an interior-exterior pressure difference, powered by the waste heat from people and equipment. These water bath models—a form of "analogue" computing, well established in the field of fluid dynamics— explore how a warm, massive envelope (dark gray) could generate the necessary updraft. A comparably cool mass generates a downdraft of equal strength.

floor. The occupants are architects who are keen to learn about buoyancy ventilation by experience so they can apply the knowledge in future designs to help stop Medellín from sleepwalking into the "HVAC trap." The client is unique in that they understand the value of Post-Occupancy Evaluation and are willing to be transparent with the results.

Thermal Texture

We adapt to seasonal changes and diurnal shifts in temperature. But there are many more subtleties of thermal sensation to explore. Some are bound to suggest energy dividends.

There is an experiment I recreate with my students that has been attributed to John Locke, the seventeenth-century philosopher.[16] I ask a volunteer to come to the front of the class, where he finds a table with three buckets of water. One is hot, one is cold, and one is at room temperature. He puts one hand in the hot bucket, and the other hand in the cold bucket. After acclimatizing to the temperatures, he takes both hands out, and plunges them both into the middle bucket—the one full with water at room temperature. When I ask him to guess the temperature, he struggles to respond: "I can't tell, because my hot hand feels cold, but my cold hand feels hot!"

These crossed wires highlight that our bodies are not objective measures of temperature. Our thermal senses are change seeking. They are tuned to cultivate an internal homeostasis, but the calibration is subjective. We sen-se comfort, discomfort, pleasure, or pain, depending on the thermal stimulus, and whether it has the potential to threaten or ameliorate our internal state of homeostasis.[17] The hardware is Paleolithic, but the software is being blunted, and the range is narrowing. Are we like tops in a spin, which can tolerate a nudge, but no longer a push?

Le Corbusier said that architecture is the "play of masses brought together in light."[18] If only he'd had the foresight to add heat. There is more to heat than temperature, just as there is more to light than lux. And more so, since heat comes in many forms. Daylight has been sculpted by architects to create scenes of drama, tension, and difference; to program social interaction; to cultivate individual calm; and to heighten group alertness. Where is the appetite for exploring heat and the subtleties of its perception? The "cold crunch" demands that we atomize the idea of thermal comfort. Without this curiosity, we will never find an antidote to HVAC infrastructure.

Smart Geometry, Dumb Materials

A camel is a horse designed by committee. This old saying springs to mind on seeing Rem Koolhaas's installation of a contemporary office ceiling, suspended claustrophobically below a soaring dome frescoed with scenes of the evolution of art, for his exhibition "Elements of Architecture,"[19] at the 14th Venice Architecture Biennale, in 2014. According to Koolhaas:

"The ceiling used to be decorative, a symbolic plane, a place invested with intense iconography. Now, it has become an entire factory of equipment that enables us to exist, a space so deep that it begins to compete with the architecture. It is a domain over which architects have lost all control, a zone surrendered to other professions."[20] I propose another name for this "surrendered space": the "clusterduct." Because while it has been handed over to a splintered pack of specialists, a rabble who do not care for Architecture with a capital A, *they are not in control of it either.*

For some years now, commentators have looked on with despair at the fragmented, chaotic state of our industry's knowledge, labor, and materials supply chain.[21] This decentralized, fickle network of self-interested, risk-adverse actors tends to reinforce the status quo, making anything more than incremental innovation unlikely. Those who lament this state of affairs used to advocate moving construction sites into factories. Now they are more likely to sing the praises of BIM (Building Information Modelling).

One futurist tale of radical, disruptive innovation is that we will ride on the coattails of busy, genius materials scientists, who have invented more new materials in the last fifty years than in the prior history of human civilization.[22] But a pair of little-discussed graphs makes for sober reading. When comparing the cost of materials we use, and the value we add to them, we fall in line at the bottom of the ladder, next to the packing industry.[23]

While shoe designers and aerospace engineers can afford to use materials that cost $10 per kilogram and up, architects, civil engineers, and packaging designers must work in the order of $1 per kilogram. This is because construction demands an especially high throughput of materials. Buildings and civil structures are big, and there are a lot of them. This is obvious but the upshot is perverse. Per unit mass, the building you are in costs the same to make as the disposable cup in your hand or the foil around your sandwiches.

This explains why insulation materials and packing materials are so interchangeable. It also explains why the usual suspects for structural materials dominate—wood, concrete, steel, glass, fired clays. As bulk structural materials, they are the cheapest and best performers per unit mass or volume.[24] The same list of candidates comes up when examining the structural performance per unit of embodied energy or carbon dioxide.[25] By orders of magnitude, they are the best bulk performers within budget.

Are we condemned to use concrete? Can we build towers with timber? Should clothing designers share responsibility for steering clear of the cold crunch? The stark reality is that we are tasked at doing better—much better—with the palette of materials we already have.

Materials scientists will not fire a silver bullet anytime soon—but we can learn from them. The majority of them are not searching for fundamentally new materials; they realize that this is unlikely. Most are working on new hybrids of existing materials. The idea is to superimpose properties and get more than the sum of the parts.[26] There are lots of basic materials to play with, lots of possible combinations, and plenty of successful precedents. Think of fiber-reinforced plastics, cellular materials, and other composites—or reinforced concrete and multilayered structural glass.

Some materials scientists even see themselves as architects. That is, they "architect" materials.[27] They design on a smaller scale, between the micrometer and the centimeter. But the variables they tinker with are undeniably architectural: the choice of materials, their relative volumes, the shapes and their connectivity, and the length scale of the features. They are in the business of organizing matter in space. The purpose is to better orchestrate phenomena.

With the new capabilities afforded by digital fabrication, in particular 3-D printing, the mesoscale tinkering of materials has fallen within remit of some architects in academia and practice. This "bottom-up" trend is nascent and bears a distinct hacker-collective spirit. Contributors seem more interested in communicating and sharing than laying claim to intellectual property.

Historically, only two types of patents gain traction in the construction industry: those for mass-production material processes, such as float-glass or rock-wool insulation, or those for higher-tech plug-in modules, such as AC units. This makes sense when looking at the special conditions of the construction industry. That is, the highly fragmented knowledge and materials supply chain, the severe constraints on material cost, and the fact that "solutions" must be flexible so they can be adapted to local circumstances, since there is not much opportunity for wholesale repetition. Either you score on bulk materials that everyone in the network can use according to the demands of their project, or you score with something that can be easily added in fit-out.

In between, there is a space where another type of innovation takes place. Here intellectual property is part of a shared commons. This commons is stored in the minds of architects and engineers who learn details, make adjustments, and pass them on. It is embodied in built examples all around.

The "solutions" are tectonic in nature: they relate to the configuration of materials and parts in space. Historically, they are configurations that can be seen clearly with the naked eye. They occur on the centimeter to the meter scale. (We are talking orders of magnitude; so the meter scale involves features that are tens or hundreds of meters in length scale too.) Now, with the growth in "architectured" materials, we can add another length scale to the commons of solutions.

To make an impact on construction, to change how buildings are built, your ideas must proliferate in the commons. To proliferate in the commons, *the ideas must be adaptable configurations of standard materials.*

Conclusion

Global energy for cooling is set to exceed energy for heating by 2060. More efficient versions of the same buildings won't buck the trend. We need to figure out how to unplug buildings from HVAC infrastructure. This is now feasible for high-density offices in certain climates, thanks to revisions in thermal-comfort standards and advances in the theory and practice of buoyancy ventilation. To make these "breathing buildings" feasible in a wider range of climates, building envelopes must be put to work as heat exchangers. The designs must be open-source, adaptable to local circumstance, and made—or "architectured"—from standard materials. Otherwise there is little chance of them being taken up industry-wide.

1. Roger Fouquet and Peter J. G. Pearson, "Seven Centuries of Energy Services: The Price and Use of Light in the United Kingdom (1300–2000)," *Energy Journal* (2006): 139–77.
2. "Birmingham Energy Institute Policy Commission: Doing Cold Smarter – University of Birmingham," accessed January 19, 2016, http://www.birmingham.ac.uk/research/activity/energy/policy/cold/doing-cold-smarter.aspx.
3. Jon Henley, "World Set to Use More Energy for Cooling than Heating," *The Guardian*, October 26, 2015, sec. Environment, http://www.theguardian.com/environment/2015/oct/26/cold-economy-cop21-global-warming-carbon-emissions.
4. Daniel Lieberman, *The Story of the Human Body: Evolution, Health, and Disease*, 1st ed. (New York: Pantheon Books, 2013).
5. Pam Belluck, "Chilly at Work? Office Formula Was Devised for Men" *New York Times*, August 3, 2015, http://www.nytimes.com/2015/08/04/science/chilly-at-work-a-decades-old-formula-may-be-to-blame.html?_r=0.
6. Gail Cooper, *Air-Conditioning America: Engineers and the Controlled Environment,* 1900–1960, Johns Hopkins Studies in the History of Technology (Baltimore, MD: Johns Hopkins University Press, 1998).
7. Ray Bert, "Losing Our Cool: Uncomfortable Truths about Our Air-Conditioned World (and Finding New Ways to Get Through the Summer)," *Civil Engineering* 80, no. 9 (2010): 82.
8. Stephen Healy, "Air-Conditioning and the 'Homogenization' of People and Built Environments," *Building Research & Information* 36, no. 4 (2008): 312–22, doi:10.1080/09613210802076351; Thomas Parkinson, Richard de Dear, and Christhina Candido, "Thermal Pleasure in Built Environments: Alliesthesia in Different Thermoregulatory Zones," *Building Research & Information* 44, no. 1 (2016): 20–33.
9. Yuval Noah Harari, *Sapiens: A Brief History of Humankind* (Random House, 2014), 84–88.
10. Daniel Lieberman, *The Story of the Human Body*, 295–98.
11. Richard J. de Dear and Gail S. Brager, "Thermal Comfort in Naturally Ventilated Buildings: Revisions to ASHRAE Standard 55," *Energy and Buildings* 34, no. 6 (2002): 549–61.
12. Torwong Chenvidyakarn, *Buoyancy Effects on Natural Ventilation* (Cambridge: Cambridge University Press, 2013).
13. Andrew Acred and Gary R. Hunt, "A Simplified Mathematical Approach for Modelling Stack Ventilation in Multi-compartment Buildings," *Building and Environment* 71 (January 2014): 121–30, doi:10.1016/j.buildenv.2013.09.004.
14. T. Chenvidyakarn and A. Woods, "Top-Down Precooled Natural Ventilation,"

Building Services Engineering Research & Technology 26, no. 3 (2005): 181–93, doi:10.1191/0143624405bt129oa.

15. Andrew Acred and Gary R. Hunt, "Stack Ventilation in Multi-Storey Atrium Buildings: A Dimensionless Design Approach," *Building and Environment* 72 (February 2014): 44–52, doi:10.1016/j. buildenv.2013.10.007.

16. Edward A. Arens, H. Zhang, and C. Huizenga, "Partial- and Whole-Body Thermal Sensation and Comfort, Part II: Non-uniform Environmental Conditions," Center for the Built Environment, University of California, Berkeley (2005).

17. Richard de Dear, "Revisiting an Old Hypothesis of Human Thermal Perception: Alliesthesia," *Building Research & Information* 39, no. 2 (2011): 108–17, doi :10.1080/09613218.2011.552269.

18. Le Corbusier, *Toward an Architecture*, Texts & Documents (Los Angeles: Getty Research Institute, 2007).

19. Rem Koolhaas et al., *Elements of Architecture* (Venice: Marsilio Editori Spa, 2014).

21. Cited in Oliver Wainwright, "Rem Koolhaas Blows the Ceiling Off the Venice Architecture Biennale," *Guardian*, June 5, 2014, http://www.theguardian. com/artanddesign/architecture-design-blog/2014/jun/05/rem-koolhaas-architecture-biennale-venice-fundamentals.

21. *Rethinking Construction: The Egan Report* (Oxford: Blackwell Science Ltd, 2008 [1998]).

22. M. F. Ashby, *Materials Selection in Mechanical Design*, 4th ed. (Amsterdam: Elsevier, 2011), 4–8; Mike Ashby, "Materials: A Brief History," *Philosophical Magazine Letters* 88, no. 9–10 (2008): 749–55, doi:10.1080/09500830802047056.

23. Ashby, *Materials Selection in Mechanical Design*, 482–83.

24. Ibid., 138–42.

25. M. F. Ashby, *Materials and the Environment : Eco-Informed Material Choice*, 2nd ed. (Amsterdam: Elsevier, 2013), 250–55.

26. M. F. Ashby and Y. J. M. Brechet, "Designing Hybrid Materials," *Acta Materialia* 51, no. 19 (2003): 5801–21, doi:10.1016/ S1359-6454(03)00441-5.

27. Mike Ashby, "Designing Architectured Materials," *Scripta Materialia* 68, no. 1 (2013): 4–7, doi:10.1016/j.scriptamat.2012.04.033.

Biopolitics on the Nile: The Toshka Project

Charlotte Malterre-Barthes

Though politics often claim hydrological infrastructure as evidence of national technological achievement, Charlotte Malterre-Barthes uses Egypt's history of managing the Nile under the auspices of food security as the control not just of water but population and territory.

Here, the political, social, national, and military battles of the Egyptian people materialize as the bulk of the great rock which blocked the old Nile waterway, to accumulate its waters into the biggest lake ever made by man, as a permanent source of prosperity.

—Gamal Abdel Nasser,
May 14, 1964[1]

Wearing a dark suit and aviator sunglasses, President Hosni Mubarak stands firmly, arm on the railing, overlooking blue waters. The pumping station that carries his name looms in the background. This scene occurred in 2005 during one of the many visits of the then President of Egypt to the Toshka Project, an infrastructural feat that includes the aforementioned pumping station—the largest in the world—and a 310-kilometer-long water channel, both of which aim to funnel water to one million hectares of irrigation fields for crops. The project is part of the "New Nile Valley"—a vision that encompasses three schemes (Toshka, Oweinat, and the New Valley oases) to convert part of the Western Desert into an agricultural and industrial area.

Fig. 1: Mubarak Pumping Station, Lake Nasser, 2003 Inaugurated by and named for then President of Egypt Hosni Mubarak, it is the largest pumping station ever built.

President Mubarak inspected the site at the Toshka Depression in the desert region west of Lake Nasser at various stages of construction. His visits, spanning the late 1990s to the mid-2000s, attest to both the political relevance of water infrastructures for Egypt's governing powers as well as the desire of the regime to express confidence in a plan posed to solve water supply, food scarcity, and overpopulation issues through one large-scale enterprise. The construction of the Toshka Project also places its instigator in the long lineage of Egyptian rulers who have embarked on similar schemes.

In Egypt, there is a legacy of presenting monumental water projects as national technological achievements, as was the case with the High Aswan Dam. Scholars argue that these projects have served as governmental instruments of political hegemony and social control, fostering national pride while diverting attention from other issues.[2] Toshka is one of the most recent additions to this extensive line of projects concerning irrigation and hydraulic infrastructures, most of which are partially inspired by colonial technocracy and associated with agricultural prosperity. Other examples include the Delta Barrages, Asyut Barrage, Low and High Aswan Dams, the Century Storage Scheme, and the Western Oasis Project. When considered within the historical nation-building discourse of monumental Egyptian schemes, Toshka appears to be another political and territorial act implemented in the name of food security that involves both foreign and national actors and financial capital. The project functions as a spatially grounded biopolitical instrument with social, economic, and political factors affecting the built environment and shaping territory beyond the national scale.

Foucault argued that biopolitics originated when politics ceased to be seen as an extension of war and instead began to be used as a tool to

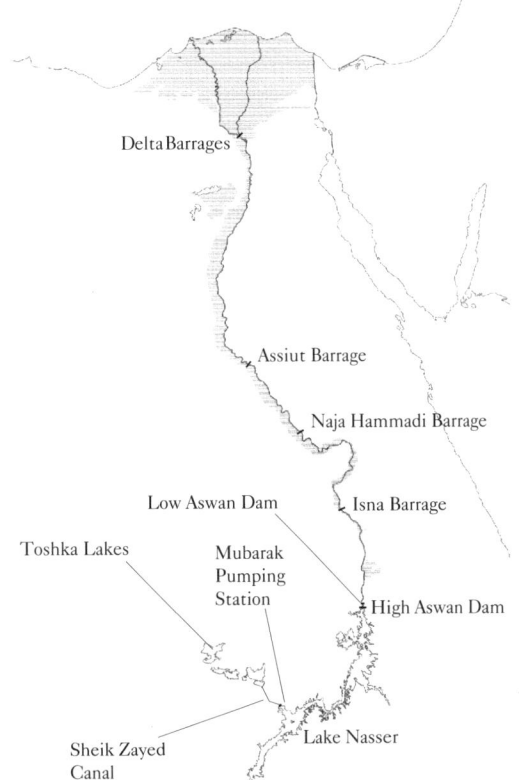

Fig. 2: An Infrastructural chronicle of the River Nile in the Egyptian territory.

control, regulate, and manage the lives of populations in the service of the state. The result of this is politics' increasing concern with the administration of life itself. Food security has therefore become a regulatory instrument with which to politically control and manage life similar to the way in which control has long been exerted over food production and supply.[3] Toshka and its preceding modern water infrastructures are the physical manifestations of this phenomenon; namely, how, under global pressure, the pursuit of national food self-sufficiency has been magnified to justify large-scale territorial transformations claiming agricultural opulence. Echoing the legacy of the High Aswan Dam, Toshka exemplifies how colossal hydro-infrastructures inserted into rural areas redefine territory—from the massive diversion of water flows to the magnitude of topographical modifications, the construction of large-scale structures, buildings, or new transportation networks, and the envisioned relocation of 20 percent of the population (around 16 million people)—resulting in tremendous political, climatic, and topographical consequences.

Evidenced as far back as biblical narratives, Egypt's fertilizing sediments carried by its major river have been imperative to ensuring local food production. Many times during the country's history, the fine balance between appropriate irrigation and flooding was a matter of life and death. For hundreds of years, Egypt has sought to secure the flow of water down the Nile to ensure its food supply through hydraulic management and artificial irrigation—often straining diplomatic relations with neighboring countries Sudan and Ethiopia in the process. In fact, the political history of the Egyptian nation-state is indissociable from that of the river and its control. Both national and colonial rulers have relied on the construction of modern infrastructures to regulate water levels and guarantee food security, resulting in territorial transformations as a physical expression of biopolitics.

Egypt's history of hydraulic management and artificial irrigation spans centuries, with the Nile having been managed since Pharaonic times, flooding annually with predictable regularity. The floodwaters were channeled into reservoirs or irrigation waterways along feddans,[4] pumped and distributed according to a complex hierarchy, and eventually released into the river in an intricate mechanism called basin irrigation. Despite claims that colonial Britain brought progress to nineteenth-century Egypt in the form of engineering, it was Khedive Muhammad Ali Pasha, Ottoman viceroy of Egypt, who first ordered infrastructural measures to harness the Nile's waters in the modern era, guided by the studies of French scientists who accompanied Napoleon's army.[5] Integrated within Ali's political project, the modernization of the irrigation system was meant to establish the nation's strength and independence. Under his rule, Egyptian agriculture, which had previously relied on yearly floodwaters to produce only one major crop a year, shifted from basin irrigation to a perennial irrigation system, expanding a network of deep canals in the delta.[6] The new system was implemented rapidly, in part due to a boost in the cultivation of cotton, with floodwaters stored in reservoirs to be used throughout the year and barrages damming the Nile to raise the water level.[7]

The first modern infrastructural works on the Egyptian Nile that aimed to increase agricultural production based on national demand were the Delta Barrages, which were planned by French engineers, located at the Nile division between the Rosetta and Damietta branches, and completed in 1862. It quickly surfaced, however, that the Delta Barrages had structural flaws and could not withstand the Nile floods. Two decades later, as financial collapse loomed, Egypt became a British protectorate. Colonial forces came to Egypt with faith in the power of technology, which took the form of irrigation infrastructures and disdain for Muhammad Ali's efforts to control floods, guarantee food security, and promote cotton production.[8] While the Delta Barrages marked the start of the irrigation works of the nineteenth century, it was their failure in restraining the floods that promoted the construction of the Low Aswan Dam. The primary motivation of the British for erecting another dam was to retain a year-round water supply, as the colonial administration was shifting from a culture of sustenance food crops to an export-oriented cotton economy. This political deviation was concealed in a discourse of modernization and rooted in a Western conception that the Nile waters had previously been underutilized. These assumptions, along with the underlying aim of serving foreign interests and fueling European banks with debt repayments generated by building the Suez Canal, resulted in increased construction of hydraulic infrastructures along the Nile.

Under British supervision, the Low Aswan Dam was completed in 1902, but it too proved insufficient and had to be raised several times. When it threatened to overflow for a *third* time in 1946, a second dam was proposed a few miles upstream—a decision that was confirmed after the overthrowing

of the monarch by Gamal Abdel Nasser's military group, the Free Officers. Following modernist rationale, the first Aswan Dam paved the way for the largest hydropower infrastructure backed by foreign expertise in Egypt: the High Aswan Dam. Motivations for its construction ranged from energy production to Cold War political arrangements, but for Nasser the primary objective was to feed the Egyptian population by improving irrigation and reclaiming desert land for agriculture. It is no surprise, then, that this massive dam (five kilometers long and 100 meters high) and the 163,000 km^3 capacity of the Lake Nasser reservoir laid the foundations for the Toshka Project.

In 1966, to prevent any downstream or backflow flooding, an overflow canal named the Toshka Spillway was excavated on the western shore of Lake Nasser, into the Toshka Depression. Though it was not used for its intended purpose, Egyptian engineers saw in it the potential to turn the Toshka Depression into a series of lakes and the opportunity to reclaim desert land[9]—an idea that was revived when, in 1996, the Nile waters overflowed into the canal.[10] A new waterway, the Sheik Zayed Canal, was created eight kilometers north of the Toshka Spillway and was supplied with Lake Nasser water by the Mubarak Pumping Station to irrigate the sands of the Western Desert. Although only partially completed, it marked the first phase of the Toshka Project. Ultimately, it is intended that the project will irrigate 540,000 feddans (approximately 560,520 acres) and become home to

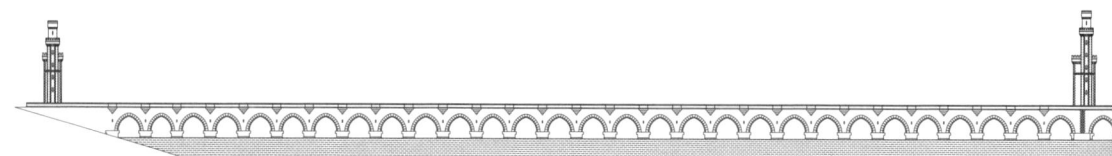

Fig. 3: Mougel Bey, Delta Barrages, Rosetta and Damietta branches of the Nile, Egypt, 1862 The Delta Barrages, ordered by Khedive Muhammad Ali Pasha, were the first modern infrastructural works on the Egyptian Nile. They never succeeded in resisting Nile flooding despite several reparation works and are currently used as bridges.

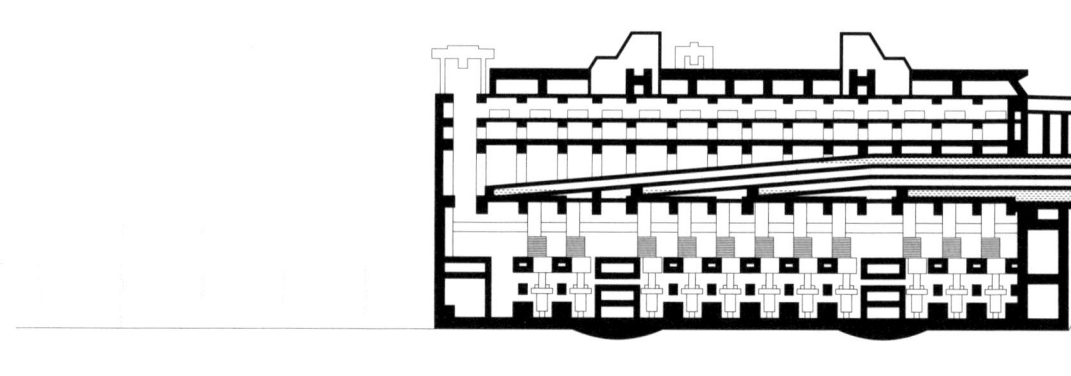

Intake canal - - - - - - - - - - - - - - - - - - - / - - - - - - - - - - - - - - - - Pumping station - - - - - - - - - -

Fig. 4: Mubarak Pumping Station, Toshka Project, Lake Nasser, Egypt, 2003 Inaugurated in 2003, the Mubarak Pumping Station supplies the Sheik Zayed Canal with Lake Nasser water to irrigate the sands of the Western Desert. It is the centerpiece of the Toshka Project. Built by a consortium of international and local companies, the station is surrounded by water in a fifty-meter-deep (164-foot-deep) intake channel with 24 vertical pumps with an intake capacity of 400 cubic meters (14,125 cubic feet) per second.

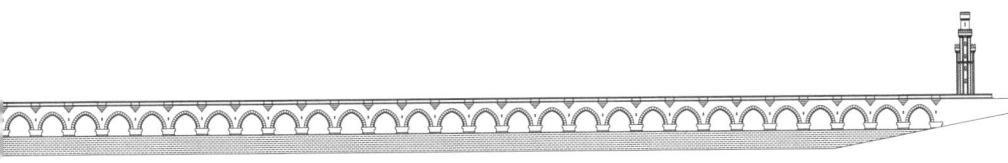

0 5   15   30 m

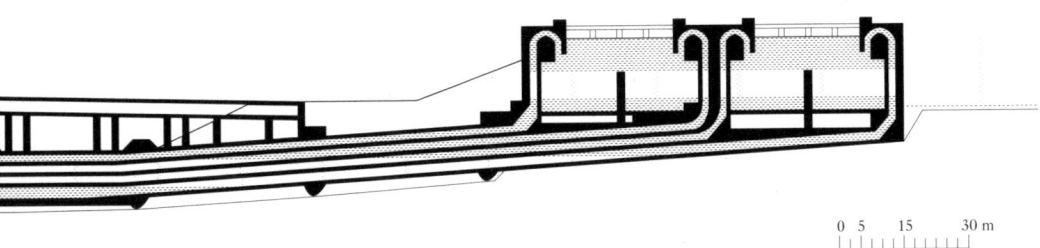

0 5   15   30 m

— — — — — — — Discharge ducts — — — — — — — — — — — — / — — — — Discharge basins —

twenty percent of the Egyptian population, to alleviate pressure on the country's crowded cities. As a public project of unprecedented scale that entails a slow pace of construction, it relies on development aid from several countries and organizations as well as on private investors. Presented as Mubarak's all-in-one solution for Egypt's urban density, food insecurity, and unemployment issues, this is a massive project involving complex arrangements of foreign investments both in terms of finance and knowledge, but one that experts claim has so far failed to deliver. High saline levels mean that the volume of available fresh water is less than expected, employment opportunities are limited, the anticipated housing and infrastructure have yet to materialize, and ultimately, food production at Toshka is concentrated on profitable export crops for foreign companies rather than on food for domestic consumption, breaking the initial promise to facilitate local agricultural production and, with it, national food security.

Fig. 6: Construction site of the Sheik Zayed Canal at Toshka, Egypt, 2010
Fed by Lake Nasser water via the Mubarak Pumping Station, the Sheik Zayed Canal is only partially completed and sustains agricultural activity in constricted fields on land that was previously desert.

The shaping of Egypt's agricultural system has meant the rearrangement of its territory and population through the ordering and managing of earth and water; namely, biopolitics as infrastructure. Fueled by a constructed image of Egypt as a country on the brink of starvation with scarce agrarian land and explosive demographics, a claim denounced by Timothy Mitchell in *Rule of Experts*, Egyptian political forces have engaged in undertaking gigantic projects against the backdrop of a historical legacy of water infrastructures. Under the cover of attempts at achieving food security, large-scale modern projects such as the one at Toshka have proved an essential element of Egyptian politics. The control over water, land topogra-

Fig. 5: One of the largest manmade lakes in the world, the Lake Nasser reservoir was created by the construction of the High Aswan Dam, completed in 1971.

phy, population, and agricultural and food production revealed by the infrastructural chronicle of the Nile is a recurrent story of power struggles over territory, people, and resources. Egypt is thus a paradigmatic case of the contemporary deployment of biopolitics, and the ensuing spatial consequences on territories, such as at Toshka, are acutely visible.[11]

A previous and modified version of this text has been published as "The Toshka Project: Colossal Water Infrastructures, Biopolitics and Territory in Egypt," in Architectural Design 86, no. 4 (2016).

1. Extract from Gamal Abdel Nasser's speech on the occasion of the diversion of the Nile River. Gamal Abdel Nasser, "The Address by President Gamal Abdel Nasser at Aswan Celebrating the High Dam Attended by Soviet Premier Nikita Khrushchev," nasser.org, May 14, 1964, http://www.nasser.org/Speeches/browser.aspx?SID=1084&lang=en.
2. Jeroen Warner, "The Toshka Mirage in the Egyptian Desert: River Diversion as Political Diversion," Environmental Science & Policy 30 (2013): 102–12.
3. See Michel Foucault, Society Must Be Defended: Lectures at the Collège De France, 1975–1976, ed. Mauro Bertani and Alessandro Fontana, trans. David Macey (New York: Picador, 2003).
4. The feddan is a unit of area used in Egypt, Sudan, and Syria. 1 feddan = 60 x 70 meters = 4,200 square meters = 0.42 hectares = 1.038 acres.
5. Timothy Mitchell, Rule of Experts: Egypt, Techno-Politics, Modernity (Berkeley: University of California Press, 2002), 35.
6. See the exhibition catalogue, Pascal Coste:, Toutes les Égypte (Marseille: Éditions Parenthèses, 1998), 40.
7. A. B. Zahlan "Established Patterns of Technology Acquisition in the Arab World," in Technology Transfer and Change in the Arab World: The Proceedings of a Seminar of the United Nations Economic Commission for Western Asia, ed. A. B. Zahlan and Rosemarie Said Zahlan (Oxford: Pergamon Press, 1978), 1–28.
8. Diana K. Davis, Edmund Burke, and Timothy Mitchell, Environmental Imaginaries of the Middle East and North Africa (Athens: Ohio University Press, 2011), 6.
9. M. M. Sayed and M. M. Kamal, "Flood Evaluation and Management after the High Dam Reservoir," in Dams and Rservoirs, Societies and Environment in the 21st Century, ed. L. Berga et al, (London: Taylor & Francis, 2006), 47–52.
10. Robert O. Collins, "Negotiations and Exploitation of the Nile Waters at the End of the Millennium," Water International 31, no. 1 (2006): 116–26.
11. Bradley Hope, "Egypt's New Nile Valley: Grand Plan Gone Bad," National, April 22, 2012, www.thenational.ae/news/world/middle-east/egypts-new-nile-valley-grand-plan-gone-bad
12. See Mitchell, Rule of Experts, 209.

Beyond the Binary: Risk, Governance and Infrastructure

Miho Mazereeuw and Claudia Bode

The steepest and most risk-susceptible topography of Peru's capital city is home to some of its most economically vulnerable residents. Miho Mazereeuw and Claudia Bode address how formal and informal realms might better interact in order to successfully manage the risks associated with building in such contexts. They make a plea for overcoming binary categorizations that tend to keep these two realms separated, acknowledging that infrastructure is not the sole property of the formal city and that true risk governance is not possible without integrated solutions.

The vast urban landscape of Lima stretches from the densely built flat plains on the Pacific coast to the perilous terrain of the surrounding mountains. These slopes, which often crumble as people climb them, are host to the majority of city's lower-income residents. This topographic segregation of the population is particularly troubling because Peru is situated in one of the most seismically active regions of the world. Seismolo-gists are concerned about the capital insofar as there has been little seismic activity since the mid-eighteenth century, a notable gap in tectonic activity, which in all likelihood points to the threat of a significant earthquake in the near future. This prospect notwithstanding, and despite the potential hazards of building on steep slopes, informal construction in the form of small brick and wooden homes perched on steep hillsides continues unabated, often with little or no infrastructural provisions.

Fig. 1: Housing covers the sloped terrain in the Villa María del Triunfo district on the outskirts of Lima.

This predicament, whereby economically weaker sectors of society are left with few housing options and thus are forced to live on dangerous, marginal land plots, is not unique to Lima. When seen in the context of decreasing municipal government investment, the issue of risk in relation to urban poverty becomes all the more pressing. This is where the concept of "risk governance" becomes timely and relevant, referring to a political framework in which multiple actors are brought together to devise ways of dealing with systemic risk in an adaptive and integrative way.[1] This concept builds on Ulrich Beck's study of what he called "risk societies," pertaining to societies that require new forms of governance to manage new—and at times unforeseeable—threats, such as nuclear fallout or global warming.[2] With this in mind, the risks in Lima's mountainous periphery raise challenging questions concerning the role of governance in risk-prone and poverty-stricken contexts, where officials are disinclined to act and where the poor are disproportionately affected by endemic marginalization, government oversight, and the ever present threat of natural disasters. More to the point, what does risk governance entail in what is essentially a state of exception?

The case of Lima foregrounds just this condition and points out the urgent need for synergies aimed at fostering social capacity-building, more responsive governance, more resilient urban structures, and more adaptive infrastructure to reduce risk. After decades of prioritizing large-scale infrastructure projects that basically cater to the formal city, alternative means to providing amenities to all sectors of society must be sought, which might require a more decentralized and incremental approach to building infrastructure. This process needs to be coupled with a durable organizational framework for citizen governance during the planning and construction

Fig. 2: Homes built upon arid slopes in the Ate District of Lima Province.

of projects, as well as for management of projects *after* they have been completed. This would be a much needed first step at including those so often excluded from the social contract, which ultimately might overturn those divisions premised on the simplistic binary distinction between the formal and informal city.

Risk and Governance

The term "risk" is often misunderstood or overly simplified. As a matter of fact, it connotes three interrelated concepts: the presence of a *hazard*, a person's *vulnerability* to that hazard, and his or her ability to *cope* with that hazard. Hazard in this case is usually considered to be of a physical nature, most often associated with a specific event and assessed in terms of its magnitude and frequency. Vulnerability may refer to a person's health, social position, economic status, age, or other attributes. Geographer Susan Cutter defines vulnerability, in particular with regard to environmental hazards, as "the potential for loss."[3] Reducing risk may mean mitigating hazards, but it may also mean lessening vulnerabilities to those hazards, especially since some may not always be manageable. A person's coping capacity can help offset these compounding effects, yet is frequently understudied.[4] The UN International Strategy for Disaster Reduction defines coping capacity as "the ability of people, organizations, and systems, using available skills and resources, to face and manage adverse conditions, emergencies, or disasters."[5] It is here where social networks, community capacity, and support mechanisms intersect with the design of shared space and infrastructure.

Furthermore, so-called "simple" risks should be differentiated from "systemic" risks, which comprise multiple components and have the potential to paralyze an entire system. Systemic risk is essentially structural, inherent to the way a society is organized and is not necessarily reduced or mitigated by short-term measures.[6] In the case of Lima, the situation on the city's outskirts is aggravated by the overlapping factors of poverty, the lack of access by the poor to the formal housing market that drives ad hoc settlement construction, not to mention a lack of available flat land. An earthquake in Lima would cause significantly more damage than in a region with similar topography but with a different type of urban development due to the extent in which multiple hazards and vulnerabilities are intertwined here.

What exacerbates the vulnerabilities of the population living on the slopes and further complicates the methods to address these conditions can be partially attributed to the common characterization of where the "formal city" ends and the "informal settlements" begin. The common oversimplification and often depoliticized understanding of terms such as "formal" and "informal" have given rise to alternative, counter urban theories of "subaltern" urbanism.[7] Such theories re-politicize this distinction by acknowledging the role of the state in creating, regulating, or perpetuating conditions of informality. Poverty scholar Ananya Roy has written about informality as a phenomenon that arises from calculated systems of deregulation, in which the state creates its own exceptions to planning rules.[8] Informal city dwellers, in this view, live within what political geographer Oren Yiftachel has called the "grey zones" that exist between the formal and informal.[9] Informality is not a result of a lack of government per se; it is a direct outcome of the power of the state to enact "states of exception." This predicament, again, is not unique to Lima, yet the unimpeded urban growth along its slopes quintessentially embodies the complexity of systemic risks within a landscape of fluctuating and politically charged interventions.

Lima: Non-Binary Urban Growth

Lima provides a telling case study of how conditions can emerge from a shifting and non-binary set of relationships between a people and the state. The city's *barriadas* (as they were referred to in the 1950s) and *pueblos jovenes* (as they were referred to in the 1960s and 1970s) are far from manifesting a homogenous mass of unregulated shantytowns and actually offer a prime example of what can be accomplished when various levels of government interact in the pursuit of more inclusive social and spatial policies.

In response to the rapid informal growth of the city during the 1950s, Lima passed a law in 1961 (the Law of Marginal Settlements and Popular Neighborhoods, or Barriadas Law) that recognized the legal status of the barriadas, while comprehensively integrating them into the city through physical upgrades.[10] Although prohibiting the construction of future barriadas, it created "popular neighborhoods," setting aside relatively flat plots of land to be settled in a coordinated manner. Throughout the 1960s and early 1970s, these plots were progressively filled by well-organized resident groups. Syndicalism shaped the structure of the barriadas as they grew, leading to neighborhoods based on the tradition of communal work. In the 1970s, SINAMOS was formed, an organization dedicated to the study of the barriadas, which led to the construction of the innovative PREVI low-cost housing projects (Proyecto Experimental de Vivienda) by renowned international and Peruvian architects.

With all due respect to such efforts, the availability of flat land has dwindled since the late 1970s and the state has withdrawn its support for upgrading and planning in accordance with neoliberal economic restructuring of the country.[11] While the state greatly reduced its direct involvement in social housing, it nonetheless distributed large amounts of property titles through the Commission for the Official Registration of Informal Property in an attempt to develop a citywide real estate market and improve access to credit for low-income homeowners; the latter, however, with little success.[12] The lack of building and planning resources for the poor has resulted in the uncontrolled growth of low-density settlements in areas that were previously deemed undevelopable due to their unfavorable topography.

Toward Integration

The complexity of Lima's situation—related to poverty, political dysfunction, and environmental risk—points to possible solutions that are adaptive and integrative to specific social and contextual challenges. To gain traction, such solutions must engage the state as the entity capable of dealing with large-scale risks. But to date, there is little incentive for the government to include the most vulnerable segments of the population, insofar as they remain disenfranchised and can thus be conveniently ignored, if not exploited outright. Metropolitan Lima contains 49 districts with no overriding mechanism of coordination for municipal planning, creating a disjunction between planning jurisdictions and actual neighborhoods that has led to a situation in which the poor are politically unrepresented.[13]

The varied urban fabric of Lima is directly tied to residents' access to state resources pertaining to planning, the provision of services, and technical advice. The mid-twentieth century saw the growth of barriadas that existed within the "gray zone" of informality: self-built, but recognized by the state, and sometimes granted legal property titles (in comparison to the illegal market of property titles).

The outer fringes of the city, however, have received little planning attention or support for construction; they exist in their current form primarily because the government has chosen to uphold a "calculated system of deregulation" that, in effect, amounts to a retrenchment of the state, and this in spite of the extreme risks posed by unfavorable site conditions for building in the hills, chronic housing shortage, persistent poverty, and the always looming possibility of earthquakes.

Fig. 3: Access and evacuation stairs in the Ate District.

In response to this dilemma, Lima's Barrio Mío program was initiated in 2012 in order to implement "Integrated Urban Projects" (PUIs) in Lima's most marginalized neighborhoods. Prioritizing health, recreation, urban development, and culture, the program aimed to combine physical improvements with social and cultural capacity-building measures. Based on a study carried out between 2011 and 2012 by geographer Jose Barreda, parts of Lima were divided into nineteen zones that corresponded to existing urban subdivisions within its poorest areas. In the end, a total of forty zones were established for the city as a whole, with an estimated 2.8 million people living in those forty priority areas situated in the steepest zones on the city's periphery.[14]

Within each zone, a PUI was to be developed via the collaboration between neighborhood residents and professional planners, engineers, and architects, all of whom aimed to upgrade physical infrastructure and implement risk mitigation strategies, while also providing social services and urban design workshops.[15] The PUIs aimed to bring together disenfranchised areas of the city by creating new administrative zones that more closely align with residents' self-determined neighborhood boundaries, giving citizens new tools for political participation and allowing them to assert themselves in a more democratic and inclusive civic process.

The Barrio Mío program focused initially on specific physical improvements, the objective being to save lives in the likelihood of an earthquake or similar disaster. The first phase of the project, carried out by geotechnical experts, included identifying those parts of the built fabric most prone to seismic failure. Teams were then brought in to plan the construction of approximately 700 access and evacuation stairways and more than a 1,000 retaining walls in unsafe neighborhoods.[16] Such interventions were meant to stabilize slopes, with the stairs also providing a more expedient escape route should an earthquake or other emergency occur.

With the slopes so stabilized, neighborhoods have been incrementally outfitted with potable water systems as well as schools and community facilities. The stairs themselves were also designed to connect communities and link with existing paths and roads, containing multiple elements such as landings with integrated benches and intermediate rest areas. Although the primary motivation for the construction of these elements has always been safety, they were also presented as anchors for current and future development, including housing and commercial spaces. In the San Juan de Lurigancho district, for example, the seven large stairways constructed included a numbering system that allows residents easier access to social services, with this small coding system also functioning as a type of address, a stipulated requirement for receiving micro-credit.

When conducting fieldwork in these sites, it became apparent that this system of decentralized risk-reduction infrastructure, as innovative as it is, constitutes still only a small remedy for much larger systemic shortfalls. Part of the problem is that the migration to the city has continued and dwellings are still being built at an alarming rate at ever-higher altitudes. Another issue is that the upgrade program, which was initially implemented to allow for collective political representation, is now being used for political gain by candidates running for office in municipal elections. A

Fig. 4: Stairway routes ascending the slopes in the
San Juan de Miraflores District in Lima Province.

representative color for the stairwells is chosen by officials, the aim being to associate the project with their particular campaign and thereby gain clout by showing presence, albeit symbolic, in local communities. It is in such cases where infrastructure becomes politicized in a very literal sense. The stairs are painted over again and again in each election cycle as a ploy to win votes and put in office an official who will supposedly serve as the people's political representative.

The irony of such tendencies notwithstanding, the social programs, tools for political organization, methods for integrated spatial design, and infrastructure for risk reduction initiated by the PUIs should nevertheless be considered as a viable model for future projects within Lima and other rapidly urbanizing fringes of cities as well. The decentralized system of physical infrastructure made up of communal stairwells and retaining walls is a relevant example to keep in mind when considering alternatives to large-scale and costly infrastructure projects. While far from perfect, these micro-engineered interventions could—and should—become part of the common repertoire of planning and design approaches to minimizing risk, specifically those risks associated with vulnerable urban settlements.

Lima's housing situation has currently reached crisis levels, as the very poor continue to build on unsafe terrain. But the solution cannot be limited to simple depoliticized technical or economic "fixes." More pertinent questions would be: Which framework would allow citizens and planners alike to question perceived binaries in the first place and enable citizens to access the resources they need to live dignified lives? How can measures be implemented to support lasting citizen governance? How can infrastructure ultimately contribute to creating places that foster greater coping capacity amongst residents? Aiming to address such questions, the concept of risk governance acknowledges the reality of complex factors that interrelate in unexpected ways to produce volatile situations like those in Lima, the solutions to which require the input of multiple actors engaging as stakeholders in a common project. But before such a concept can ever be translated into practice, we ourselves must take the risk to scrutinize those essentializing narratives of poverty that, by underwriting the distinctions between formal and informal worlds, constitute the real hazard to any inclusive civic vision.

1. Eugene Rosa, Ortwin Renn, and Aaron McCright, eds., *The Risk Society Revisited: Social Theory and Governance* (Philadelphia: Temple University Press, 2013), 154.
2. Ulrich Beck, Risk Society: *Towards a New Modernity* (London: Sage Publications, 1992).
3. Susan Cutter, Bryan J. Boruff, and W. Lynn Shirley, "Social Vulnerability to Environmental Hazards," in Susan L. Cutter, *Hazards, Vulnerability, and Environmental Jusis, At Risk, Natural Hazards, People's Vulnerability and Disasters* (New York: Routledge, 2004), 112.
5. 2009 UNISDR *Terminology on Disaster Risk Reduction* (Geneva: United Nations International Strategy for Disaster Reduction, 2009), 8.
6. Rosa, Renn, and McCright, *Risk Society Revisited*, 123.
7. Ananya Roy, „Slumdog Cities: Rethinking Subaltern Urbansim," *International Journal of Urban and Regional Research* 35, no 1 (March 2011): 235.
8. Ann Varley, "Postcolonialising Informality?," *Environment and Planning D: Society and Space* 31, no. 1 (2013): 5.
9. O. Yiftachel, "Theoretical Notes On 'Gray Cities': The Coming of Urban Apartheid?," *Planning Theory* 8, no. 1 (February 1, 2009): 88–100.
10. Ana María Fernández-Maldonado, 2007. "Fifty Years of Barriadas in Lima: Revisiting Turner and de Soto," ENHR 2007 International Conference 'Sustainable Urban Areas', 13.
11. Ibid., 15.
12. Ibid., 14.
13. Gustavo Riofrío, "Urban Slums Reports: The Case of Lima, Peru," *Understanding Slums: Case Studies for the Global Report on Human Settlements* (2003), 3.
14. Luis Rodriguez Rivero, *Vivienda en Ladera Hacía una política pública en la periferia de Lima* (PLAM2035, 2014).
15. Luis Rodriguez River, professor at the Pontificia Universidad Católica del Perú, in discussion with the authors, February 2015.
16. Emily Culver, "Social Program Barrio Mio to Complete 350 Projects in Lima's Poorest Districts," *Peru This Week*, July 2, 2013.

Land as Project:
On Territorial Construction

Milica Topalović

The scale and speed at which earth-work projects can now be implemented warrants an examination of the *problematic* of land reclamation for territorial expansion. Touching upon the role of major infrastructure projects that have reshaped Singapore's coastline, Milica Topalović charts a route through the history of what are not just constructions of land and infrastructure, but also of political power relations.

ture: the newly built sites for **Chinese** bases controlling the maritime **bas**in constitute a territorial encroa**chme**nt, in "violation of the United Nations Convention of the Law of the Sea" and "causing 'irreparable harm' to the marine environment."

Apart from provoking an international uproar in disturbing the global geostrategic hierarchies, this case also speaks in a clear, and even spectacular, manner about the nature of earthworks. This example helps lift infrastructure and land construction out of the mundane world of engineering and muddy construction pits in order to remind us of what philosophers of land or territory have long since established: that land (and infrastructure) are never innocent, or purely technical and utilitarian, but always strategic, political, and ecological.

When Chinese military ships and warplanes took position in the South China Sea in 2014 in order to ensure an undisturbed realization of an infrastructural project, the earthworks filling the shallow waters and coral reefs of Spratly Islands suddenly found themselves at the center of media attention worldwide. It was fascinating to see the photographs of a typically unnoticed landscape of land reclamation—sandy islands growing in the sea, surrounded by batteries of dredgers and sand barges—garnering so much attention. Of course, these new patches of *terra firma* being constructed in the middle of the South China Sea are more than infrastruc-

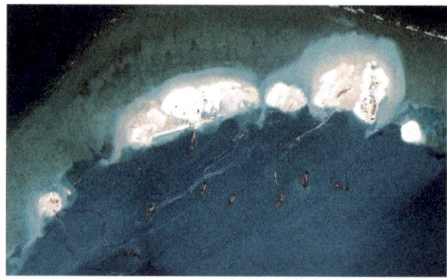

Fig. 1: Land construction is political and strategic: Reclaimed land in the South China Sea at the service of China's campaign of territorial claims.

What has taken place in the South China Sea illustrates that ecology and politics of land are intertwined in ways that lead to fundamental questions about the nature of governance in the globalized world, capitalist urbanization, and urban sustainability. For example, new land construction often involves increasing the scale and complexity of resource politics; a growing patch of new land often links to long distance resource extraction and transport, to networks of sand trade and geopolitical games in transnational sand hinterlands: "sand wars" among governments and other entities, corporate, local, and international.[2]

This case also shows that new land construction exceeds the commercial motivations behind, for example, Dubai's Palm Islands, or the purpose of environmental engineering for transport or industry, as seen in Chinese and South Korean ports, such as Shenzhen and Saemangeum. Land construction is also a tool of territorial appropriation and even of encroachment on sovereign borders. Enabled by ever more powerful construction technology, earthworks now serve as a strategy of colonization—much more than infrastructure works were thought or meant to do.

Importantly, the South China Sea case also helps remind us that earthworks, and infrastructure in general, still constitute an activity lacking public visibility and critical study, in particular from the social sciences and design disciplines. "Many aspects of infrastructure are singularly unexciting," points out ethnographer Susan Leigh Star, launching her call "to study boring things." Many characteristics of infrastructure "appear as … technical specifications, or as hidden mechanisms subtending those processes more familiar to social scientists. It takes some digging to unearth the dramas inherent in …" these systems, and "to restore narrative to what appears to be [a] dead…" bulk of data. But to study a city or an urban territory and to neglect its sewers, power supplies, or reclaimed lands and landfills, is to miss essential aspects of aesthetics, change, distributional justice, and planning power.[3]

In one of his seminal essays on philosophy of land, French-Swiss urban historian André Corboz describes land as a multidimensional entity, not solely physical in nature. Land, according to Corboz, originates from culture and politics as much as it is shaped by direct human intervention, and by "nature's forces" deriving from climate or geology. In other words, land is a *process*, a *product*, and a *project* at the same time.[4] There is no doubt then that land can be understood as problem of critical research, and of design. But how can we elevate earthworks out of the realm of the utilitarian and rethink them in the domain of the political and the ecological? How can we approach land as project?

Land Construction: A Lexical Entry

A great many concepts are used to describe human interaction with the surface of the earth, its transformation, exploitation, structuring: *land*, *landscape*, and *territory* are the most essential. None of them connote only "nature," but always imply some degree of "construction"—of "the transformation of earth into land."[5] Herein are phenomena both physical (natural and man-made) and social. *Land construction* describes extensive morphological alterations of the earth's surface by displacing large quantities of material—soil, gravel, rock, etc.—in order to create a buildable or inhabitable land, often in shallow water or swamp, where no land existed previously. Terms such as *man-made land*, *artificial land*, and *artificial landscape* are used with similar meanings, while expressions such as *earthworks* and *terraforming* point to techniques and technologies of land construction, such as cutting and filling, levelling, dredging sand, and stabilising and compressing soil. All of them relate to the many types of modified landscapes including polders, reclaimed lands, and landfills.

Land construction abounds throughout history—the notable projects are never seen as purely technical achievements, but as reflections of socio-cultural value systems and political priorities. The high culture and prosperity of Egypt's Old Kingdom is thought to be evidenced by alterations to the Giza plateau, starting in 2650 BCE—the Cheops Pyramid alone consisted of 2.6 million cubic meters of gigantic blocks, weighing in total some 7 million tons.[6] Distinctive cultures developed around the problem of constructing the interface between the sea and the land in naval states and cities—the water-and-land matrices of Venice and Amsterdam are remarkable works of engineering. While being a cultural and technical artifact, man-made land is also understood as a means of expression of power—absolutist rulers intervened in a territory to bestow upon it royal or imperial character. Louis XIV, for example, had Versailles built on swampy terrain, which he had cleared, filled, and redesigned—a demonstration of personal power subsequently emulated by many other rulers in Europe. Similarly, Peter the Great founded St. Petersburg in 1703 and built the city on swampy floodlands in an extremely raw climate—he then extolled the virtues of his new capital city as "Eden," a splendid "paradise" on the Neva river.[7]

Highly elaborated land and water landscapes in agricultural civilizations—such as Angkor and Nile Valley—have indicated stable, if not harmonious, socio-cultural systems and practices. In the eleventh century, Dutch polder landscapes of drained wetlands, sea inlets, and lakes were associated with evolving social structure and governance—a society Whose image took the form of its territory. The water board—*het waterschap*—was the first democratic form of Dutch society, and corresponded precisely to the organization of water management in the landscape, while the metrics of agricultural polder land were seen as the ideal measure for the organization of cities and buildings.

Unlike today's infrastructures, which are by definition invisible and commonly understood only as systems of substrates forming merely a background for other kinds of activity, in the sophisticated practice of polder-making, the water network is open and visible, and it structures the land—the technical (the infrastructural), the ecological and the social are interwoven with each other to create an aesthetic (land) form.

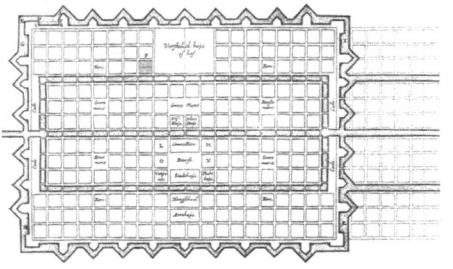

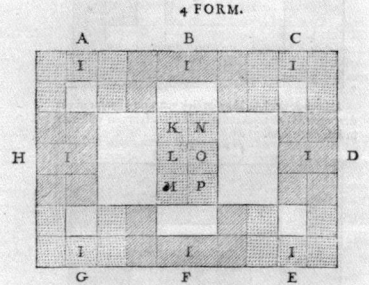

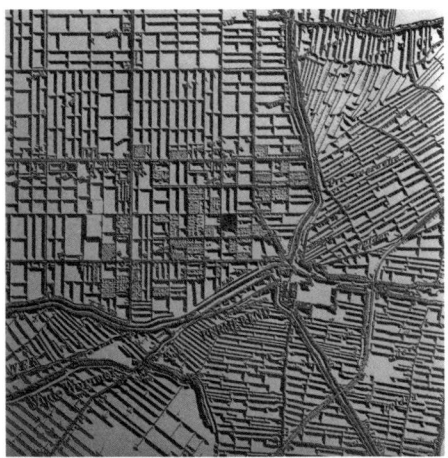

Fig. 2: Land tectonic as imprint of social organization: This reconstruction of the landform of polders near Purmerend, North Holland, in the early seventeenth century, reflects one of the oldest forms of Dutch governance: The water boards. During the twentieth century, the landscape has lost much of its clarity, due to urban growth, modern irrigation technology, and mobility infrastructures (source: Reh, 2005).

With polders and other intricate socio-cultural landscapes in mind, André Corboz wrote of "land as palimpsest"—this is the land (or territory,

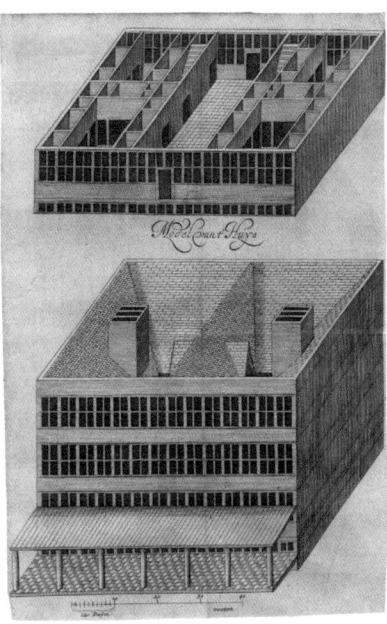

Fig. 3a-c: Simon Stevin, Plan for an Ideal City, Ideal Metric of a City Block, and Model for a Town House, c.1600; co-evolution of land, city and society. The measurements of constructed polder land in Holland were seen as ideal measures for the laying out of cities and buildings (source: Reh, 2005).

or landscape), seen not as a passive object of construction, but as an entity evolving through social practice. Land bares a name; it can be parsed and semanticized, and projections of all kinds are attached to it. It therefore transforms from a passive object of construction, into an active *subject* that exerts its own will—and that may contribute to the stability and the reproduction of social relations.[8]

During the nineteenth century, the industrial revolution, the rise of industrial capitalism, and the creation of modern (national) states gave rise to new conceptions of land, as well as greatly increased human ability to transform land. Laying infrastructures and land-shaping became conjoined operations with enormous physical impact—*de facto* able to set new topographic laws for the modern times. For railway lines, or any infrastructural system, to achieve optimal performance with minimum expenditure of energy, a considerable levelling of terrain must take place. The new conditions of flatness and horizontality coupled with the space-time compression as a result of acceleration of movement shaped the new spacetime topology of industrial modernity.[9]

Mediated via technology and the machine, perceptions of nature—and of land—began to oscillate between the views of Positivism and Romanticism—between the land seen as an *object* available to humanity for industrial exploitation and extraction of profit, and the land seen as a divine *subject* with whom relationship is lost and needs to be restored.

American cultural historian Leo Marx observed, in *The Machine in the Garden* (1964), that spatial ideologies of modernity have dual and contradictory character and lead to a new kind of hybridity in the landscape. Marx observed that "the free economic competition and technological progress are valued equally with the tradition of landscape pastoralism"; thus, "in our landscape the machine is accommodated in the garden." Today it is fair to say that machine has become indistinguishable from the garden,[10] the land is inextricably intertwined with technology. Infrastructures and soils blend together with human and other ecologies in hybrid, engineered systems, the planet's second skin.

Fig. 4: Flatness and horizontality—the fundamental diagram of urbanization and modernization: Laying out any modern infrastructure, such as a railway, requires leveling the irregularities of the terrain. Modern infrastructures and tabula rasa are direct correlates.

The processes of industrialization and urbanization translate into new scales and morphologies of land and landscape. The morphological figures registering social practices in the form of land—"the material record of

136

humans upon the landscape and the areal association of the physical and cultural phenomena"—such as land use and the water system, settlement and property patterns, continue to change through the agency of modern industrial culture.[11] Since the first steam-pumping station was used in reclaiming the Zuidplaspolder in 1825, for example, Dutch communities have been steadily liberated from their duty to control water, resulting in a more arbitrary relationship to the land, and ultimately in more random and dispersed land-use patterns. Similarly, modern transportation and the mechanization of farming have relativized or loosened social ties to the land everywhere.

At the turn of the twentieth century, the consequences of the Fordist organization of the economy and of the nation state's interventionist policies in the territory, such as land nationalization, mono-functional industrial land production, or the opening of fast transportation corridors, have completely reshaped the morphologies and metrics of the land and landscape. André Corboz noted that, "under these conditions … land can no longer serve as the unit of measurement of human phenomena."[12]

Now, at the onset of the anthropocene, with population numbers and the use of modern machinery growing, scientists have pointed out that "our ability and motivation to modify the landscape by moving earth in construction and mining activities have also increased dramatically. As a consequence, we have now become arguably the premier geomorphic agent sculpting the landscape, and the rate at which we are moving earth is increasing exponentially."[13]

Land and the City: Promiscuous Stories of Tabula Rasa

In the realm of architectural and urban design, the concept of land (or territory) does not appear as part of modern architecture's repertoire during the twentieth century, save for the intermittent interest during the period of critical reappraisal of the modern movement in the 1960s, '70s, and '80s, for example in the work of Vittorio Gregotti (Il territorio dell'architettura, 1966) and Aldo Rossi (Construzione del territorio, 1979).[14] Rather, it appears that for much of the twentieth century, the land as concept disappeared in the "blind spots" of modern architecture and urbanism. Instead, modern technology gave architecture the instruments to revolutionize its relationship with the land and reinvent it as an artifact, disengaged from nature. This new relationship can be traced through the idea of the ground. In modern architecture, ground is not in any measure an external natural given, but a fully controlled surface, an object of conception and construction.

The romantic current of architectural modernism cultivated a reverent relationship to the idea of ground, emphasizing efforts to "liberate" it, in order to minimize the impact of buildings and cities. In his description of the design principles structuring Villa Savoye, Le Corbusier described the first of five modern canons as the "recovery of building ground," achieved by lifting the house on *pilotis*. The ground that would have been lost to building is in this manner "recovered"; a garden or a landscape can pass under the house, and the same ground can be doubled on the roof.[15]

Fig. 5: Land as emblem of resistance: In 2007, the Chongqing nail house, and other similar cases, became emblematic of neoliberal recklessness and resistance to it, in the redevelopment of Chinese cities.

Now lifted and detached from the ground, the modern building also embraced its newfound emancipation from the physical site, the metaphor of "weightlessness," and the levitation of the *bel étage*.[16] The consequence of this conceptual and factual detachment from the ground has been the removal of context. The (natural) conditions of the site—topography, soil, water, vegetation—generally ceased to define the building. Instead, modern architecture can presuppose and construct a quasi-abstract site or context, which corresponds to the

vision of architecture of non-specific, universal characteristics. Throughout the twentieth century, the idea of the ground appears in modern architecture in many different forms, their common horizon being the building of an artificial plane or of a more complex system of surfaces and infrastructures often completely detached from the actual ground level. In the process, the artificial ground develops as a refined technological instrument for organizing all elements of urban life.

There is thus a deep and uneasy affinity between modern architecture and (artificial) land. The idea of land in its long-term dimension, as a result of slow processes of stratification of human and natural traces, a palimpsest, generally stays in architecture's "blind spot." Instead, it could be said that in modern architecture and the modern city, every land is constructed land—a product of urbanization and an urban mentality that creates land surface as a projection of its desires, goals, and needs. These are governed in turn by different sets of relationships than in traditional societies. The effort that bound rural inhabitants to the land has dissolved; the city-dweller has assumed a more emancipated and arbitrary relationship to the land. Artificial urban land—a *tabula rasa*, a *clean slate*, an *unscripted tablet*—is thus not an exception—it is the central concept of the modern city: the product and the habitat of urban culture.

In cities across the globe, the *tabula rasa* was often deployed as urban strategy in the hands of the state

Fig. 6: Ashael Curtis, *The Leveling of the Hills to Make Seattle*, 1910. Cut-and-Fill: The basic earthworks technique used to realize a buildable urban plane consists in breaking hills and dumping them into the sea, swamps or other low-lying areas.

and other protagonists, for different symbolic and political purposes. In Seattle, a staggering work of erasure, the so-called "regrading" of the city, was portrayed in the photographic work "Levelling of the hills to make Seattle," by Asahel Curtis in 1910. (Fig. 5). Arguably one of the largest physical alterations of terrain ever performed—outside natural disaster and wartime destruction scenarios— it mobilized America's tremendous technological capabilities and can-do spirit, in a fervour to modernise the city's infrastructures and buildings as a response to the gold rush and rising real-estate values. In some places the ground level in the city was lowered by nearly 90 feet (nearly 30 meters),

with the help of steam shovels and hydraulic mining techniques.[17]

In recent examples, the idea of land as unscripted tablet was also connected with neo-liberal forms of urban development radicalism, for example in the cases of "flattening of the Riyadh" for building villas[18] and the Chongqing nail house in 2007.[19] In both, cut hills and levelled terrain surfaced as synonyms of state-organized destruction and appropriation of land and property for the benefit of political-economic elites.

Many other cities today—including highly visible cases of terraforming spectacle from Bahrain and Dubai to Hong Kong and Shanghai—have embraced *tabula rasa* and land con-

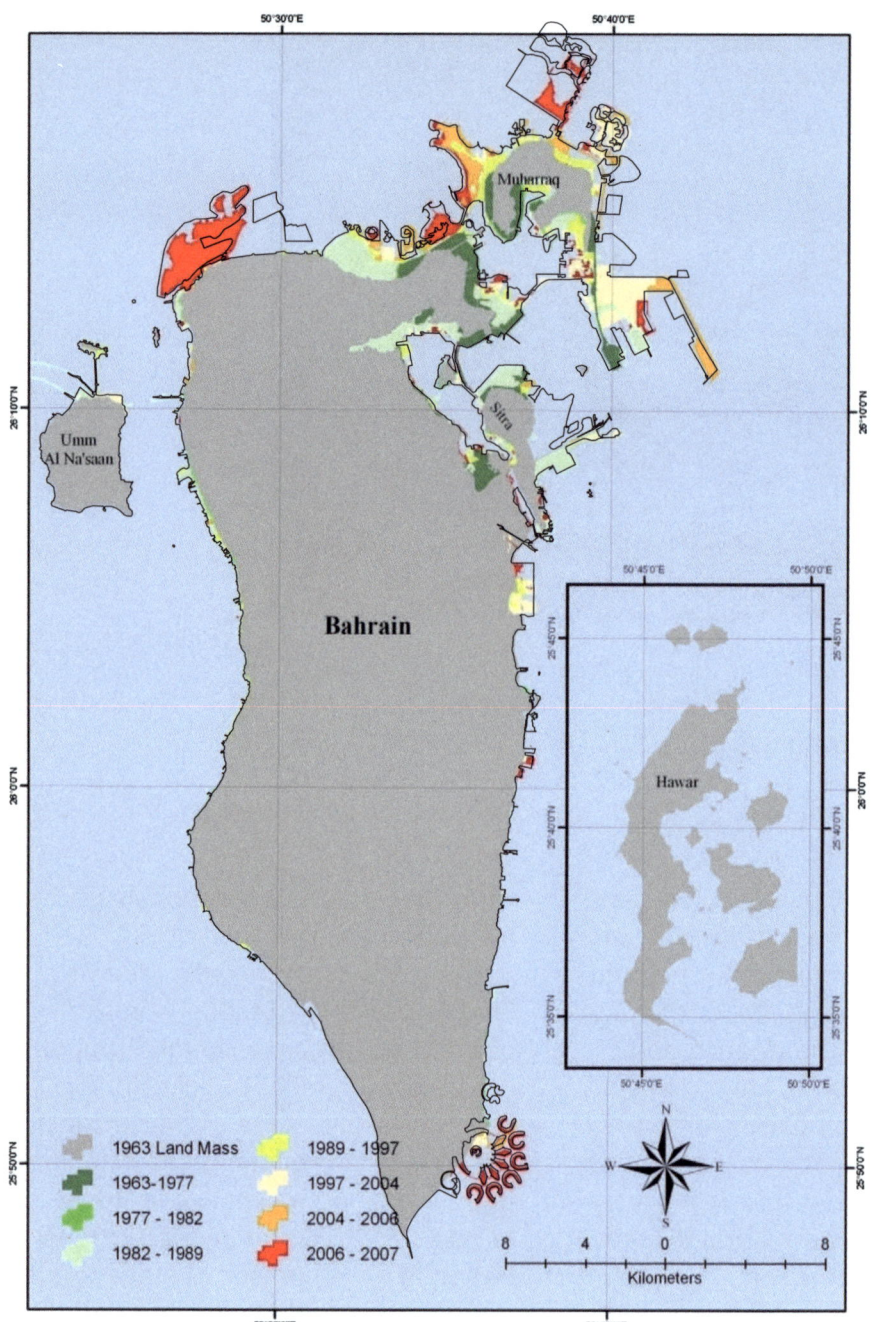

Fig. 7: Territory liquefied—Bahrain's land reclamation 1963–2007:
Owing to the radically liberalized authoritarian state, stabilizing
ideologies such as soil and ground have lost any meaning.
The black line shows the extent of Bahrain in 2016. In forty
years, Bahrain's land area has been enlarged by 315 square
kilometers, doubling its original size (source: Khadija Zainal et
al., 2012).

140

struction as a key element of their development repertoire (Fig. 7). The generic character of the reclaimed land projects—their often-repeated forms (palms, islands, and other protrusions) found all over the world—may seem surprising. The urbanistic logic of the reclaimed land is equally generic and widely shared. The basic programmatic ingredients are the same—large-scale facilities involving logistics, oil and gas, and extravagant real estate for investment—only the relative amounts vary. These resonances are in part due to long-distance sharing of experiences and know-how in the field, disseminated by the multinational dredging industry. Dutch dredging company Van Oord, for instance, has taken part in every major land-reclamation project of the past few decades from Singapore's Tuas and Changi to Palm Jumeirah.[20]

But, there are other affinities: most of the leading land reclamation cities are coastal cities (or city-states), sharing high population density, strong economic growth, and scarcity of coastal land—these characteristics make them prone to land reclamation. Ultimately however, it is their common political feature of entrepreneurially minded and authoritarian state governments with unrestricted authority that are able and willing to push territorial expansion forward.

The state governments and agencies exploit—legitimately or not—the economy of the reclaimed-land prototype, which offers remarkably low prices for building land. The total reclamation costs are usually below 250 EUR per square meter (by comparison the seafront land prices in Singapore are more than twenty times higher, in Hong Kong even a hundred times higher).[21] Additional revenues from activities at those sites can further multiply the profits. Thus, for a select group of cities where politics and geography come together in the right formula, land reclamation amounts to a form of alchemy for creating prime sites and exorbitant returns "out of nothing" (Fig. 8a).

The case of Bahrain, where more than 90 percent of the reclaimed land (315 square kilometers in total, half of the original land area) is in the hands of private investors,[22] also illustrates the shameless affinity that has developed between terraforming and private security. Private estates on reclaimed land, protruding into the sea like castles surrounded by defensive ditches, speak of the fact that exclusive assess has become a *bon ton* of the real estate business, in which the high-security regime functions as a business compliment paid by the government to the private entities and multinationals residing and operating in their territory. As a result, less than ten percent of Bahrain's coastline is now accessible to the public.[23]

I indiscriminate land reclamation has also been linked with wide-ranging cultural and ecological destruction, from the depletion of marine life and the demise of local fishery, to the erasure of cultural heritage sites and the lack of drinking water. Ironically, it appears that, in the process of the

141

Fig. 8a: Bas Princen, Bahrain (Durrat Marina), 2016
State-organized terrain for speculation: Despite vehement
public opposition, Bahrain continues with land reclamation.
Critics claim that the ruling elite has benefited personally from
land deals; more than 90 percent of the reclaimed land is in
the hands of private investors.

Fig. 8b: Bas Princen, *Bahrain (Investment Gateway)*, 2016
Terraforming for Security: Private estates on reclaimed
land, protruding into the sea like castles surrounded by
defensive ditches, illustrate the fact that exclusive assess has
become a *bon ton* of the real-estate business. Less than ten
percent of the newly created coastline in Bahrain is
accessible to the public.

territorial overhaul, some of the same resources have been appropriated by the ruling class and economic elites. But this is not a surprise: *tabula rasa* and the reation of new land routinely bring about the erasure of local history and ecology—in exchange, they open space for construction of new historical narratives and ecological imaginaries, reinforcing the given social order. For example, the private estates occupying Bahrain's new coastal areas have access to an abundant water supply, ensuring their verdant oasis experience in contrast to the conditions of the water scarce-city;[24] and the erasure of the historical pearling economy and sites is compensated symbolically by "The Pearling Trail"—Bahrain's successful inclusion into UNSECO heritage register in 2012—that will allow its government to (re)construct some of the previously erased culture and heritage. The issues around access to the land, the sea and to their resources came into focus during the public anti-government protests in Bahrain in 2011, during the events of the Arab Spring.[25] These issues, elsewhere correctly framed as issues of human rights and social justice in relation to the landscape—"the right to the landscape" [26]—point to the vital importance of, and necessity for, a democratic politics of (urban) land: questioning and negotiating who ultimately has the right to imagine it, to transform it, and to use it.

By contrast to Bahrain, Singapore's new land is not identifiable as a spectacle of image-urbanism in the littoral zone. Singapore deploys *tabula rasa* as a long-term strategic project of "nation building"[27]—an all-encompassing three-dimensional transformation of both old and new land and landscape, used as a fundamental tool of social, political, and economic transformation following post-colonial independence in 1965. The process of change from a backwater colonial port, predominantly rural, to the new nation of industrial middle class housed in public high-rise, was dubbed a "territorial revolution"[28] with many layers: the social, political and economic dimensions of the national territory have been sculpted by the hand of the state, using topography as the main medium (Fig. 9).

Singapore also shows that construction of urban land usually doesn't come without a (vast) hinterland. The city-state is known as the world's largest importer of sand for construction, as is located at the center of the sand-trade region whose radius extends to South China, Cambodia, and Myanmar. With nearly a quarter of its land area, around 140 square kilometers, added over the years, it has been estimated that three-quarters of this is "built on foreign soil."[29]

Up to the 1970s, the material for construction of land and buildings used to come from the island's granite quarries, levelled land, and clay pits. But in the 1980s, the flows of sand, gravel, and rock to the city-state began to extend across the border to Malaysia and Indonesia, and further afield—in other words,

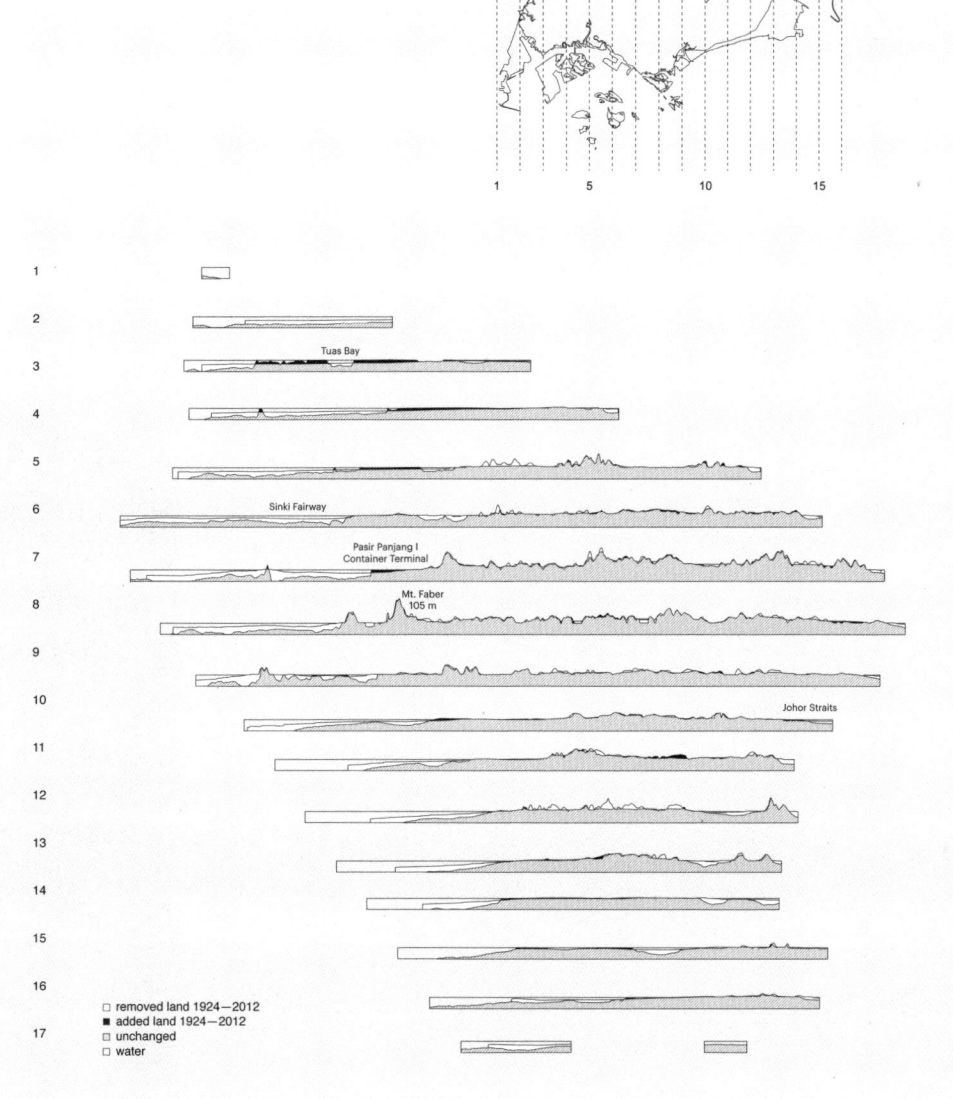

Fig. 9: Constructing the Nation—Sections through Singapore
in 1924 and 2012: Constructed land should be understood as
a central paradigm on which Singapore's urban development
has been based. The socio-political, economic and cultural
spheres are "sculpted" by the hand of the state, together with
the territorial form (source: Hassler and Topalović, 2014).

Fig. 10a: Bas Princen, *Sand quarry (Batam)*, 2013.
Sand hinterlands: In the booming industrial periphery of
Singapore, on the Indonesian island of Batam, a hill is cut in
order to obtain sand for land reclamation and to leavel the
terrain for development. Singapore is known for having razed
and remodelled its own terrain in the 1970s and '80s.

Fig. 10b: Bas Princen, *Oil cavern (Jurong Island)*, 2013.
Going underground: Despite the vast land area claimed from the sea, the territorial expansion vector in Singapore increasingly points underground, as in the recently completed artificial caverns for storing crude oil on Jurong Island.

Singapore's sand hinterland begun to "disintegrate,"[30] and assume geopolitical scale (Fig. 10a, b).

The expanding sand hinterland has problematized Singapore's claims to sustainability. Critics have pointed out that the state must do more to reduce the negative impacts of its demand for sand—the reliance on illegal trade, on corruption of its trading partners, and on ineffective national and international regulation in the field.[31]

The shifting sands and the liquefied territorial contours in the region have also exposed national tensions and older colonial and postcolonial borders that continue to problematize the current geography of governance. For example, land reclamation and dredging in the Singapore Straits led to national border disputes (Singapore-Indonesia and Singapore-Malaysia) in front of international arbitrage, and at huge collateral costs. This and other similar reasons were cited by Indonesia and Malaysia when they introduced successive bans on sand trade with Singapore, followed by Cambodia and Vietnam.[32]

Analogous to diaspora, a barge of traded sand floating in the sea from one country to another is an offshore territory symbolically attached to the mainland. Just as newly reclaimed land can become synonymous with "territorial expansion" and "occupation," selling sand to a foreign country has been rendered equivalent to "sell-out of the nation's pride" and an "act of treason."[33] In the unstable political geography of the region, sand trade and reclaimed lands have become themes of war-gaming exercises and conflict simulations—negotiation agents testing and localizing frictions.

Proponents of globalization have argued that the world is becoming "flat": a level playing field in terms of commerce where all competitors have an equal opportunity, and where historical and geographical divisions are being neutralized due to communication technologies, transport, and the worldwide synchronization of various systems of rules.[34] This has been coupled with more lamentable manifestations of cultural flattening: a widespread acceptance of generic cultural production and consumption at the expense of authentic forms of culture. This discussion can gain unexpectedly when approached from the angle of physical geography: If not economically or culturally flatter, the world is becoming flatter, literally.

In Bahrain, Singapore and other cities attached to flatland production, economic and technical rationalities have often taken precedence over other values in urban space; the priorities of speed, efficiency, and profit have brushed other concerns aside. Heritage, ecology and social equality have been assigned lower priorities, but the cases show that the shortage of gravitas can also help liberate the city's identity from restrictions. The preference for artificiality and newness, and the untroubled pursuit for more, also constitutes a specific flatness (Fig. 10c, d).

The question is, do these choices matter? Does twenty-first century culture permit, or possibly even favor, the innocent charm and frivolity of instant history, ready-made identity, do-it-yourself nature, and topography on demand? Ultimately, can design make a difference in these decisions?

Epilogue: Designing Land Better?

Cities inevitably modify their surroundings—their actual sites and their hinterlands. Over the last century, despite the extraordinary increase in our ability to transform land and topography through the construction of urban structures and infrastructures, both land and infrastructure as problems of design—as "wilful configuration(s)"[35]—have barely been articulated. Neither architecture and urbanism nor landscape architecture seem to have a firm grip on the problem; among the three disciplines, the (under)world of messy earthworks, machines, cables, and pipes, exists largely unnoticed.

The reasons for this can be sought in the way land is constituted as an object of modern scientific and technical expertise, the ways different fields of knowledge interact with one another, and the ways their authorities are engaged in urban space. Since the late nineteenth century, expert cultures dealing with land multiplied, from those engaging with the earth's dynamic processes (geology, hydrology), or the chemical processes and biosphere (soil science, ecology), to those engaged in the new ways of mapping the earth (areal archaeology, geomatics) and projecting new so-

cio-spatial realities (geography, planning). Among this growing number of expert cultures, land as object of study and intervention has been fragmented: generally speaking, design disciplines now focus on the surface; science and engineering capture the "subsurface." In the gaps between the fragmented disciplinary pursuits, knowledge and opportunities are lost. For example, scientists now recognize that built areas have been ignored and omitted in soil mapping and in studies of soil formation and behavior.[36] Other researchers have pointed out that "through the hegemony of efficiency and scientific positivism, civil engineering has become central to the design of urban environments as the premier design service discipline," despite the lack of attention in this professional segment to social conditions, ecology, politics, theory, etc.[37] These and similar symptoms hinder the possibility of a holistic approach to (urban) land, and of transdisciplinary work in the potentially new and exciting areas of contact among sciences, engineering, and design.

No doubt, land does invite opportunities for design—precedents abound. Sensibility to territorial form goes back to the Italian Renaissance, which invented landscape as a pictorial genre and looked for ways to reconcile the necessities of production and "beautiful landscape."[38] Agrarian landscapes grown over time became cultural artifacts of great value and are sometimes protected as such. For expressionist architect Bruno Taut, who envisioned the reconstruction of

Fig. 10c: Bas Princen, *Straits (sand trade)*, 2013.
Sand trade: Sand travels to Singapore largely over water
from the Southeast Asian hinterland. Each sand barge carries
approximately 1,500 tons of sand, used for land reclamation
and building construction.

Fig. 10d: Bas Princen, *Artificial island (Garbage of Eden)*, 2014.
Landfilling: Since the 1950s, through the building of coastal retaining walls, most of Singapore's coastline has transformed from soft to hard. At Pulau Semakau, dubbed the "Garbage of Eden," these walls enclose ash shipped from Singapore's incineration plants to form the landfill island.

Alpine summits into crystalline cities, land was a medium though which human society could shape itself—the work of art by the state and the people. For land artists such as Robert Smithson or Michael Heizer, land became the medium of artistic protest against the perceived artificiality, plastic aesthetics, and commercialization of urban life.

Inevitably, land is always a project, a made entity. "The necessity of a collective relation between a topographic surface and a population established in its folds permits drawing a conclusion that there is no land without imagining a land."[39] The value attributed to the land and landscape, its form and configuration—its design—is and can only be cultural. Culture supplies the program, the underlying vision to any design.

The question of the city's relation to the land is essentially the question of its relation to its place, its geographical and cultural setting. The choices with which the city approaches these specific limitations are political. It may seem that these choices are indifferent, but this would be a simplification—cities are always forms of their politics, the signs of their collective will.[40]

Land (or territory) is not merely a utility or a product, part of the invisible infrastructural (under)world we have created, but an entity with highly complex performance and function, and an object of relations of appropriation that involve geo-strategic, economic, symbolical, and other intentions. Instead of maintaining the distance between infrastructure as a problem of engineering, and city or urban space as domains of landscape architecture and urban design, these areas need to be brought together. In addition to the currently simplified conception of (urban) land as an abstract surface with technological character, land has to be recovered in terms of its stabilizing ideologies[41]—soil, fertility, history, place, permanence. Conversely, infrastructure is not a neutral technical apparatus, but a political, ecological, and ethnographic entity.

This is an expanded field where previously remote disciplines—from soil science to geomatics, and from transport engineering and biology to landscape, urbanism, and architecture—have a chance for coaction.

This essay is based on: Milica Topalović, "Constructed Land: Singapore in the Century of Flattening," in Constructed Land: Singapore, 1924–2012, ed. Uta Hassler and Milica Topalović (Zurich and Singapore: ETH Zurich D-ARCH and Singapore-ETH Centre, 2014), 56-57.

1. Rupert Wingfield-Hayes, "China's Island Factory", BBC News, September 9, 2014.
2. Peter Dupont, "Sand Wars," trans. Rafael Njotea, working grant proposal for the Pascal Decroos Fund, 2013/995, http://www.fondspascaldecroos.org/en/inhoud/werkbeurs/sand-wars
3. Susan Leigh Star, "The Ethnography of Infrastructure," American Behavioral Scientist no. 43 (1999): 377–9.
4. André Corboz, "The Land as Palimpsest," Diogenes, vol. 31 no. 121 (1983): 16–18.

5. Ibid., 13.
6. André Corboz, "Disregarding the Environment: An Ancient Tradition," in: *Landscapes Abused / Missbrauchte Landschaften*, A. Corboz et al. (Zurich: ILA ETH Zurich, 2007), 13.
7. Ibid., 17.
8. Corboz, "The Land as Palimpsest," 18–19.
9. Wolfgang Schivelbusch, *The Railway Journey: The Industrialization of Time and Space in the 19th Century*, (University of California Press, 1986), 22.
10. See Gary L. Strang, "Infrastructure as Landscape," *Places* 10 (1996): 3, 8–15 and Leo Marx, *The Machine in the Garden. Technology and the Pastoral Ideal in America* (Oxford University Press, 1964).
11. Carl O. Sauer, "The Morphology of Landscape," *University of California Publications in Geography* vol. 2, no. 2 (1925): 19–54.
12. Corboz, "The Land as Palimpsest," 16.
13. Roger LeB. Hooke, "On the history of humans as geomorphic agents," *Geology*, vol. 28, no. 9 (2000): 843.
14. See Vittorio Gregotti, *Il territorio dell'architettura* (Milano: Feltrinelli, 1966) and Aldo Rossi, Fabio Reinhart, Bruno Reichlin et al., *Costruzione del territorio e spazio urbano nel cantone Ticino* (Lugano: Fondazione Ticino Nostro, 1979).
15. Werner Oechslin and Wilfred Wang, "Les Cinq Points d'une Architecture Nouvelle," *Assemblage* no. 4 (1987): 82–93.
16. Ilka and Andreas Ruby, *Groundscapes: The Rediscovery of the Ground in Contemporary Landscape* (Barcelona: Editorial Gustavo Gili, 2006), 11.
17. V. V. Tarbill, "Mountain-moving in Seattle," *Harvard Business Review* (1930): 482–89.
18. Joumana al Jabri, "The Flattening of Riyadh, *Volume 23 Al Manakh 2 special edition*, eds. AMO et al., (Amsterdam: Stichting Archis, 2009), 430–1.
19. "Demolition ends China house row," *BBC News*, April 3, 2007.
20. Jan Schaart, "Mega Reclamations: Opportunities and Challenges," presentation, CEDA Conference on Dredging and Reclamation, Doha, (May 2008). http://www.cedaconferences.org/documents/dredgingconference/downloads/2/qatar2008_2008-18-05_41_schaart.pdf
21. ibid.
22. Cynthia O'Murchu, Simeon Kerr, Russel Birkett, and Aleksandra Wisniewska, "Explaining Bahrain's Land Reclamation Controversy," *Financial Times* video, December 10, 2014; and Mohammad Noor Al-Nabi, *History of Land Use and Development in Bahrain* (Bahrain: Kingdom of Bahrain Information Affairs Authority, 2012.), http://www.housing.gov.bh/en/PublicationsLibrary/6681%20book%20resized.pdf
23. O'Murchu, et al., "Explaining Bahrain's Land Reclamation Controversy."
24. Gareth Doherty,"Bahrain's Polyvocality and Landscape as a Medium,"in: *The Right to Landscape: Contesting Landscape and Human Rights*, ed. Shelley Egoz, Jala Makhzoumi, and Gloria Pungetti, (Farnham: Ashgate Publishing, Ltd., 2011), 185–96.
25. O'Murchu, et al., "Explaining Bahrain's Land Reclamation Controversy."
26. Gareth Doherty,"Bahrain's Polyvocality and Landscape as a Medium."
27. Peggy Teo, Brenda S. A. Yeoh, Ooi Giok Ling, and Karen P.Y. Lai, *Changing Landscapes of Singapore*, (Singapore, National University of Singapore: McGraw-Hill Education, 2004).
28. Rodolphe De Koninck, "Singapore or the Revolution of Territory. Part One: the Hypothesis," *Cahiers de geographie du Quebec* 34(92) (1990): 209–16.
29. Lee, S. L. et al., "Layered Clay-Sand Scheme of Land Reclamation," *J. Geotech. Engrg.* 113(9) (1987): 984–995.
30. Neil Brenner and Christian Schmid, "Planetary Urbanization," in *Urban Constellations*, ed. M. Gandy (Berlin: Jovis Verlag, 2011), 10–13.
31. "Shifting sand: How Singapore's demand for Cambodian sand threatens ecosys-

tems and undermines good governance." *Global Witness*, report, (London: Global Witness Limited, May 2010).

32. "Singapore's sand shortage: The hourglass effect," *The Economist*, October 10, 2009.

33. Various newspaper articles on the subject have appeared in the Malaysian and Indonesian press.

34. Thomas L. Friedman, *The World is Flat* (New York: Farrar, Straus and Giroux, 2005).

35. Corboz, "The Land as Palimpsest," 19.

36. David G. Rossiter, "Classification of Urban and Industrial Soils in the World Reference Base for Soil Resources," *J Soils Sediments* 7 (2) (2007): 96.

37. Pierre Belanger, "Landscape Infrastructure: Urbanism Beyond Engineering," *Infrastructure Sustainability & Design* eds. Spiro N. Pollalis, Daniel Schodek, Andreas Georgoulias, and Stephen J. Ramos (London: Routledge, 2012): 278–279.

38. Corboz, "The Land as Palimpsest," 21.

39. Ibid., 18.

40. Aldo Rossi, *The Architecture of the City*, (Cambridge, Mass: MIT Press, 1982 [1966]), 10.

41. Joshua Comaroff, "Built on Sand: Singapore and the New State of Risk," *Harvard Design Magazine*, No. 39 (2014): 140-143.

Image Sources:

Wouter Reh, Clemens Steenbergen, and Diederik Aten, *Zee Van Land: De droogmakerij als atlas van de Hollandse landschapsarchitectuur*, (Stichting Uitgeverij Noord-Holland: 2005), 14.

Wolfgang Schivelbusch, *The Railway Journey: The Industrialization of Time and Space in the Nineteenth Century* (The University of California Press, Berkeley, 1977), 22.

Khadija Zainal et al., "The cumulative impact of reclamation and dredging on the maritime ecology and land-use in the Kingdom of Bahrain," *Marine Pollution Bulletin* 64 (2012): 1452–1458; ETH Architecture of Territory.

Uta Hassler and Milica Topalović, *Constructed Land: Singapore 1924-2012* (ETH Zurich DARCH and FCL, Singapore, 2014), 25-41. Reworked drawing based on first publication.

A Visual Atlas

Part 2

Compiled by Something Fantastic

Fig. 44: Hyllie Water Tower
in Malmö, Sweden

Fig. 45: Tramstation Bellevue in Zurich, Switzerland

Fig. 46: McMath–Pierce solar telescope
at Kitt Peak Observatory in Tucson, USA
The long shaft focuses light from the sun
towards the telescope's primary mirror,
the largest of its kind in the world.

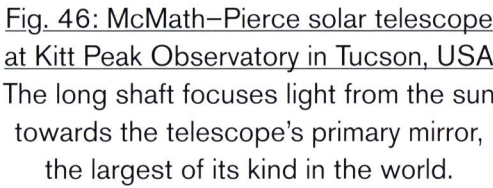

Fig. 47: Handrail at the Universidad Nacional
Autónoma de Mexico in Mexico City, Mexico

Fig. 48: Traffic viaduct
in Wentbridge, England

Fig. 49: Tubular railway bridge in Conwy, Wales

Fig. 50: Elevated pedestrian crossing in Detroit, USA
The bridge on the 14th floor was built as a connection in the 1980s, when
One Woodward Avenue housed the *Consolidated Gas Company* and the
other, the Guardian Building, the *American Natural Resources* offices.

Fig. 51: Suspension bridge across the Rhine
in Cologne-Rodenkirchen, Germany
Initially begun in 1938, construction was interrupted
by the Second World War, and finished in 1954,
after doubling the amount of lanes and adding a
second set of arches.

Fig. 52: Inner-city parking under an elevated road in Stuttgart, Germany
This centrally located, partly covered parking lot holds 220 cars and was built in 1961 during the redevelopment that saw Stuttgart become a "car-friendly city".

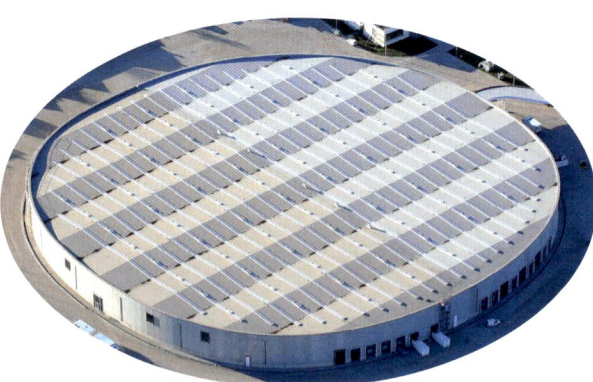

Fig. 53: Vitra distribution center in Weil am Rhein, Germany
Designed by SANAA, the building's shape allows trucks to circulate inside the building.

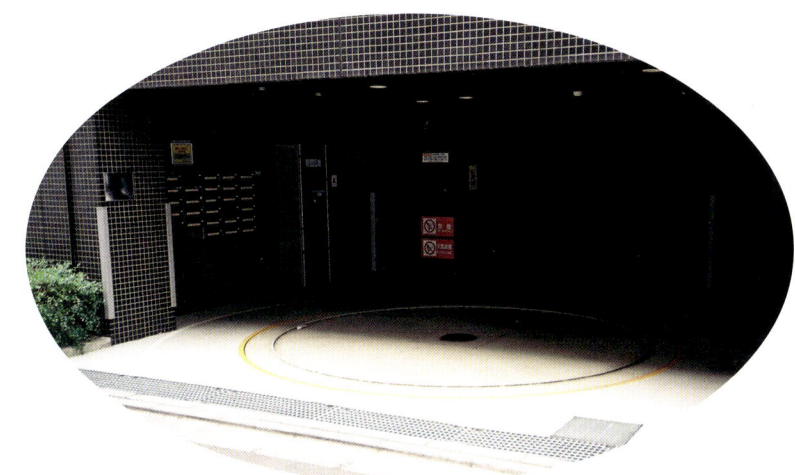

Fig. 54: Car turntable in Tokyo, Japan
A turning platform allows cars to enter and exit a parking
garage in an otherwise too narrow street.

Fig. 55: Cattle enclosure in Zambia

Fig. 56: Oil refinery in Linden, USA

Fig. 57: Hand rail in the Paimio Sanatorium, Finland
Designed by Alvar Aalto in 1929, this building's hallways feature
handrails with a functional, lacquered waterproof coating.

Fig. 58: Janitor's house
at the government complex in Chandigarh, India
Narrow pillars support the roof.

Fig. 59: The aircraft carrier
USS Theodore Roosevelt (CVN 71)
in the Atlantic

Fig. 60: Parking lot in Hong Kong, China

Fig. 62: Parking lot in Cairo, Egypt
An empty lot is temporarily used as
parking space until construction begins.

Fig. 61: John F Kennedy Airport
in New York City, USA

Fig. 63: Highway E40, west of Kiev, Ukraine
Spanning a distance of over 8,000 kilometers,
Route E40 is Europe's longest highway and connects
Calais in France with Ridder in Kazakhstan,
close to the Chinese border.

Fig. 64: Loggia and Piazza Grande
in Arezzo, Italy

Fig. 65: Protection barrier for a pipe in Kyoto, Japan
The barrier is additionally marked by white paint
on the ground.

Fig. 66: Differently colored traffic lanes in Tokyo, Japan

Fig. 67: Sports pitch in Tavares Bastos favela
in Rio de Janeiro, Brazil The pitch doubles as courtyard
and entrance to some of the houses.

Fig. 68: Pacific Highway, Peru
This stretch of road interupts the
Nazca Lines, a series of ancient geoglyphs
in the Nazca desert.

Fig. 69: Europa Bridge in the Wipp valley
near Innsbruck, Austria

Fig. 70: Suez Canal, Egypt
Major trade route connecting the Mediterranean Sea
with the Red Sea, built between 1859 and1869.

Fiv. 71: Covered Walkway in Milan, Italy
Part of the Gallaratese II housing project from 1972,
the walkway designed by Carlo Aymonino crosses the interior courtyard.

Fig. 72: Farmhouses in Grünwald, Switzerland
Evenly distributed farmhouses create a net
of infrastructure across the sloped landscape.

Fig. 73: Palms on a street
in Goa, India

Space Frames

Fig. 74: Jacob K. Javits Convention
Center in New York City, USA
The complex, designed by Richard
Rogers and James Free, opened in 1986.

Fig. 75: Racks for drying the harvest in Shirakawa
on the island of Honshū, Japan

Fig. 76: Bridge under construction with
wooden scaffolding in Moulin-des-Pierres, France

Fig. 77: Railway bridge dating from 1875,
crossing the River Inn near Königswart, Germany

Fig. 78: Silo in France
The silo, factory and administrative spaces
are located in the same building, designed
by Francois Hennebique.

Fig. 79: Winding road on the
Amalfi Coast near Ravello, Italy

Fig. 80: Carajás Mine
in Para, Brazil

Fig. 81: Highway ramps at
Charles de Gaulle Airport in Paris, France

Rectangular Troughs

Fig. 82: Light shafts in
Heidelberg, Germany

Fig. 83: Light shaft of the
Glass House in São Paulo, Brazil
The glass panels of this "house as an aquarium"
unify the inner spaces with the surrounding landscape.

Document:

The following is a transcript of a keynote address delivered by Carlos Lopes, United Nations Under-Secretary-General and Executive Secretary of the United Nations Economic Commission for Africa, at the 5th International Forum of the LafargeHolcim Foundation for Sustainable Construction in Detroit on April 7, 2016. Entitled "Africa's Infrastructure Appetite," the lecture foregrounds a particular pro-development narrative, as opposed to a narrative of despair, concerning the future of the continent's course. Lopes's optimistic account promotes infrastructure as the catalyst of widespread economic growth, capable of taking what was once viewed as a "hopeless continent" to the era of "Africa rising."

Africa's Infrastructure Appetite

Carlos Lopes

We all know the importance of infrastructure in fostering growth and development. Africa is no different. However, because the continent lags behind other regions in almost all infrastructure indicators, the issue deserves—in the African context—particular attention. Accelerating infrastructure development is not only essential for maintaining a trajectory of growth, but it is also a prerequisite for preparing the continent for mega-trends. Deficits in roads, railways, ports, airports, information technology, and energy are daunting. It is estimated that these deficits hamper national economic growth by two percentage points every year and cut business productivity by as much as 40 percent.[1]

Lack of proper infrastructure is a serious bottleneck for private business. Transport costs, for example, remain uncompetitive in Africa compared to other regions. Freight costs account for 13 percent of the value of imports in the continent, against an average of 8.8 percent for the rest of the developing countries and 5.2 percent for industrialized countries. Against this background nobody will be surprised that African leadership is so focused on the need for large investments in the sector, despite the challenging global economic landscape. In Africa, a number of mega-initiatives at the continental level, driven by the Programme for Infrastructure Development in Africa (PIDA) and the Presidential Infrastructure Champion Initiatives (PICI), are making the business case for connecting African countries.

Let me mention a few of these initiatives: a US $23.7 billion natural-gas pipeline running from Nigeria to Algeria and then from Algeria to Spain; a 8,715 kilometer road and rail transport corridor all the way from Dakar to Djibouti, linking the largest horizontal west-to-east stretch of the continent, estimated to cost over US $18 billion; the construction of a multimodal (road, railways, and ports) transcontinental interconnector that will ultimately link Cape Town in the south to Cairo in the north; the construction of a navigation line between Lake Victoria and the Mediterranean Sea to enable intermodal transport by integrating river, rail, and road transport along the Nile corridor; the Lappsset Corridor that will connect Kenya's Lamu Port to South Sudan and Ethiopia; or a high-speed standard-gauge modern railway from Kenya's Port of Mombasa to Kigali in Rwanda and Juba in South Sudan. In the field of electric power projects, two examples stand out. First, Ethiopia's Grand Renaissance Dam project to develop a 5,250-megawatt hydropower plant in the Nile basin. It will be Africa's largest hydroelectric power plant, with a storage capacity of 74 billion cubic meters of water. Second, the Zambia-Tanzania-Kenya interconnector project that will integrate the countries' individual grids into one comprehensive infrastructural network covering a distance of 2,206 kilometers.

Africa is also embarking on a major renewable energy initiative in the order of US $70 billion to add ten gigawatts of electricity capacity by 2020 and at least 300 gigawatts by 2030. Several countries are also driving their own ambitious plans: between 2010 and 2014, Cape Verde increased its renewable power capacity by 200 percent, to 33 megawatts—mainly from wind and solar power; between 2011 and 2015, South Africa invested over 190 billion rand to add 6.3 gigawatts of renewable energy to its energy mix; Morocco increased its installed renewable energy capacity by roughly 24 percent between 2010 and 2014; Mauritania installed a fifteen-megawatt solar plant in 2013 and is planning to install another twelve megawatts by the end of 2016 in collaboration with Masdar of the United Arab Emirates; and Kenya now ranks as third in the world in terms of with installed geothermal power capacity, at approximately 600 megawatts in 2014.

The financial implications of what is the largest drive for infrastructure in the last sixty years are substantial, so it is normal for people to ask whether Africa has the money to accomplish its objectives. Between now and 2020 about US $93 billion is needed to overhaul Africa's infrastructure. About two-thirds, or US $60 billion, is to build new infrastructure, and US $30 billion is for the operation and maintenance of existing facilities. These financial needs represent about 10 percent of the GDP of

III

Africa's middle-income countries, and about 15 percent of the GDP of its low-income countries. Thus the shortfall to meet the desired target is substantial; however, it only represents between 1 and 2 percent of Africa's fiscal pressure.

Contrary to popular belief, domestic financing remains the single main source of infrastructure financing. Recent estimates suggest that Africa finances about 65 percent of its infrastructure expenditure. Resources have increased thanks to increased revenue collection, gains from commodity prices, a demand boom that lasted one decade, and, more generally, improved macroeconomic and institutional policies. Africa has the potential to generate significantly more domestic financial resources. Its fiscal pressure is the lowest in the world, at around 17 percent; for instance, by simply improving internal tax efficiencies, Africa has the potential to generate more domestic resources. It is a known fact that African governments have a weak capacity to collect taxes.

Although tax revenues are the largest domestic resource, many African countries have a tax-to-GDP ratio below 10 percent. Mobilizing alternative sources of investments, such as private equity, pension funds, and sovereign funds, has the potential to generate significant local capital. By the end of 2014, private-equity firms were estimated to have assets worth US $25 billion in Africa. The size of Africa's pension-fund assets is growing at an impressive pace; for instance, South Africa saw assets grow from US $166 billion in 2007 to US $277 billion in 2011, and Nigeria from US $3 billion in 2008 to US $14 billion in 2010.[3]

Boosting regional integration and the establishment of a continental free-trade area are all significant channels for increasing the domestic resource base. Curtailing illicit outflows will also free up capital for the infrastructure project. Data by the United Nations Economic Commission for Africa (ECA) from 2015 show that annual average illicit financial flows out of the continent reached US $50 billion between 2000 and 2008 against a yearly average of only US $9 billion for the period from 1970 to 1999.

I am not saying all of this to paint an optimistic picture of African financing capabilities. Africa still needs foreign domestic investment for its infrastructure development. But I am conscious that this avenue is not an easy one, because such investments are long-term and based on return calculations that are more complex. For these types of investments, stability is a must. Foreign investors are normally worried about investing in Africa or any frontier market. The perception is that Africa is a risky place to invest and a continent in crisis. But the news is not as bad as most think. My primary responsibility in the framework of United Nations institutions is actually to demonstrate that misconceptions exist. Allow me therefore to briefly highlight a few narratives that are misconstrued.

Let me start with the falling commodity prices. The "Africa rising" narrative has dominated international coverage until quite recently, when falling commodity prices and recessive demand from large economies like China as well as currency volatility have yet again sounded alarm bells. Low commodity prices in particular are causing lower export revenues, fiscal imbalances, and current account deficits across several African countries. In 2015, Africa had the highest negative account balance over the past ten years. African countries remain exposed to volatility and trade shocks as a result of their dependence on commodity and natural-resource exports. However, taken in context, the current volatility of most commodities (oil excluded) is not out of the ordinary when compared to past trends. Most African countries are net importers of commodities and therefore are set to gain from lower prices. The recent drop of the price of oil to around US $30 per barrel is estimated to have cost oil-exporting countries around US $47 billion in trade losses; however, this represents only 8 percent of the total value of Africa's exports in 2014. While it is difficult to predict how the current downturn in commodity prices will affect Africa's development trajectory, let's keep in mind that other commodities exported from Africa such as uranium, gold, coffee, cocoa, or orange juice are experiencing record prices. Equally, a fall in oil prices presents good incentives for governments to relocate economic resources away from commodity production into more diversified activities.

The second issue I would like to comment on is the supposition that Africa's debt is reaching unsustainable levels: Africa's total foreign debt has been higher than 30 percent of GDP since 2010 and it was projected to rise to approximately 37 percent by the end of 2015. However, net foreign debt as a share of GDP is only 1 percent, having been negative since 2006 because of Africa's international reserves. This debt level is also comparable to other developing countries and is well below that of advanced economies. For example, the total debt for OECD countries was nearly 80 percent of the OECD GDP in 2008 and was expected to grow to 111 percent in 2015. As of mid-2015, Africa's public debt-to-GDP ratio has been at its lowest in decades. The debt level is also comparable to other developing countries and well below that of advanced economies. As of 2014, 35 out of 42 African countries had reserves double the amount of short-term external debt. In similar fashion, as of 2014, forty out of 46 African countries had external-debt-to-gross-national-income ratios lower than 50 percent. Part of the challenge is that there is no coherent mechanism to govern any future sovereign debt crises, which overshadows what should be an important debate on quantitative easing that has created easy credit for debilitated economies of developed countries since the beginning of the 2008 financial crisis. Moreover, the discourse on debt should be contextual, giving African countries the flexibility in placing debt ceilings without unduly burdening their fiscal stance.

The third area that investors harp on about is the perception of security and conflict: perceptions of a continent burdened by conflict persist, despite facts calling for a more nuanced view. Between 2014 and 2015, armed conflict decreased by 14 percent, the first negative trend since 2009.[4] Conflict-related fatalities dropped by 10 percent in 2016 and confrontations between armed groups comprised approximately 27 percent of all conflict events and more than half of total related fatalities, despite a relative annual decrease. Patterns of conflict across the continent are changing fast, which should mitigate the perception of a conflict-prone continent: while overall political violence decreased in 2015, civil wars, armed insurgencies, and violence against civilians remain a major source of instability, but are now concentrated in a few countries. In Asia almost a third more people are killed by conflicts than in Africa. But the UN Security Council continues to make Africa's conflicts an active part of their agenda while those in Ukraine, Colombia, Malaysia, the Philippines, Indonesia, India, Thailand, or Myanmar are not on that agenda. Nor do we see a military foreign mission to tackle the piracy of the Strait of Malacca, bordering Malaysia and Singapore, despite having twice the number of attacks the Somali coast had at the height of its crisis.

These negative headlines create a gap between perception and reality regarding the investment climate in Africa. Despite the fact that over the last few years, over half of the ten fastest growing economies are consistently in Africa, and the continent ranks as the second most attractive investment destination in the world, the prevailing narrative is about the problems.[5] It is important that we contextualize risks, understanding what the reality is and what is an externally driven perception, so that Africa is not short-changed. In fact, current mega-trends are in Africa's favor: a demographic boom, rising middle class, and rapid urbanization. It is a continent where the state of the economy offers some of the best prospects for the future; but more precisely, it is a continent where the need for the development of innovative and sustainable infrastructure systems is the most acute in the world.

1. Vivien Foster and Cecilia Briceño-Garmendia, eds., *Africa's Infrastructure: A Time for Transformation* (Washington, DC: World Bank, 2010).
2. Ibid.
3. United Nations Economic Commission for Africa, *Innovative Financing for the Economic Transformation of Africa* (Addis Ababa: ECA, 2015).
4. Therése Pettersson and Peter Wallensteen, "Armed Conflicts, 1946–2014," *Journal of Peace Research* 52 (2015).
5. Ernst & Young, *Executing Growth: EY's 2014 Africa Attractiveness Survey* (Ernst & Young, 2014).

Infrastructure as Network

Essays, Part 2

Kathy Velikov and Geoffrey Thün, Carlotta Darò, Sven Stremke, Ross Exo Adams, Nancy Couling, Tom Avermaete, Keller Esterling

Territorial Infrastructures: Recognizing Politico-Environmental Ecologies

Kathy Velikov
and Geoffrey Thün

When it comes to the recognition of infrastructure, there are a multitude of different "ways of seeing," none of which are necessarily neutral. Kathy Velikov and Geoffrey Thün investigate how different modes of representation can engender different readings of infrastructure and, in turn, new infrastructural design.

Recognition is both an act of seeing and an act of identification. Infrastructure, because it often literally exists *infra* (below, or underneath), is not always seen, not always easy to identify. Whereas some infrastructure is manifest in physical artifacts—roads, bridges, dams—most infrastructure is largely invisible and can only be recognized through its partial physical evidence, such as nodal objects—faucets, drains, cover plates, switches—or by organizational patterns. To recognize infrastructure, one often has to not only go below the surface of things, but also learn to see infrastructure's organizational technologies, such as rules, codes, protocols, standards, as well

as its ephemeral technologies, such as electromagnetic or wireless signals.[1] Therefore, central questions in working on and thinking about infrastructure are: How do we recognize it? How can we make it visible? How can we make it public? How can the design disciplines practice new ways of seeing, of representing, to enable meaningful discourse and action on infrastructure?

To think infrastructure demands systems thinking. It requires thinking relationally, thinking through dynamic and interacting models, thinking temporally. Systems thinking is a way of recognizing things. Christopher Alexander wrote: "A system as a whole is not an object but a way of looking at an object. It focuses on some holistic property which can only be understood as a product of interaction among parts."[2] However, ways of seeing, mental models, and the representations we produce to communicate them are not benign—they have significant ontological, political, and physical ramifications within our societal and built environments.[3] For example, the ways that society has understood the solar system, and the various representational structures that have been created to visualize and model it, have had immense political and social ramifications—consider the histories of Copernicus and Galileo.

In the following pages, we elaborate on three modes of representation, or ways of seeing and recognizing, that have been central within our work on infrastructure—thick cartographies, relational mappings, and projections of urban society. These are situated within the theoretical concepts of ecology and apparatus, which we argue are critical frameworks in the conceptualization of infrastructure space.

Fig. 1: "The ways in which man has viewed the solar system have resulted in many ideas about its structure. A single set of objects may be thought of as a system in a number of different ways." Christopher Alexander, *Architectural Design*, 1968.

The representational approaches described here are not meant to be prescriptive or exhaustive, but rather are intended to open a discussion around the instrumentality of representation, and to enter into discourse with other representational strategies and conceptual approaches mobilized by authors in this volume.

Ecology and Apparatus

The concepts of ecology and apparatus are two ways to approach thinking in systems. Each offers specific nuances in the subsequent recognition and representation of infrastructure as a system. *Ecology*, in its most general sense, can be defined as a study of relations among dynamic agents interacting in coevolution with their environment. It has developed as a science within multiple fields, evolving closely with concepts of general systems theory, cybernetics, and self-organizing emergent processes, and has become a central paradigm for many disciplines beyond the biophysical sciences—from social studies to political theory to economics.[4] Recent urban and landscape thinking has not only embraced the conceptual framework of ecology and interrelated systems, but has placed this domain of inquiry at the center of their respective disciplinary efforts.[5]

Within these practices, questions of infrastructure are being rethought. It is no longer possible to consider infrastructure as a compartmentalized and bounded system, manifest through the design and detailing of specific artifacts that are planned, constructed, and managed within silos of expertise and governance. Constructed infrastructure is now increasingly understood as dynamically intertwined with biophysical and human systems, exchanging matter, energies, and information beyond the artifacts that are present in these systems.[6] Designers engaging questions of sustainability are beginning to comprehend how, in the words of David Orr, "properly engaged, nature will in fact do a great deal of the work in engineered systems for free."[7] This precipitates a paradigm shift in how infrastructure is being conceived and implemented. As opposed to centralized, energy-intensive, monofunctional systems, designers, planners, and policy-makers are increasingly considering distributed, low-energy, multifunctional, and often redundant systems, which are believed to be more resilient to disaster and risk, and can be more adaptive over time. Biological models that prioritize solving tasks through low-energy expenditure (as opposed to energy-intensive mechanical operations) have been argued as models for solutions to technical challenges in ways that are very different from traditional engineered systems.[8]

Michel Foucault has framed apparatus not as a thing or a device, but rather as a "system of relations" established between the elements of a "thoroughly heterogeneous ensemble consisting of discourses, institutions, architectural forms, regulatory divisions, laws, administrative measures, scientific statements, philosophical, moral, and philanthropic propositions."[9] Within urban theory, the notion of apparatus becomes useful in describing the "instrumentalized network of relationships" that produce urban processes, subjectivities, and modes of participation.[10] Since infrastructure serves an organizational and utilitarian role for societies, it is also a highly strategic political and economic instrument, and a primary technology in the construction of territory.[11] Apparatus implicates a critical

dimension to contemporary theories of urban analysis, such as actor-network theory, that might be activated to produce new readings and understandings of regional interactions.[12] It also gives designers and planners a framework with which to think about the production of new infrastructures—particularly the hybrid and multifunctional infrastructures of the future, which will operate interdependently with biotic and social systems. The realization of such works requires the assembly and mobilization of multiple actors, financial instruments, policies, codes, public-relations campaigns, and material and technological artifacts in order to be brought into being, and thus design thinking can be expanded beyond physical objects to entail elements of the entire infrastructural apparatus.

The frameworks of ecology and apparatus connote networks of relations that are not visible as objects and therefore necessitate the production of diagrams, maps, and models to render their structures, rules, and behaviors legible and apparent. Not only do these forms of representation have agency in enabling the apprehension of the schema patterns, relations, and coevolutions among things, but by visualizing these systems, they allow designers to postulate within a representational field how the system and its networks might be rewired, how new networks could be assembled to identify places where intervention might be most effective, and to envision and enact future possibilities.[13]
Ways of Seeing: Thick Cartographies

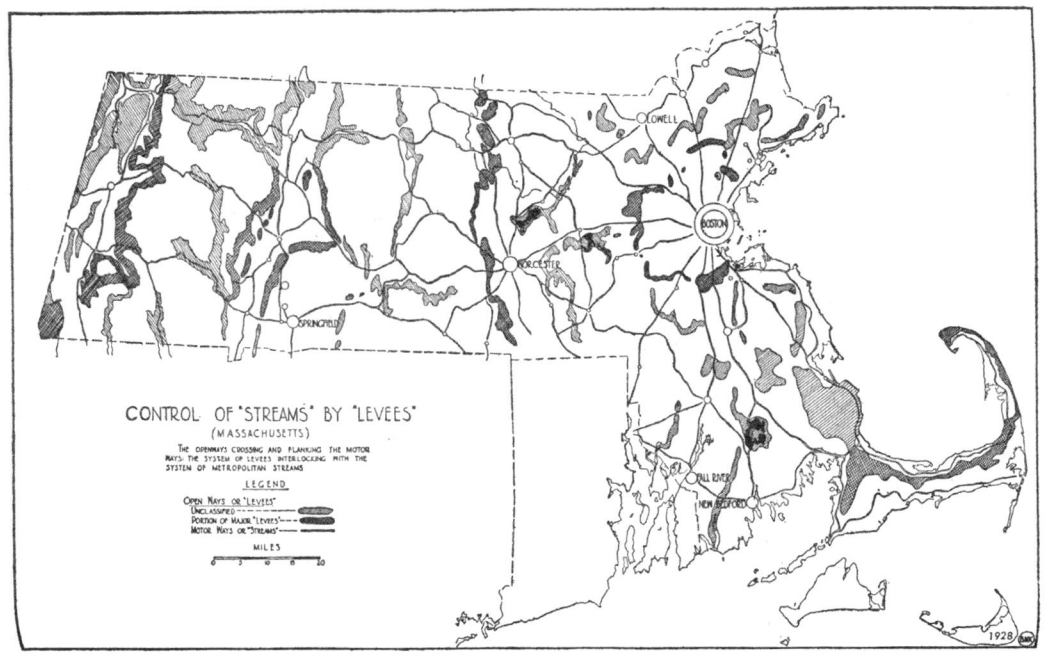

Fig. 2: Map showing the control of "streams" (motorways) by "levees" (openways) in Massachusetts. Benton MacKaye, *The New Exploration*, 1928.

Territorial infrastructures inscribe geographies and geopolitics, structuring flows, landscapes, and subjectivities. The lens of territory implicates the infrastructures of border and boundary as well as the geography of authority and of political forces, implicating local power structures and extending across vast globalized value chains. Cartographic practices, primary technologies in the construction and control of territory, also enable ways of seeing new imaginative potentials.[14] We refer to "thick" cartographies as the techniques of mapping that layer and combine complex and interacting human and nonhuman agents and flows within geographic space. The inherent flatness of the map is conceptually and descriptively "thickened" with relational information.

Forester, planner, and conservationist Benton MacKaye was one of the first to conceive of and visualize commodity, energy, and resource flows as related to geography and geology, and as formative agents in urban development and planning. In the 1920s he argued that geography—mapping, plans, charting, sections—was a form of "discovery" of the new "wilderness" and "physiology" of industrial America, and proposed that mappings of industrial flows overlaid with constructed and natural systems could be instrumental tools in reconceiving future regional infrastructures and urban developments according to geographic logics.

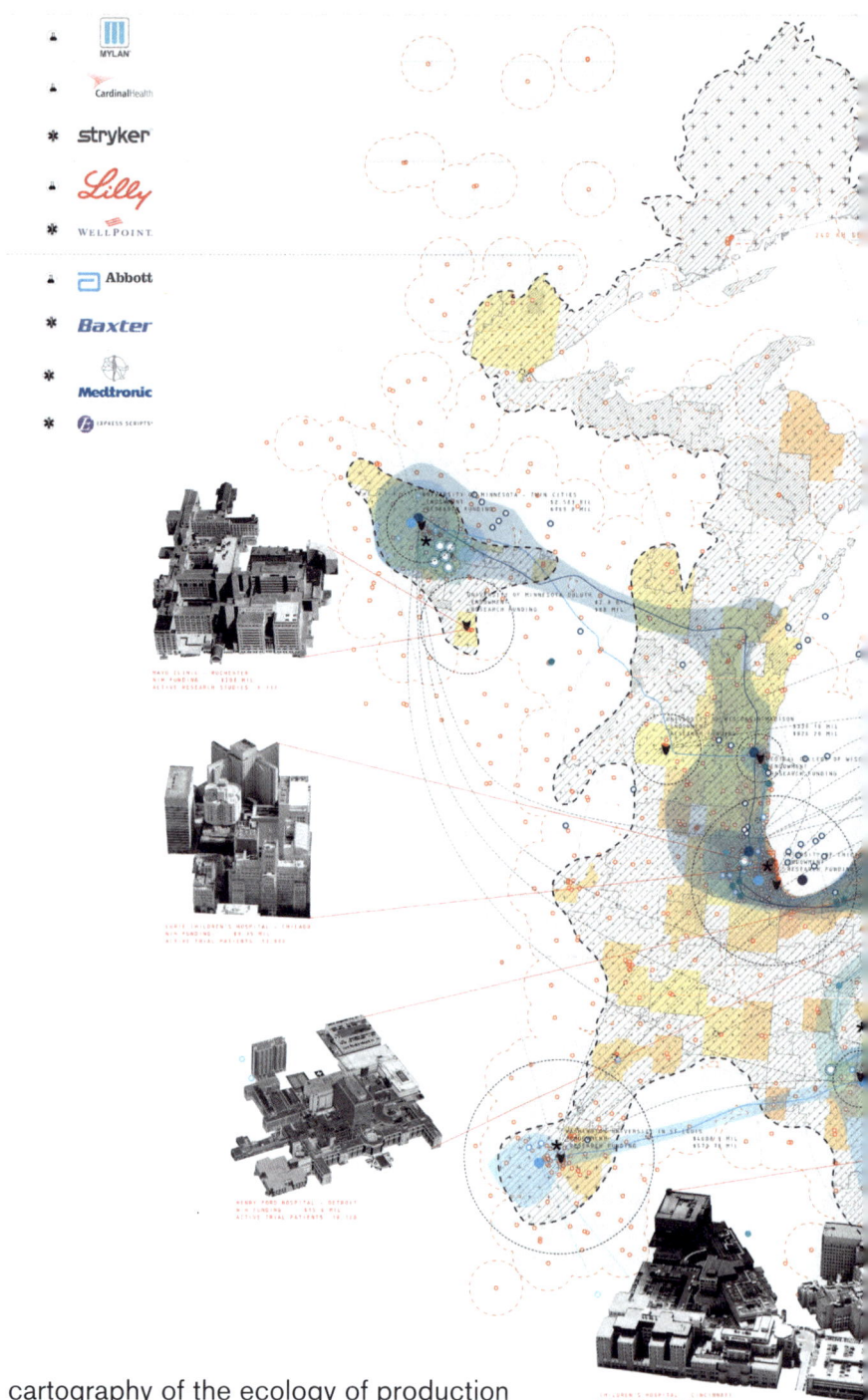

Fig. 3: "MediShed" cartography of the ecology of production and exchange among emerging industries linked to medical provision in the Great Lakes Mega-region. The cartography reveals a complex and interwoven network of health-service delivery as well as pharmaceutical and biotechnological research, production, and distribution.

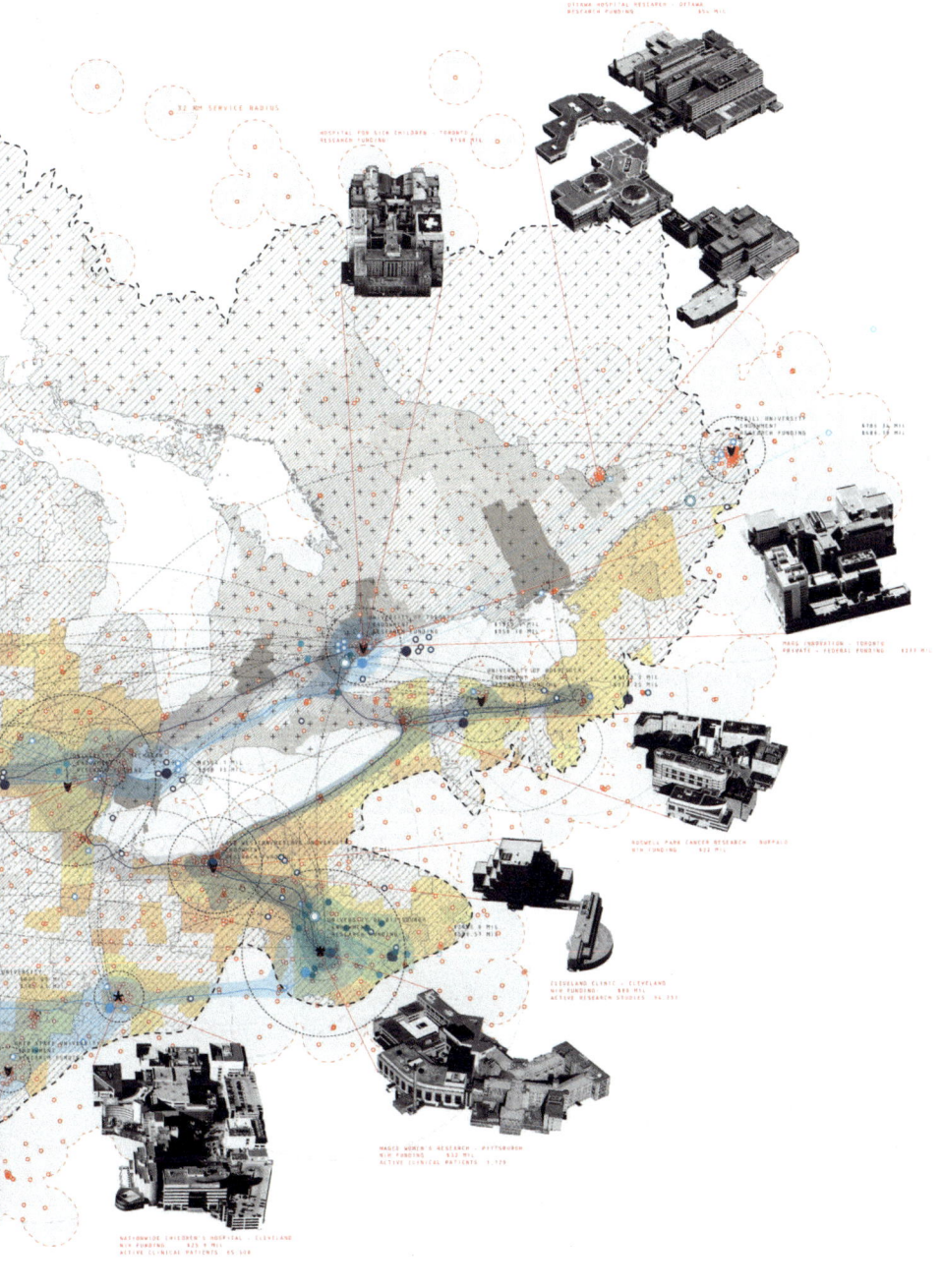

Our "shed cartographies" of the Great Lakes Mega-region are a series of mappings that build on the ideas of MacKaye, as well as on the broader history of methods for regional planning, mapping, and analysis informed by ecological and systems-thinking paradigms.[16] As in the well-known term "watershed," sheds are geospatial areas within which elements of a specific system, such as an ecosystem, retain a high degree of interconnectedness, interdependency, and coevolution.[17] The identification of the shed, whose boundaries are often elastic, is dependent on the agents, infrastructures, and processes brought into interrelation in a given geography. These cartographies describe a complex relational territory of human and biophysical systems through the superimposition of multiple geo-spatialized data sets combined with physical and nonphysical spatial information. They aim to empower the strategic capacity of regional planning and design by revealing interacting spatial agents and helping to make apparent current and potential synergies, possibilities for reorganization, and strategic sites of leverage.

Within our work, we also use the descriptive capacity of thick cartographies to reveal the contexts of uneven access to the products of infrastructure that condition participation within urban domains. In the project Protean Prototypes, thick cartographies are used to visualize urgent contemporary conditions of urban injustice and exclusion, while simultaneously making apparent the local agents current-

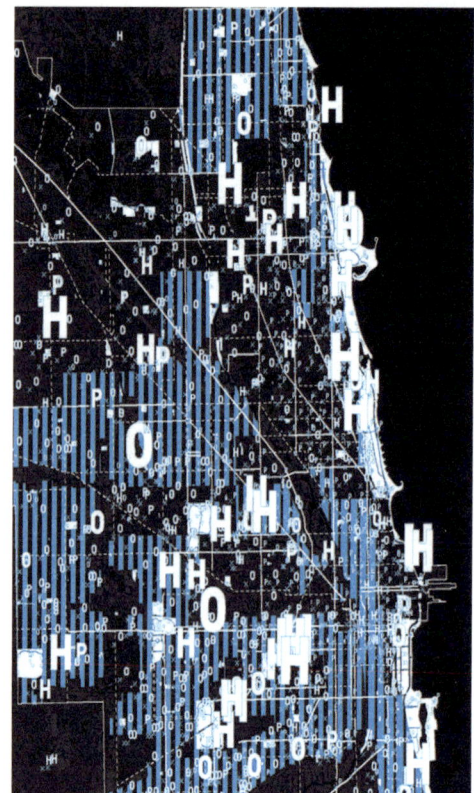

Fig. 4: "Chicago Geography of Access and Exclusion for Health: A thick cartography that combines GIS data sets for medically underserved areas with related "agents of access." These agents include hospitals, emergency rooms, CVS pharmacies and MinuteClinics, community centers, clinics for women and infants, Planned Parenthood, sexual health clinics, condom distribution, Chicago public schools, cooling centers, senior centers, YMCAs, youth centers, parks, and bicycle lanes.

ly working to provide access to vital urban services. Through the assembly of opposing information (urban-exclusion data sets with access-enabling agents) in cartographic space, we are able to begin to conceive of sites of need and local mechanisms of transformation in a synthetic way.[18]

Ways of Seeing: Relational Mappings

Whereas the geospatial depiction of cartography provides insight into the spatial relations between infrastructure and territory, the networks of power relations and exchanges that structure infrastructural ecologies are often more productively described through nonspatial relational network diagrams and mappings. In the field of industrial ecology, nested exchanges and thermodynamic cascades are often depicted in constructed ecosystem diagrams; the network diagrams of the closed-loop industrial ecology of Kalundborg, Denmark, are some of the best-known examples (Fig. 5).[19]

Territorial infrastructure mobilizes not only material and thermodynamic ecologies, but also a political and economic apparatus. Such infrastructural works are inherently understood as materializations of power structures that assemble multiple political, institutional, and economic actors, and that structure subjectivity, participation, and identity. Actor-network theory and assemblage theory inform our approach in developing relational mappings that

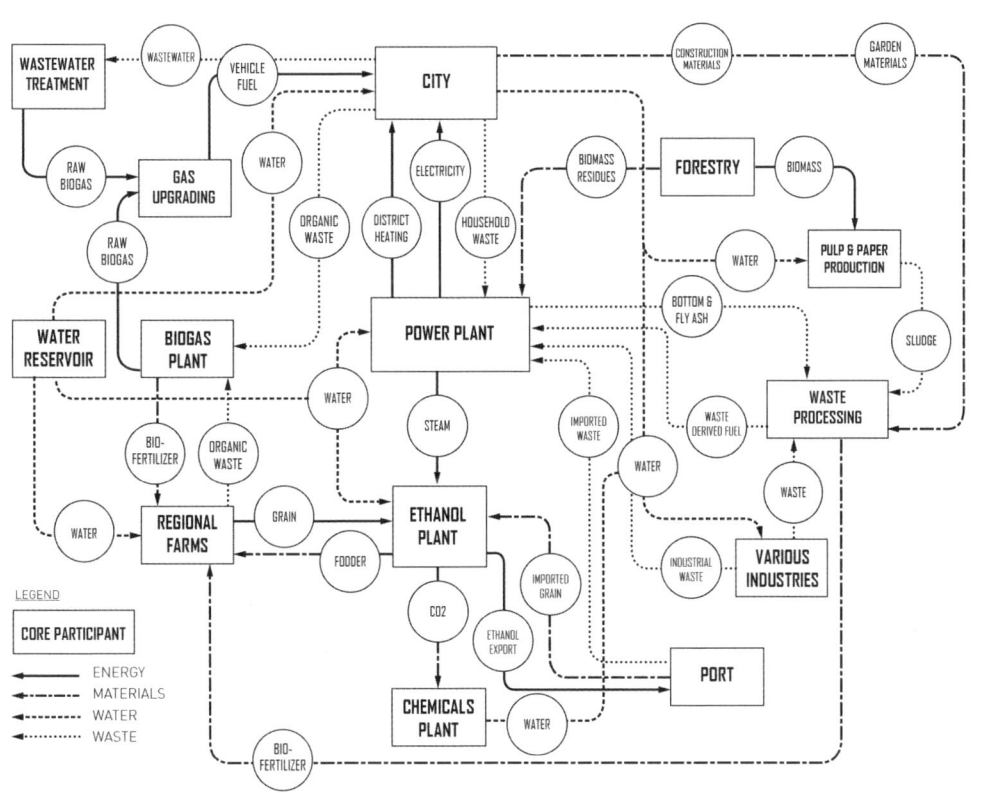

Fig. 5: Industrial-ecology network illustration of Kalundborg, Denmark.

allow us to think both the production of urban space and its design possibilities through the dynamics of networks, associations, and socio-technical assemblages. We deploy these theories to develop illustrations used for both analysis and envisioning future scenarios.

It is important to not only imagine urban change through the strategic design and redesign of infrastructure, but to also understand and speculate on the other mechanisms by which proposed transformations might take place: from urban community and political actors, to zoning or legal codes, to funding programs and enterprise. The Protean Prototypes project is a strategic, hybrid infrastructural project that speculates on how the existing space of transit infrastructures might as well become physical platforms that enable access to a broader variety of urban needs beyond the provision of public transit, while also facilitating the emergence of new encounters, associations, and adjacencies.

The illustration "System-Wide Network of Instruments and Actors" (Fig. 9) assembles current and proposed *access-enabling* physical infrastructures and technologies along with the governmental, institutional, community, and financial agents that participate in their maintenance, control, and support.

It is important that we not only imagine urban change, but also understand and speculate on the mechanisms, co-operations, and synergies through which transformation can take place. We are interested in the urban actors that are involved, what they produce and deliver, and how their work is spatialized. We consider how actors operating in disparate domains can be brought together. We investigate what amendments to zoning or other city codes and policies need to be made to facilitate modification of existing spaces, or how existing city-owned lands might be assembled. We explore what funding mechanisms or business enterprise might be leveraged to mobilize these changes and to sustain their operation. We envision how new technologies might be able to transform systemic components at a low cost and with a lightweight spatial implication while increasing possibilities for collaboration. Considerations such as these inform the development of design proposals that operate as complex assemblages. The combinatory spatial and nonspatial actor-network representations enable us to envision the production of urban space through the context of its interrelated processes. The project develops a tool-kit of instruments and actors, assembled into illustrations of relational networks at the scales of the entire urban system and the sites for which proposals are developed.

Ways of Seeing:
Projections of Urban Society

In the United States there is a tradition of referring to infrastructural projects undertaken as a cooperation between federal and state governments as "public works." Beginning with a broad range of transportation-related "internal improvements," these infrastructures expanded to include public-service infrastructures, as well as public buildings (schools, hospitals, municipal buildings) and public recreational spaces, especially during the Roosevelt-era WPA program.[20]

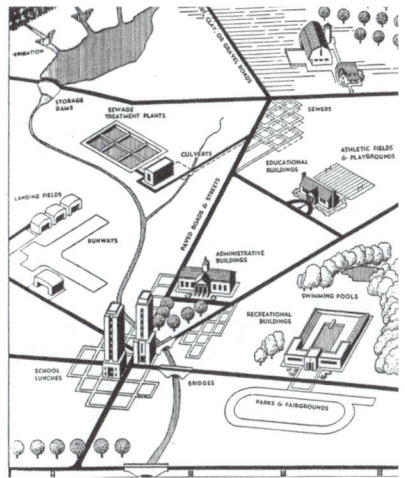

Fig. 6: US government poster from the 1940s, summarizing the Works Progress Administration's achievements.

This notion of public works looks beyond infrastructural efficiency and effectiveness to a conceptualization of infrastructure that has the capacity to produce new community, recreational, and public-space systems. Moreover, this conceptualization implies the possibility of combining service infrastructures and public spaces, as can be seen in the infrastructural/ recreational projects of the Tennessee Valley Authority, or Benton MacKaye's vision for the Appalachian Trail as an organizational spine for public access

and public utility, connecting transportation, hydroelectric networks, coal mining, and communities, while also serving as a firebreak and lookout for forest fires.[21] In contemporary practice, some of the most successful and resilient infrastructural projects are ones that are planned and realized in combination with public access and amenities.[22]

Fig. 7: Detail of *Along the River during the Qingming Festival*, by Zhang Zeduan. 1085–1145.

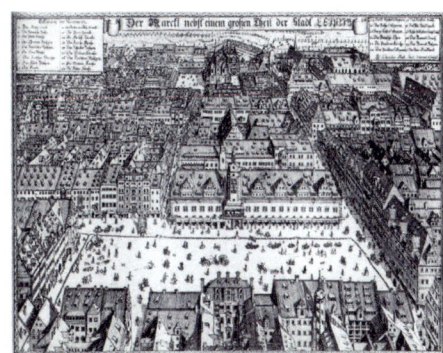

Fig. 8: Johann Georg Schreiber, *Leipzig, Market Square*, copper engraving, 1712.

A representational genre that is productive in recognizing infrastructure as public space is pre-aerial-view

Fig. 9: System-Wide Network of Instruments and System-Wide Network
of Instruments and Actors: Protean Prototypes detail, in the City of Chicago.

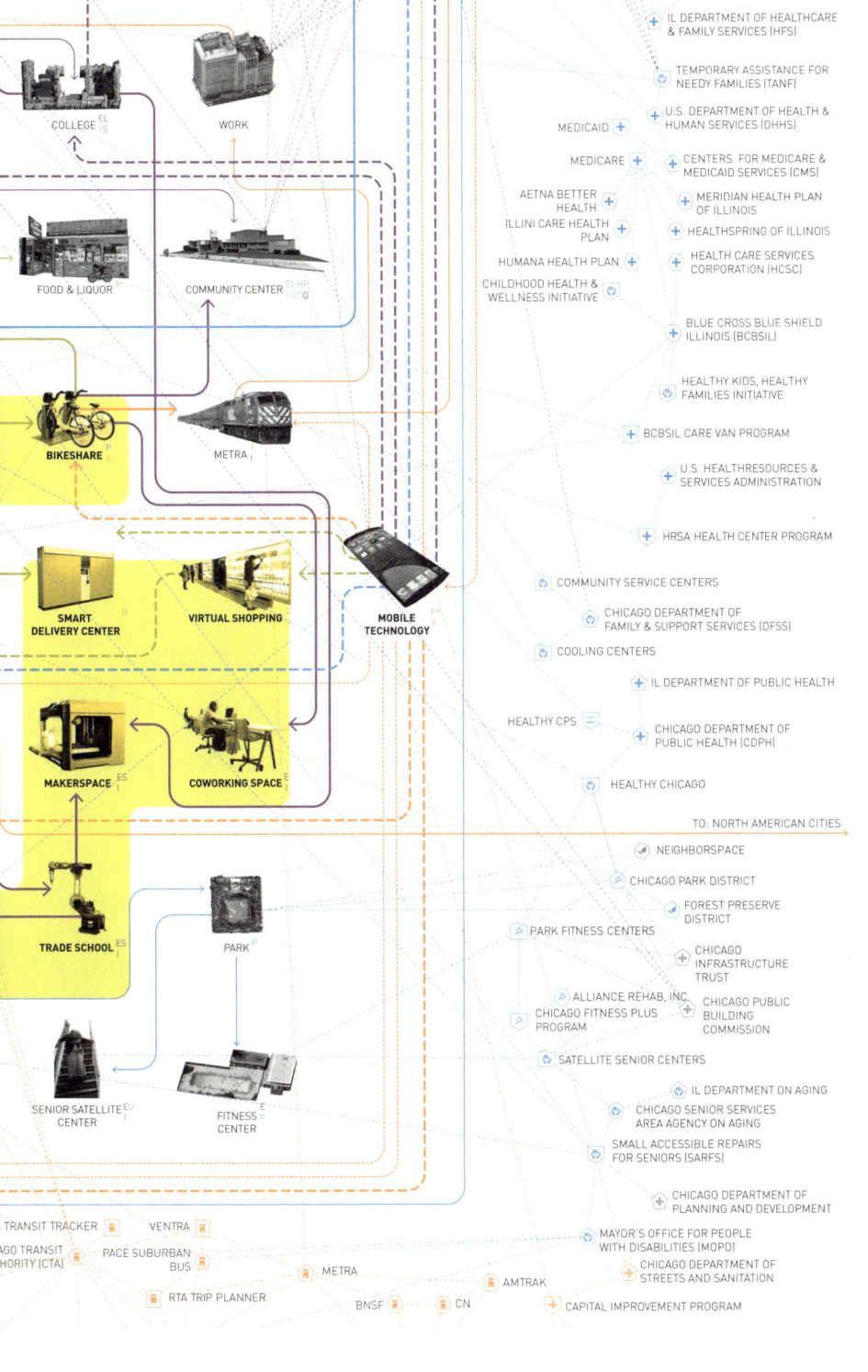

COLLEGE

WORK

FOOD & LIQUOR

COMMUNITY CENTER

BIKESHARE

METRA

SMART DELIVERY CENTER

VIRTUAL SHOPPING

MOBILE TECHNOLOGY

MAKERSPACE

COWORKING SPACE

TRADE SCHOOL

PARK

SENIOR SATELLITE CENTER

FITNESS CENTER

IL DEPARTMENT OF HEALTHCARE & FAMILY SERVICES (HFS)

TEMPORARY ASSISTANCE FOR NEEDY FAMILIES (TANF)

MEDICAID

U.S. DEPARTMENT OF HEALTH & HUMAN SERVICES (DHHS)

MEDICARE

CENTERS FOR MEDICARE & MEDICAID SERVICES (CMS)

AETNA BETTER HEALTH

MERIDIAN HEALTH PLAN OF ILLINOIS

ILLINI CARE HEALTH PLAN

HEALTHSPRING OF ILLINOIS

HUMANA HEALTH PLAN

HEALTH CARE SERVICES CORPORATION (HCSC)

CHILDHOOD HEALTH & WELLNESS INITIATIVE

BLUE CROSS BLUE SHIELD ILLINOIS (BCBSIL)

HEALTHY KIDS, HEALTHY FAMILIES INITIATIVE

BCBSIL CARE VAN PROGRAM

U.S. HEALTHRESOURCES & SERVICES ADMINISTRATION

HRSA HEALTH CENTER PROGRAM

COMMUNITY SERVICE CENTERS

CHICAGO DEPARTMENT OF FAMILY & SUPPORT SERVICES (DFSS)

COOLING CENTERS

IL DEPARTMENT OF PUBLIC HEALTH

HEALTHY CPS

CHICAGO DEPARTMENT OF PUBLIC HEALTH (CDPH)

HEALTHY CHICAGO

TO: NORTH AMERICAN CITIES

NEIGHBORSPACE

CHICAGO PARK DISTRICT

FOREST PRESERVE DISTRICT

PARK FITNESS CENTERS

CHICAGO INFRASTRUCTURE TRUST

ALLIANCE REHAB, INC.

CHICAGO FITNESS PLUS PROGRAM

CHICAGO PUBLIC BUILDING COMMISSION

SATELLITE SENIOR CENTERS

IL DEPARTMENT ON AGING

CHICAGO SENIOR SERVICES AREA AGENCY ON AGING

SMALL ACCESSIBLE REPAIRS FOR SENIORS (SARFS)

CHICAGO DEPARTMENT OF PLANNING AND DEVELOPMENT

A TRANSIT TRACKER

VENTRA

MAYOR'S OFFICE FOR PEOPLE WITH DISABILITIES (MOPD)

CAGO TRANSIT
THORITY (CTA)

PACE SUBURBAN BUS

CHICAGO DEPARTMENT OF STREETS AND SANITATION

METRA

AMTRAK

RTA TRIP PLANNER

BNSF

CN

CAPITAL IMPROVEMENT PROGRAM

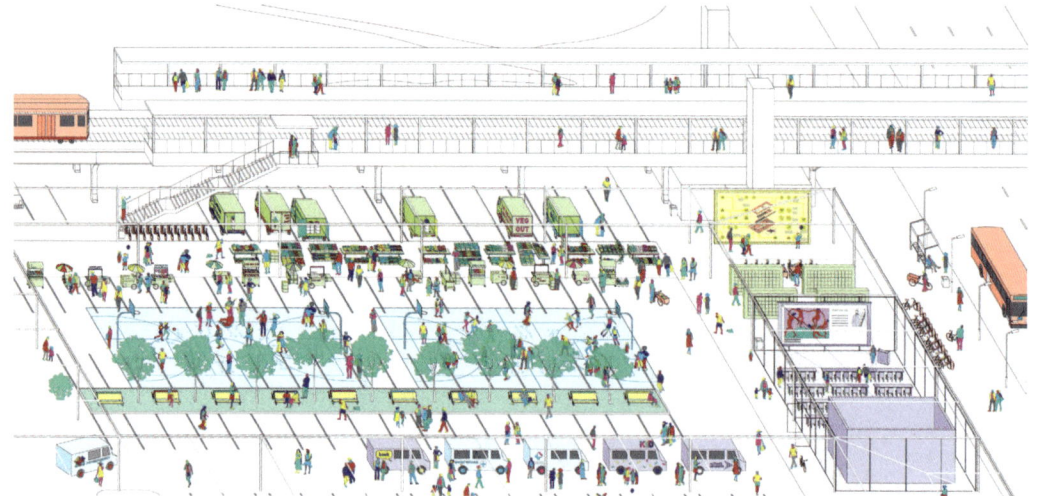

<u>Fig. 10:</u> Protean Prototypes detail of an illustration of urban society for the Washington Park/Garfield Station prototype.

urban mapping, where the infrastructure of the city, projected isometrically, is visualized simultaneously with the public life of citizens. The Song dynasty artist Zhang Zeduan's twelfth-century painting of the Quingming Festival (Fig. 7) and Johann Schreiber's early eighteenth century engraving of Leipzig's market square (Fig. 8) are both early examples of this genre of illustration, increasingly common in contemporary practices, that articulates politics of representation within urban space.

In eschewing perspectival or photo-realist representation, the oblique point of view allows the illustration to depict both public space and the various infrastructural instruments and actors that are mobilized within it. Placing urban infrastructure and urban space in the same representational sphere emphasizes the public role of infrastructure, and reasserts its central role in urban society.

Conclusion

Visual representation is central to recognizing infrastructure as a system; its design must be thought through the frameworks of ecology and apparatus. Within this context, we have outlined three possible representational models: thick cartographies, relational mappings, and projections of urban society. Each offers potentials that are equally instrumental and imaginative. Each offers a specific perspective on the politico-environmental ecologies of infrastructure, and enables urban theorists and designers to envision the actors, agencies, instruments, practices, and codes that may be mobilized toward infrastructural design.

Acknowledgements

The authors wish to thank Dan McTavish, Andrew Wald, Ya Suo, and Nick Safley for their work on the illustrations of the Protean Prototypes project; Mary O'Malley, Zain AbuSeir, and Dan McTavish for their contributions to the production of the shed cartographies for *Infra Eco Logi Urbanism*; and Kallie Sternburgh for her work on the Kalundborg diagram.

Protean Prototypes was supported by grant funding from Alan and Cynthia Berkshire to Taubman College at the University of Michigan, the University of Michigan Office of Research, and the US Department of Transportation: Nextrans Region V Center. The cartographic research for *Infra Eco Logi Urbanism* was funded through a Research Creation Grant from the Social Science and Humanities Research Council of Canada (SSHRC).

1. Keller Easterling, *Extrastatecraft: The Power of Infrastructure Space* (London: Verso Books, 2014), 12–13.
2. Christopher Alexander, "Systems Generating Systems," *Architectural Design* 12, no. 68 (1968): 90–91.
3. See James Corner, "Aerial Representation and the Making of Landscape," in *Taking Measures across the American Landscape*, by James Corner and Alex S. MacLean (New Haven, CT: Yale University Press, 1996), 15–19; and D. Graham Burnett and Jonathan Solomon, "Masters of the Universe," in *Models*, ed. Emily Abruzzo, Eric Ellingsen, and Jonathan D. Solomon (New York: 306090 Books, 2007), 44–51.
4. See Fritjof Capra, "Systems Theory and the New Paradigm," in *Key Concepts in Critical Theory: Ecology*, ed. Carolyn Merchant (Amherst, NY: Humanity Books, 1994), 334–41; James J. Kay, "An Introduction to Systems Thinking," in *The Ecosystem Approach: Complexity, Uncertainty and Managing for Sustainability*, ed. David Waltner-Toews, James J. Kay, and Nina Marie Lister (New York: Columbia University Press, 2008), 3–14; and Chris Reed and Nina-Marie Lister, "Parallel Genealogies," in *Projective Ecologies* (Cambridge, MA: Harvard Graduate School of Design, 2014), 22–39.
5. See Pierre Bélanger, *Going Live: From States to Systems*, Pamphlet Architecture 35 (New York: Princeton Architectural Press, 2015); Reed and Lister, *Projective Ecologies*; Daniel Ibañez and Nikos Katsikis, eds., *New Geographies 6: Grounding Metabolism* (Cambridge, MA: Harvard Graduate School of Design, 2014); and Mohsen Mostafavi, *Ecological Urbanism* (Baden: Lars Müller Publishers, 2010).
6. See Hillary Brown, *Next Generation Infrastructure* (Washington, DC: Island Press, 2014), 7; and Pierre Bélanger, "Landscape as Infrastructure," *Landscape Journal* 28, no. 1 (2009): 79–95.
7. David Orr, foreword to Brown, *Next Generation Infrastructure*, xii.
8. Julian Vincent, "Biomimetics of Skins," in *Functional Properties of Bio-inspired Surfaces: Characterization and Technological Application*, ed. Eduardo Favret and Nestor Fuentes (London: World Scientific Publishing, 2009), 3–15.
9. Michel Foucault, "Confessions of the Flesh," in *Power/Knowledge: Selected Interviews and Other Writings, 1972–1977*, ed. Colin Gordon (New York: Pantheon Books, 1980), 194.
10. McLain Clutter, *Imaginary Apparatus: New York City and Its Mediated Representation* (Zurich: Park Books, 2015), 29.
11. Stuart Elden, *The Birth of Territory* (Chicago: University of Chicago Press, 2013), 16–17.
12. See Neil Brenner, David J. Madden, and David Wachsmuth, "Assemblages, Actor-Networks, and the Challenges of Critical Urban Theory," in *Cities for People, Not for Profit: Critical Urban Theory and the Right to the City,* ed. Neil Brenner, Peter Marcuse, and Margrit Meyer (London: Routledge, 2012), 117–37; and

Ignacio Farias and Thomas Bender, *Urban Assemblages: How Actor-Network Theory Changes Urban Studies* (London: Routledge, 2010).

13. Geoffrey Thün, Kathy Velikov, Colin Ripley, and Dan McTavish, *Infra Eco Logi Urbanism: A Project for the Great Lakes Megaregion* (Zurich: Park Books, 2015), 90–93.

14. See Denis Cosgrove, *Geography and Vision* (New York: I. B. Tauris & Co., 2008); Charles Waldheim, "Aerial Representation and the Recovery of Landscape," in *Recovering Landscape: Essays in Contemporary Landscape Architecture*, ed. James Corner (New York: Princeton Architectural Press, 1999), 121–39; and Corner, "Aerial Representation."

15. Benton MacKaye, "The New Exploration: Charting the Industrial Wilderness," *Survey Graphic* 65 (May 1925): 153–57, 192–94.

16. Kathy Velikov and Geoffrey Thün, "Shed Cartographies," in *Third Coast Atlas*, ed. Daniel Ibañez, Charles Waldheim, Mason White, and Clare Lyster (Barcelona: Actar, forthcoming/2016).

17. Thün et al., *Infra Eco Logi Urbanism*, 30–31.

18. Geoffrey Thün and Kathy Velikov, "Protean Prototypes: Urban Platforms for Appropriation," *OASE* no. 96, (forthcoming/2016).

19. John Ehrenfeld and Nicholas Gertner, "Industrial Ecology in Practice: The Evolution of Interdependence at Kalundborg," *Journal of Industrial Ecology* vol. 1, no. 1 (1997): 67–79.

20. Harlan D. Unrau and G. Frank Williss, "Public Works Administration," in *Expansion of the National Park Service* in the 1930s: *Administrative History* (National Parks Service, 1983), https://www.nps.gov/parkhistory/online_books/unrau-williss/adhi3d.htm.

21. Benton MacKaye, "An Appalachian Trail: A Project in Regional Planning," *Journal of the American Institute of Architects* 9 (1921): 325–30.

22. See Brown, *Next Generation Infrastructure*, 97–125; and *Sandy Success Stories* (BuroHappold Engineering, 2013), http://issuu.com/burohappold/docs/sandysuccessstories_june2013__1_

Sound Networks, the Private, and the Public Sphere

Carlotta Darò

The apparatus of telecommunication networks constitutes an infrastructure space that was once regarded as a highly visible occupation of the street, rendering ever more elusive the ine between architecture and infrastructure. In turn, the boundary between public and private space has become blurred, increasingly defined not by the physicality of the built environment but rather by the non-static properties of use, suggests Carlotta Darò.

If architecture is traditionally a static and fixed object, then infrastructure, conversely, represents a system that includes dynamic and fluid items. However, both share the prerogative of occupying and bringing functional values into space, including its immaterial and environmental proprieties. What, then, happens to the nature of that space when it becomes involved in telecommunication systems, henceforward designated here by the phrase "sound networks"? How do objects that comprise architecture and infrastructure face up to the dimension of the private and, consequently, to that of the public, when they are all together part of a unitary functioning circuit?

In order to begin, and to tackle the question of the unitary circuit, the following discussion will start by addressing what comes from outside the built environment—or rather, what is commonly called the public domain—before focusing on the actual architectural object; namely, the physical space of the home: the house. This physical progression also reflects a theoretical issue stemming from the difficulty, as soon as we begin speaking about infrastructural systems and functioning movements, of isolating the architectural scale from urban and territorial ones. As we will see, addressing the private and the public dimension of space is a complex question, and the action of inscribing it within a singular object can hardly do it justice.

This is what each vacuum tube repeater does for your words.

Fig. 1: Explanation of a telecommunications repeater from a John Mills "tell-you-how" story entitled _The Magic of Communication._

As others have noted, the notion of privacy is legislated and circumscribed, primarily, by the law; thus, it is less strong and universal than the idea of intimacy.[1] The term "intimate" derives from the Latin _intimus_, the superlative of _interior_, which designates what is hidden from an external gaze.[2] While intimacy is supposed to be secret, invisible, and silent, privacy, by contrast, can be visible, tangible, and audible, yet judicially it remains understood as something that must be protected from external invasion. Conversely, the term "public" originally indicates what belongs to and comes from the people.[3] Since antiquity, this authority—the public—has been represented by the state. The *res publica* designates, then, what belongs to the collectivity and what cannot be altered by law. In the end, the distinction between private and public is not a matter of physical sites, but rather an issue of power distribution.[4] Consequently, the law becomes the actual subject of that regulation. In light of this, we might then ask: How did modern telecommunications develop legally? Was the expansion of sound networks through cities and territories a smooth or, on the contrary, a controversial process? And how have different cultural and political contexts, North America and Europe in particular, administered over divergent issues of private rights and public uses?

At the end of the nineteenth century, lawyer Edward Q. Keasbey published *The Law of Electric Wires in Streets and Highways*. In this book, Keasbey evoked a number of controversial cases dealing with the installation of networks and the use of transducer systems, which were undergoing a substantial development across the United States at the time: "It has been found that the wires will carry the sound of the voice and send

spoken as well as written messages. […] For all these uses the electric current must be distributed from central sources and carried by wires throughout the city and across the country."[5]

Fig. 2: Telecommunications infrastructure soon took over the space of the street.

In the early years of telecommunications, the number of wires and poles was perceived to have increased significantly. What could be termed their "occupation" of streets and highways made these objects obnoxious to property owners. Keasbey observed that poles disfigured the appearance of streets and, to a certain extent, obstructed their use as well. Wires obstructed access to buildings in cases of fire and they even gave rise to different kinds of damage in cases of storms or floods. Some of them carried high electrical currents that could potentially be deadly to passersby, and in cases where various kinds of wires with different applications intermingled, it was not unusual to see one current interfering with another.

These issues gave rise to public concern over the use of electric wires on streets and highways, a public opposition that eventually led to litigation.

Fig. 3: Streets began hosting a different kind of traffic: that of communication.

Fig. 4: Such infrastructure was vulnerable to damage from the elements.

However, Keasbey continued, the wires were too useful to be dispensed with, and the purposes they fulfilled were viewed as desirable by many. He compared these purposes to those of networks of transportation—that is, to highways—and he emphasized that it was only by using highways themselves that poles and wires could fully serve their function: "Their relations, therefore, to the public and private rights in the highways must be defined, conflicting rights must be adjusted, and the manner of using the streets must be controlled."[6] According to Keasbey, issues of street regulation were then both a public and a private matter. "The streets are opened for public use," he wrote, "but only for use as a street."[7] The title of the land that would be subject to this use remained, however, in the name of the owners of the adjoining lands. This discussion, in other words, asked questions about the proper uses of streets and to what extent streets were being underserved by the installation of electric wires. Ultimately, it also inquired into public and private rights with respect to street regulation and other possible applications. The North American development of sound networks was indeed tricky in terms of legal definition. Even if their services were considered public (at least as stated by telecommunication propaganda), these networks were owned by private companies that, through their infrastructures, occupied fragments of lands, streets, and subterranean as well as subaquatic corridors administrated by both private and public legislatures. As a result, Keasbey identified a triangular potential conflict that involved private networks, public services, and private ownership of space.

The context and terms of this issue were rather different in Europe, where public space has traditionally enjoyed a stronger presence, a fact that finds itself reflected in the urban landscape. In his brilliant essay "Savoirs de la ville et de la maison au début du 19eme siècle," François Béguin draws on a range of British and French examples to explore the rise of what he calls *politique de l'habitat* (housing politics) during the nineteenth century.[8] Through a study of various reports and surveys from that period, the author brings to attention the way in which housing politics at the time tended to be defined mainly in terms of uses, functions, legislations, and services, rather than through spatial and architectural concerns. Water regulation, the cleanliness of houses and cities, and climatic comfort (air and lighting) were all new elements brought forth by the salubrious machine of nineteenth-century housing politics. At first, cleaning and distribution services were administrated by dwellers themselves, but soon they were taken over by new specialized professions. Civil engineers, rather than architects, engaged in infrastructural research and projects that aimed to find solutions to the often fatal problem of insalubrities.[9] In the case of Europe specifically, the early private companies that had sought to tackle these issues were soon taken over by apparatuses of state administration. Indeed, the managing of waste, water and gas, and lighting—and later of telecommunications as well—became a fundamental concern within a European conception that positioned public space, broadly, as a shared and state-owned good. Béguin, however, concludes his study by describing a complex switch between private and public spheres that took place during the nineteenth century: a number of practices that had previously been public—meaning, that they took place outside the home—were being progressively privatized—or rather, domesticated—through the appearance of domestic appliances such as running water, gas, electricity, the telephone, radio, and then, ultimately, television.[10] Yet these systems depended entirely on extensive urban and territorial networks that belonged to the public sphere and occupied public areas. Consequently, the very idea of the home as a physical container that defined the private sphere would have to be radically questioned, since connections and other manners of communication with the outside world tore through the walls of what others have called the home's "shell of privacy."[11]

Fig. 5: The advent of the telecommunication age blurred the boundaries between the "exterior" and "interior" of the home.

From a visual and material standpoint, the border between the private and the public sphere is traditionally defined—at least within the domestic realm—by relying on the notions of "interiority" and "exteriority." In other words, the difference between private and public spheres is defined by opposing that which takes place on the inside of enclosed walls to that which is to be found outside of them. Thus, the intimacy of domestic space might be said to correspond to the ultimate idea of privacy as that which is opposed to the exposed and heterogeneous notion of public space. From a media-history perspective, this traditional distinction came under fire during modernity when architects, such as Le Corbusier, took to using the window as a frame that would simultaneously look out onto the exterior and serve as a showcase for elements of private life.[12] Put differently, in the modern period, the "publicity of the private" would give rise to innovative architectural conceptions. However, what remained, in essence, a fundamentally visual way of approaching architecture becomes more pervasive once the environmental proprieties of space, such as air, light, and sound, are taken into account. Walls and other material barriers have never offered an absolute guarantee in terms of acoustic isolation, since sound is a transducer agent that travels through air, water, and solids. Indeed, in their application to communication, modern technologies further extended this characteristic of sound, leading it ultimately to entirely overcome the limits of distance and

physical fences, with the most blatant result being that one could now hear the voice of another person located several kilometers away.[13] From a sonic perspective, then, the limits between private and public spheres have always been explicitly nuanced, since sound is essentially a phenomenon that moves between a source and a receptor (physiological and/or technological), rather than a static object easily apprehensible and spatially determined. Consequently, the fact of considering architecture and infrastructure as part of a whole circuit requires us to turn away from a purely formal understanding and, instead, to think more in terms of performative devices and mechanical functions. Yet, with the advent of telecommunications—notably the telegraph, the telephone, and the radio—came the assumption that the phenomenon of sound transmission is also a material agent involving physical objects and effects. It follows that technologies and infrastructures—and sound itself—were now seen as giving rise to a merger between private and public spheres that was both highly explicit and, at times, problematic.

Perhaps, then, it is the very idea of associating privacy to the physical dwelling, the house, that is in need of further questioning. The original Greek term for "house," *oikos*, designates both the physical space of the home and the group of people living in it, each pursuing his or her own activities.[14] Historians remind us that conceptions of, for instance, the Roman or the medieval town house necessarily included the presence of the public at large.[15] Within, the manufacturing locale, the counting house, the store, and the shop added a variety of other services to the family home, whose related spaces offered connections to the exterior world. Beginning in the seventh century, the rising economic prosperity of the bourgeoisie came to be reflected in the conversely declining presence of the public realm within the home.[16] As the European bourgeoisie and the American middle class significantly grew in number during the nineteenth century, the presence of the public within the private realm diminished dramatically, meaning that fewer and fewer people—employees, servants, clients, guests, etc.— entered the home on a regular basis.

Fig. 6: Headphones allowed for individual access of the public sphere.

At the same time, a keen interest in the outside world was fueled by the incursion of a flurry of media into the home. Books, maps, newspapers, magazines, and journals: these allowed access to the exterior world, and were notably located in specific rooms within the house, such as the studio or the library. This way of accessing the public sphere individually, or sometimes via a restrained collectivity, would subsequently be significantly augmented by the use of early modern telecommunications. Consider, for instance, the highly confidential ear-to-ear telephone system, or the way the use of radio evolved over time—in its early beginnings, the radio offered a private experience accessible only through individual headphones capable of isolating the very first weak wireless signals. During the 1920s, after the technology had improved and the radio became a popular device, listening to the radio came to be associated with moments of restrained socialization among groups of people and families. From car audio systems to the Walkman and the wireless smartphone, technology made it increasingly possible to bring along one's own piece of sonic environment. These aural bubbles would then become transportable entities that could be taken outside the private dimension of the home. The increased mobility achieved through the development of modern means of transportation, associated with the technological possibility of always remaining connected to one's private environment, is described by Raymond Williams in terms of "mobile privatization."[17] This phenomenon reflects the atomization of modern societies, where individuals, perpetually in motion, take their intimate sphere with them wherever they go.

Following this perspective then, the distinction between private and public dimensions appears to be defined, not by architectural static properties, but rather by uses, regulations, and everyday activities that have the potential to change and overlap over time. Thus, domestic space can be either public or private according to users' behavior. Likewise, public space can be traversed by private environmental bubbles that are attached to moving individuals.

Fig. 7: Gathering around the wireless became a social pastime.

More generally, this history of telecommunications opens a significant avenue into the way we define architecture and infrastructure in relation to their uses. Keasbey's overview of early infrastructural developments reveals a complex legal definition surrounding them. Architecture and infrastructure can hardly be taken as isolated objects, since one always already belongs to the other and each gives the other its functional meaning: indeed, the moment one focuses on usages rather than on objects, separating the architectural scale from the exterior becomes an artificial operation. As discussed above, modern technologies such as the telegraph, the telephone, and the radio emphasized the role of communication and physical networks—notably sound networks—by connecting the private with the public sphere. In other words, modernity "made the housing more explicit."[18] The increased specialization of networks, brought about by advances in technology, led to a separation between the functions that were imputed to the physical space of the home and those that lent its systems legibility through the presence of pipes, cables, outlets, and switches that are always connected to the exterior world. This distinction of functions produced similar consequences in terms of users' perception and has been acknowledged as a prerogative of modernity.[19] Consequently, one user could communicate with another by speaking (and hearing) without physically moving, seeing, and feeling the presence of that other user. This is the decisive separation between the hearing and the seeing subject that first emerged when, on March 10, 1876, Alexander Graham Bell placed his first phone call to his assistant Thomas Watson. Telephoning from one room of his Boston laboratory to another, Bell, in just a few words, made explicit the possibility of isolating different layers of communication by piercing "the shell of privacy": "Mr. Watson. Come here—I want to see you."

1. See Gérard Wajcman, *Fenêtre: Chroniques du regard et de l'intime* (Lagrasse: Verdier, 2004), 439–41; and Georges Teyssot, "Windows and Screens: A Topology of the Intimate and the Extimate," *Log*, no. 18 (2010): 75–88.
2. Wajcman, *Fenêtre*, 439.
3. Georges Duby, "Ouverture" in *Histoire de la vie privée*, ed. Philippe Ariès and Georges Duby, vol. 2, *De l'Europe féodale à la Renaissance* (Paris: Seuil, 1985), 19–24.
4. Ibid., 22–23.
5. Edward Q. Keasbey, *The Law of Electric Wires in Streets and Highways* (Chicago: Callaghan and Company, 1900) reprinted by Biblio Bazaar in 2009, 1.
6. Ibid, 2.
7. Ibid, 2.
8. François Béguin, "Savoirs de la ville et de la maison au début du 19ème siècle," in *Politiques de l'habitat*, 1800–1850, ed. Michel Foucault (Paris: Corda, 1977), 211–324.
9. Ibid., 247–51.
10. Ibid., 317–24.
11. Stephen Kern, *The Culture of Time and Space*, 1880–1918 (Cambridge, MA: Harvard University Press, 1983), 187; and Christoph Asendorf, "Telefon: 'Piercing the Shell of Privacy,'" *Arch+*, nos. 191/192 (March 2009): 118–23.
12. Beatriz Colomina, *Privacy and Publicity: Modern Architecture as Mass Media* (Cambridge, MA: MIT Press, 1994), 7–11.
13. Conversely, according to Stephen Kern, during the nineteenth century, a number of inventions such as the microphone, in 1877, "pierced the shell of privacy." The author refers to Frank Lloyd Wright's "prairie-style" home, whose interior was developed as a shelter from the outside. This conception was part of a broad reconsideration of the relationship between public and private sphere. Kern, *Culture of Time and Space*, 187.
14. Evelyne Patlagean, "Bysance Xème-XIème siècle," in *Histoire de la vie privée*, ed. Philippe Ariès and Georges Duby, vol. 1, *De l'Empire romain à l'an mil* (Paris: Seuil, 1985), 547.
15. Ibid., 547–48; and Spiro Kostof, *A History of Architecture: Settings and Rituals* (New York: Oxford University Press, 1985), 361. See also Terence Riley, *The Un-Private House* (New York: Museum of Modern Art, 1999), 10.
16. Riley, *The Un-Private House*, 11; and Roger Chartier, "Les pratiques de l'écrit," in *Histoire de la vie privée*, ed. Philippe Ariès and Georges Duby, vol. 3, *De la Renaissance aux Lumières* (Paris: Seuil, 1986), 165–67.
17. Raymond Williams, *Television: Technology and Cultural Form* (London: La Fontana, 1974).
18. Peter Sloterdijk, *Ecumes: Spheres III*, trans. Olivier Mannoni (Paris: Hachette Litteratures, 2005), 443. My translation.
19. See Caroline A. Jones, ed., *Sensorium: Embodied Experiences, Technology, and Contemporary Art* (Cambridge, MA: MIT Press, 2006), 5–49.

Image Sources:

Fig. 1: John Mills, *The Magic of Communication* (American Telephone and Telegraph Company, 1937).

Fig. 2, 4: AT&T Archives and History Center.

Fig. 5: Warshaw Collection of Business Americana, Archives Center, National Museum of American History, Smithsonian Institution.

Fig. 4: James Robb, *The Biography of Telephone*. AT&T Archives and History Center.

Figs. 6, 7: George H. Clark Radioana Collection, Archives Center, National Museum of American History, Smithsonian Institution

Fig. 5: Warshaw Collection of Business Americana, Archives Center, National Museum of American History, Smithsonian Institution.

Energy Transition at the Regional Scale: Building Sustainable Energy Landscapes

Sven Stremke

While the transition towards more sustainable energy systems is a pursuit across all scales, Sven Stremke argues that the regional scale is the most appropriate for the planning and design of sustainable "energy landscapes"—in which infrastructure manifests as the physical artifacts of this transition.

Before the era of fossil fuels, there was a direct relation between spatial organization of the physical environment and energy sources. Renewable energies shaped landscapes and vice versa. Over the past century or two, however, we've become addicted to an ever-increasing amount of fossil fuels while most of us have lost sight of the energy infrastructure that is necessary to exploit, process, store, and transport crude oil, natural gas, and their derivatives. More recently, we can observe that the reintroduction of renewable energy has serious implications for the spatial organization and appearance of the physical environment. I want to explore here the regional planning and design of sustainable "energy landscapes"—a physical environment (or territory) that can evolve on the basis of locally available renewable energy sources without compromising landscape quality, biodiversity, food production, and other life-supporting ecosystem services.

The first objective for the designer of energy landscapes is the energy-conscious organization of land use, since both energy supply and demand are influenced by the spatial organization of the environment. The second objective is to design resilient infrastructure that can transport and transmit energy of different qualities effectively—district heating networks, for example, allow the use of residual heat from power plants. The third objective is to increase the assimilation of energy by means of renewable energy technology. On this point, both the spatial claims and the appearance of renewable energy technologies ought to be taken into account.

A full transition to renewable energy is expected to take decades and necessitate energy-conscious interventions that range in scale from the architectural (e.g., heat pumps) to the continental (e.g., gas networks). Spatial planners, landscape architects, and other environmental designers working at the intermediate scales are challenged both by the long-term nature of this transition and the spatial complexity of energy landscapes. Until very recently, research within spatial planning was limited to energy use in relation to commuting and the resulting implications for city planning.[1] In architecture and urban design, renewable energies have been considered more thoroughly.[2] Energy-conscious urban-design principles have been formulated in pursuit of sustainable urban development.[3] In the field of landscape planning and design, energy is also addressed; historically, the focus here was limited to energy conservation through vegetation and site planning. More recently, the assimilation of renewable energies has become a scope for landscape architects. In spite of the relative novelty of the subject for the environmental design community, there is consensus among scholars about the need to rethink the spatial organization of the physical environment, and to develop resilient infrastructure and promote renewable energy technologies.

There are many calls to pursue sustainable energy transition at the regional scale.[4] How to define the term "region" is a crucial question to the planner or designer of sustainable energy landscapes. Geographers, economists, and politicians all have their own understandings of what a region might be. Regions can be as large as a continent, or as small as a city and its immediate surroundings. The scale of "regional planning" is thus considered highly elastic. In my use of the term here, "region" is understood as a large territorial system that is smaller than a country and comprises several municipalities.

In spite of the potential benefits of regional energy landscapes—to increase energy assimilation and optimize energy flows—there are few publications that examine the possible implications of designing at the regional scale for so-called energy-conscious planning and design; for instance, how the region should be conceptualized in the context of energy-conscious planning and design. I will consider this issue via the exploration of three key concepts from systems theory: open systems, optimum system size, and hierarchy.

Open Systems Approach to Energy Transition

Cities are thermodynamically open systems, far from a state of equilibrium. Their future depends on the activities within city limits as well as external life-support systems providing, for example, food, water, and energy. Regions too are open systems, because they "receive causes from or generate effects to other systems."[5] Whereas energy regions are thermodynamically open systems, most if not all renewable energy is derived from sources *outside* the system, with emissions leaving the system. It is important to stress that energy self-sufficiency is substantially different from the notion of autarky, which implies being disconnected from other regions. Self-sufficient regions may utilize infrastructure to export and import energy from other regions, whereas autarkic regions represent apparently closed systems—an outdated idea that has been abandoned in the context of present-day energy transition.

The energy supply of any region consists of a number of (sub)systems with regard to energy sources, carriers, and networks.[6] Heat grids, for example, typically serve a neighborhood or a town. Their spatial extent is limited by heat losses. Electricity grids, on the contrary, are capable of transmitting energy over longer distances without significant energy loss. Spatial proximity of sources and sinks can reduce transportation costs and, more importantly, help to minimize energy degradation. This applies, in particular, to energy carriers with relatively low densities, such as heat and biomass. When considering the different energy carriers and their mode of transportation and transmission at the global scale, a picture of overlapping energy systems emerges (Fig. 1). The largest system is defined by the global "service area" of coal, oil, and liquefied natural gas (LNG), followed by gas networks, electricity grids, biomass systems, and finally heat and cold grids.

Determining the spatial boundaries of energy systems can be a rather difficult task. On the one hand, geographic indicators can help in defining "zonal regions."[7] Solar, wind, or hydro regions can be determined based on the hours of sunshine, wind speed, and topography. On the other hand, there also exist "functional regions," especially as one considers energy infrastructure: the

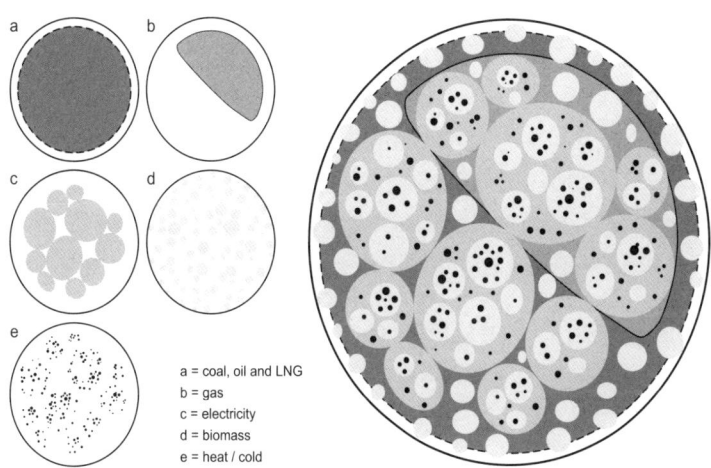

a = coal, oil and LNG
b = gas
c = electricity
d = biomass
e = heat / cold

Fig. 1: Overlapping energy systems with relative system extent. The "service area" of coal, oil, and liquefied natural gas (LNG) is the entire planet. Gas networks, on the contrary, extend only over certain parts of the planet. Electricity networks are again smaller but interconnect. Second-generation biomass is usually utilized within a region. Yet heat/cold networks are smaller, extending over a just a neighborhood or parts of a town.

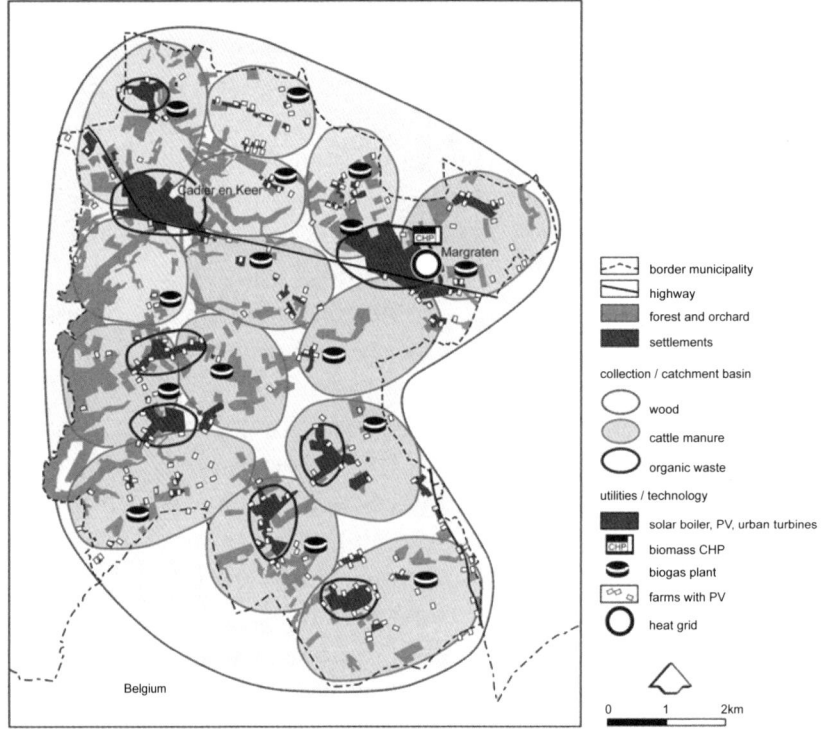

Fig. 2: Proposal for sustainable energy landscape in Margraten, the
Netherlands. The spatial extent of the different energy systems is indicated
by means of continuous lines.

"service area" of a power plant that is connected with consumers via the electricity grid presents a functional region. Nevertheless, many functional regions are somewhat flexible, both in size and structure, depending on the kind of energy network. When designing energy regions that make use of renewable energy, one has to deal with relatively open zonal and functional regions.

Another distinction has to be made based on the spatial structure of an energy system. Let us imagine an island with two possibilities for fulfilling electricity demand. One option is a large biomass-fired power plant that generates all the electricity needed. The electricity is distributed from one single "source" to the consumers. Another option is a set of combined heat and power plants (CHP) that run on locally available biomass. In both cases, electricity and heat are distributed via energy networks to the consumers. The latter energy system is considered multinodal, the former uninodal. Energy systems are thermodynamically open systems—their spatial extent and relation with a particular energy region can be described making use of geographical, spatial, and energetic indicators.

Optimum Size of Energy Systems

The optimum size of each energy system has great relevance for the planning and design of energy regions. This is because once the size of a system is beyond its energetic optimum (in either direction) it requires *additional* energy to maintain that system. Here, I am using "optimum system size" to refer to the spatial extent of a system at which energy supply and demand can be matched most effectively in space and time (Fig. 2). Whereas a certain minimum system size is necessary to match supply and demand, unnecessarily large systems should be avoided to reduce energy loss (the principle of subsidiarity).

The optimum system size of renewable energy systems is generally smaller than that of fossil fuel systems. The distance woody biomass can be transported, for example, is limited by the quantity of fuel needed to power trucks. The amount of energy invested for transporting an energy carrier to a centralized plant should not exceed the efficiency wins of converting energy at that plant.

Hierarchy between Energy Subsystems

Hierarchy is the third critical concept for the planning and design of energy landscapes at the regional scale. Scientists conceptualize systems as consisting of levels (or subsys-

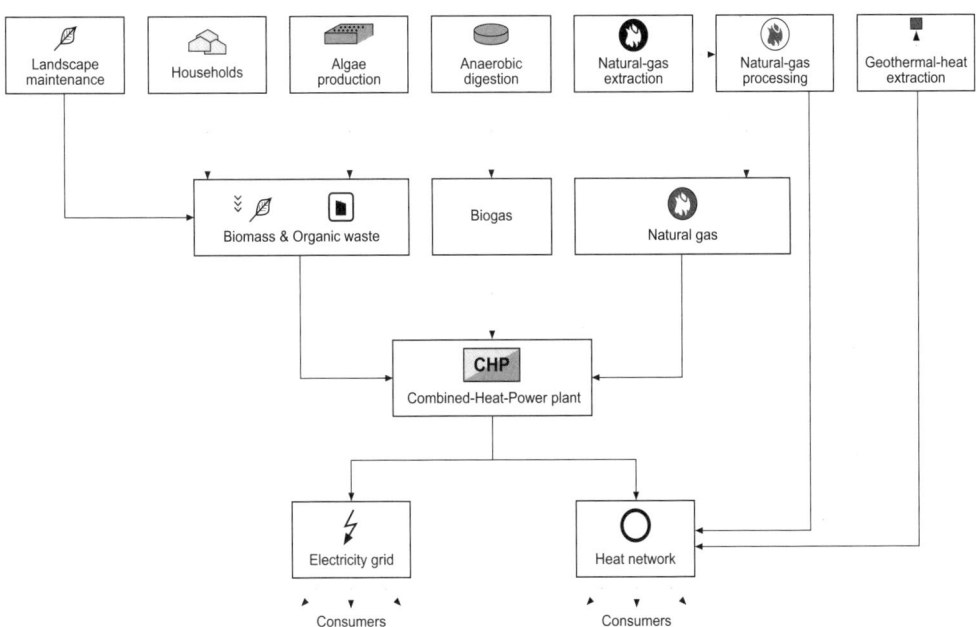

Fig. 3: Interdependencies between the energy-system levels of a combined heat and power plant (CHP): energy sources, energy carriers, conversion technology, networks, and consumers (from top to bottom).

tems) defined by physical or spatial structure. The following levels have been suggested in the past: energy sources, energy carriers, conversion technology, networks, and consumers. It is important to remember that each of these levels is part of a hierarchy.

Interdependencies among the energy system levels can be illustrated as follows, using a CHP as an example (Fig. 3). Access to the electricity grid is a first prerequisite for both the plant and the consumers. Local conditions, such as the presence of a heat network, determine whether it is possible to utilize residual heat. Without fuels, however, it is not possible to run the CHP. Several options exist: The plant can be powered by biomass from landscape maintenance, households, or algae production. Biogas from anaerobic digestion might be another energy source. All input/output relations of the CHP plant have direct feedback in both directions.

Most conventional fossil fuel energy systems, on the contrary, have control hierarchies. There exists only limited control from the consumer to the utility. Recently, however, consumers can not only choose between different energy utilities, but can also "upload" energy into the networks; in doing so, they become so-called prosumers.

Hierarchy is thus also relevant to the discussion on feed-in tariffs and open access to energy infrastructure. Sustainable energy transition not only depends on physical infrastructure; producers of renewable electricity, biogas, and heat must also have the right to feed their energy into the res-

pective energy networks. Systems can only be optimized if energy can "travel" in both directions. The concept of hierarchy is especially useful for understanding energy systems at the regional scale; each system can be seen as part of a larger supersystem and, in turn, may comprise several subsystems. The following case study of the Southeast Drenthe energy region, in the north of the Netherlands, illustrates how the aforementioned concepts of openness, optimum system size, and hierarchy have been employed.

Southeast Drenthe Energy Region

In the Netherlands, forty COROP areas have been defined based on a nodal classification principle linked to land-use patterns.[8] Each of those regions contains a spatial center (i.e., city) that provides services to the surrounding area. Southeast Drenthe is one of the COROP regions in the northern Netherlands, comprised of three municipalities (Fig. 4). The two municipalities of Emmen and Coevorden (covering a total area of 646 km^2) were the subject of the project "Synergies between Regional Planning and EXergy" (SREX).

To begin, the significant energy-related features of Southeast Drenthe were mapped onto an energy landscape map (Fig. 5). First, energy sources and consumers were localized (e.g., power plants, hospitals, heavy industry, waste-water treatment plants, and housing areas). Then, energy infrastructure, such as power lines, gas grids, main roads, and rail-

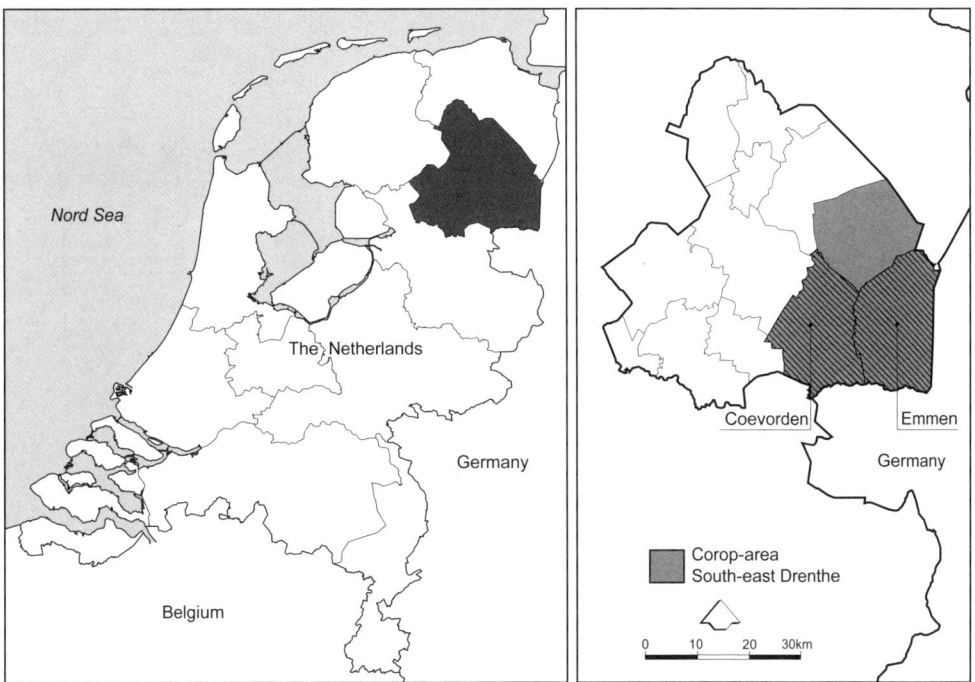

Fig. 4: Location of the province of Drenthe in the Netherlands (left) and the COROP region of Southeast Drenthe and the municipalities of Coevorden and Emmen (right).

roads were plotted on the map. The reason for mapping the present-day energy systems was to "visualize" the components of this complex system. Although many energy features are not yet considered in land-use planning, they are important for the development of a sustainable energy landscape.

Boundaries of the Open Energy System in Southeast Drenthe

The region of Southeast Drenthe is open and relatively fuzzy in terms of boundaries; people, information, goods, materials, and energy both enter and leave the region. A freeway, several highways, and a railroad connect the region with other parts of the Netherlands and Germany. A high-voltage power line transmits electricity from Eemshaven, in the north of Groningen, to the densely populated areas in the south of the Netherlands.

It is important to recognize that external factors influence energy flows that cross the region. In Eemshaven, for example, at time of writing, new

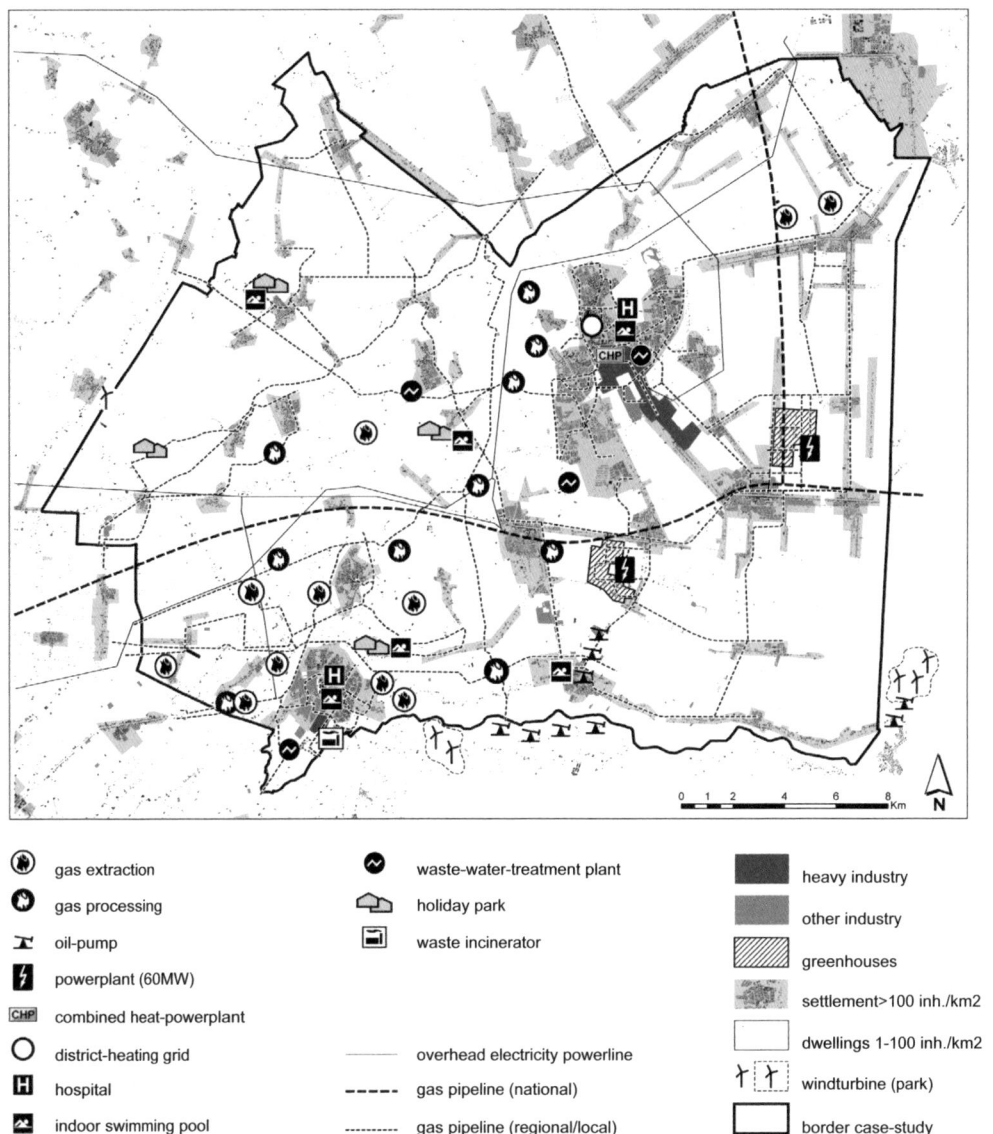

⊛	gas extraction	⊘	waste-water-treatment plant	■ heavy industry
◕	gas processing	⌂	holiday park	■ other industry
⊥	oil-pump	⊡	waste incinerator	▨ greenhouses
⚡	powerplant (60MW)			▦ settlement>100 inh./km2
CHP	combined heat-powerplant			☐ dwellings 1-100 inh./km2
○	district-heating grid	⎯⎯	overhead electricity powerline	
H	hospital	-----	gas pipeline (national)	⋎ ⋎ windturbine (park)
⌇	indoor swimming pool	---------	gas pipeline (regional/local)	☐ border case-study

Fig. 5: Map of the present-day energy landscape in the Southeast
Drenthe region.

power plants are under construction. Electricity generated in Eemshaven will be transmitted to other regions in the country and possibly abroad by means of the high-voltage power line that transects the case-study region. In doing so, Eemshaven electricity competes with renewable electricity generated in Southeast Drenthe because no preferred "right-of-way" for renewable electricity exists on the high-voltage power line. Next, converting renewable electricity from low to high voltage requires substantial amounts of energy; that's why it would make sense to create regional energy infrastructure such as low-voltage electricity networks, low-pressure biogas grids, and local heat networks.

Added to this is the fact that in terms of oil and natural gas, the region of Southeast Drenthe can be considered open. The extraction of oil is still taking place here; its output is transported through a pipeline to a refinery in Germany. Although the physical distance is only 35 kilometers, oil crosses the national border and therefore enters a different socio-economic system. Refined products such as petroleum enter the region via pipelines and trucks. A similar situation applies to natural gas. The gas that is extracted in Southeast Drenthe is transported via the gas grid owned by the Dutch Gasunie (Gas Union). This nationwide grid uses high pressure to bridge long distances. Although there are interregional and local gas grids with lower pressure, natural gas is injected into the national grid first and then distributed across the country.

System Sizes and Hierarchies in Southeast Drenthe

For energy-conscious planning and design, it is necessary to determine the spatial extent of the existing energy systems. One could conceptualize the electricity system (that is, electricity generation and transmission) as the top "layer" in Southeast Drenthe. The present electricity system is top-down, centralized, footloose, and stretches across the entire Netherlands. The nearest large coal- and gas-fired power plants are located in Eemshaven, about eighty kilometers to the north of Emmen. Those power plants generate electricity that is transmitted, via Drenthe among others, to the south of the country.

When it comes to gas networks, two perspectives have to be considered. The existing natural gas system extends far beyond the region of Southeast Drenthe. Gas is extracted across the northern parts of the Netherlands and transported via an extensive network of pipelines throughout the country. There are, however, more and more initiatives producing local biogas. It is disadvantageous to transport biogas via the national gas network for two reasons: first, the biogas needs to be "cleaned" before it can be injected into the natural gas network, and secondly, a great deal of energy is needed to pressurize biogas before it can enter the natural gas network. The construction of new regional biogas grids, as proposed for Southeast Drenthe, offers an alternative approach. Such smaller scale (and low pressure) gas networks further strengthen the case for studying energy systems at the regional scale.

Heat and cold networks represent a third type of energy network. In a number of countries—Denmark, for example—the combination of heat network and CHPs is very common. CHPs are an energy-efficient alternative to conventional power plants, where residual heat is simply emitted into nearby bodies of water or into the atmosphere. Most heat grids extend over a district (district heating) or a city (urban heat network). In some countries such as Germany and Austria, however, heat networks have been created in villages and low-density rural landscapes. If a heat grid transports heat of different caloric values between various kinds of consumers, it is also referred to as a "heat cascade." Such a heat cascade has been proposed for Emmen to further improve the already existing heat network in the city.

Finally, a certain hierarchy exists between the various interrelated energy systems in Southeast Drenthe. On the one hand, some energy systems (e.g., electricity grids) operate beyond the region. On the other hand, the region contains several smaller energy systems (e.g., existing heat grids with heat plants in Emmen). It remains important to stress that the proposed low-pressure biogas network and heat cascade are context-specific interventions that highly depend on other (higher order) levels in the energy system (e.g., biogas plants and CHPs). There is no single system; several interrelated energy systems coexist at various spatial scales. It is expected that the number and diversity of energy systems will increase as part of the energy transition. Such a development would be beneficial to create a resilient energy landscape because diversified energy systems are capable of coping with possible shortfalls of a source while diversification may also, in a market economy, help to balance fluctuating energy prices.

Conclusion

There is a great potential to develop sustainable energy landscapes beyond the architectural and urban scale. In the Netherlands and beyond, an increasing number of provinces and regions are committed to becoming self-sufficient with regards to energy. They are looking for knowledge to develop alternative energy landscapes that can be sustained on the basis of locally available renewable and residual energy sources.

Three concepts from systems thinking are pertinent to the pursuit of an energy transition at the regional scale. Energy systems are thermodynamically *open systems*; their spatial extent and relation with a particular energy region can be described making use of geographical, spatial, and energetic indicators. A certain *system size* is necessary to match supply and demand; unnecessarily large systems should be avoided to reduce energy loss. Finally, the concept of *hierarchy* is useful for the understanding of energy systems at the regional scale; each system can be part of a larger supersystem and, in turn, may comprise several subsystems.

A first important step for the development of alternative energy regions is to map present-day energy systems. A second step is to map renewable and residual energy potentials. Although the case study examined here focuses on the municipalities of Coevorden and Emmen, it is also useful in mapping networks that cross the region. Existing superregional energy networks could influence, for example, the location of new wind turbines within the region. Not only are sufficient wind speeds needed, so is access to high-voltage power lines.

A regional approach to the design of sustainable energy landscapes also implies looking for synergies among the different urban and rural uses of land. Both the finance and costs of energy distribution depend on the spatial characteristics of a region. A regional approach to energy transition also necessitates considering possible future developments—regional developments (e.g., increasing the number of greenhouses), as well as developments outside the region (e.g., new coal-fired power plants in Eemshaven), may affect the regional energy landscape.

To conclude, a regional approach to energy transition can assist the synchronization of energy-conscious interventions that take place in various locations and across different scales. It also has the potential to bridge the gap between (inter)national targets and local initiatives. At the regional scale, long-term strategies and short-term actions can be integrated effectively to transform today's fossil-fuel dependent environment into a more sustainable energy landscape. More importantly, stakeholder values and preferences can be accommodated effectively in the regional design process. The Southeast Drenthe study presented here revealed concrete energy-conscious interventions, facilitated lively discussions, and raised the attention of key decision-makers in the region—three key ingredients for a successful energy transition.

Acknowledgments

Earlier research for this essay was conducted in collaboration with Dr. Ferry van Kann (Groningen University, the Netherlands) and Prof. Dr. Jusuck Koh (Wageningen University, the Netherlands). The author also wishes to acknowledge the other researchers of the SREX research project funded by SenterNovem/Ministry of Economic Affairs.

1. S. E. Owens, "Energy and Spatial Structure: A Rural Example," *Environment and Planning* A 16, no. 10 (1984): 1319–37, doi:10.1068/a161319.
2. Carla Balocco and Giuseppe Grazzini, "Thermodynamic Parameters for Energy Sustainability of Urban Areas," *Solar Energy* 69, no. 4 (2000): 351–56,

doi:10.1016/S0038-092X(00)00069-4; P. Droege, "Renewable Energy and the City: Urban Life in an Age of Fossil Fuel Depletion and Climate Change," *Bulletin of Science, Technology & Society* 22, no. 2 (2002): 87–99, doi:10.1177/0270467602022002003; Thomas Herzog, Norbert Kaiser, and Michael Volz, *Solar Energy in Architecture and Urban Planning* (Munich: Prestel, 1996).

3. Alexander J. Boelen and Taeke M. de Jong, *Ontwerp-ingrepen op de hectare en hun energie-effect* (Delft: Technische Universiteit Delft, Faculteit der Bouwkunde, 1995); T. Elkin, D. McLaren, and M. Hillman, *Reviving the City: Towards Sustainable Urban Development* (London: Friends of the Earth, 1991); H. Frey, *Designing the City: Towards a More Sustainable Urban Form* (London: E & FN Spon, 1999).

4. J. Benner, *Energietransitie begint in de regio: Rotterdam, Texel en Energy Valley onder de loep* (The Hague: Rahtenau Instituut, 2009); Michael Narodoslawsky and Gernot Stoeglehner, "Planning for Local and Regional Energy Strategies with the Ecological Footprint," *Journal of Environmental Policy & Planning* 12, no. 4 (2010): 363–79, doi:10.1080/1523908X.2010.528885; Philipp Späth and Harald Rohracher, "'Energy Regions': The Transformative Power of Regional Discourses on Socio-technical Futures," *Research Policy* 39, no. 4 (2010): 449–58, doi:10.1016/j.respol.2010.01.017; Petra Wächter, Michael Ornetzeder, Harald Rohracher, Anna Schreuer, and Markus Knoflacher, "Towards a Sustainable Spatial Organization of the Energy System: Backcasting Experiences from Austria," *Sustainability* 4, no. 2 (2012): 193–209, doi:10.3390/su4020193.

5. Bernard C. Patten, "Systems Approach to the Concept of Environment," *Ohio Journal of Science* 78, no. 4 (1978): 206.

6. In Patten's system approach theory, he conceptualized a "system" as part of larger "supersystems," while at the same time consisting of various "subsystems." This model is referred to as "triadic structure."

7. Max Blatter, *Geografie der erneuerbaren Energien* (Münchenstein: Energie-Atlas GmbH, 2006).

8. COROP stands for *COördinatie commissie Regionaal Onderzoeks Programma* (Coordinating commission for the regional research program).

On Scaleless Urbanization: Cybernetic Infrastructures, Resilient Design and the Becoming of Planetary Space

Ross Exo Adams

What if "planetary urbanization" does not simply describe processes that operate at the scale of the planet and, instead, contemporary modes of urbanization have no scale? What if to understand a "planetary" ontology is to understand one that eludes scale altogether? Ross Exo Adams reflects upon how we can experience the planetary without a map of the world.

"Planetary" would perhaps be best understood as a signifier for the scale*less*—a name for the growing sensibility of a world that sees scalar difference as a matter of technological overcoming; a condition whose exploration I hope will broaden our understanding of contemporary forms of urbanization by exposing their uniquely political resolution. In doing so, we stand not only to gain more insight into precisely what urbanization itself consists of, but we may also be better able to strategize contemporary practices of resistance to it: Living in a time of planetary urbanization, how can we begin to formulate effective responses to something that, through its predominantly cartographic optic, may give the appearance of a planetary totality, inaccessible to human agency? Research on the urban, both historically and in its present modalities, points not only to its constant expansion across scales, but to the ways in which *scale itself* may perhaps be a tenuous concept by which to reliably assess urbanization[1], just as it has proven for grasping many other spatiotemporal phenomena today (ecology, cybernetics, geopolitics, etc.).[2]

My contention is that "planetary" is not a scale, nor even a particularly emergent discursive notion, as we may tend to think. Our use and consciousness of it today may instead be a confirmation of an epistemological horizon that has been quietly taking form over the last two centuries, and whose truths, objects, and relations derive from even more distant referents. Planetary, perhaps more than a particular scalar octave, may be better understood as the signature of a trans- or even non-scalar ontology characteristic of our present epistemological horizon. Here, we encounter questions such as: At what scale can we measure, experience, or know climate change? At what scale does contemporary warfare take place? Has neoliberal economics not reduced scale to something of an opportunistic, floating signifier? And what of urbanization today?

Such a suggestion entails a different way of seeing the urban, less concerned with registering its *effects* (shipping lanes, global infrastructures, "operational landscapes,"[3] etc.) than with understanding its *commands*—as a logic that organizes and orders space, infrastructures, domesticity, processes of control, expansion, destruction, networks and circulations, and so on. By treating the urban as a logic, we may begin to question its very nature as *both* the concrete abstraction of capitalism *and* the spatial organization of political form—a reading that remains somewhat obscured by the predominant overemphasis of its relation to capitalism.

Scaleless Space

Under the name of "resilience," a practice of urbanism has emerged whose strategies appear to hinge on their ability to organize circulations and technologies, bodies and ecologies, regions and infrastructures fluidly across scales. Rebuild by Design (RBD) is a flagship project of resilience urbanism. Launched in the summer of 2013, following the devastation of Hurricane Sandy, RBD is an ongoing project that intends to implement corrective measures across the New York City metropolitan region's coastal zones and the aging infrastructural networks they depend on. The practices underpinning the project are generative of an urban space whose consistency and conditions of possibility are located in planetary and extra-planetary infrastructures, yet whose effects are registered in and across all scales at once. What makes this form of urbanism unique is that it

hints at the possibility that large-scale infrastructure is no longer the sole, privileged medium through which subsequent processes of urbanization proceed. Rather, it suggests that the urban can be entirely rethought *around the body*, with the body itself treated as a medium of urbanization—as a site through which both macro and micro processes of accumulation, consumption, circulation, control, and subjectivation are mediated.

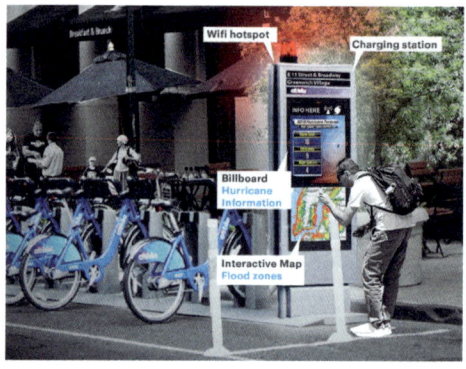

Fig. 1: Alternative information delivery via the retrofitting of already existing infrastructure, as designed by the OMA team.

RBD is a pragmatic response to the reality of climate change and its promise for more extreme weather to come. As an initiative of the Rockefeller Foundation, in coordination with municipal, state, and national agencies, RBD has brought together ten teams of architects, urbanists, engineers, marine ecologists, climate scientists, and economists to propose a new approach to design in the age of climate change. Peddled as the "love child" of Jane Jacobs and Robert Moses[4], the projects assembled by RBD unanimously seem to abstain from any radical transformations to the physical spaces of greater New York City, employing strategies instead that appear to operate at a fine grain, all the while deploying themselves across the tristate area, some of which extend quite far along the Eastern Seaboard.

Superficially more Jane Jacobs than Robert Moses, the resilience urbanism of RBD appeals to a certain "back to basics" attitude—an urbanism more intent on celebrating the life of the city than its proposed infrastructural interventions. Appearing to promote agency rather than heavy-handed design, the project comprises largely "reclaimed" spaces at the interface of land and water, appropriated by the bodies who inhabit them—shoppers at a local market, families playing on docks, tai chi under the freeway—all of which seem to accentuate the everyday behaviors of individuals. It achieves this by treating the totality of existing urban space as infinitely augmentable through cybernetic technologies. Cybernetic space, it is suggested, coordinates a new sense of public exchange: Citi Bike stands double as real-time hurricane and flood information stations with public Wi-Fi hotspots and cell-phone charging points; news kiosks distribute "Flood Risk" flyers; and flood-risk apps will be made widely available in order to communicate with and coordinate the population of the coastal urban region. All of which will assure the wi-despread integration of a new public knowledge of climate emergency and its spatio-social management.

These strategies, set out in renderings, drawings, and project descriptions from RBD proposals, make the integration of cybernetic infrastructures a unanimous component of resilience urbanism. In the final round of RBD, several of the winning proposals suggested that, through the use of distributed Internet and Communications Technology (ICT) infrastructures, new feedback loops of data—relevant for government, first responders, insurance companies, and the general population—could be created to streamline the management of climate emergency situations in time scales both immediate (first responders)[5] and long-term (recalibration of risk by insurance companies).[6] And like all cybernetic urbanism projects, the real-time distribution of bodies provides the basis on which a new knowledge of the city and its permanent management can play out across all scales of the metro region.

This form of urbanism appears to privilege two distinct scales of intervention: On the one hand, this project is an attempt to address a regional site that stretches across much of the Eastern Seaboard—a scale that brings to mind Jean Gottmann's "megalopolis." On the other hand, RBD deploys its strategies at a much more immediate scale, where concepts like resilience, climate change, coastal geographies, ecology, and even nature itself suddenly appear in vibrant, fluctuating colors and displays, creating a space sensible to the body, from which citizen groups, "communities," and individuals can all participate in the real-time construction of the urban as a totality of data. However, to read it as such is to miss the point: the eco-cybernetic space of RBD is one without scale. That is to say, it proposes a system whose management of space occurs *across* scales. While this is in part a consequence of deploying cybernetic infrastructures across a metro region, it is not merely a question of technology that drives this change: rather, it is the *product* of the relation between cybernetic infrastructures and an emergent form of "resilient governance" that this technology makes possible.

Scaleless Government

More recently, RBD has begun to aggressively advocate far-reaching legal reforms that they assert will help to achieve resilience. In June 2014, it published a report aimed to direct conversations that would take place during a roundtable held later that month. RBD asked its ten design teams to identify areas in which their proposals would likely encounter legal and policy-based obstacles. The results of this were distilled into three main topics of discussion: how to formalize "civic infrastructures," or how community and civic groups may esta-

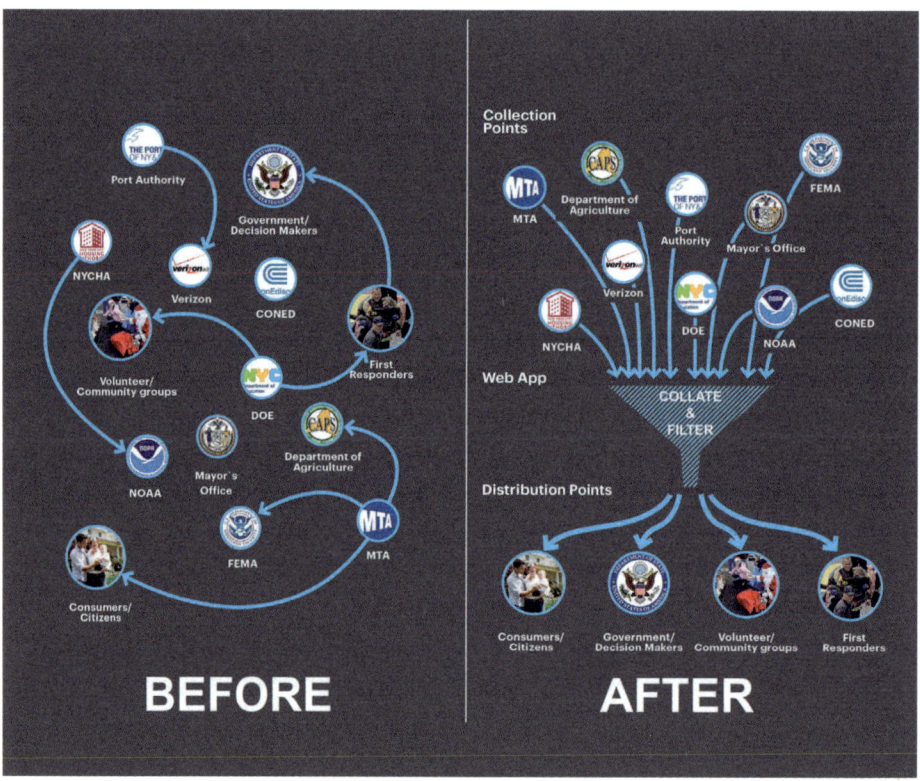

Fig. 2: Data management and communication system as envisaged by the OMA team.

blish formal positions in government planning; how governmental models could be reformed to "balance human, ecological and economic needs in coastal areas"; and lastly, how to expand "nature-based solutions" as a form of urban design. The three topics intended to address a realm of design exposed in the initial process, yet go beyond what spatial design itself is able to prescribe: the design of law.[7]

What came out of this meeting was summarized in a report published a year later addressing ways in which governance should be reformed to accommodate the mandates of resilience.[8] In this summary, RBD participants emphasize the need to coordinate governance across all scales. The current model, described as "fragmented," operates through clumsy and often nonexistent mechanisms to coordinate federal, regional, state, municipal, and local authorities when faced with an emergency on the scale of Hurricane Sandy. What RBD participants propose in response they call "administrative continuity," which is an effort to restructure government, collapsing all layers of governance into a single, fluid machine of government tuned to respond to the imminent emergencies that climate change promises. This makes sense: since the climate is not bound to a single scale, neither too should the governmental response to its effects. "To address emerging environmental and social challenges, we must operate at the scale of climatic and ecological regions, and in a way that puts communities first."[9]

In its proposal to restructure government, the administrative-continuity model highlights the figure of "the community" as not simply the beneficiary of a reformed governmental structure, but as a central figure in the governmental space of resilience itself. "Communities must be drivers of resilience," headlines the "Collaboration by Design" section, a statement that poses questions about how community efforts connect with governmental planning, and what gaps exist in the span between the two. If it was "the community" that was the victim of poor governance in the recovery efforts following Sandy, it is now "the community" that must be endowed with new powers within a framework of resilient governance. Just as government must adopt resilience, so too, the participants of RBD suggest, must communities and civic groups be encouraged to "fully embrace resilience as part of their mission."[10] Through an "engaged partnership" between government and the local coastal communities of Greater New York City, the notion of community is transformed into a key site in which a new governmental knowledge relevant to resilience may emerge.

Indeed, if resilient government must work across scales, it must also become inclusive. The government's expanded field of operation within the category of community thus requires a kind of layered pedagogical campaign that would elucidate the knowledge and set of values that communities must adhere to within the framework of resilient governance. The role ascribed to design here takes on new importance, which the participants of RBD highlight. Not only is design a matter of proposing legible strategies for the city, but it must also serve as a pedagogical interface through which to both include communities in the design process and, more importantly, narrate the values embedded in the program of resilience more broadly.

Described as "awareness," design becomes both a medium and a practice through which to penetrate the opacity of "community," disciplining it to speak in a common language. If, through the design of images and spatial diagrams, this language makes transparent the way in which space is to be reorganized, infrastructures reworked, and climate reimagined, it uses this visual/spatial language to construct and make operational new relations relevant to resilient government.

Of course, "design" goes much further than this. One of the key forms of design that has been embraced by RBD teams is the so-called nature-based solution—"sand engines" and oyster beds that can absorb storm surges, breakwaters modified to shield from flooding, water basins optimized to absorb floodwaters more efficiently, and so on. These proposals constitute ways in which "nature" can be incorporated into the design of the urban in ways that selectively cancel out its negative effects.[11] Yet, unlike traditional infrastructure, they all seem to require perpetual monitoring. Draped with sensing technologies, nature-based solutions are environ-mental sensing systems that demand vast assortments of data-collecting technologies, sensors, and computational models to present a real-time image of climate at the interface of land and ocean.[12] "Nature" becomes at once celebrated in its opposition to old-fashioned, man-made infrastructures, while at the same time being transformed into a multi-scalar technology known through the copious data it produces. Whether monitored centrally or through the "bottom-up" stewardship of community groups, nature-based solutions present themselves as eco-cybernetic technologies whose disposition tends to elude the notion of scale altogether.

In such an eco-cybernetic space, data must be comprehensive, high quality, and perpetual. Just like resilient governance, the data collected must be consistent across multiple geographies. According to the agenda of administrative continuity, it must extend a new span of knowledge from the individual "user" to the climatic space of extreme weather, filling in the inevitable gaps of data by including communally driven data clearinghouses. For resilience to operate through nature-based solutions, the data pertaining to it must be total; but it must also be compelling. It must not only translate itself in an accessible manner to a broader public; it must *seduce* that same public. Its seduction comes in part because it illuminates itself to the inhabitants of the urban in the real-time unfolding of nature, captured in brilliant colors on LCD screens and endless updates

234

communicated through smartphone apps. Less the crisis of climate, what becomes the object of a total visibility in the space of resilient urbanism is a climate of crisis.

RBD, we could say, consists of a set of strategies that, by conceiving themselves as eminently trans-scalar, work in direct relation to a parallel restructuring of law itself. What RBD proposes is a radical transformation of governmentality through a coordinated set of spatial technologies.[13] If modern urbanism gained "scientific" consistency by organizing its knowledge and technologies as a hierarchy of discrete scales, resilience urbanism, as evidenced by RBD, is an attempt to invert this logic: it is a program of scalar *coordination*. Its technologies, strategies, and innovations all stem from the ambition to smooth scalar differences into a single, coordinated space of governance—a regional (and indeed *planetary*) technology designed for efficient management of the bodies that dwell within it.

Scaleless Urbanization

Similar to how many discourses have responded to the rise of a planetary consciousness with uniquely trans- or non-scalar methodologies, ontologies, and conceptual apparatuses, the planetary urbanization thesis, I believe, can expand its critique by dislodging the planetary from its status as a somewhat fixed scale to one denoting an entirely new scalar epistemology. We can understand how it may be tempting to treat the planetary as a scalar referent, in part because of an inherited form of knowledge of "scaling up" indebted to its Marxian roots with thinkers like Neil Smith and David Harvey.[14] While this has been incredibly useful in opening new approaches to the "field formerly known as urban studies," it also often has a flattening effect on the urban, presenting it as something that can only be understood through a scalar correlate to "the planet." This may also be because the discourse of planetary urbanization is one that tends to see the urban as a resolutely capitalist formation—a process whose questions of politics, power, legal, and administrative logics, and forms of subjectivation all seem to bear relevance only insofar as they can be mapped onto the demands and processes of capitalism. Rather, by assuming the urban to persist in excess of itself—always exceeding its own capitalist modalities that drive it to become both a space and process—by assuming it to be a *spatio-political order*, we immediately open onto new questions about *the urban in itself*: how to grasp the urban historically, how to map it as a technology of subjectivity and power; how to chart the ontological and biopolitical roles that infrastructure plays, the way territory is both a fundamental concept of the urban and a marker of its historical distinction from the city.[15] Urbanization as such may appear instead as a process of deterritorialization and reterritorialization that works across scales, one that binds the discreteness of life to the ubiquity of infrastructure and thus makes the notion of scale something of a linguistic shorthand rather than any metric that is epistemologically or ontologically stable. Our critique of the urban today must focus both on the radically expanded realms in which it operates, and on the way it works across scales—the way it coordinates materialities and circulations, freedoms and securities, access and prohibition, technologies and natures, wealth and bodies, inclusions and exclusions, barriers and penetrations—all without regard to scalar referents like "city," "region," "territory," and yes, indeed, "planet."

What we are seeing emerge today, what we may call "planetary urbanization," may not simply be processes that are jumping scales upwardly, moving toward the scale of the planet, but rather a *rationality* that seeks to coordinate spaces and circulations, bodies and quantities *across scales*—a political technology intent on smoothing scalar differences into a spatio-governmental continuum—a logic that, as Anna Tsing has shown, attempts to reduce worlds to a single planetary space of complete scalability.[16] By shifting our focus from the planetary as a discrete scale to the planetary as *non-scalar spatial ontology*, we may be able to identify an entirely new political disposition from which to situate effective forms of resistance within the increasingly trans-scalar continuity of power, law, capital, and subjectivity that constitutes the urban as a spatio-political order unique to the modern world.

Notes

An earlier version of this essay appeared in *Climates: Architecture and the Planetary Imaginary*, ed. James Graham, Caitlin Blanchfield, Alissa Anderson, Jordan Carver, and Jacob Moore (New York: Columbia Books on Architecture and the City; Zurich: Lars Müller Publishers, 2016).

1. Ross E. Adams, *Circulation and Urbanization* (London: Sage Publications, forthcoming).
2. See, for example, Timothy Morton, *Hyperobjects: Philosophy and Ecology after the End of the World* (Minneapolis: University of Minnesota Press, 2013); Benjamin H. Bratton, *The Stack: On Software and Sovereignty* (Cambridge, MA: MIT Press, 2015); and Bruno Latour, "Some Advantages of the Notion of 'Critical Zone' for Geopolitics," *Procedia Earth and Planetary Science* 10 (August 2014): 3–6.
3. A recent exhibition held in the Melbourne School of Design, "Operational Landscapes: Towards an Alternative Cartography of World Urbanization" (March 17–March 29, 2015), presented the work of Neil Brenner's Urban Theory Lab (Harvard Graduate School of Design), looking specifically at "the wide-ranging sociospatial and environmental transformations that are currently unfolding in supposedly 'remote' or 'wilderness' regions," as integral to the expanded fabric of planetary urbanization.
4. Henk Ovink, Senior Advisor of the Hurricane Sandy Rebuilding Task Force, is working closely with RBD; he made this comment in his keynote address at the LafargeHolcim Forum 2016. See "Henk Ovink: "We need the transformative capacity of collaboration" – LafargeHolcim Forum 2016, YouTube video, 27:03, posted by LafargeHolcim Foundation, April 15, 2016, https://www.youtube.com/watch?v=aBcyUKeWLS4.

5. See OMA's proposal for "communications systems," *Rebuild by Design*, accessed June 28, 2016, http://www.rebuildbydesign.org/project/information-systems/.

6. See the proposal by WXY / West 8, *Blue Dunes: The Future of Coastal Protection*, http://www.rebuildbydesign.org/wordpress/wp-content/uploads/briefing/WXY__IP_Briefing_Book.pdf; esp. 9–12, and "Catastrophe Risk Engineering," 106–9.

7. Rebuild by Design, *Policy by Design: Promoting Resilience in Policy and Practice*, June 27, 2014, http://www.rebuildbydesign.org/wordpress/wp-content/uploads/briefing/RBD_policysession_briefingbook-FINAL.pdf, 2.

8. Rebuild by Design, Policy by Design: Promoting Resilience in Policy and Practice; June 2014 Roundtable Discussion Summary, June 2015, http://www.rebuildbydesign.org/wordpress/wp-content/uploads/2015/07/Updated-Policy-Doc.pdf.

9. Ibid., 7–8.

10. Ibid., 4–5.

11. See Bruce P. Braun, "A New Urban Dispositif? Governing Life in an Age of Climate Change," *Environment and Planning D: Society and Space* 32, no. 1 (2014): 49–64; and Ross E. Adams, "Notes from the Resilient City," *Log* no. 32 (2014): 126–39.

12. See Jennifer Gabrys, *Program Earth: Environmental Sensing Technology and the Making of a Computational Planet* (Minneapolis: University of Minnesota Press, 2016).

13. Michel Foucault's well-known notion of governmentality identifies the ensemble of modern power whose increasingly administrative character developed over the nineteenth century by tying together political economy (as its form of knowledge), population (as its subject-object), and "mechanisms of security" (as its means of intervention). For more on this notion, see, among others, Michel Foucault, *Security, Territory, Population: Lectures at the Collège de France, 1977–1978*, trans. Graham Burchell (London: Palgrave Macmillan, 2009).

14. See, in particular, Neil Smith,. "Homeless/Global: Scaling Places," in *Mapping the Futures: Local Cultures, Global Change*, ed. John Bird, Barry Curtis, Tim Putnam, George Robertson, and Lisa Tickner (New York: Routledge, 1993), 87–119.

15. See Adams, *Circulation and Urbanization*.

16. See Anna Tsing,. "On Nonscalability: The Living World Is Not Amenable to Precision-Nested Scales," *Common Knowledge* 18, no. 3 (2012): 505–24.

The Urbanization of the Ocean: Extractive Geometries in the Barents Sea

Nancy Couling

The world's ocean system is urbanized by trade, extraction and production but defies the metrics developed for land-based systems. Through the case study of petroleum production in the Barents Sea, Nancy Couling describes the geographic, legislative, and economic ordering of a complex, contested ocean.

Scale Relationships in Ocean Space

A container ship classified as 15,000 TEU (twenty-feet equivalent units) defines the maximum capacity of the Suez Canal. In the marine transport sector, both locks and vessels are measured according to their cargo capacity—the vessel itself is merely an empty site with high-density loading potential. A rearrangement of the "Suez-max" volumes on one vessel could produce a metropolitan neighborhood of seven six-story-high city blocks.[1]

Until recently, the actual space occupied by ocean activities has been of scant interest. But in the Baltic Sea, wind parks nudge against the outer limits of International Maritime Organization–designated shipping lanes, which are in turn restricted by the depth and width of the straits. A quantum shift in the scale and intensity of activity in all sectors has resulted in cumulative areas that now match the geographic scale of the sea itself. Offshore exclusive economic zones (EEZs) have been marked out as an extension of national territory.

Can measuring units of area and volume be transposed from the unfamiliar *oceanic* to familiar *urban* contexts, and vice versa? Vessels, cargos, and petroleum-license areas hold their own urban ground in terms of size, but fall short in terms of density and heterogeneity. Offshore hardware is visibly thin and shipping transient compared to urban yardsticks. Developed ocean sites are monofunctional and remote from human settlement.

As I argue below, these porous and uneven scale relationships are an indicator of the advanced urbanization processes in ocean space. Neil Brenner and Christian Schmid argue against *methodological cityism*[2] and the persistence of the outmoded parameters of size, density, and heterogeneity in defining the urban.[3] Urban formations have exploded beyond this corset and imploded within it, simultaneously rendering internal configurations obsolete and annexing vast external operational landscapes. Ocean space is drawn into these processes.

The urbanization of the ocean takes place within discreet, deep, remote, contingent, and constitutionally ambiguous spaces that have shielded its progression and obscured it from critical view. Unpacked cargo loads can illustrate the physical dimensions of urban indicators—however the ocean is differentiated, inter-scalar, and kinetic, and therefore outside standard conceptions of density and mass. The urbanization of this realm has therefore created dispersed intensities within largely invisible ordering systems of planetary force.

This discussion firstly examines the inherent scalar properties of the ocean itself, including the infusion of urbanization's flow through the very materiality of this medium. These dynamics stand in contrast to the bounding of ocean space through the United Nations Convention on the Law of the Sea (UNCLOS). A close-up view of the otherwise intangible Barents Sea petroleum "provinces"[4] in the second part, leads to an analysis of the scalar mechanisms and spatial processes unfolding in this region. The results illuminate the convergence of environmental and urbanization systems and the instrumentalisation of geometrical ordering systems to systematically investigate, establish, and extend petroleum production activities in ocean space.

Ocean Scale

The dimensions of the ocean's surface have become significant due to the intensification of activities and the urge to logically distribute expanding spatial demands. Hence the ocean gains recognition as a sedentary space of strategic economic importance. However, looking below the surface and beyond what Philip E. Steinberg calls "the great void idealization,"[5] the ocean is a full and intricate spatial system in its own right, within which a myriad of distinct environments are embedded: the topographical bottom surface, the upper surface, and oscillating water masses occupying the water column. Water masses are highly spatial; although fluid, their form is determined by salinity and temperature gradients, resulting in volume, density, and cores—properties normally associated with solids. Water masses are not static, but transform continuously at rates determined by currents, winds, chemical exchange, and the interaction with physical bathymetry (Fig. 1).

Ocean space is dense, fluid, malleable, and emergent. According to the combination of organic conditions—the logic of periodic parameters and broad thresholds—its dynamics can be precisely located in space and time. Rather than subscribing to a metricized notion of scale, however, the ocean operates according to the mechanisms of biological scale.

The world's oceans form one interconnected planetary system; it is the main driver of weather, produces 70 percent of our oxygen, and stores vast amounts of CO_2. The ocean is both distributor and collector, both a common resource and a common sink.[6] In the ocean, the minute is directly connected to the vast. An investigation by London's Architectural Association on form in relation to energy makes these relationships clear: "The notion of energy subverts the concept of a homogeneous space-time continuum—with each proposal interacting

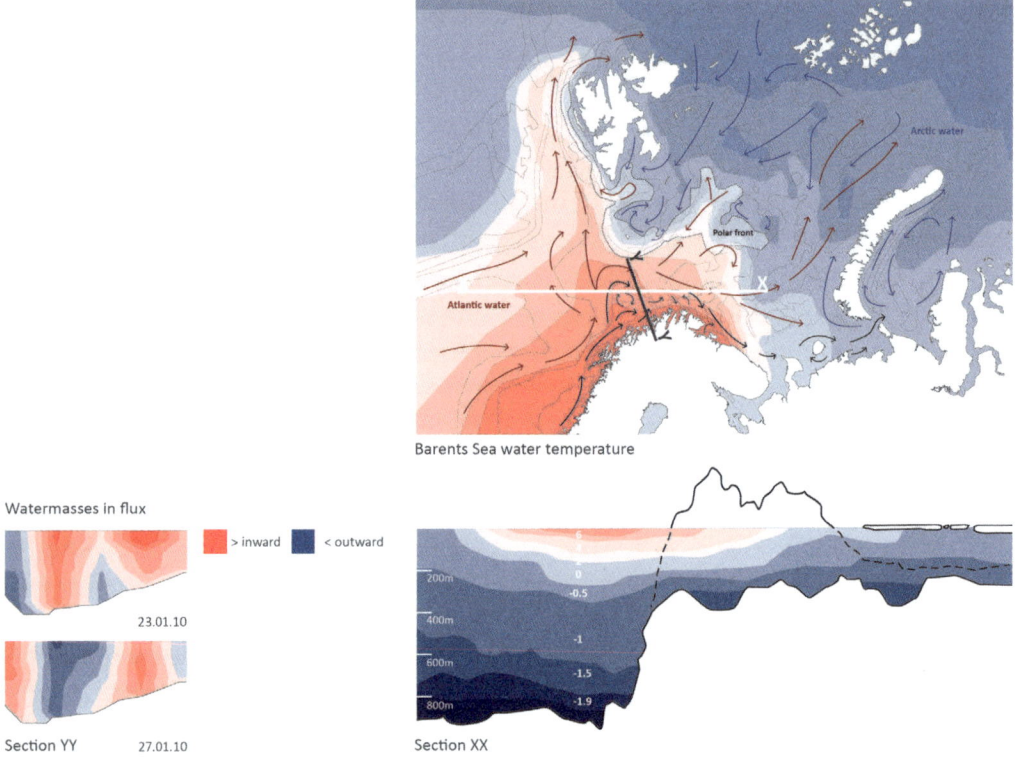

Barents Sea water temperature

Watermasses in flux

> inward   < outward

23.01.10

Section YY   27.01.10

Section XX

Fig. 1: Water-masses in the Barents Sea according to water temperature.

with its temporal and spatial context. […] The continual subdivision of scale from big to small is subverted by the continuous emergence of the very big within the very small."[7]

We know that it takes close to 1,000 years for water to circulate completely around the globe, but the time scales involved in the breakdown of plastics in the ocean are still not well understood. Tiny plastic particles are distributed throughout the water column and across the seabed in all areas of the ocean, regardless of their proximity to land. They have entered the food chain. This complete immersion of urban residue into biological scales is a further indicator of the effects of total urbanization. Research has shown that almost no part of the global ocean remains free from human impact.[8] It therefore offers no wilderness,[9] no outside.[10] What we have previously understood as nature is now part of a continuous if unevenly "cultivated" realm, including the planet's oceans. Along with inside/outside, the urban/nature divide has been dismantled in the age of the Anthropocene, resulting in the condition described by Harry Gugger and Barbara Costa as the forced co-existence of two antagonistic conditions.[11]

The spatial dynamics of the inherently inter-scalar ocean augment the extreme juxtapositions, inversions, and systematic illegibility characteristic of urbanization on a planetary scale. Ocean space therefore serves as a case study par excellence for the investigation of scalar relationships under "extended urbanization."[12]

Territorialization

Intersecting the kinetic, transboundary, and highly differentiated space of the ocean, land-based territorialization systems have defined static slices of space from above-sea air to the sub-sea crust. Historically based on the range of a hypothetical cannon-shot of three nautical miles, territorial limits in ocean space have never been legible and only-just tangible, since from a viewer's position at sea level, perception drops off the horizon at a distance of roughly five kilometers (2.6 nautical miles). In response to heightened territorial disputes, in 1958 UNCLOS (United Nations Convention on the Law of the Sea) fixed the territorial zone to twelve nautical miles offshore, followed by a further 200-nautical-mile exclusive economic zone in 1982.[13] Within this economic zone, coastal states enjoy the right to exploit resources, protect the environment, and carry out research for "peaceful" purposes. In theory, the 200-nautical-mile limit is based on the geological transition from the continental crust to the ocean crust, hence the extent of "land" on the seafloor (Fig. 2).

The formation of an extended national economic zone subsequently unleashed further legislation and planning efforts. Despite coastal nations not having sovereign territorial rights to ocean commons, their right to the exploitation of resources plus the international right to unimpeded shipping, cable- and pipe-laying, quickly dominated planning objectives in the national EEZs and established economic priorities as the zone's foremost function. The following case study of the Barents Sea's hydrocarbon ecology vividly illustrates this point.[14]

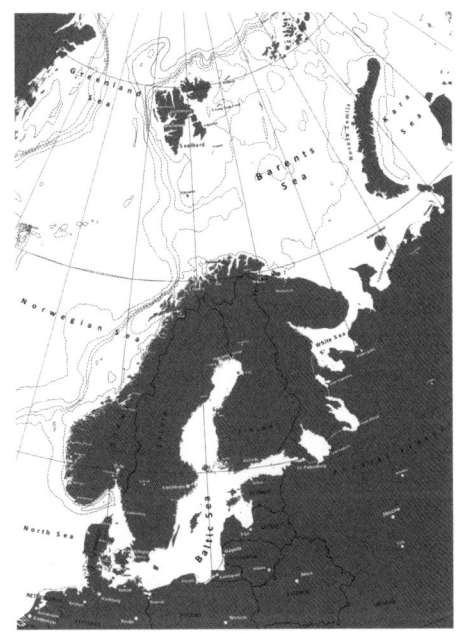

Fig. 2: The Barents Sea's location within the Arctic Circle.

Case Study: Extractive Geometries in the Barents Sea

As well as being one of Europe's last clean and intact marine ecosystems, the Barents Sea—located to the north of Norway within the polar circle, and

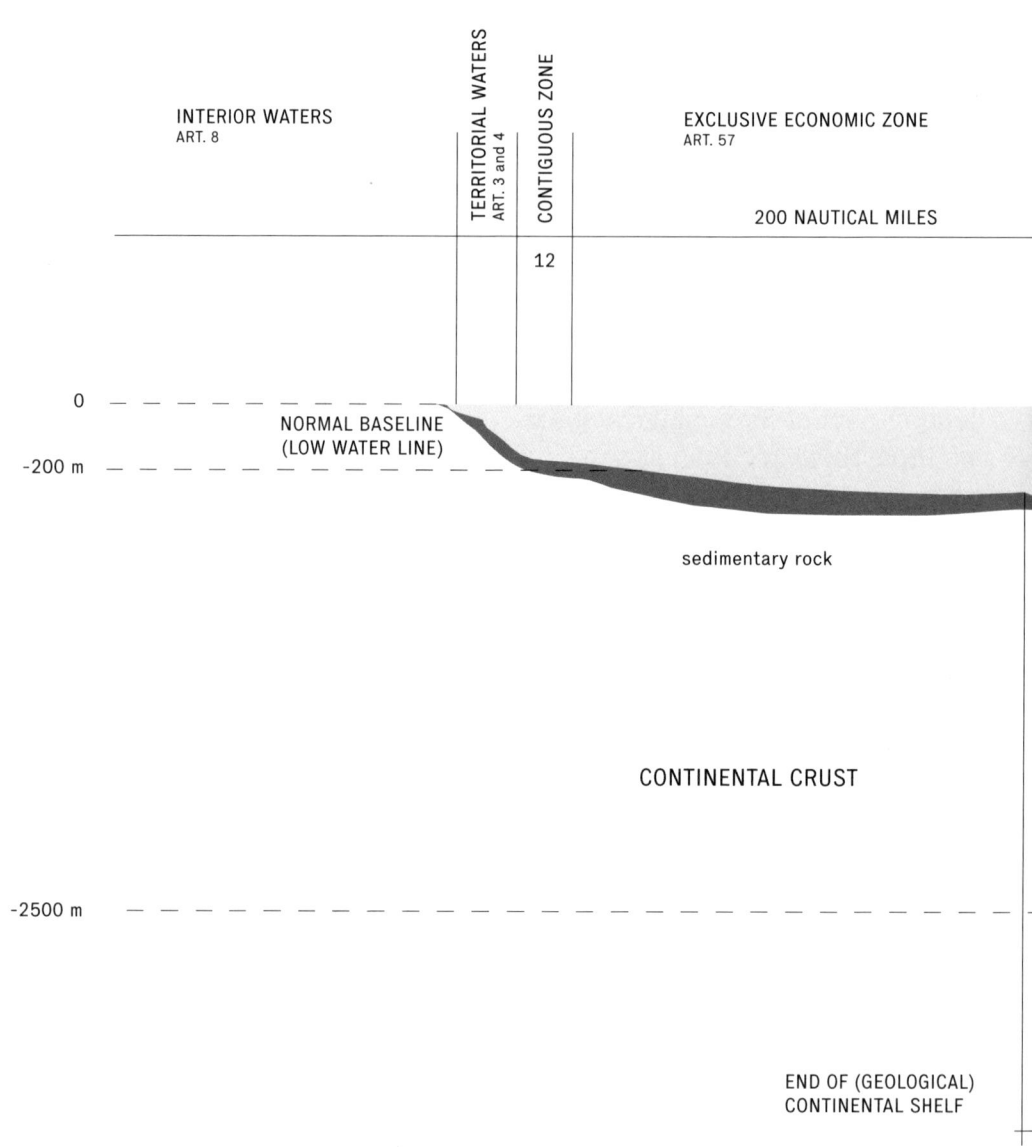

Fig. 3: Ocean zones, as defined by the United Nations Convention on the Law of the Sea (UNCLOS) in 1982.

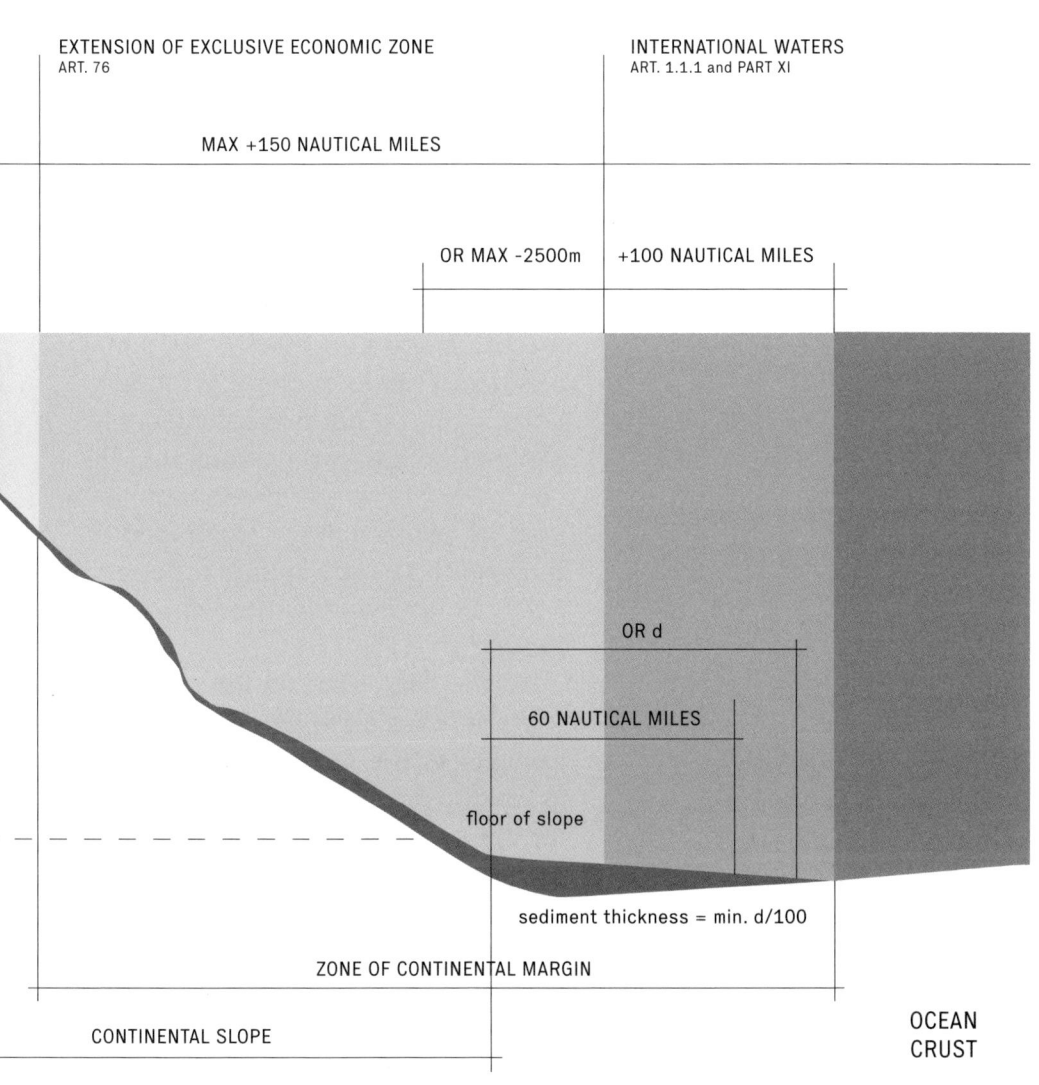

EXTENSION OF EXCLUSIVE ECONOMIC ZONE
ART. 76

INTERNATIONAL WATERS
ART. 1.1.1 and PART XI

MAX +150 NAUTICAL MILES

OR MAX -2500m   +100 NAUTICAL MILES

OR d

60 NAUTICAL MILES

floor of slope

sediment thickness = min. d/100

ZONE OF CONTINENTAL MARGIN

CONTINENTAL SLOPE

OCEAN
CRUST

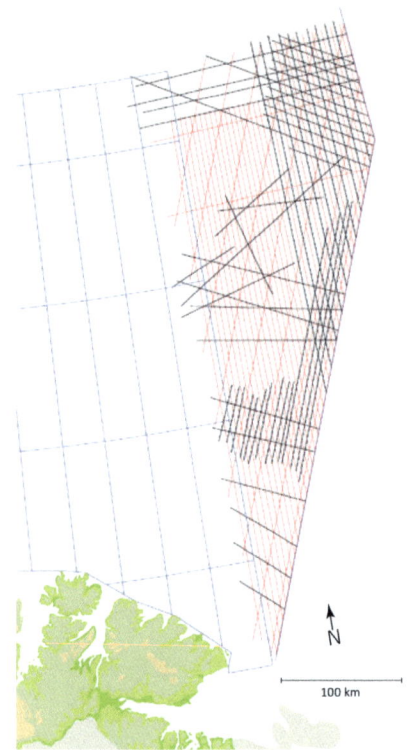

100 km

Fig. 4: An example of the regular 5 x 20 km seismic survey grid for the southeastern Barents Sea.

base serving the expansion of petroleum activities. Mareano survey locations were selected in 2006 *"because they were of interest for the oil and gas industry and had also been identified as particularly valuable and vulnerable."*[15] Almost as a by-catch to petroleum activities, valuable environmental data on the Barents Sea is collected throughout the phases of hydrocarbon exploration.

Specialized scanning and mapping technologies lay the foundations for a new "petroleum province" in the Barents Sea—a new type of urbanized territory. Rania Ghosn describes how the seascape becomes significant as a series of deep geological formations, mapped out through scientific exploration and representation: "The verticality of the environment, no less than its horizontality, is produced through the intertwined practices of scientific fieldwork and political authority."[16]

almost evenly divided between Norwegian and Russian EEZs, holds an estimated 30 percent of the world's gas and 25 percent of the world's oil reserves at subsea depths of 2,500 to 5,000 meters (Fig. 3). Large amounts of geological data have been accumulated by the Norwegian Petroleum Directorate, which carries out continuous seismic surveys (Fig. 4). This involves letting off small explosions and sending shockwaves into the sub-surface. Together with data from the Norwegian Defense Research Establishment and the interdisciplinary government-initiated Mareano mapping program, information is collated into a knowledge

At the same time as the underwater crust is revealed in its richness and complexity, the surface seascape is (re)constructed as a regular grid for the same purpose (Fig. 5). In March 1965, the Norwegian and UK governments jointly agreed to divide the North Sea into quadrants according to the median line principle of one-degree latitude by one-degree longitude. On the Norwegian continental shelf, quadrants were then subdivided into twelve blocks of fifteen minutes latitude x 20 minutes longitude, corresponding to circa 10 x 25 km. This subdivision of the North Sea was undertaken in response to

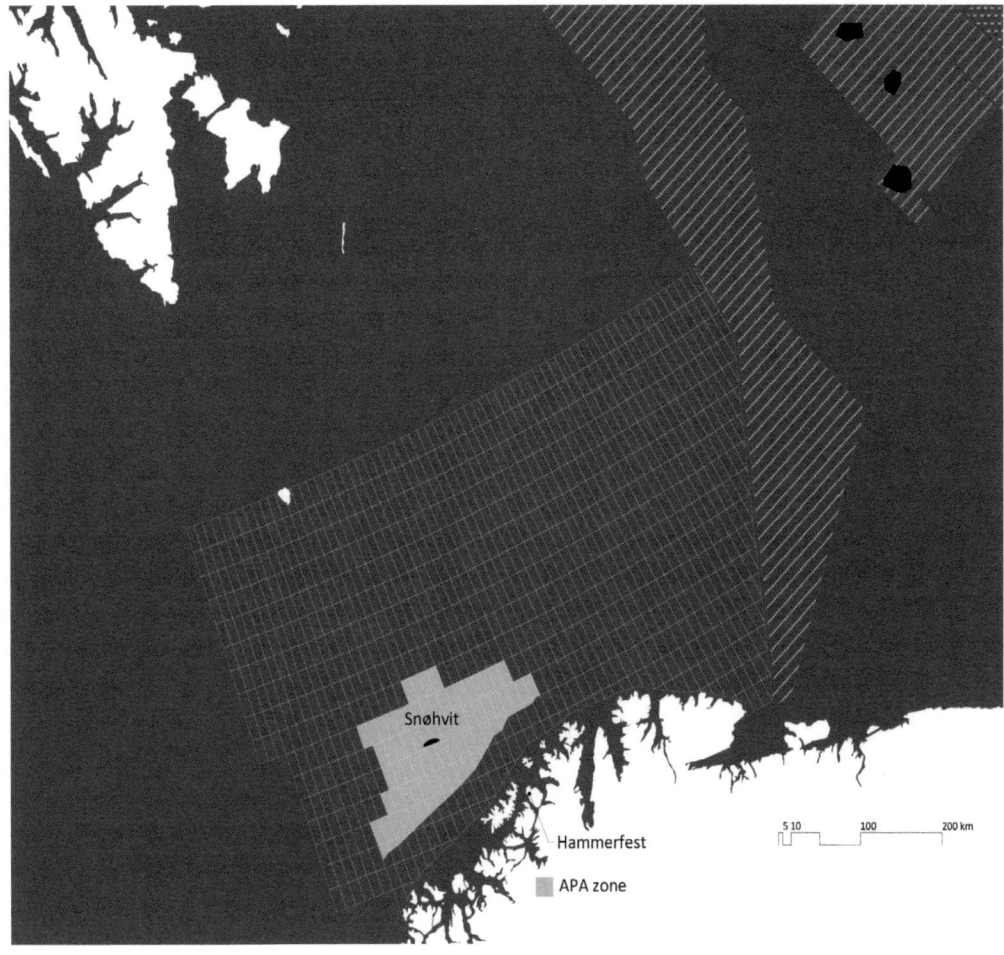

Fig. 5: Petroleum grid, Norwegian continental shelf, Barents Sea.

pressure from the petroleum industry and directly subsequent to the United Kingdom and Norway passing national legislation on sovereignty over the seabed and natural resources.[17]

The orthogonal grid is a device of preliminary colonization and the primary hydrocarbon infrastructure. It is infinitely extendable. Despite the organic form of the deposits themselves, the differentiated nature of the Barents Sea's ecologically valuable and vulnerable areas, and

the sophistication of today's mapping techniques, the grid establishes an immutable, orthogonal, and highly resilient referential layer, presupposing the possibility of development anywhere within its range.

At 2,140,000 square kilometers, Norway's total marine area amounts to 6.5 times the size of its land area. Of this marine area, 50 percent contains sedimentary rocks potentially containing petroleum and which are progressively being released for exploration. By 2011, 25 percent of the total marine area was open for petroleum activity.[18] The Barents Sea South province covers 190,000 square kilometers, with a further 44,000 square kilometers in the previously disputed southeast area toward the Russian border (Fig. 6). In December 2015, first applications for the exploration of these new southeastern blocks were filed in Norway's 23rd licensing round.[19] As production in the "mature" North Sea fields winds down, the new Barents Sea fields are vital for sustaining petroleum growth in Norway, hence the opening of new exploration blocks is a national priority.

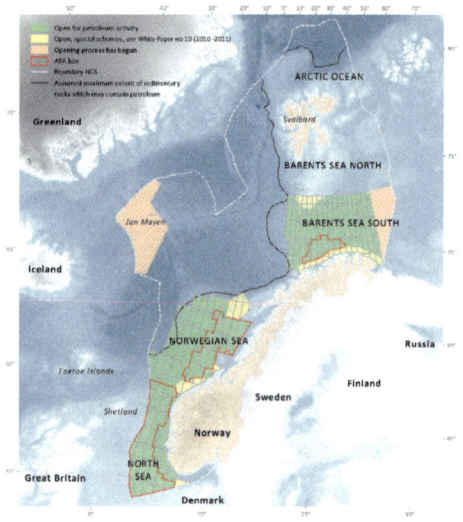

Fig. 6: Area status of the Norwegian Continental Shelf, June 2013.

Petroleum's strategic geometries in the Barents Sea create a loose but precise mesh of coordinates over a vast area, thereby constructing a solid foundation for exploration and extraction activities. As a result, this part of the Norwegian continental shelf has been drilled with approximately 100 wells since the beginning of exploration activities in 1979.[20]

Of these wells, to date the only producing fields are Snøhvit—a gas field located at latitude seventy degrees north, in water depths of 300 meters (Fig. 5), and the Goliat oilfield. Snøhvit gas came on-stream in 2007 and has an average daily production of 20.8 million standard cubic meters of natural gas liquids and condensate. The Goliat oilfield, located fifty kilometers to the southeast in water depths of 340 to 400 meters, began production on March 13, 2016.

The petroleum grid provides an electronic girder over half of the Norwegian Barents Sea to support what first appear to be singular, isolated production sites. However hydrocarbon extraction is a continuing process, with high preproduction activity over long phases, resulting in irregular infrastructural intensity. The Snøhvit "neighborhood" is a combination of seven production licenses distributed across three fields; Snøhvit, Albatross, and Askeladd, with a combined total of twenty wells and an area the size of the City of Los Angeles[21] (Fig. 7). Snøhvit utilizes an extraction system located directly on the seabed with a 6.8-meter-diameter pipeline transporting gas condensate 145 kilometers to the Melkøa Island processing plant near Hammerfest. From Melkøa, the CO_2 produced during processing is piped back to the field and re-injected into adjacent geological formations. Through these extensions, technology enables the excess "products" of urbanization to be stored in depths reaching 2,500 meters below the seabed.

The deep organic geological formations, the infrastructural network on the seafloor, and the orthogonal licensing grid at the Snøhvit field are each separate spatial systems occupying discrete ocean layers. Their material distance and morphological diversity is overcome and integrated through technology. Hence, the operating systems swiftly link highly divergent singular elements and condense scale. The state-of-the-art seafloor installations at the Snøhvit field have no connection to tangible physical scale

or context—they are highly abstract, remotely controlled, autonomous, and far from the public eye.

Snøhvit is exemplary of a new hydrocarbon frontier in colder, deeper waters[22]; the result of a process of incremental offshore extension beginning on the Californian coast in the 1890s and driven by the increased difficulty of finding large new fields in established locations.[23] "Constructing" this frontier requires large-scale territorial reorganization, the establishment of new laws, securing international expertise, and the laying of long infrastructural lines. Operating the frontier requires the mobilization of ever more sophisticated equipment, a dispersed

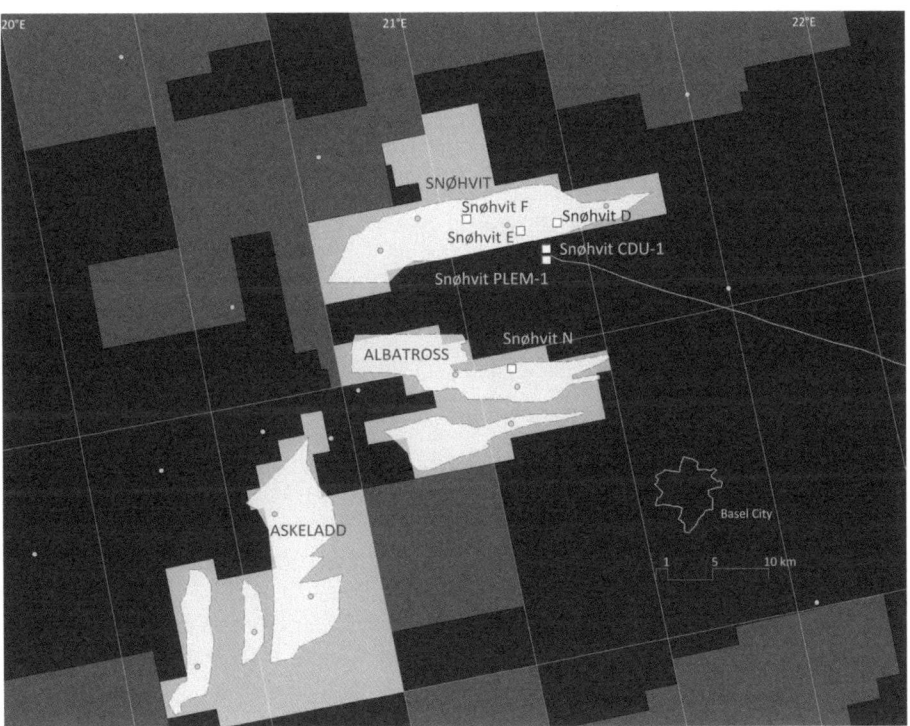

Fig. 7: Snøhvit field showing production templates (E, D, N), distribution center (CDU 1), pipeline end manifold (PLEM-1), and the gas injection well (F).

workforce, and the delicate disposal of accrued waste, including the dismantling of decommissioned equipment itself—a task necessitating the further large-scale reorganization of territory.

At this frontier, the planetary dimensions of both urban and environmental systems merge. The Barents Sea exemplifies this uncomfortable alliance most beautifully: the marginal ice-front traditionally formed midway across the Barents Sea, thereby creating a natural barrier for hydrocarbon development. But the ice front is receding at an alarming rate, indirectly "opening" new territory for production. The Norwegian Petroleum Directorate has already carried out seismic surveying in Barents Sea North, in preparation for this possible extension. In addition, the directorate works in close coordination with the Ministry for the Environment—the common objective being to increase the predefined licensing areas.

Research shows that ecological issues are spatiotemporal issues, therefore ecosystems as well as energy, need space. What if the petroleum industry were to abandon the grid and draw up organic areas of renewable energy production tuned to the spatiotemporal dynamics of the ocean and to differentiated biological scale? Our understanding of complex ocean systems would then have the potential to enrich and inform our understanding of urban systems and steer a radically different urbanization of the ocean.

1. A city block is calculated as 100 x 100 x 22 meters, the standard dimensions of a Berlin block in late nineteenth century Gründerzeit, with the containers stacked around the block perimeter.
2. Hillary Angelo and David Wachsmuth, "Urbanizing Urban Political Ecology: A Critique of Methodological Cityism," in *Implosions / Explosions: Towards a Study of Planetary Urbanization* (Berlin: Jovis, 2014), 372–85.
3. Neil Brenner, "Introduction: Urban Theory without an Outside," in *Implosions / Explosions : Towards a Study of Planetary Urbanization* (Berlin: Jovis, 2014), 14–30.
4. Harry Gugger, Nancy Couling, and Aurélie Blanchard, eds., *Barents Lessons. Teaching and Research in Architecture* (Zürich: Park Books, 2012), 4.
5. Philip E. Steinberg, *The Social Construction of the Ocean*, Cambridge Studies in International Relations 78 (Cambridge [etc.]: Cambridge University Press, 2001), 125.
6. John Vogler, *The Global Commons: Environmental and Technological Governance*, 2nd ed (Chichester [etc.]: John Wiley & Sons, 2000), 3.
7. Stefano Pansera, *Beyond Entropy : When Energy Becomes Form* (London: AA Publications, 2011), 109
8. B. S. Halpern et al. "A Global Map of Human Impact on Marine Ecosystems," *Science* 319, no. 5865 (15 February 2008): 948–52, doi:10.1126/science.1149345.
9. Neil Brenner and Christian Schmid, "Planetary Urbanization," in *Urban Constellations*, ed. Matthew Gandy (Berlin: Jovis, 2011).
10. Brenner, "Introduction: Urban Theory without an Outside."
11. Harry Gugger and Barbara Costa, "Urban-Nature: The Ecology of Planetary Artifice." *San Rocco* 10, no. Ecology (2014): 40.
12. The thesis that *extended urbanization* is one of three mutually constitutive moments of urbanization is elaborated in: Neil

Brenner and Christian Schmid, "Towards a New Epistemology of the Urban?," *City* 19, no. 2–3 (4 May 2015): 151–82, doi:10.1080/13604813.2015.1014712.

13. UN, "UNCLOS 1982," 1982, http://www.un.org/Depts/los/convention_agreements/convention_overview_convention.htm.

14. Arne Næss and David Rothenberg, *Ecology, Community and Lifestyle: Outline of an Ecosophy* (Cambridge: Cambridge University Press, 1989). Arne Naess defined ecology as "the interdisciplinary scientific study of the living conditions of organisms in interaction with each other and with the surroundings, organic as well as inorganic."

15. Royal Norwegian Ministry of the Environment, "Meld. St. 10. Report to the Storting (White paper) First Update of the Integrated Management Plan for the Marine Environment of the Barents Sea—Lofoten Area," 3 November 2011, http://www.regjeringen.no/en/dep/md/documents-and-publications/government-propositions-and-reports-/reports-to-the-storting-white-papers-2/2010-2011/meld-st-10-20102011.html?id=682050.

16. Rania Ghosn, "The Expansion of the Extractive Territory," in *The Petropolis of Tomorrow* (New York: Actar Publishers and Architecture at Rice, 2013), 236.

17. Alex Kemp, *The Official History of North Sea Oil and Gas: Vol. I: The Growing Dominance of the State* (Routledge, 2013), 1-85. In the United Kingdom, the Continental Shelf Act was passed in 1964. In Norway, the Royal Decree of 31 May 1963 establishing Norway's sovereignty over the seabed was followed by the Act of 21 June 1963 Relating to Exploration and Exploitation of Submarine Natural Resources. The basis for this legislation had been established at the 2nd Convention on the Law of the Sea in Geneva in 1958.

18. Norwegian Petroleum Directorate, "Petroleum Resources on the Norwegian Continental Shelf 2013: Exploration," (Stavanger: Norwegian Petroleum Directorate, 2013), http://www.npd.no/en/Publications/Resource-Reports/2013/

19. Ministry of Petroleum and Energy, "Meld. St. 28 (2010–2011)," 16 November 2014, https://www.regjeringen.no/en/dokumenter/meld.-st.-28-20102011/id649699/.

20. "CO2 Storage Atlas Norwegian Continental Shelf." (Stavanger: The Norwegian Petroleum Directorate, April 2014), http://www.npd.no/Global/Norsk/3-Publikasjoner/Rapporter/CO2-samleatlas/Preface.pdf.

21. Circa 40 x 40 square kilometres

22. Alberto Serna Martin, "Deeper and Colder: The Impacts and Risks of Deepwater and Arctic Hydrocarbon Development," *Research report, Unconventional Oil & Gas* (Amsterdam: Sustainalytics, March 2012), http://www.sustainalytics.com/deeper-and-colder-impacts-and-risks-deepwater-and-arctic-hydrocarbon-development-0.

23. Joseph A. Pratt, Tyler Priest, and Christopher J. Castaneda, *Offshore Pioneers Brown & Root and the History of Offshore Oil and Gas* (Houston, Tex: Gulf Pub. Co, 1997).

24. Nancy Couling, "The Role of Ocean Space in Contemporary Urbanization," (EPFL, 2015), http://infoscience.epfl.ch/record/212706

25. Rania Ghosn, "Energy as a Spatial Project," in *Landscapes of Energy*, New Geographies 2 (Cambridge, Mass: Harvard University Press, 2009), 7–10.

The Infrastructure of Bare Life: Another Definition of Housing from and for the Global South

Tom Avermaete

was equated with a map showing "the chaos of networks" in the metropolitan Detroit area.[2] On the basis of this visual analogy, Doxiadis argued that the role of the architect was no longer that of a simple form-giver but more that of a coordinator of various infrastructural networks: "We must coordinate *all* our Networks *now*. All networks, from roads to telephones."[3]

Tom Avermaete demonstrates how the work of Constantinos Doxiadis, Michel Ecochard, and Otto Koenigsberger expanded the definition of infrastructure, making it part of the development agenda. Regarding plans as an integrating framework rather than a fixed vision, these figures, despite their shortcomings, helped emphasize agency over one's environment as a fundamental need.

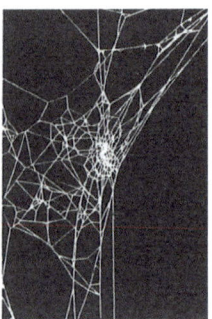

Fig. 1: A spider's web before and after the animal had been drugged with amphetamines (source: Doxiadis, 1972).

A continuous network of centers and lines of communication [in which] all parts of the settlement and all lines of communication will be interwoven into a meaningful organism[1]

—Constantinos A. Doxiadis

In 1963, the Greek architect and urban planner Constantinos Doxiadis described the city of the future as a complex network of infrastructures. Doxiadis substantiated his viewpoint by publishing photographs of a spider's web before and after the animal had been drugged with amphetamines. The distorted organization of the doped spider

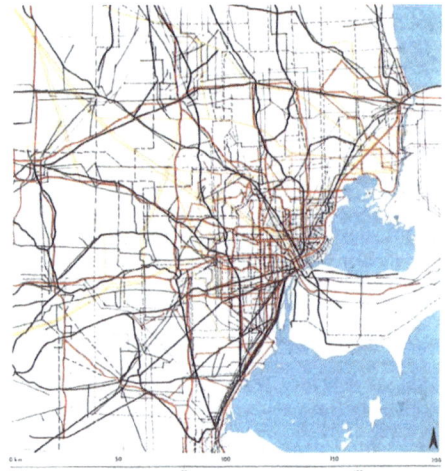

Fig. 2: the chaos of networks in the metropolitan Detroit area (source: Doxiadis, 1972).

Doxiadis, typecast by *Life* magazine as the "Busy Remodeler of the World," was not an exception but rather an exemplary representative of a generation of architects and urban planners that worked globally during the decades following the Second World War under the regime of development aid. These designers—including well-known names such as Michel Ecochard, Otto Koenigsberger, Georges Candilis, Shadrach Woods, Maxwell Fry, and Jane Drew—initiated a broader debate on the character, role, and potential of infrastructure. This essay is an attempt to probe into these other definitions of infrastructure that not only changed architectural and urban discourse at the time, but are also relevant for contemporary design thinking and practice.

Otto Koenigsberger: Climatological Apparatus of Urban Growth

An initial contribution to such a definition came from the German-born architect Otto Koenigsberger, one of the main protagonists of postwar development aid.[4] In a 1971 report for the Ford Foundation, *Infrastructure Problems of the Cities of Developing Countries,* Koenigsberger signalized that the discipline of architecture and urban planning had been overly focusing on "the master plan, sugar-cube or Lego approach to cities," and therefore had bluntly forgotten about the issue of infrastructure.[5] In the early stages of his own career, he had claimed that "the greatest area

of non-research is into [...] the collective or individual sectors of urban infrastructure."[6]

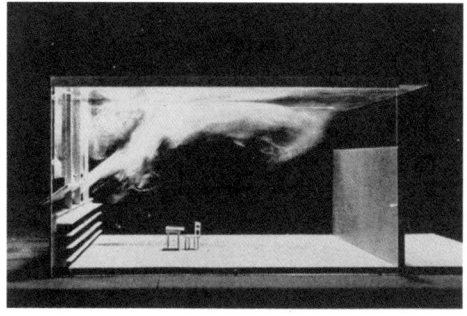

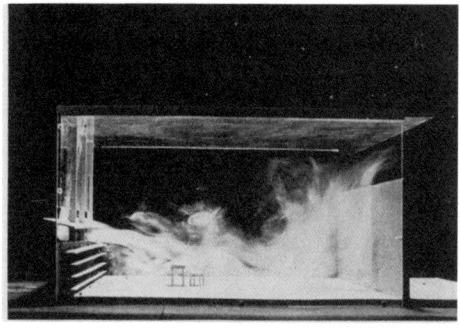

Fig. 3: Koenigsberger's study into the building as a performant climatological infrastructure in modern and vernacular built environments.

Koenigsberger suggested that the house could be looked upon as the infrastructure par excellence through which problems of population growth, health, and urban development could be addressed.[7] In well-known publications such *Roofs in the Warm Humid Tropics* (1965) and *Manual of Tropical Housing and Building* (1974), Koenigsberger started to cast a new definition of the house: no longer a passive container of dwelling practices, but rather a performative technical infrastructure that could regulate phenomena such as heat conduction, ventilation, and rain, and thus had the capacity to provide a comfortable basis for everyday life. In a panoply of publications and lectures, Koenigsberger started to typecast the house as a climatological apparatus that was assembled from components like roofs, walls, windows, and ventilator openings—all understood as regulators of interior climate and therefore dwelling comfort.[8]

Fig. 4: A residence built from components produced by the "housing factory", 1950.

Koenigsberger maintained that this infrastructural understanding of the house was nothing new and that lessons could be drawn from the low-tech solutions in vernacular construction, simultaneously maintaining that in modern times climatological infrastructures could be mass-produced. In 1949, out of this perspective, he initiated for the Indian government of Nehru a so-called housing factory that mass-produced a set of basic components, including walls, roofs, windows, overhangs, and louvers. Koenisgberger's idea was that these prefabricated elements could be easily and swiftly composed to be the climatological infrastructure of the house, which he was able to demonstrate in various Indian locations that were facing the pressing issue of refugee housing.

It is interesting to notice that, for Koenigsberger, this infrastructural understanding of the house did not only concern the interior climate. On the contrary, the well-tempered environment of the housing unit became a precondition to think about new ways of grouping houses. Koenigsberger maintained that: "the subject of housing forms part of the larger and more comprehensive subject of town planning and can not be treated separately."[9] The very capacity of the house to act as a well-performing climatological infrastructure was, for Koenigsberger, a precondition for new forms of clustering, and thus enabled new urban formations. Hence, in many of his projects he explored how the "house as infrastructure" allowed for combinations of new clusters and neighborhoods. These new urban morphologies were quantitatively explored in diagrams and schemes, but also in real-life experiments in many test sites in India, such as Jamshedpur, in the very eastern part of the country, where well-performing houses were combined into a garden-city development. In all of these studies, Koenisgberger illustrated how the house, understood as a performative climatological apparatus,

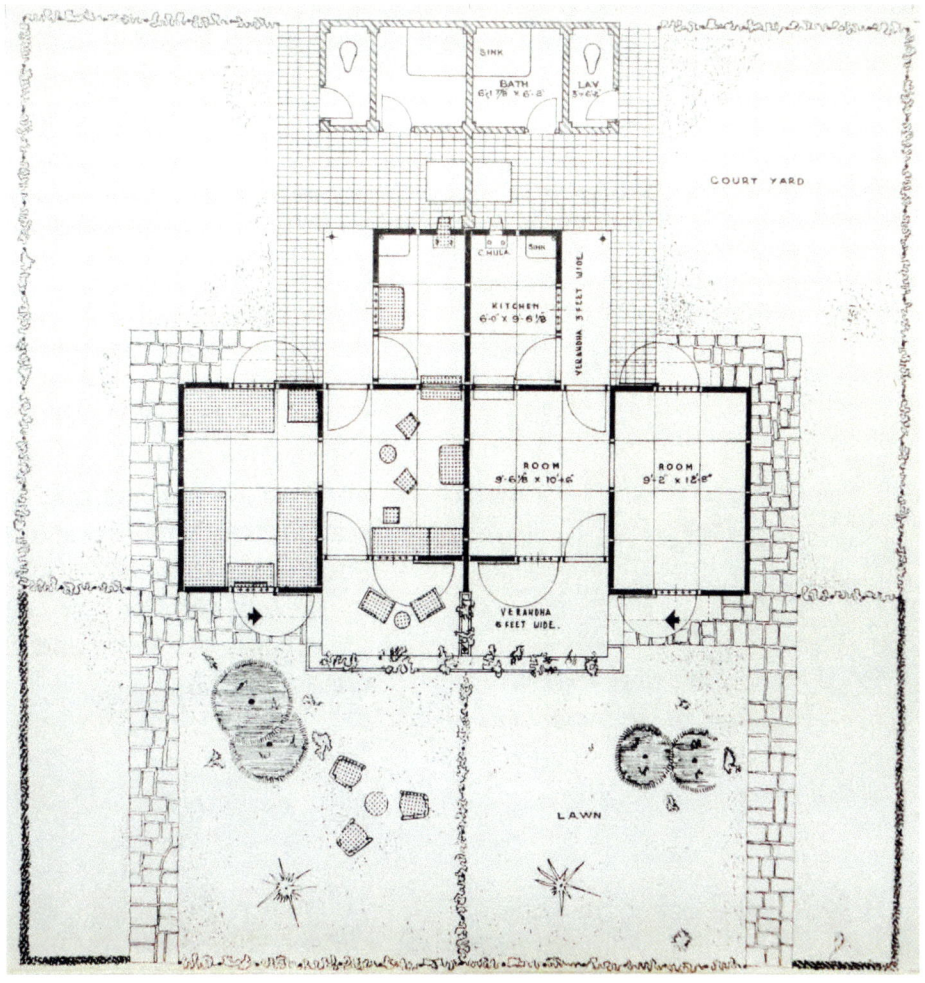

Fig. 5: Factory-made houses arranged as a group.

became an enabler of new forms of urban living. It acted as true infrastructural mediator between the realm of dwelling and the city.

Michel Ecochard: An Armature for Autarky and Publicity

A second contributor to the international debate on infrastructure and development was the French archaeologist, urban planner, and architect Michel Ecochard, who spent most of his career working in the non-Western world—under colonial and then later development-aid regimes.[10] As with Koenigsberger, Ecochard also saw the house as playing the role of a mediating infrastructure, but not in terms of climate. For Ecochard, the house was the prime unit of urban planning. During his career he developed a particular urban design instrument, the *trame Ecochard*, or Ecochard grid, based on a module of eight by eight meters, and used for the development of new urban neighborhoods.

Fig. 6: Echochard believed that the open courtyard of the house could provide the family with a certain form of self-reliance.

However, the Ecochard grid consisted not only of a system of guidelines for allotment, construction, and equipment, but also functioned as an integrator of single family houses into a dense, regular, and low-rise urban pattern.[11] For Ecochard, the house, also called the *minimum économique*, was an infrastructure that had the capacity to mediate between urban and rural ways of living, between individual and collective life.[12] Ecochard maintained that this capacity depended upon particular architectural features of his (otherwise quite rudimentary) dwelling units. The open courtyard, in particular, was a central feature of the house for Ecochard.

It was not only a space of distribution from which all of the interior rooms could be accessed, it was also a place in which the production and reproduction of the household could take place. In Ecochard's view, the courtyard of the house provided the family with a certain form of self-reliance, since it could provide for spaces where more rural-oriented practices such as the cultivation of herbs or the drying of grains could take place, even within its urban environment. In addition, he saw the courtyard as the place where small additions to the house could be made, providing the family with additional space for living or working, as needs and aspirations changed.

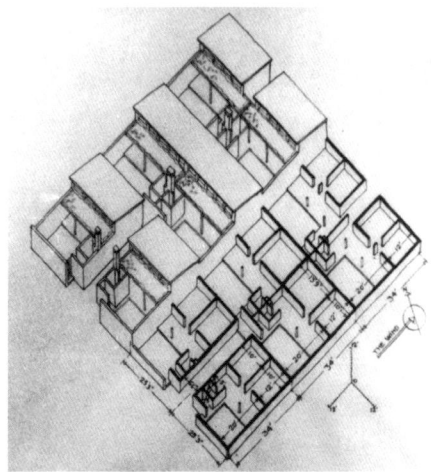

Fig. 7: Courtyard houses on 8 x 8 meter grid for refugees in Karachi, 1954.

As illustrated by his 1954 design proposal for refugee housing in Karachi, the house not only played the role of infrastructural support for the production and reproduction of the single family, but the courtyard dwelling was also the basic building block for the collective environment of the neighborhood and, by extension, the city at large.

Fig. 8: A combination of houses provides the counter-form for the many collective and public spaces of the city—its alleys, streets, avenues, and plazas.

In a 1960 article entitled "Urbanism in Developing Countries," Ecochard stated: "In this discipline we constantly strive to see the mass problems that are imposed on our time. […] This does not mean that we ignore the individual, but if we really want to comprehend him, really want to know him, we will find him ubiquitously in the collective."[13]

In the approach of Ecochard, the house, or a combination of houses, is literally creating the city by providing the counter-form for the many collective and public spaces of the city—its alleys, streets, avenues, and plazas. Ecochard maintained, "The study of the house should be conducted with that of the quarter because then it will be possible to group the houses and obtain great economy in matters of common walls, roads, water supply, drainage and sewerage." This becomes visible in the project that Ecochard developed in 1954 for the extension of the Pakistani city of Karachi. The juxtaposition of the individual domains of the houses creates a literal public counter-domain. In between the houses there are collective and public domains at both the scale level of the neighborhood and the scale level of the entire city.

The very typology, materiality, and form of the houses plays a central role in enabling the emergence of these collective and public domains. Ecochard's houses create a strong border between the collective and individual realms; a high wall separates the individual realm of the house from the collective realm of the street. The form and material articulation of the "house as infrastructure" installs the conditions for coexistence: it separates the temporalities and practices of the house from that of the city, while keeping them in close proximity. This double capacity has also contributed substantially to the life span and sustainability of Ecochard's neighborhoods. The houses have been extended to comply with the

Fig. 9: Doxiadis Associates, Master plan for Korangi
Township, Karachi, 1959-1961.

changing needs of individual families, while contributing to the emergence of a new collective realm and a new urbanity.

Constantinos Doxiadis:
A Common Aggregate

The primacy of the house as "the main element inside most human communities" was also shared by Constantinos Doxiadis, who, like his two peers, was working during the 1960s in the developing world—in the Middle East, Africa and South-East Asia, for instance—and concei-ving of large urban extensions. The house—understood as infra-structure and sometimes simply called "structure"—was looked upon as the building block of new urban environments that had the capacity to integrate various practices and networks—which becomes apparent from Doxiadis's many diagrams. In these visual representations, Do-xiadis depicts the house as a knot that ties the various infrastructural networks together—he also regar-ded it as the infrastructural entity par excellence from which to build the city rationally:

Fig. 10: Korangi Township, Karachi, 1959-1961. In between the houses a rich figure of streets, squares, market galleries, and other public spaces emerges.

257

The room, the smallest nucleus of a house must have straight walls and these must be at right angles to each other so that they can be connected with the other rooms, otherwise there is no house. The house and its plots should have straight walls at right angles to each other so that they can be connected with other houses and other plots. The plots as a whole form a block and the blocks, too, should have straight walls at right angles to each other so that they can be connected in a rational way to the other blocks. More blocks form a neighbourhood, more neighbourhoods form a city.[16]

This rational aggregate approach is evidenced in his master plan for Korangi Township, one of the two new urban poles that he developed in the eastern part of Karachi. In this project, Doxiadis illustrates that he intentionally designed the dwelling typologies in a rudimentary way (few partitions, simple spatial layouts) to cater to the changing dwelling needs of individual families, but also to allow for simple aggregation and thus contribute to the establishment of a collective urban realm. Doxiadis writes: "The house we build must be coordinated with other houses, buildings, squares, open spaces and traffic. [...] All these aspects must be integrated with one another."[17] In the plan for Korangi the juxtaposition of elementary housing typologies constitutes the form of the public realm. In between the houses a rich figure of streets, squares, market

galleries, and other public spaces emerges, rudimentary in character but advanced in the way that they accommodate everyday collective practices and generate public spaces for the citizens of the township (Fig. 10).

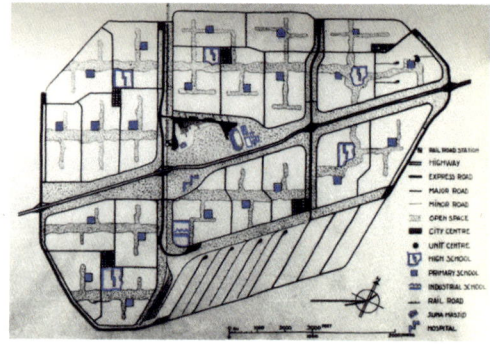

Fig. 11: Plan of the Korangi Township, Karachi. Schools, playgrounds and the hospital are marked in blue.

Similarly, in Doxiadis's plans for the extension of Baghdad (1955-1958), the house is also seen as a building block and enabler of a common realm. In between the repetitive configuration of houses, Doxiadis envisaged a diversified public realm that was composed of alleys, streets, and avenues, but above all of common urban domains that corresponded to Iraqi culture. The aggregate of houses installs the backdrop for collective spaces that attempt to provide a place for an old tradition within the contemporary city. These so-called gossip squares were attuned to storytelling in public spaces, which have an age-old pedigree the local culture. The houses carved the counter-form for these common spaces while also giving them substance.

Fig. 12: A Baghdad "gossip square". (Source: Doxiadis Associates, 1958)

The inhabitants populate and animate these spaces. As with Koenisberger and Ecochard, Doxiadis sees the "house as infrastructure" providing not only the frame for private life, but also the rudimentary counter-form for a rich variety of public practices.

Doxiadis's approach resonates with Koenigsberger's in that the house is also considered as a climatological infrastructure. The rudimentary typology of Doxiadis's houses partially stems from concerns regarding shade and cross-ventilation. Doxiadis also shows affinities with Ecochard in that they both provide outdoor spaces where the family can maintain the household and secure its autarky through various routines and practices. Moreover, Doxiadis also maintained that the infrastructure of the house should accommodate change, and adapt to dwelling practices over time. Doxiadis wrote of the house

as "a changing organism" that had to be thought of "in transition."[19] He looked upon housing as a collective infrastructure, a commons, in which private life could be situated and resituated throughout time—in response to changing needs and aspirations as well as to transformations in technology and habits.

Fig. 13: Housing within Baghdad extension plan by Doxiadis Associates, 1955-1958.

As he illustrates in his project for Tema, in Ghana from 1960, this continuous resituating of private life was enabled by a rich variety of housing typologies in a single neighborhood, so that "people will be able to move from a small unit to a large one and vice versa"[20] (Fig. 14). At the same time, it relied on a logic in which "the basic frame is going to remain the same while internal partitions and fittings might be changed from time to time."[21]

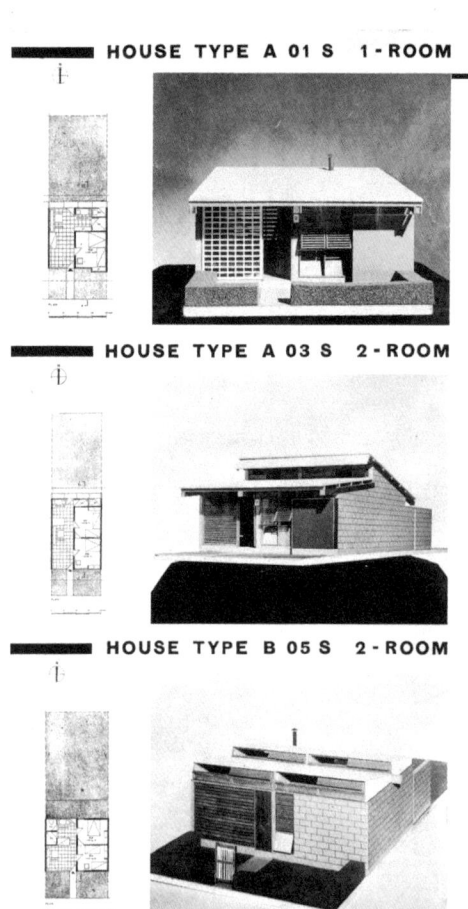

HOUSE TYPE A 01 S 1-ROOM

HOUSE TYPE A 03 S 2-ROOM

HOUSE TYPE B 05 S 2-ROOM

Fig. 14: House types designed by Doxiadis Associates in various sizes for Tema, Ghana, 1960.

Doxiadis's housing infrastructure was diversified in its variety of housing typologies and diversifiable in its intrinsic capacity to respond to growth and change. The architect held that "this kind of idea will lead to a radically different design of hous[ing], one allowing for natural and gradual growth, to be followed perhaps by its redivision and re-allocation among more families, yet still providing for its final reunification into a single house if and when that

proves necessary."[22] An exceptional viewpoint that Doxiadis and his team of collaborators held—including renowned architects such as Hassan Fathy and Jacqueline Tyrwhitt—is that "housing as infrastructure" was not a permanent given but needed to be maintained and renewed. In Doxiadis's approach, the reproduction of the house as infrastructure became an important concern, and the inhabitants were explicitly called upon as caretakers of the house so that it could continue to fulfill its role as a common infrastructure.

Recalibrating the Notion of Housing

The works of Koenigsberger, Ecochard, and Doxiadis illustrate that in the postwar period of development aid for the Global South, a new notion of infrastructure was articulated. "Housing as infrastructure" became a commonly held notion among a group of architects and urban planners. This infrastructure was alternatively looked upon as a guide of urban growth that did not act as a container but an active enabler of urban development; a social armature that regulates the balance between collective interest and self-reliance in the built environment; and a "commons" understood as a resource to the city and its citizens, reproduced collectively on an everyday basis.

Though these approaches to housing as infrastructure for and from the Global South also became the subject of fierce criticism that lamented, for instance, the political framework from which they emerged, or their low-quality materiality, they also represent an approach that reaches beyond simultaneous experiences in Europe and North America. The idea that housing can be conceived as an infrastructure that supports collective and public life while having the capacity to adapt to changing individual dwelling needs and patterns was largely absent from European and North American discourse and practice. In addition, the perspective "housing as infrastructure" redefines canonical conceptions of what an urban project entails, and rearticulates the agency of the designer in relation to the agencies of others, such as constructors and inhabitants.

It was most probably Koenigsberger who discussed this changing role of the architect and urban planner most clearly in stating that "planners must learn to think of themselves not as controllers, but as initiators, and leaders of development."[23] Koenigsberger believed that architects and urban planners would become, through initial design choices, the public initiators of a process of urban development, which would further rely strongly on the actions of both rich and poor investors. In his seminal 1963 article "Action Planning," Koenigsberger abandoned the idea that design and planning should be about determining exact or even idealized outcomes. He claimed that planning no longer entails the conception of blueprints, but rather the initiation and coordination of a set of processes in which various other urban stakehol-

ders play a prime role.[24] Against this background, the work of Koenigsberger, Ecochard, and Doxiadis invite us not only to rethink the urban project as a matter of housing infrastructure, but also to reconceive the role of architect as an initiator and steward of processes related to this infrastructure.

Though many critical remarks can be made vis-à-vis the success of the work of architects like Koenigsberger, Ecochard, and Doxiadis, their particular approach to housing as infrastructure challenges us to rethink our conceptions of the architecture-infrastructure nexus. It not only invites us to consider the possibilities of conceiving of housing as infrastructure, but also to understand it as a complex integrator of climatological and social concerns, of individual and collective practices, of architectural and urban considerations—an integrator that is not permanent but requires constant curation and renewal. This layered understanding might help us to move our debates on housing beyond a matter of style or typology and toward more fundamental social, cultural, and political categories.

The most important contribution of this group of architects and urban planners is that they recalibrated the notion of housing in the economically and politically restricted conditions of development aid. They conceived of the architecture of housing not only as providing the necessary spaces, technical equipment, and comfort for the inhabitant, but also as an armature for the inhabitant's essential praxis of intervening in his dwelling environment by building and rebuilding. The essence of the infrastructure of housing was located in this simultaneous catering to the biological and praxeological needs of man. In this respect, the Italian philosopher Giorgio Agamben speaks of the concept of "bare life" as situated between a definition of life as biological existence (*zoe*) and of life as political speech and action (*bios*). Agamben's concept offers us a perspective though which to look anew to the definition of housing as infrastructure not only as a technocratic solution to pressing urban issues, but as the provision of the bare necessities for everyday existence and simultaneously an urban collective realm in which the political and existential action of the bios can take place. It invites us to reconsider, from a historical and contemporary perspective, if housing can be considered an infrastructure of bare life.

1. Constantinos A. Doxiadis, *Ecumenopolis: Towards a Universal Settlement*, Document R-GA 305 (Athens: Athens Technological Institute, 1963), 116.
2. Constantinos A. Doxiadis, "The Two-Headed Eagle: From the Past to the Future of Human Settlements," *Ekistics* 33 (May 1972) : 406–20. See also Mark Wigley, "Network Fever," *Grey Room* 4, no. 4 (2001): 82–122.
3. Doxiadis, "The Two-Headed Eagle," 418.
4. For a more elaborate introduction to the career of Koenigsberger, see Vandana Baweja, "A Pre-history of Green Architecture: Otto Koenigsberger and Tropical Architecture, from Princely Mysore to Post-colonial London," (PhD diss., University of Michigan, Ann Arbor, 2008), http://deepblue.lib.umich.edu/handle/2027.42/60709; Rachel Lee, "Otto Koenigsberger: Bringing Modernism to India," (PhD diss., TU Berlin, 2014); and Tile von Damm, Anne-Katrin Fenk, and Rachel Lee, OK—*Otto Koenigsberger: Architecture and Urban Visions in India* (Liverpool: TAG Press, 2015).
5. Beverly Bernstein and Otto H. Koenigsberger, *Infrastructure Problems of the Cities of Developing Countries* (New York: International Urbanization Survey, Ford Foundation, 1971).
6. Otto Koenigsberger, "Town Planning and Housing," *Mysindia Annual* (1948): 10–11.
7. Ibid., 33.
8. See, for instance, O. Koenigsberger, J. S. Millar, and J. Costopolous, "Window and Ventilator Openings in Warm and Humid Climates," *Ekistics* 9, no. 56 (1960): 417–23; and Otto H. Koenigsberger, Carl Mahoney, and Martin Evans, *Climate and House Design* (New York: United Nations, 1971).
9. Koenigsberger, "Town Planning and Housing," 33.
10. An introduction to the work of Michel Ecochard can be found, for example, in Eric Verdeil, "Michel Ecochard in Lebanon and Syria (1956–1968): The Spread of Modernism, the Building of the Independent States and the Rise of Local Professionals of Planning," *Planning Perspectives*, no. 27 (2012): 243–260; *Urbanism: Imported or Exported? Native Aspirations and Foreign Plans*, ed. Joe Nasr and Mercedes Volait (West Sussex: Wiley-Academy, 2003); Eric Verdeil, "Une ville et ses urbanistes: Beyrouth en reconstruction," *Strates*, no. 11 (2004); Joos Van Den Dool, "Le rôle professionnel de Michel Ecochard en architecture, archéologie et en urbanisme français à l'étranger" (PhD diss. University of Ghent, 2004); and Luce Beeckmans, "The Adventures of the French Architect Michel Ecochard in Post-independence Dakar: A Transnational Development Expert Drifting

between Commitment and Expediency," *Journal of Architecture* 9, no. 6 (2014): 849–71.

11. For a more elaborated introduction to Ecochard's approach, see Tom Avermaete, "Framing the Afropolis: Michel Ecochard and the African City for the Greatest Number," *OASE*, no. 83 (2010): 77–101.

12. The rationales of this system were explained in drawing and text in, for example, Michel Ecochard, *Karachi: Mission de l'ONU 1953–1954: Etude sociale et d'urbanisme; Non suivie de realization* (unpublished paper, Agha Kahn Foundation, Geneva, 1954).

13. Michel Ecochard, *L'urbanisme dans les pays en voie de développement* (Paris: Fondation Nationale des Sciences Politiques, 1960): 1. Translation by author.

14. Michel Ecochard, Karachi First Report: *Note on Refugee Work* (unpublished, IFA archives, 1959), 1.

15. Constantinos A. Doxiadis, *Architecture in Transition* (London: Hutchinson, 1963), 115. For more on Doxiadis see, for instance, Panayiota Pyla, "Back to the Future: Doxiadis's Plans for Baghdad," *Journal of Planning History* 7, no. 1 (February 2008): 3–19; Hashim Sarkis, *Circa 1958—Lebanon in the Pictures and Plans of Constantinos Doxiadis* (Beirut: Dar An-Nahar, 2003); Viviana d'Auria, "From Tropical Transitions to Ekistic Experimentation: Doxiadis Associates in Tema, Ghana," *Positions* 1 (2010): 40–63; and Ray Bromley, "Towards Global Human Settlements: Constantinos Doxiadis as Entrepreneur, Coalition-Builder and Visionary," in *Urbanism: Imported or Exported? Native Aspirations and Foreign Plans*, ed. Joe Nasr and Mercedes Volait (Chichester: Wiley-Academy, 2003), 325–30.

16. Matthew S. Hull, Government Paper: *The Materiality of Bureaucracy in Urban Pakistan* (Berkeley: University of California Press, 2012), 51.

17. Doxiadis, *Architecture in Transition*, 88–89.

18. P. Pyla, "Gossip on the Doxiadis 'Gossip Square': Unpacking the Histories of an Unglamorous Public Space," *Architectural Histories* 1, no. 1 (2013), doi.org/10.5334/ah.bb.

19. Doxiadis, *Architecture in Transition*, 115.

20. Ibid., 118.

21. Ibid, 116.

22. Ibid, 115.

23. Otto Koenigsberger, "The Role of the Planner in a Poor (and in a Not Quite So Poor) Country," *Habitat International* 7, no. 112 (1983): 52

24. Otto Koenigsberger, "Action Planning," *Architectural Association Journal* 79, no. 882 (May 1964): 306–12.

Image Sources:

Constantinos A. Doxiadis, "The Two-Headed Eagle: From the Past to the Future of Human Settlements," *Ekistics, The Problems and Science of Human Settlements* vol. 33, no. 198 (May 1972): 406–420.

Doxiadias Associaties, "'Tribal' Housing in Iraq," special to the *New York Times* from Baghdad, Iraq, Ekistics—Housing and Planning Abstracts,HIB-GA 33, vol. 5 (June 1958): 280–282.

Split Screen

Keller Easterling

In the following transcript of her keynote address at the 5th International Forum of the LafargeHolcim Foundation for Sustainable Construction on April 6th, 2016 in Detroit, Keller Easterling advocates for viewing the world as a split screen and looks at the protocols that generate space across the globe, arguing that they are fertile grounds for repeatable, responsive, and sly design—even in politically gridlocked environments.

In my work, I am asking that we look at the urban world and see not only buildings with shapes and outlines, but also the infrastructural matrix in which buildings are suspended. This *infrastructure space* is not just an infrastructure of pipes and wires hidden underground; rather, it's a spatial operating system for shaping the city. That operating system is like a rule set for repeatable urban formulas and spatial products—the cartoon of skyscrapers, malls, resorts, franchises, parking lots, airports, golf courses, greenhouses, ports, lounges, or free zones that press into view and look the same whether in Texas or Taiwan or Inner Mongolia. Bankers, develo-

pers, World Bank specialists, and 28-year-old McKinsey consultants are coding infrastructure space, which is often largely regarded to be merely a by-product of laws, econometrics, informatics, logistics, or global standards. Wrapped in TED talk locutions, it is assumed that these technical languages or the latest digital technologies may have the most authority in contemporary problem-solving.

But while it might be difficult to see at a moment of digital ubiquity, the lumpy heavy solids of urban space themselves constitute a technology and an information system in the same way that Gregory Bateson said a man, a tree, and an ax is an information system. The spatial technologies of infrastructure space are overwriting the planet. That spatial language or code is creating *de facto* forms of polity, and it is even a secret weapon of stealthy political forces. However unlikely it may seem, and beyond the authority of other technical languages, I am arguing that space is currently the underexploited medium of innovation, with the potential to bring designers different aesthetic pleasures and political capacities—an expanded repertoire of form-making but also a surprising and unorthodox approach to political activism.

Infrastructure space prompts a different habit of mind about design. But it also turns out to be an adventure in thinking with broader cultural significance, offering nothing less than new instruments of global governance. This different habit of mind about design and politics might begin with one simple observation: culture is well rehearsed at pointing to things, calling their name, or recognizing their shape, but *under*-rehearsed at describing the interactivity or chemistry *between* things. Infrastructure space is thus productively imponderable because it is not a thing; it is a large socio-technical system—with a nod to Rosalind Williams, it is too large to be in any one place. It can be assessed not by its name, shape, or outline, but rather by its *disposition*—its latent properties that unfold over time and territory, its propensities within a context, or the potentials in its arrangement. That disposition, that agency in arrangement, acting like an operating system or a growth medium, decides what will live or die—what will constitute information.

While designers are good at making buildings and landscapes, they might also be particularly astute when it comes to detecting and adjusting disposition—the capacities, even the political temperaments, latent in organization. This faculty, which may be only under-indulged or under-rehearsed, allows us see the world as a split screen. Utilizing this view, we see not only objects and declarations but also a matrix: the activity and disposition that have been hiding in the atmosphere, right in front of our eyes.

Those engaged in this kind of work strive to make responsible and reasonable decisions, seeking out the right answer to design issues, building consensus, or following best practices. But having the right answer isn't enough in a world with global-warming naysayers and Donald Trump to contend with. Reasonable innovations can easily be outmaneuvered by unreasonable politics. But an ability to adjust disposition in infrastructure space offers another approach to design that is not always about meeting exact standards and having the right answer. Rather, it is an approach that allows design to exploit the powers of these large systems by reaching into time and giant macro-organization strata with moves that are potentially sneakier or more politically agile.

The stories of infrastructure space are usually stories where reasonable things don't happen and where innovation comes up against political superbugs and bulletproof forms of power. I am often asked to tell the story of one of these super-nodes of infrastructure space: the free zone, a space that denotes the crossroad of many networks under consideration within this publication. In the mid-twentieth-century, the free zone was a warehousing or manufacturing compound for storing custom-free trade. Later, it mutated into the export-processing zone (EPZ), a formula promoted by the United Nations for jump-starting the economies of developing countries. In the last thirty years, it has become the germ of a building epidemic that produces the glittering mimics of Dubai, Singapore, and Hong Kong all around the world. Free-zone promotional videos tend to always take the same form: a zoom from outer space drops through the clouds to reveal the new center of the earth, at which point a deep movie-trailer voice repeats all the neoliberal mantras of free trade and incentivized urbanism to which foreign investment has become addicted. Free from the laws of its host country, the zone offers no taxes, no bureaucracy, streamlined customs, and deregulation of labor or environmental law. The stirring music that typically soundtracks an epic adventure or fast-moving western accompanies a swoop through shimmering cartoon skylines, resorts, and suburbs, the image dotted with sun flares.

This very same zone harbors labor and environmental abuse, and it continues to fail to deliver on its economic promises. But egged on by global institutions and consultancies, the zone is often bathed in redemptive rhetoric and treated as the necessary signal for entry into a global marketplace, to such an extent that the next poorest country wants its mirror-tiled skyline at any cost. The promotional videos become more and more delirious as the zone becomes more and more contagious. Taking the "split screen" view, you can see the objects and declarations—the skyscrapers and fictions about openness, relaxation, luxury, and freedom. But you also see the autonomous island free from any law or urban circumstance that obstructs corporate profit—a major organ by which corporations avoid regulations. In the split screen you see not only a skyline but, if you are good at detecting disposition, an organization as a closed loop that erases inconvenient information.

Traveling on through infrastructure space, look at a place like Kenya that, in the wake of fiber-optic submarine-cable landings, is exploding with new broadband capacities and skyrocketing numbers of cell phones. These digital information technologies are most productive when they work together with other information systems that have different lineaments. Countering some myths of the smart city, regardless of whether or not it is coated with digital sensors, space itself is an information system. It is *already* a network and a router. Space computes. Spatial information systems are more robust when people access each other and multiply their exchanges. And when the intelligence of cities and landscapes is more robust, digital information systems are also more robust. But rather than innovative spatial arrangements, in Kenya the spatial vessels that accompany digital technologies often *erase* information. They might be large highways that decrease exchanges by inflating the distances between people or zone enclaves with the disposition of a closed loop. As the spatial information system gets dumber, the digital information system gets dumber as well.

Or look at Bangladesh, a country with an extremely shallow coastal plain, where the rising tide due to global warming can race deep into the interior. The people who are displaced as a result relocate to cities and work in factories like those in the Dhaka Export Processing Zone—site of the Rana Plaza collapse in 2013, a tragic example of the deadly dispositions immanent in infrastructure space. We try to regulate labor and environmental abuse in these factories with the standard making that occupies another strata of the infrastructure-space operating system. The International Organization for Standardization (ISO) is one global parliament of this soft law that determines technical details like the thinness of credit cards or the pitch of screw threads as well as often hilarious *patois* of the ISO 9000 quality management with its acronyms, bullet-pointed lists, mandalas, and motivational aphorisms. Sometimes management standards from ISO or other NGOs raise awareness or change behavior, and sometimes watchdog groups are funded by the very companies that contract for the factory service that is to be observed. Often these auditing groups only provide nonbinding and often self-certifying seals of approval that inoculate against further regulation. Taking the split-screen view, however, you can see the discrepancy between what the organization is saying and what it is doing. Whatever its labels and certificates, the organizational disposition is again a closed loop that is tightening to eliminate inconvenient information about human rights and environment. The house always wins.

Infrastructure space constitutes a kind of extrastatecraft—a realm of governance outside of, in addition to, and often in league with the state. In this system some receive excessive immunities and others are consistent losers. It is a place of profound failu-res, a list that includes Rana Plaza or the Shenzhen collapse (2015), ongoing climate-change denial, the financial meltdown of 2008, or the contemporary refugee crisis. It is often fueled not by cast-iron economic logics but by powerful habits and fictions. Within this matrix, conventional organs of design and governance—buildings and master plans or standards and laws—have great authority, even when they are spectacularly inadequate and unimaginative. This prompts the question: Might the spectacular failures and powers of infrastructure space inspire nothing less than a different organ of design, different ways to register the design imagination? Might they engender form making in another gear? Designers and architects are very good at making buildings, but working in infrastructure space is less like making a thing and more like having one's hands on the faders and toggles of organization. Studying it trains you to see the field—akin to being able to anticipate several moves ahead in a game of chess.

Any attempt to adjust the disposition in infrastructure space benefits from an artistic curiosity about reagents and spatial mixtures, or spatial *wiring*. The interest should orient not toward designing a single object form, but toward designing an active form that inflects a population of objects or sets up relative potentials within them. The active forms that manipulate dispositions of infrastructure space are time-released forms or dynamic markers. They are like little bits of code in the spatial operating system—multipliers, switches, or other network adjustments. Amy Mielke and Caitlin Taylor, winners of the 2014 Holcim Awards Gold, designed an example of active form. Poreform is a concrete detail able to absorb urban floodwater. The detail assumed many incarnations in different scales, from a curb all the way up to a gigantic gathering space the size of Tate Modern's Turbine Hall in London. Mielke and Taylor were designing an active form, designing not only the detail but also the way in which it becomes a multiplier, and eventually a network, in the city. Alternatively, when not dealing with these little bits of code, the designer of active form thinks about adjusting a larger network by changing one switch within it. It is possible, for example—as I have long been advocating—to change a highway system by making smarter intermodal switches within it? It is worth noting even now that, without these switches for upshifting and downshifting into different transportation capacities, even the smartest things, like new driverless vehicles, might be as dumb as a mid-twentieth-century car.

How, then, might you hack into the world's dominant types of software by combining forms like multipliers and switches into organs of interplay? How do you shape global agreements not only as buildings, master plans, declarations, laws, or standards, but also as bargains, chain reactions, or ratchets—protocols to recondition spaces over time? When considering these questions I often refer to a simple spatial software of interplay,

like the eighteenth-century city of Savannah in the US state of Georgia. Its founder, James Edward Oglethorpe, did not design a master plan or object form but rather designed a growth protocol. The town would grow by wards, each of which contained a quotient of public, private, or green space, as well as agricultural space beyond. You did not know the shape of the town's outline but you had an explicit, measured spatial instruction for relationships between things. It was like a governor or thermostat—an interplay between counterbalancing spatial variables or a time-released instruction for the ongoing activities of urban space.

Or consider a protocol for the subtraction of building through interplay—something like an inversion of Savannah. If you allow yourself to think about active form as well as object form, you can design not only a means of putting the development machine into forward motion but also into reverse. In cities like Detroit after the 2008 financial crisis, failure was so spectacular that a magical thing happened. Many properties stopped being financial abstractions or trafficked mortgage products and returned to being heavy buildings on land collected and traded by land banks. Using this more physical portfolio, the protocol suggested several ways of simply counterbalancing toxic and densifying properties. The revenues from one property might relieve another, and if cities can, as a result, acquire and aggregate land for infrastructures or other projects, the properties can also generate dividends for each other. A subtraction protocol might be very useful in many parts of the world, from distended McMansion suburbs to coastal flood plains to sensitive environmental landscapes like the Amazon rain forest. Different from the designer's desire for a *tabula rasa*, a subtraction protocol might even be a safeguard against more violent ecologies of disenfranchisement. Through interdependence and exchange no property is ever worth nothing.

In those flooding coastal areas, in addition to all the other things we design, we might make a macro-organizational move that changes the terms of a problem. For example, what if mortgages were simply considered in pairs or groups? With the benefit of intelligence from urbanists, landscape architects, and regional environmentalists, an index could target and rate properties for *complementary or counterbalancing* attributes that reduce collective risk.

Such an approach could take the form of a matchmaking website—an exchange that would rate not single properties but pairs or groups of properties. For example, a shoreline owner moves to higher ground; a year-round coastal property becomes a seasonal vacation home; a municipality is able to aggregate land for levees, water retention, or sand-replenishing programs. For transactions that result in more resilience or a net move to high ground, banks and insurance offer lower rates and streamlined deals. The mortgage that has been a

multiplier of financial, environmental, and social disaster is finally rated not for virtual financial abstractions but for environmental properties that offer more tangible risks and rewards.

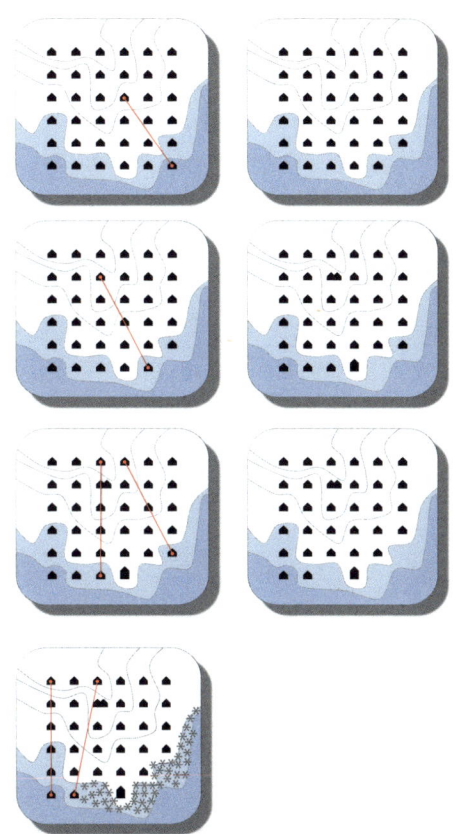

Fig. 1: Figure Coastal protocol

What if, in addition to our buildings, master plans, and low aerial views, we left behind another kind of code or shorthand like this, designing simple linkages or counterbalancing interdependencies that could be established and, like software, updated? If they then became contagious they might change a landscape in only a little more time than it takes to construct a single design. In this way, a city like Nairobi might better bargain with their assets—assets like millions of cell-phone users. Similarly, some countries have made access to their oil and gas resources contingent on investment in other industries that they need—an "offset" that leverages sustaining resources. So maybe one way to hack the zone is to use foreign investment to leverage benefits for existing cities rather than newly minted exurban zone enclaves. Just like the interplay between public and

private in Savannah, the interplay can link investment to shared resources like transit (in red) that benefit the city while delivering workers to business. This urban "rewiring" settles the intelligence of people in the city,

Fig. 3: Broadband/Road-protocol

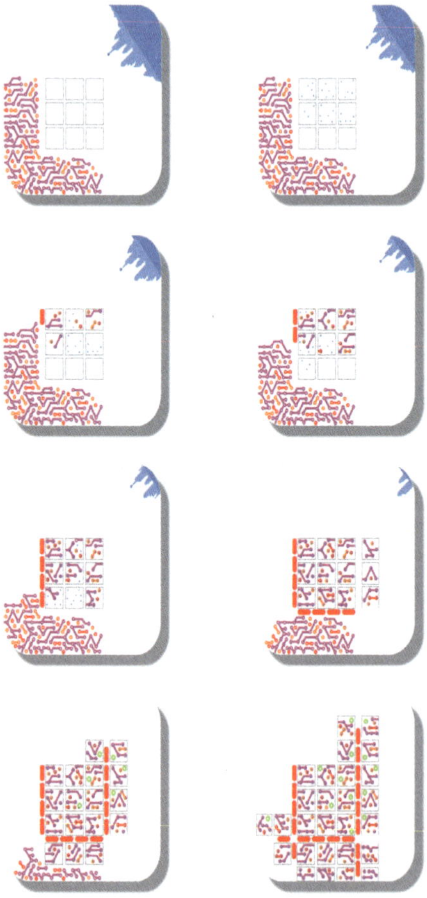

increases security, saves the costs of ill-advised development, more directly returns financial benefits to the domestic economy, and perhaps, most importantly, returns the enterprise and its workers to the protections and regulations of law.

Fig. 2: Anti-zone protocol

In sensitive landscapes like the jungles of Kenya or the biodiverse rain forests of Ecuador, in addition to a subtraction protocol, might there be an interplay between digital and spatial information systems? As noted earlier, spatial information systems are more robust when people can access each other and landscapes more intelligent, when they preserve their atmospheric powers, their biodiversity and indigenous culture. And while roads are typically regarded as conduits of progress and opportunity, in rural or wilderness areas (here in pursuit of oil) they can erase the information immanent in cities, villages, and landscapes. It might be more productive to dial down roads (gray lines) when dialing up broadband (the red radiating circle) to preserve farms and forests—the green information system—that attracts more global resources for tourism or education. Just as changing a bit of code can hack a telecommunications network, so too can changing a road.

In a final urgent example, infrastructure space has streamlined the movements of tens of millions of tourists and cheap laborers and products around the world, and the sharing economy has linked millions one-on-one in 190 countries in the world. Yet at a time when sixty million people in the world are displaced, more than at any other time in history, the problem of moving five to six million people away from a global atrocity is one that simply can't be solved. The nation-state employs a dumb on-off button to grant or deny citizenship/asylum and the aid organizations are often equally innovation-free. To address these and other problems, is it possible to slither in between the state and the NGOcracy as another kind of design entrepreneur? How about taking not the role of policy expert but rather that of social/political design entrepreneur, offering spatial urban variables that change the terms of the problem? Can the resources and logistics of infrastructure space be hijacked for other purposes?

How do you diagram not solutions, but rather things that shouldn't always work—not because they are marginal or weak, but because they need to be agile enough and with sufficient temporal dimensions to be able to respond to the moment when they are outmaneuvered? These alternative organs of design might come with different sorts of documents, but they also inspire another kind of knowledge or practice. With a tip of the hat to thinkers like Gilbert Ryle, designing interplay and adjusting disposition is less about "knowing that" and more about "knowing how." It is not about knowing the *right* answer. One can only "know *how*" to navigate a river, feel for the potentials of bread in dough, land a plane in high wind, sling plaster, hustle, kiss, or tell a joke. Knowing how requires an artistic comfort with unfinished processes. But that indeterminacy is not about forestalling decision, but about developing forms that can be more responsive over time as a matter of practicality. Forms that are time-released also have the political capacity to remain in place to respond to a countermove.

The discrepancy highlighted by the split-screen view offers additional political capacities. Relying on fluid undeclared intentions, global powers in infrastructure space are masters of the split screen. Decoupling their official declarations from their dispositions—saying something different from what they are doing—can confound dissent. Our clanking left-right politics or neoliberal labels are completely inadequate when it comes to handling these moving targets. It should be noted that dissent that is itself a closed loop of right answers and ultimate righteous solutions is especially vulnerable. There are certainly moments when dissent must stand up and declare opposition. Yet as important as knowing what to oppose (knowing *that*) is knowing *how* to oppose it. Two can play at this game. More than just the tool of political bullies who play dirty, the split screen inspires a sly approach to spatial activism. The dispositions that can hide in the atmosphere right in front of us can be tilted toward alternative politics and surrounded by the same camouflaging bluffs. With a nod to Latour, it's a world where sociologist Gabriel Tarde is as important as Karl Marx. Being able to separate what an organization is *saying* from what it is *doing* is the first step in learning to manipulate both sides of the screen with sneakier techniques, like the gifs, pandas, rumors, meaningless distractions, and other totemic fictions that are so effective in culture.

Anyone who knows how to get things done never relies only on proper declarations, laws, and standards. The designer can hardly hope to be successful without knowing how to design the spatial change, as well as the spin that propels it—the irrational desires that accompany any innovation. Recalling the aforementioned observations of the character of infrastructure space, we know that it is too big to apprehend, it is in no one place, and many problems are only exacerbated by duels or righteous binary conflicts. Given this, perhaps it is sneakier when David never bothers to actually *kill* Goliath if he can instead use the giant's large size and many multipliers to amplify a change. It is the activist who is too smart to be right who can also manipulate the split screen, stealing some of the powers of infrastructure space and designing a snaking chain of moves to worm into and generate leverage against intractable politics.

A Visual Atlas

Part 3

Compiled by Something Fantastic

Fig. 84: Via Elevada Presidente Costa e Silva
in São Paulo, Brazil On Sundays, cars are banned
from this inner-city, elevated highway to make room for
cyclists, pedestrians and street musicians.

Fig. 85: Hospital in Freiburg, Germany
The surgical ward, built in 1928,
offers generous balconies
for sunbathing while recuperating.

Fig. 86: Miyashita Park in Tokyo, Japan
Designed by Atelier Bow-Wow in 2011, the
park spans a street and a parking garage
and includes a football field, a rock
climbing area and skating facilities.

Fig. 87: Panathenaic Stadium in Athens, Greece
Excavated and restored during the nineteenth century,
the structure is built entirely from marble.

Fig. 88: Entrance steps
in Lonedo, Lugo di Vicenza, Italy

Fig. 89: Highway bridge
crossing the Lahn valleynear Limburg, Germany
The bridge was built in 1937 and destroyed
just a few years later, in 1945.

Fig. 90: Exhibition space at the Sir JJ College
of Applied Arts in Mumbai, India
Lamps and fans occupy the upper part of the room.

Fig. 91: Parking lot in Detroit, USA
The vast area of event parking during the
opening weekend of the baseball season.

Fig. 92: Cane bridge crossing the
Waria river in Papua New Guineag

Fig. 93: The opening of the Golden Gate
bridge in 1937 in San Francisco, USA
The wider a bridge span spans, the higher
its tower. The arc of the parabolic wires is
in turn defined by the laws of physics.

Fig. 94: Cellulose storage, Sunila, Finland
The concrete structure was designed
by Alvar Aalto in 1936.

Fig. 95: Airship hangar
at Marine Corps Air Station in Tustin, USA

283

Fig. 96: North Hoyle Offshore Wind Farm
in Liverpool Bay, Wales

Fig. 97: Lake water work Lengg
in Zurich, Switzerland Most of the drinking
water in Zurich passes through the slow
filtration basins pictured above.

Fig. 99: Bissina Dam in
Adamello Trento, Italy

Fig. 100: Lakeshore Drive in
Chicago, USA

Fig. 101: Pedestrian crossing on
Paulista Avenue in São Paulo, Brazil

Fig. 102: Ramp climbing a building
in Ahmedabad, India

Fig. 103: External staircase
in Ahmedabad, India

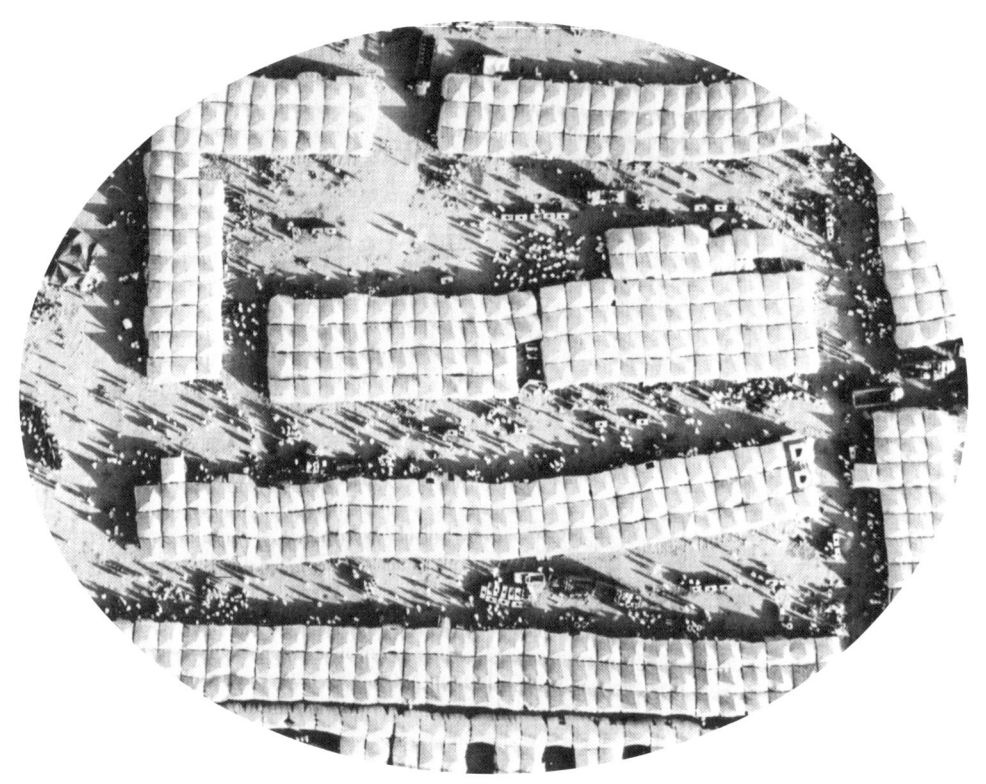

Fig. 104: Tent city outside of Mecca
on the Plain of Arafat in Mina, Saudi Arabia
Every year temporary city quarters are rebuilt to
house more than two million pilgrims during the Hajj.

Fig. 105: Landslide barrier in Genova, Italy

Fig. 106: Trellis in the gardens
of Schwetzingen Palace, Germany

Fig. 107: Beach huts at the
Lido in Venice, Italy

Fig. 108: Mountain hut in the
Bernerse Oberland region,
Switzerland

Fig. 109: Covered chimney
at a mill in Berlin, Germany

Fig. 110: Windbreaker hedges in the Shimane Prefecture, Japan

Fig. 111: Carport in Kyoto, Japan

Fig. 114: Public Baths
opened in 1910 in Berlin,
Germany

Fig. 113: Water pumping
station in Wrocław, Poland

Fig. 115: Bus stop near Shymkent,
Kazakhstan

Fig. 116: Market arcade in Ghardaia, Algeria

Fig. 118: Zoloti Vorota underground
station in Kiev, Ukraine
Located 100 meters underground,
the station is equipped
to double as a bomb shelter.

Fig. 117: Sanatorium in Paimio, Finland
The rounded corners in the hallways
of this former tuberculosis sanatorium,
opened in 1932, make cleaning easier.

Document:

The following is a transcript of an impromptu summation by Simon Upton, Director of the Environment Directorate of the Organisation for Economic Co-operation and Development (OECD), at the 5th International Forum of the LafargeHolcim Foundation for Sustainable Construction in Detroit on April 9, 2016. Entitled "The Planet's Infrastructure," Upton's statement asserts that the planet is by any means *not* "too big to fail." Upton argues that both the "soft infrastructure" of our societies—governance, policies, regulations, etc.—and the "hard infrastructure" of the man-made environment—energy systems, transportation networks, logistics conduits, etc.—must be made to align with what he terms the "infrastructure" of the planet: a rewiring done in accordance with the demands set forth by the planet itself.

The Planet's Infrastructure

Simon Upton

Infrastructure is not only deeply political but is also linked to discourses, narratives, and imaginaries. These broad concerns are a reminder that the objective of infrastructure is well-being; there is a long history of technophilic infrastructural utopias that promise new modes of living. Our infrastructural future will certainly be decided by politics. I would like to

I

contend, however, that the choices available to us might be more limited than our imaginations sometimes lead us to believe. Rather than ask how we would like to live, perhaps we should focus on how we will be forced to live by the physical constraints of the planet on which we are living. These constraints emerge from very physical things, like water and waste, ecosystem services, and climate stability.

Put simply, the planet's infrastructure is an intricate, interconnected web of living processes that cycle finite elements within an enclosed space drawing on incoming solar energy. What we term "infrastructure" is in fact an artificial superstructure superimposed on those natural systems. That very superstructure—based on human intelligence—is starting to cause some massive perturbations in the earth's system. As a species, we have leveraged those natural cycles to our benefit without knowing where we should set limits. Yet if you look at how we are treating the planet's infrastructure, it is as though we have decided, like with Lehman Brothers and others, that it is "too big to fail."

Industrial entropy generates environmental interconnections at the planetary level (see

Fig. 1). In light of this, I think it is not so much a question of debating how we might want to live, as of coming to terms with some ways we definitely will not be able to live. This suggests a radical transformation in the physical claims we make. As scientist and policy analyst Vaclav Smil illustrates, we have created a physical superstructure completely at odds with the sort of energy harvesting we need to be pursuing (see Fig. 2 and Fig. 3)—a graphic display of the mismatch between space and built infrastructure. Generations of policy decisions have created a path of dependency that will be very difficult to break.

Yet, even governments seem to have realized that there are limits that cannot be breached, and that the whole edifice may not be too big to fail. The Paris Agreement (COP21 2015) confirmed, for the second time, the goal of limiting warming to two degrees, and even made wistful references to 1.5 degrees. This is a hard, physical goal, with demanding material consequences for infrastructure. Reaching it will require systems thinking about the transformation in the energy demands of a subset of planetary spaces (Sven Stremke's paper offers one example of this challenge).

To transform infrastructural systems and their energy demands requires a rewiring of the soft infrastructure—policy and regulations—that underlies these systems. Global infrastructure policies are messy and overlapping, designed for a world in which fossil energy was the default option. And now, late in the day, we are trying to impose climate policies on top of all the existing policies. So even really good policies, like an ambitious carbon tax, can be blunted, with new technologies and business models not able to be effective, because the rules were not designed with them in mind. But instead of listing the roadblocks—subsidies, investment restrictions, local content requirements, and fragmented metropolitan and regional governments—we need to align our demand for resources with the tolerances and margins of natural systems that deliver most of our essential services. We have to value the scarcity of those reservoirs into which we pour our waste. To do that, we need to align the "soft wiring" of our societies with the "hard wiring" of the infrastructure we need to build.

The future may not be Masdar City. But it will be one in which very different technolo-

A story of industrial entropy
... running against the earth's balance sheet?

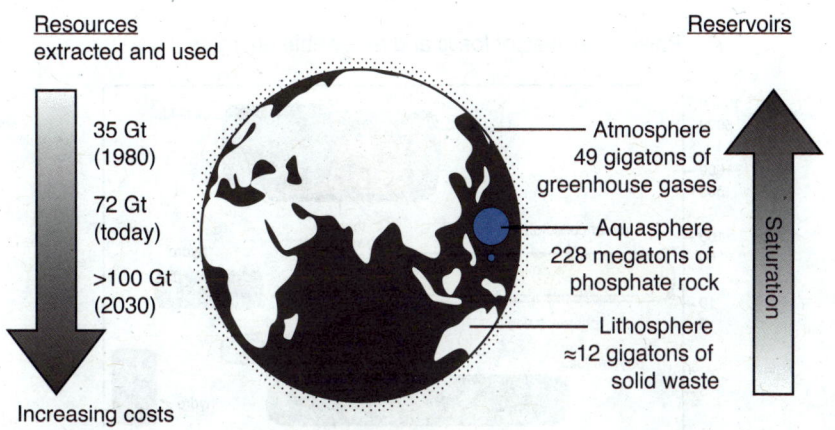

Resources
extracted and used

35 Gt
(1980)

72 Gt
(today)

>100 Gt
(2030)

Increasing costs

Reservoirs

Atmosphere
49 gigatons of
greenhouse gases

Aquasphere
228 megatons of
phosphate rock

Lithosphere
≈12 gigatons of
solid waste

Saturation

Fig. 1: Extraction doubled from 1980 to 2015. As easily
available reservoirs diminish, extraction costs increase.
Accordingly, the earth's natural reservoirs are increasingly
saturated with waste: 49 gigatons of greenhouse gases
were released into the atmosphere in 2010 alone (IPCC,
2014); 228 million tons of phosphate rock were mined in
2013 (USGS, 2014), mainly for use as fertilizer, with runoffs
polluting the aquasphere; 12 gigatons—approximately 10
percent of total global biomass—is solid waste (Chalmin
& Gaillochet, 2009). The aquasphere is represented by
two spheres: the larger one shows all water on the planet
amounting to 1,386,000,000 km3 and less than 1 percent
of the earth's volume; the smaller sphere represents the
earth's fresh water of 10,633,450 km3. The total volume of
fresh water is equal to just over four times the volume of the
Greenland icecap (USGS, 2016).

V

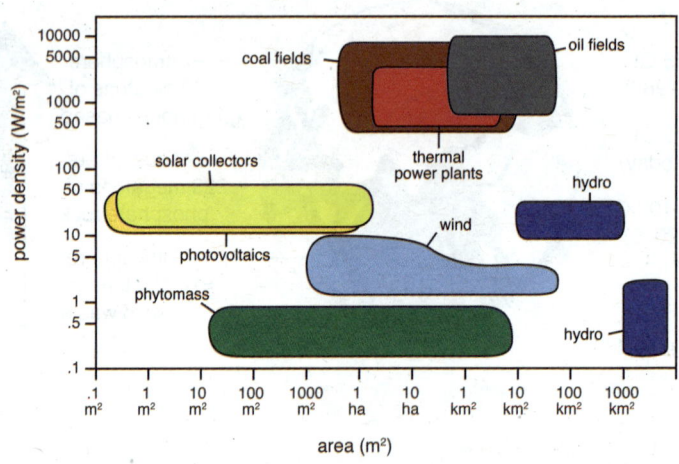

Power densities of fossil and renewable energies

Fig. 2: Current infrastructural systems are at odds with the type of energy harvesting that needs to be pursued. Shown here are the power densities of fossil and renewable energies.

Comparison of power densities of energy consumption
and renewable energy production

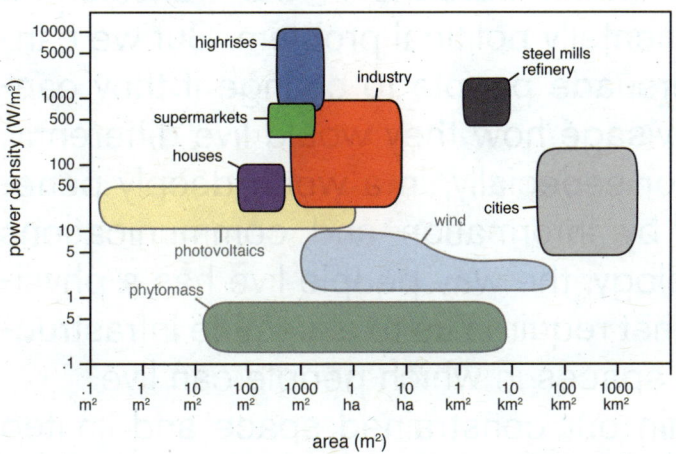

Fig. 3: A comparison of power densities of energy
consumption and renewable energy production. This and
the previous graph—based on research by Vaclav Smil—
reveal the discrepancy between space requirements and
built infrastructure(source: Vaclav Smil, Energy at the
Crossroads, MIT Press, 2005).

gies are deployed and a very different sort of path dependency laid down. The problem will not be the technologies, but rather who carries which burdens in the transition—a fundamentally political problem. But we cannot persuade people to change if they cannot envisage how they would live differently. Even, or especially, in a world deeply penetrated by information and communications technology, the way people live has a physicality that requires us to assemble infrastructure in spaces in which people can live.

Within our constrained space and limited time, policy makers need advice grounded in practical solutions on how to address our unavoidable reality. This is what I hope this conference and its subsequent publication can help policy makers envisage.

Infrastructure as Agency

Essays, Part 3

Ricky Burdett, Diane Van Buren, Paul N. Edwards, Henk Ovink,
Anuradha Mathur and Dilip da Cunha, Rania Ghosn and El Hadi Jazairy

Infrastructures of Equality Versus Inequality

Ricky Burdett

When planning infrastructure at a large scale it can be easy to lose sight of its effects upon the individuals who actually use it, as well as its capacity to act as a multiplier of social equity. Joining up the dots between the data, density and development, Ricky Burdett explains how policy choices have emboldened infrastructure's social impact in Bogotá and London—and could do so elsewhere.

There is a tendency to be negative when it comes to talking about infrastructure. Though I had originally titled my essay "Infrastructures of Inequality," I would like instead to take a positive approach and focus on infrastructure's capacity to foster social integration. When one thinks of the negative aspects that are often associated with infrastructure, one should not forget that there is a flip side. Whereas infrastructural systems always benefit those who have access to them, one could also invest in infrastructure in order to improve existing conditions and modes of operation—to do things better and with better results. This is what we should be most interested in learning.

Exploring the physical and political impacts of infrastructure on urban life necessitates a different way of thinking about design as a form of political action in order to effectively solve the problem of using economic means in a positive, inclusive, and equitable way. To pursue such an agenda requires a twofold perspective—on the one hand, a big-picture approach vis-à-vis infrastructure and, on the other, the particular view of affected individuals on the ground.

One of the most important things in contemporary discourses concerning infrastructure is that academics and practitioners have broadened their view, not exclusively addressing sewers, transportation systems, water distribution networks, or social institutions as isolated components, but asking how they actually *interconnect*. This shift of perspective is particularly important when looking at those parts of the world that are currently urbanizing at an unprecedented rate, requiring more and more investment in infrastructure in the years to come. Statistics back this up. When it comes to urbanization, the cities that are growing faster—*much* faster than those we typically think of in China or Latin America—are metropolitan regions such as those of Nairobi, Lagos, Kinshasa, Kabul, and Addis Ababa. These agglomerations, at least today, are located in regions of the world with societies marked by relatively low levels of income and energy consumption. What are the appropriate models to follow and what are their consequences when trying to address such challenges? Beyond the very visible problem of a lack of "big infrastructure," there is also a range of less discernible sociopolitical issues, most explicitly revealed by the fact that large portions of populations in places such as these are living in slum conditions. While the term "slum" per se is a problematic one, it nonetheless stands for a lack, not only of infrastructure as it's normally understood, but most importantly a lack of infrastructure fostering common well-being—a lack of schools, housing, medical clinics, communal institutions, and so on, not to mention a lack of the transportation network connecting them.

Fig. 1: Infrastructure has a profound effect on the lives of the increasing number of urban dwellers across the globe, as evidenced by the success of the *ciclovías* in Bogotá, which have not only reduced commuting times and pollution levels, but have also positively affected the quality of life of individuals and families.

When talking about infrastructure at such a large scale, one must acknowledge its effects on social agency in general and individuals in particular—for example, a father taking his two children to school on his bicycle in Bogotá. As straightforward as this example might be, it nevertheless points to the role that infrastructure can play when trying to improve social conditions. Important in this discussion is the relationship between infrastructure and social equity. One way of measuring social equity is access to education. It is a well-accepted fact that if children do not get education early on in life, in a safe environment and in close proximity to their home, they lose out on the benefits that a society might be able to offer. Discussing transport as a means to access education is a proxy for talking about social integration. If one takes education levels of the population in different parts of the city, the quality of education utterly correlates with the availability of and accessibility to transit facilities, whether a subway, bus rapid transit system, or bicycle network. In other words, the better the infrastructure, the higher the educational levels. It is fundamental to remember that decisions made about whether to invest in one form of public transport over another have an impact on the way our children and grandchildren are educated. The critical relationships between those different aspects have been understood by successive mayors of Bogotá, who introduced a bus transit system as well as a network of bicycle paths in their city, placing bus stops close to bicycle lanes, which can be used by parents to take their children to school. Infrastructure in this case positively affects

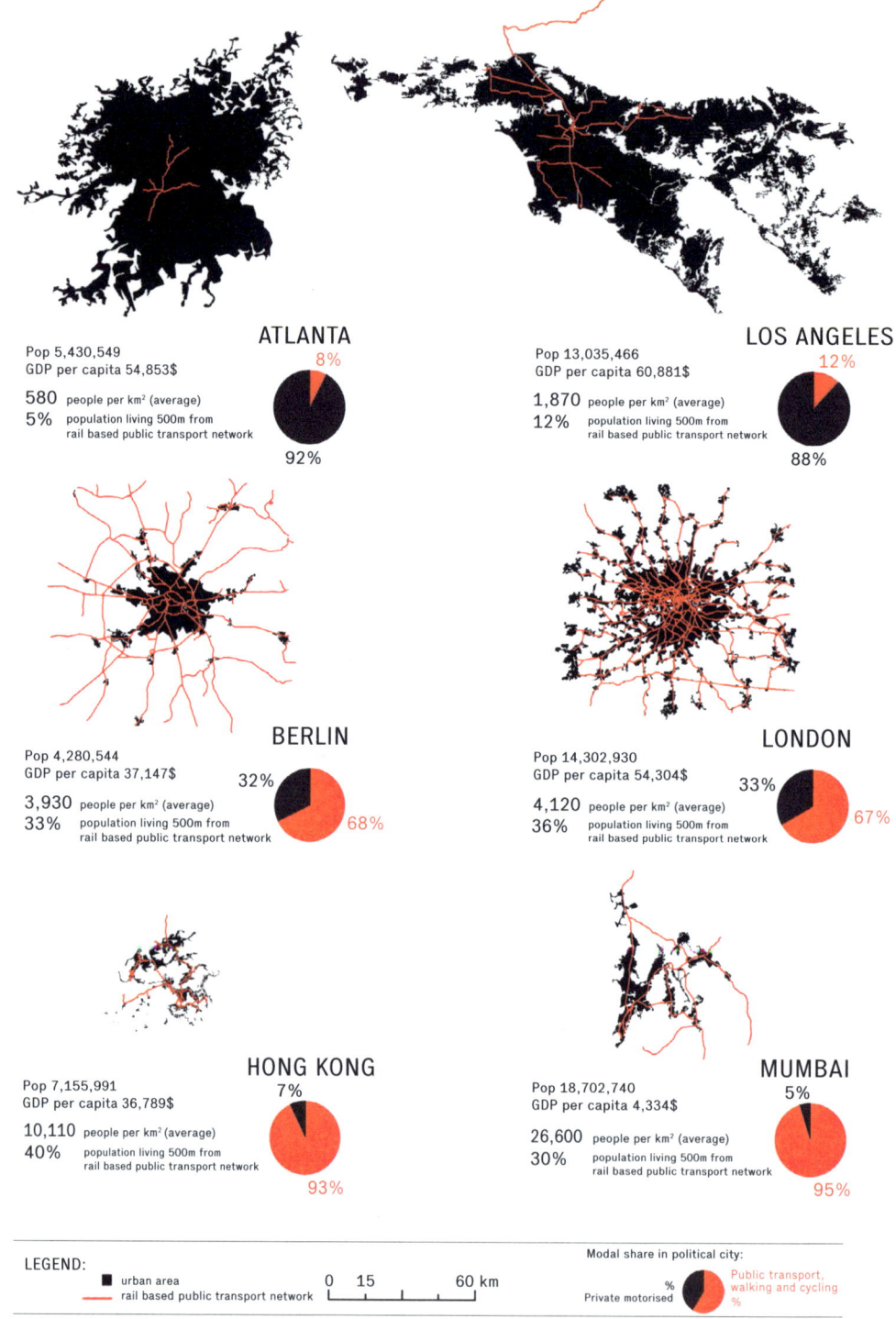

ATLANTA

Pop 5,430,549
GDP per capita 54,853$

580   people per km² (average)
5%   population living 500m from
      rail based public transport network

8%
92%

LOS ANGELES

Pop 13,035,466
GDP per capita 60,881$

1,870 people per km² (average)
12%   population living 500m from
       rail based public transport network

12%
88%

BERLIN

Pop 4,280,544
GDP per capita 37,147$

3,930 people per km² (average)
33%   population living 500m from
       rail based public transport network

32%
68%

LONDON

Pop 14,302,930
GDP per capita 54,304$

4,120 people per km² (average)
36%   population living 500m from
       rail based public transport network

33%
67%

HONG KONG

Pop 7,155,991
GDP per capita 36,789$

10,110 people per km² (average)
40%   population living 500m from
        rail based public transport network

7%
93%

MUMBAI

Pop 18,702,740
GDP per capita 4,334$

26,600 people per km² (average)
30%   population living 500m from
        rail based public transport network

5%
95%

LEGEND:
■ urban area
▬ rail based public transport network

0   15   60 km

Modal share in political city:

%   Public transport,
               walking and cycling
Private motorised   %

Fig. 2: While Atlanta and Berlin have roughly the same population size, their urban footprint varies by a factor of seven. A third of all Berliners live 500 meters from a rail-based public transit network, while the number drops to 5 percent in Atlanta.

people's living conditions. Bogotá's transport policies have furthermore taken the locations of public schools into account, the result being that the city now has the highest literacy rate in Latin America. Consider the effect such projects might have on parents who spend four or five hours commuting a day in order to reach their places of work and secure their family's livelihood. Being denied accessibility, in other words, adversely affects populations. This is by no means a perfect example, but it clearly demonstrates a way of dealing with infrastructure at the macro level in order to foster social change at the micro level.

We must understand how to deal with infrastructure at both scales. The broad discussion on sustainability is concerned with how to increase human well-being, but also with how to reduce the energy footprint per person. At the heart of this discussion is the relationship between physical form, infrastructure, and sustainability. Societies have to decide on how to bring these components into a fruitful and positive relationship. Choices are to be made. It is a public-policy choice, but it is also a choice of how much one should allow the market to dictate policy. In cities such as Detroit or Los Angeles, for example, the tram systems that were built early on were removed decades ago, turning the car into the primary mode of transportation and thus foregrounding the role of a particular branch of industry. Now both cities are spending a tremendous amount of money to reintroduce public transport systems. By the same token, the effects of such choices can explicitly be discerned when comparing cities like Atlanta and Berlin (Fig. 2). Both have a population of roughly five million people, but the difference in size of their physical footprint when compared is vast. Given this difference, one should not be surprised that more than 90 percent of Atlanta's population use cars to get to work or school, while one-third of Berlin's population live 500 meters away from rail-based public transport stations.

Similar observations can be made when comparing London, New York, and Hong Kong in view of the relationship between physical form and infrastructure efficiency. London has had a costly investment in sophisticated transit for over 150 years; New York has the same population as London but double the density, with a high-priced and a well-maintained transit system; and Hong Kong is incredibly dense and has a highly efficient public transit system. In London, with nearly one million people commuting into the center each day, a rather extensive system of transport infrastructure is needed to allow the city to function. In New York City, despite having taller buildings and people living even closer together, more people come into the center on a daily basis. In Hong Kong, with an even greater density of residents as well as workplaces, people live not only closer together, in thirty to forty-story buildings, but their relative travel distance to work is also less. What does all this have to do with the theme of infrastructure space? The relationship between physical density and infrastructure has a lot to do with these interwoven facets of well-being, infrastructure efficiency, and energy footprint. Considering the effects of the physical model of Hong Kong, with a high density of residents and a high density of work, just above 90 percent of its population use public transport to get to work. Why? Because it is the quickest and most efficient way to move within the city, the average commuting time being less than fifteen minutes.

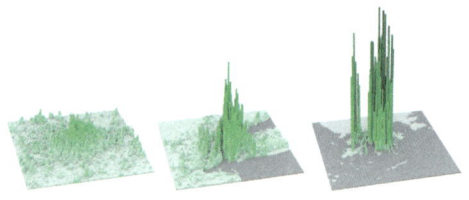

Fig. 3: London, New York, Hong Kong. The level of urban density determines the efficiency of complex metropolitan systems that require investment in infrastructure to create more sustainable cities.

London, at the opposite end of the spectrum, is a widely dispersed, relatively low-density city, with many clusters around its edges that are all very well connected. Unlike most Western cities or cities of the Global North, London has faced an increase in population over the last ten to fifteen years, currently bringing it to its historical high, potentially reaching ten million inhabitants by 2035. London is not at all a perfect city; it suffers

from divisions, it is expensive, and it has fundamental social problems that are physically translated in the reality of the city. The street confrontations that took place in 2011 are evidence of these underlying problems, which in turn are reflected in statistics and maps. London's Public Transport Accessibility Map, for example, shows a well-connected center, reachable in less than an hour when using public transport (the purple area on the map, fig. 4). The city's suburbs, on the other hand, have a deficiency of access, with commuting times into the center of over two hours. Taking into account that public transport accessibility level (PTAL) maps can be drawn for every city, the question that must be addressed is what to deduce from particular relationships between urban form and public infrastructure accessibility, not only at an abstract level, but most importantly in terms of the social impact of infrastructure on the ground.

Another statistical map of London highlights the relationship between social equity and infrastructure accessibility (Fig. 5). The areas in dark red are the most deprived of London—districts with higher rates of teenage pregnancies, unemployment, and lower life expectancy. As the map shows, East London is more deprived than other parts of the city, while those living in the suburbs are quite affluent and better educated. To state the argument otherwise, if a man born today in West London takes the Jubilee Line to the Olympic site in East London, his life expectancy will be reduced by one year at every tube stop. This is not

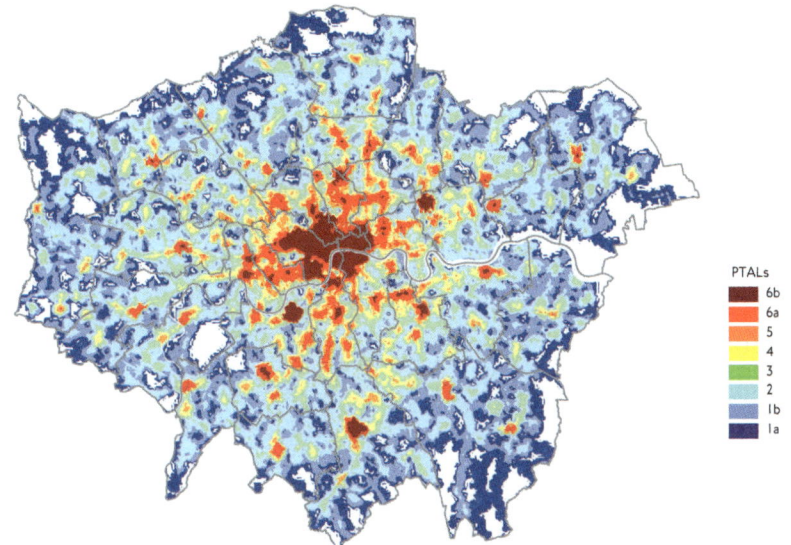

PTALs
- 6b
- 6a
- 5
- 4
- 3
- 2
- 1b
- 1a

Fig. 4: The Public Transport Accessibility Map of London shows the areas that can be accessed in less than an hour using public transit (in red and purple), demonstrating an imbalance in provisions between west and east and between the center and the periphery. The Crossrail high-speed transportation line is set to improve connectivity across London, linking currently deprived areas in the east of the city to the rest of the metropolitan region, which includes its job market and public services.

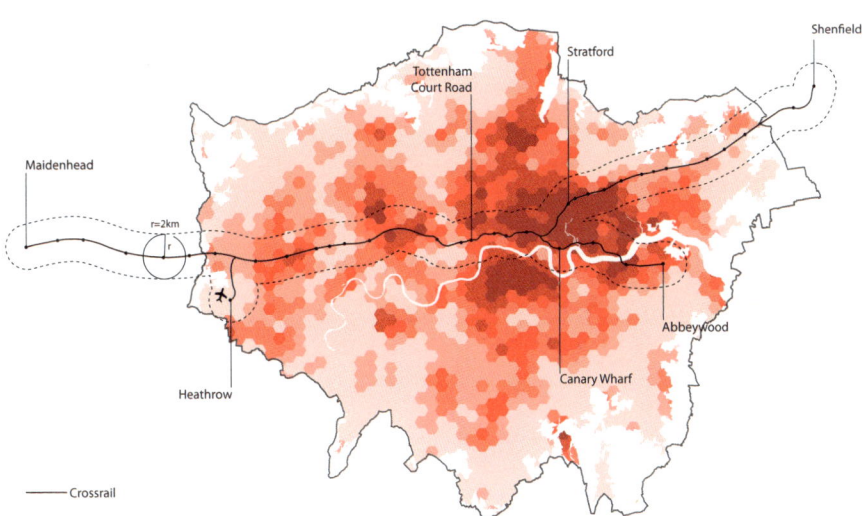

Crossrail

Fig. 5: The 2012 Summer Olympics in London has provided an opportunity to rebalance London's unequal distribution of social disadvantage, creating new jobs and improving life chances in the eastern boroughs that have suffered from decades of underinvestment in infrastructure and services.

just a condition; it is a problem that could be resolved through planning, investment, and infrastructure. Compared to the previous map depicting the inequality of access to public transport, one can argue that infrastructure planning has been biased in favor of the western parts of the city. Trying to remedy the situation, the policies of two London mayors and several governments have very simply been to spread the quality of the center—the purple area on the map—to other parts of the city. The result has been major investment in public transport. One particular case concerns the Crossrail project, a high-speed-tunnel rail route that goes all the way from Heathrow Airport in West London to the county of Essex, east of the city. The project has substantial public support, and will cost approximately $25 billion. It is already regarded as being so successful in bringing jobs and providing opportunities, that a Crossrail 2 project is being planned for 2030, going from the northeast to the southwest of London. Other infrastructure projects have been equally successful, effectively connecting parts of the city in an orbital way, which has seen much new housing and development.

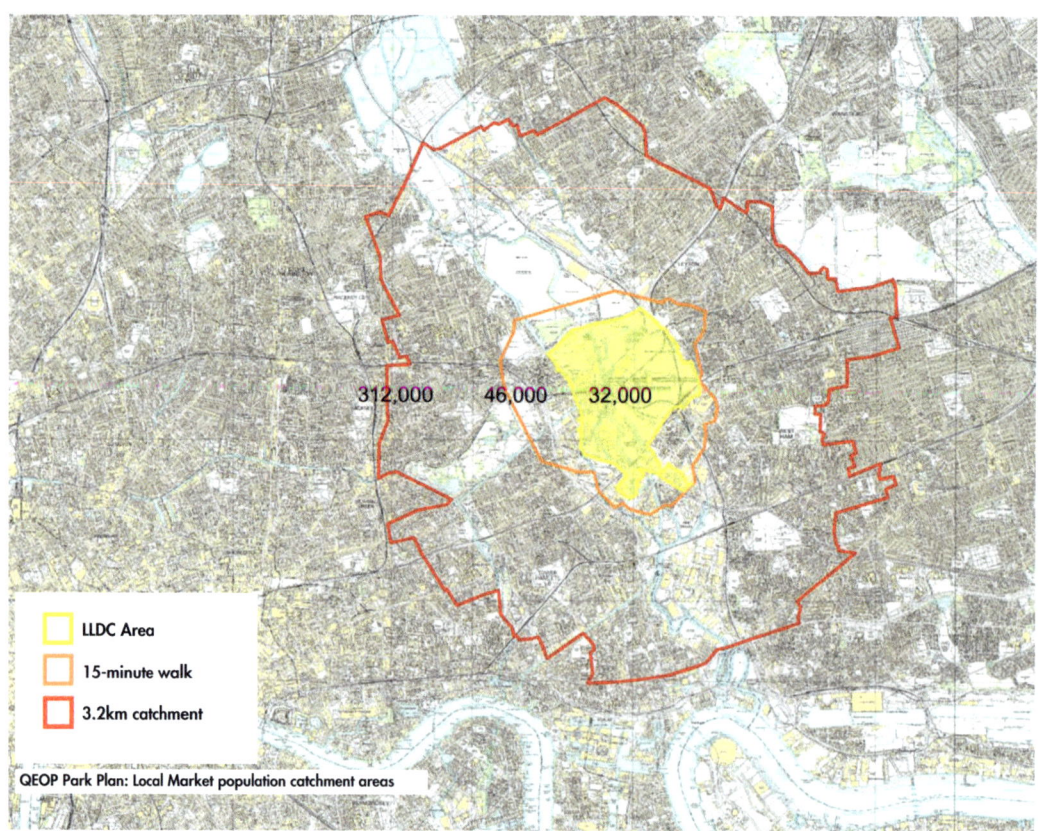

Fig. 6: Map showing the catchment of the Queen Elizabeth Olympic Park in 2016, for a local population of 312,000 people.

As far as East London is concerned, one must consider such large projects as Canary Wharf and the site of 2012 Summer Olympics. Canary Wharf, though heavily criticized when it was being built during the 1990s, has contributed to the creation of 100,000 new jobs in London. What is interesting are the synergies created between the Crossrail line and Canary Wharf, demonstrating how infrastructure and planning can come together. Sites on which nothing happened for years were suddenly developed, with 8,000 new residencies planned, of which 25 percent are affordable. More recently, the Olympic development was a project underpinned by the ambition of integrating a neglected part of the city into London's fabric, both physically and socially. The political language that was used during the planning phase was concerned with the notion of convergence, for which infrastructure would play an important role—fostering equity being a central objective of the undertaking. The master plan has since evolved, encompassing housing as well as sports facilities open to the public, such as a velodrome and Zaha Hadid's swimming pool, which was used by one million people in its first year. Many new bridges and connections have been built. There are parks and cultural institutions, like the Victoria and Albert Museum, the Smithsonian, and others venues coming to the area. Thirty thousand new jobs were created over the last decade. All in all, the economy of East London has changed dramatically. Its five boroughs— also known as the Olympic boroughs,

and considered some of the poorest in London—have significantly improved. Statistics show that the boroughs of Hackney and Newham, which in 2010 were the sixth and fourteenth most deprived areas in the United Kingdom, have now shifted position to the fiftieth and 104th, respectively. This is tangible evidence that infrastructure, not by itself but rather when planned in concurrence with other elements like schools, health, investment in social welfare, and affordable housing, can be a positive force for both growth and social integration.

Image Sources:

Fig. 1: Urban Age/LSE Cities.

Fig. 2: LSE Cities, NEC Paper 03 Accessibility in Cities: Transport and Urban Form (London: London School of Economics and Political Science, 2014).

Fig. 3: Residential density, London; Urban Age/LSE Cities LSECiti.es/u25691340; Residential density, New York City; Urban Age/ LSE Cities LSECiti.es/u159812b4; Residential density, Hong Kong; Urban Age/LSE Cities LSECiti.es/u52351432.

Fig. 4: Source: TfL Planning, Strategic Analysis.

Fig. 5: Urban Age/LSE Cities, Transport and social equity: London, Crossrail; LSECiti.es/ u33181391.

Fig. 6: London Legacy Development Corporation, 2011.

From Railroad to Greenway: Healing the Detroit Beltline

Diane Van Buren

In 1897, a rail spur was built to ease the flow of goods from Detroit's urban factories to regional waterways. Manufacturing boomed and then relocated, trade shifted from rail to road, and the "Beltline" lost its original function. Diane Van Buren explains efforts to use the space of the former rail line for sustainable infrastructure but also as the backbone of a community of disparate groups now brought together by common cause.

The former three-mile beltline rail corridor traverses the radical restructuring of Detroit, and consequently runs through the American economic, industrial, and transportation infrastructure of the twentieth century as well as current attempts to heal the local landscape through sustainable reuse and renewable energy. Physical remnants of the beltline infrastructure retain traces of this history, revealing the rapid rise of Detroit's automobile and manufacturing industries, their eventual decline, and the recent recovery to overcome environmental issues. Contributing to the revival of the area are numerous stakeholders, including business owners, nonprofit organizations, and artists, who have become interconnected through a shared vision of transforming the remnants of a pioneering district through sustainable environmental and economic development. Through the collective efforts and innovation of planning for resiliency and renewable energy, this district is poised to serve as a model for Detroit and other cities struggling to find new uses for aging infrastructure.

Historic Beltline

The Detroit riverfront that once provided access to eighteenth-century French settlers was transformed into shipping wharfs and dry docks by the mid-nineteenth century. Recreational use and public space were new concepts in American cities, and through the influence of Frederick Law Olmsted, a newly formed City parks department designated nearby Belle Isle Park (the country's largest island park) and the Grand Boulevard greenway at the city's edge. The year was 1885, when Detroit's population of just over 200,000 neatly fit within this fifteen square mile boundary; about one tenth of the present-day size of 140 square miles that contains about 700,000 residents. The location of the beltline also owes its origins to this period, as Detroit's expanding industry capitalized on its prime position within the vast Great Lakes shipping trade routes that connected Michigan's rich store of natural resources (lumber, iron ore, silica, and copper) with coal, rubber, and minerals from afar. Rail lines to the river were thus developed as a "belt-line" system connected to larger transport rail lines to the city and beyond. This confluence of raw materials, shipping routes, and capitalist wealth would play a major role in the nascent auto industry that sprang to life in the coming decade.

Constructed in 1897, the beltline sliced a three-mile rail spur that extended from the main trunk line to the Detroit River through a modest neighborhood of workers' housing at the far eastern edge of the growing city. The impact was immediate—housing development gave way to lumber mills, glassworks, and other assorted industries largely required to support the frenzy of growth. A veritable array of entrepreneurship was built along the beltline: Leverenz Lumber, Pfieffer Beer, E. P. Juis Flour Mill, Chas Schuknecht Coal and Wood Yard, John Breitmeyer Florist greenhouses, and Manzelmann Brooms and Brushes reflected late nineteenth-century German immigration to Detroit. Pfieffer Beer stretched over a city block to house beautiful outdoor beer gardens and other late nineteenth century remnants of German social life. Residential-scale businesses and housing gave way to coal storage, gasification plants, and rubber-tire manufacturing, along with the noise of industry and switching yards, although few businesses extended beyond the narrow reach of the beltline and housing filled adjacent streets since it was desirable to live along the Grand Boulevard greenway.

The Influence of the Automobile

At the turn of the twentieth century all standards of transport manufacturing began to rapidly change. The Packard Motor Company at the north end of the beltline became the first large automobile plant in Detroit, giving rise to the career of Detroit architect Albert Kahn.

From 1903 to 1905 Kahn designed a series of buildings that revolutionized factory construction, moving the drudgery of work from dungeon-like to light-filled spaces. Most important to the future of large-scale construction was the tenth addition to the complex, which tested the first use of the Kahn system of reinforced concrete construction, patented by his younger brother Julius, allowing for massive interior space to accommodate the modern assembly line. The innovative Kahn brothers eliminated all the deficiencies of millwork in factory spaces and guaranteed their future as designers for modern plants across the world. (It is worth noting that Kahn's next revolution would occur through his partnership with Henry Ford, in automating this new type of space with the assembly line, which resulted in the return of the drudgery of work.) The sprawling campus of Packard buildings was made possible through the rail network laced within and alongside each of the buildings. Factories were no longer required to be located on the riverbanks. Water lines, sewerage disposal, electricity, worker transportation routes, and shipping were all possible within the boundaries of the beltline.

315

The Columbia and Saxon automobile companies further along the beltline also required multiple blocks for their operations built along the rail lines. The rail was central to these companies, albeit on a smaller scale, along with the belching steel furnaces, engine works, stamping plants, tire companies, and tool and die manufacturers. In its current bucolic condition it's difficult to image the deafening noise, stench, and commotion of this once 24-hour working district. Numerous residential blocks remained at the south end of the district, housing workers in a city struggling to keep up with population growth. Leaping forward to 1922 the district had transformed from a location on the "edge of town" to being central to a city several times its earlier size. The population had nearly quadrupled to 993,678 and by 1930 would encompass 1,568,662 residents within a boundary of 139 square miles, laying claim to the title of fourth-largest city in the United States. The beltline had ballooned to accommodate eleven rail lines and switching yards that serviced delivery of raw materials and shipment of goods from factories.

Along the beltline in 1935, fewer of the early businesses had survived. Both Columbia and Saxon closed as the shift to larger companies forced mergers and collapsed companies that eventually dwindled down to the Big Three—Ford, Chrysler, and General Motors. By the mid-twentieth century, the auto industry that shaped the landscape and social structure of Detroit had evolved. As the Big Three swallowed smaller companies, new freeway systems and trucking replaced the dependence on rail lines, and newer factories in a global economy replaced the early forerunners. Those that could not compete, shut down. The massive forty-acre Packard site was closed in 1958. The beltline rail spur was sold off in 1981 and all but a mile of track was removed and absorbed into the landscape. The shifting economy left miles of vacant land and buildings in its tracks as well as an economic depression from lost employment that continues to this day.

A Sustainable Future

Now in its third century of development, the beltline landscape has retained much of the historic building stock but has seen much of its space revert to fields and vacant lots. The confluence of water transportation, natural resources, and a skilled workforce has been replaced by a new paradigm of need—namely, the same nexus as other disadvantaged communities worldwide: water, food, and energy. New uses for the district have emerged to utilize the historic building stock, and together with the valuable land, formed new land-use patterns to respond to urgent needs in the adjacent declining neighborhoods. Garden programs, food production and distribution, social services, and youth programs have been attracted to the district.

The opportunity to reinvigorate the beltline district through sustainable practices will repair the damage of the twentieth-century and provide solutions to urban challenges of aging infrastructure and shrinking municipal budgets. Current issues of flooding during storms, power outages, blighted and toxic abandoned property, and high unemployment can be addressed through resiliency planning that incorporates the connectivity of renewable energy systems, storm-water reuse through enhanced ecological functions, comprehensive urban design, and building renovations that save energy and create new uses. Several major planning efforts are underway with community participation, rethinking how the linkages of the beltline from the Packard plant to the river now constitute an asset for public use. At the north end of the district, the Beltline Solar Project will convert a blighted parcel of the former Packard plant and the rooftop capacity of several large industrial buildings into a two-to-three-megawatt utility-scale community solar array. The further development of the area as a renewable energy district will combine with a greenway redevelopment of the former beltline for the recapture of rooftop drainage, reducing the high infrastructure costs of storm-water recovery in Detroit. Up to one million gallons of rainwater will be redirected from the wastewater treatment plant and harvested for multiple non-potable and gray-water systems, allowing for entrepreneurial opportunities in landscaping, construction, and manufacturing. Overflow water will be devoted to creating a constructed wetland and soft outlet to the Detroit River. Originating at the river's edge, the recreational Iron Belle trail is planned to follow the former beltline with green infrastructure, bike lanes, and connectivity to the nation's longest bike and hiking trail system.

Social equity and NGO participation in the district is equally critical for its redevelopment into a twenty-first-century environment. Former industrial buildings are occupied by organizations such as the Gleaners Community Food Bank, providing surplus food to hundreds of food pantries in the area, and the Downtown Boxing Gym, offering tutoring and physical-fitness programs for youth. Large-scale food production and community building is a main part of the mission of the Earthworks community garden, and social equity is the core mission of the highly successful Avalon Bakery, whose goal, as the owner proudly states, is to help Detroiters "eat well and do good." Additional newcomers include artists and workshops that find great value in deconstructed materials from Detroit neighborhoods, which they then use to create both whimsical and functional pieces. The Packard plant was once the most progressive auto plant in the world; today plans are underway to redevelop several of the massive structures as artist residences, music studios, and film studios with the backing of global developers.

As Detroit becomes more visible on the sustainability map, its opportunities for new development cannot be limited to the downtown and

museum districts. Former industrial corridors, while left in great disarray from years of abandonment, can serve as a valuable model for economic re-development. This is an approach that utilizes renewable energy and green-way practices for future redevelop-ment, and creates jobs for residents in other aging commercial corridors. Through civic engagement and lea-dership, this model is working in the beltline district.

Views of the transformation of the beltline's infrastructure shot by Elke Eichmann during the mobile workshop as part of the LafargeHolcim Forum in Detroit, April 2016.

Image p. 318: https://whatgoodcrafts. wordpress.com

The Mechanics of Invisibility: On Habit and Routine as Elements of Infrastructure

Paul N. Edwards

Infrastructure is rendered invisible through familiarity. From transit to the toilet, Paul N. Edwards shows how the invisibility of infrastructure also contributes -to the persistence of injustice long after a change in governance through the example of post-Apartheid South Africa.

Infrastructures are often said to be "invisible" or "transparent," in the sense that they typically recede into the background of everyday life. Because mature infrastructures "just work," they almost never enter our consciousness. (When was the last time you thought much about your municipal sewage treatment plant, or the sewers that connect you to it?) When they fail—with consequences ranging from minor inconvenience to national catastrophe—maps, manuals, and how-things-work sites sprout like digital mushrooms on the Internet. Once the crisis passes, we forget them again. The lights come on, the levees hold, the toilet flushes away our waste, and cute animal videos flow freely on the Internet. We go back to living in and on infrastructures we rarely notice.

When you read the preceding paragraph, some of you—most likely from prosperous parts of the Global North—probably nodded to yourselves: "Yes, it happens like that." Others—most likely from the Global South, or poor areas of the North—thought, instead: "Not in my world." For the majority of people, a lot of infrastructure never becomes transparent. Electricity goes on and off randomly, or is only available at specified hours. Water in the pipes (if they exist) isn't reliably clean or free of poisons. Absent a sewer system, human waste can't be flushed away, but only bagged, buried, or left to dry. Internet access is too expensive or completely unavailable, as well as useless for most day-to-day concerns. So the infrastructural transparency that concerns me here is a state of privilege, one that remains nonexistent or merely aspirational for billions of people. Acknowledging this limited perspective, it's still worth asking: Exactly how does infrastructure become transparent to users? What are the mechanics of its invisibility?

Socio-technical Systems and Individual Behavior

Most infrastructures can be characterized as complex, adaptive socio-technical systems, made up of many interacting agents and components. Some of these components are technological: buildings, devices, software, and other artifacts. Others may be social:

organizations, standards, laws, budgets, or political arrangements. Finally, some components are the individuals who contribute to the infrastructure's development and maintenance, or simply make use of it in their daily lives.

Over time and in differing circumstances, relationships among these elements often shift. One typical trajectory reduces the role of individual action (choices, skills, behavior) by replacing it with social mechanisms such as organizations, laws, and standards, and/or technological elements such as sensors and software. Yet it is equally possible, and sometimes desirable, to move in the other direction, replacing social and/or technological mechanisms with individual choice and action.[1]

Consider just one aspect of the automobile-roadway-fuel infrastructure: the speed limit. What socio-technical configurations create and support this limit? Normally, speed limits are set by law, in a process that involves legislatures, traffic engineers, and standards, but there are other aspects as well. The car's top speed is of course restricted by technical characteristics of its drivetrain, but since top speed is typically much higher than the legal speed limit, it's not really a constraint. Airbags and other safety technology can raise the threshold of socially or politically reasonable speeds. The technical characteristics of roadways also play a role. A deeply pitted, wet, muddy dirt road can slow drivers to a crawl, while the radius and banking of a highway curve sets a higher but equally absolute limit. Liability law governing traffic accidents in turn influences the cost of automobile insurance. The latter often rises dramatically if drivers receive multiple speeding tickets, with significant effects on subsequent driver behavior. The speed limit may be enforced by traffic police (human individuals) using radar guns and police cars (technology), backed by the authority of the legal system (social)—but in some jurisdictions, police officers have been partially or entirely replaced by automatic cameras and sophisticated software that photograph speeding cars, read their license numbers, and send out notices of violation, all with virtually no human or organizational participation.

In this example, the effects of different socio-technical configurations on driver behavior are striking. With enforcement by police officers, actual average driving speeds are typically 10 to 30 percent above legal limits, but in countries where automatic traffic cameras are widely deployed, such as France and South Africa, most drivers have adapted to keeping within the legal limit. A traffic-calming technique successfully used in the Netherlands involves removing all traffic controls from intersections, under the logic that lacking stop signs, yield signs, or traffic lights, drivers will pay greater attention to the immediate situation.[2] In the United Kingdom, speed bumps are known as "sleeping policemen," a name that clearly captures how they replace human enforcers with lumps of asphalt. The fact that human drivers rarely follow traffic laws to the letter has recently been underscored by accidents involving Google self-driving cars, which *do* follow laws to the letter—behavior unexpected by human drivers.[3]

Hiding in Plain Sight

One major mechanism of infrastructural transparency is obvious: we deliberately hide it. Wallboard conceals electrical wiring, plumbing, and gas lines. Cellular telephone transceivers peek out from the leaves of fake palm trees. In office buildings, routers, Internet servers, and telephone switches are relegated to closets, while Ethernet cabling snakes unobtrusively through drop ceilings. A lot of infrastructure is literally buried: natural gas lines, sewer systems, subway trains and stations, underground parking garages, stormwater drainage systems, and cables for television, telephone, and electric power.

A second way that infrastructures become invisible is through the perceptual mechanism of *habituation*. Human attention naturally focuses on what changes, rather than what remains constant, in any situation. Whether natural or human-made, elements of the environment that remain stable tend to disappear from our awareness. You notice the refrigerator's hum when it starts up, but after a few seconds it fades entirely from your consciousness—until it stops and you briefly notice it again.

Infrastructure also becomes transparent in another, less obvious way: it becomes embedded in the *habits and skills* of individuals. In a process I sometimes facetiously call "infrastructuration" (punning on Giddens's notion of "structuration"), infrastructure both shapes and is recreated by the continual performances or rehearsals of agents.[4] In addition to their skill in piloting their own cars and reacting appropriately to traffic signals and signs, drivers' reactions become finely attuned to minute signals from other vehicles that express the driver's state of mind: hesitation, drunken or distracted weaving, timidity, aggressiveness. Experienced motorists can drive safely while conducting complex conversations or listening to music, traveling for long periods with little or no conscious awareness of what they are doing. These habits and skills, acquired through frequent and ongoing practice, play vital roles in the smooth functioning of virtually all infrastructures.[5] At the same time, they shape the infrastructure itself, governing, for example, what counts as a safe speed, and other norms of driving.

Encounters with unfamiliar versions of infrastructure are part of what makes foreign travel both so interesting and so exhausting. Deeply entrenched habits must be deliberately, and with effort, suppressed in favor of (first) slow, cautious, conscious decision-making and (later, as they become ingrained) new habits.[6] Take driving on the "other" side of the road (whichever that may be for you). I lived in South Africa in 2003 and 2004, driving on the left-hand side (the opposite of my native American pattern). By the time I left, it had become so habitual that when I watched an American film, my right foot would press involuntarily on an imaginary brake when somebody sped off in the right-hand lane. Everybody who's made this transition knows that the most dangerous moments lie not in the new situation, whose strangeness makes you nervous and alert. Instead, it's returning to your old situation, where you relax too quickly, expecting your old reflexes to return.

The social analogues of individual habits and skills are *social norms* and *organizational routines.*[7] These, too, are ways of black-boxing action patterns that may once have been deliberately chosen or designed. Norms and routines reduce the burden of decision-making and limit uncertainty in interactions by providing ready-made scripts. In the case of infrastructure, they do more than this; they become, in a sense, *components* of infrastructure, elements of its function on which users, maintainers, and builders can all tacitly rely. An intriguing example of this is how the habit of left- or right-lane driving carries over into other contexts, becoming a social norm in informal rights-of-way as well. If you're descending a staircase and meet someone coming up, which way do you move? In the United States it's to the right, but in South Africa, the United Kingdom, or Australia, it's to the left. You get in your lane, as it were. The same goes for sidewalks, unmarked parking lots, queues, and virtually any other public space. This quasi-automatic behavior is a manifestation of an infrastructural standard that exists as law on the road, but equally as social norm and individual habit in other rights-of-way.

Another simple example is the standard placement of light switches. In American buildings, these are usually at approximately the elbow height of an average man. An architect friend of mine designed several of his own houses with light switches placed, instead, about sixteen inches lower. When I asked him why, he replied: "Because that's where your hand is." Fair enough—but because most buildings use the elbow-height standard, when I spent a few weeks in two of his houses, I found myself constantly fumbling for the switches in the wrong place. The standard height, by contrast, permits the habit of flicking the switch to transfer among most buildings—functioning effectively as a component of the infrastructure's operation and a mechanism of its transparency.

Apartheid as Infrastructure

South Africa, where I lived with my family for thirteen months from, provides a striking illustration of how the mechanics of invisibility aid in the persistence of social norms, laws, and standards. During the apartheid era (1948–1994), South Africa's central government was controlled by a white minority determined to subordinate and control the people of color on whose criminally inexpensive labor it mainly relied. Supported by the vast wealth of its white-owned mining industry, that government grew powerful in large part by building new infrastructures. Apartheid ideology promoted "separate development" paths for the various races and ethnic groups, so major infrastructures were built or improved chiefly to benefit the white population. In white-run cities and towns, government departments and government-owned "parastatal" corporations constructed superhighways, railroad lines, water supply systems, electric power grids, a telephone system, television networks, and all the other apparatuses of developed societies. These projects helped apartheid leaders to construct an image of South Africa as part of "the West," holding the line against African communist insurgencies as a key Cold War partner of the United States and the United Kingdom.[8] Meanwhile, black townships and rural areas, especially the so-called homelands, fell far behind—not only because the government invested far less money in those areas, but also because it chose much lower quality standards and focused on different things: housing, schools, and health services, rather than transportation, electrification, and communication.

"Separate development" meant different yet intricately interconnected and overlapping infrastructures for blacks and whites. As in the segregated American South, laws required separate public facilities for blacks and whites, including bathrooms, waiting areas, railway cars, and buses. In other words, the architectural principles of virtually all South African infrastructure were technopolitical:[9] just as in the segregated American South,

many infrastructures were deliberately designed to enforce, perpetuate, and strengthen the separation of racial groups. Yet these infrastructures also had to facilitate the massive daily movement of black labor into (and out of) white spaces.

The inherent contradiction between these two aims often forced secondary elaborations of infrastructure. In the 1960s, blacks living close to Johannesburg were forcibly resettled in the South Western Townships (known today as Soweto), about fifteen kilometers from the city center. Public buses and a railway line provided commuter transport to inner-city workplaces. (In the late 1960s, with the advent of "bullet trains" in Japan, apartheid planners fantasized about moving black workers to "homelands" hundreds of kilometers from the city, linked to white urban areas by high-speed commuter rail. Planning went quite far before the South African railway services nixed the idea on the basis of cost and practicality.) The inadequate speed and capacity of "their" transport system forced Soweto-based workers to spend up to five or six hours commuting each day. Walking the fifteen kilometers (over nine miles) to work was often the fastest way to get there. Meanwhile, whites-only buses and train cars often rode empty.

Demolishing apartheid's politico-legal context was easy and fast compared with eliminating these infrastructural forms of segregation. To this day, city neighborhoods and townships remain strongly identified with particular racial groups. Though a few white people have moved into areas like Soweto, for the most part whites regard black areas as too dangerous to enter. The irony, of course, is that millions of black people enter white areas on a daily basis—just as they did under apartheid—to service their homes and gardens, care for their children, and staff their businesses.

Fig. 1: Rubbish piles up next to chemical toilets in the township of Dunoon in Cape Town during April 2009 as a row over who will get jobs in a new Cape Town waste removal tender remains unresolved.

Public Transportation

South Africa's public transport systems, too, remain racially coded. When the influx control laws preventing blacks from living in white areas were abolished in 1985, poor black people poured into the major cities. Existing public transport couldn't handle the load. Bowing to pressure, the government deregulated taxi services in 1987, and hundreds of black operators began acquiring fifteen-seat minibus-

es. The "kombi taxi" or minibus taxi industry rapidly mushroomed into the country's single largest black-owned business sector, with revenues of R39.8 billion (about $3.7 billion) on an estimated 250,000 vehicles by 2014. It plays a huge role in the lives of urban poor people, not only by providing transport but through knock-on economic opportunities, such as vehicle maintenance services and the street markets that spring up around taxi ranks (pickup points). The minibus taxi system operates in parallel with much more expensive radio taxis (cars) of the type more familiar to Americans or Europeans; most of the faces emerging from these vehicles are white.

The kombi taxis are typically Toyota vans with three or four bench seats. They are designed for a maximum of fifteen passengers, but it is not uncommon to see twenty or more people crammed into a single vehicle. These vehicles account for some 65 percent of all passenger travel in South Africa—yet it is rare to see a white face inside one. The system extends to most of the country, not only within cities but even on long-haul intercity routes such as Johannesburg to Cape Town (about 1,400 km). In rural areas, there is a similar system of "bakkie taxis" (pickup trucks) for travel on dirt roads too rough for the minibus suspensions.

Driving in Johannesburg one morning with my radio tuned to a popular talk show, I listened in disbelief as an outraged white caller railed against South Africa's supposed lack of good public transport. The well-meaning caller expressed, unknowingly, the habitual racial division surrounding transportation. It is true that the minibus taxis are privately owned, and they do have limits; few minibus taxis, for example, operate after around 7:00 p.m. Furthermore, they can be dangerous, and not only because of overloading and risky driving. Territorial "taxi wars" over access to passenger loading zones extend to gunfights and murders; while we were there, taxi drivers fought half a dozen pitched battles in various parts of Durban, sometimes in the midst of crowded commute-hour taxi ranks. To stem the violence, the government has engaged in efforts to regain regulatory control[10], as well as to "recapitalize" the aging and increasingly dangerous taxi fleet. Though initiated in 1999, these efforts still have not fully succeeded in their goal of bringing the minibus taxi system into the formal economy as a mainline public transport service.[11]

Still, they operate more cheaply and efficiently than many American or European public transit systems. The minibuses nearly always travel filled to capacity (or beyond). In 2004, the city of Johannesburg, its roadways choked by rush-hour traffic, began debating construction of new subway and rail lines. Yet if all the commuters in their private cars would hop into minibus taxis instead, Joburg wouldn't need them. Like infrastructure planners everywhere, those in South Africa thus find that their greatest challenges involve unseating entrenched habits and norms.

The Apartheid Toilet

The physical architecture of apartheid extended into private spaces as well as public infrastructure. Separate, outdoor bathrooms for nonwhite domestic workers were a typical feature of housing built for well-to-do whites throughout the period. When we lived in Durban in 2003–4, our house had one of these, in a filthy spot behind the garage, next to the garbage cans.

Fig. 2: The City of Cape Town's installation of toilets without enclosures in the area of Makhaza, Khayelitsha, as part of service delivery, stirred violent protests in May 2010 over issues of dignity following the African National Congress Youth League's complaints to the South African Human Rights Commission. The City claimed residents agreed more toilets could be provided with the available budget if they took on the responsibility of completing their own structures around the toilets.

It was a flush toilet without a seat, with a shower directly in front of it, so that you would be staring into the toilet bowl while showering. It had no roof or any other enclosure, though some minimal privacy was provided by its position between the garage and the wall of the compound. When I first discovered this a few weeks after arriving, I thought it was abandoned. We were astonished to learn that our housekeeper Henrietta had been using it throughout the sixteen years she had worked in that building under various owners. Henrietta was equally shocked when we asked her to please use the bathroom inside. Old habits die hard; it took her a few weeks to take us at our word.

Fig. 3: An informal settlement resident uses the water tap outside toilets which are locked by certain residents. Calls for the ward councillor to resolve the situation have been ignored.

We soon learned that this expectation was still widely accepted. At an expensive B&B in trendy Melville, near Johannesburg, the white owner—a well-known journalist, now deceased—constantly and ostentatiously dropped what South Africans would call her "struggle credentials," such as a prom-

inently placed picture of herself with Nelson Mandela. She herself used the indoor toilet near the sitting room. Yet her black staff were required to use the apartheid-era outdoor toilet. She gruffly ordered our black nanny—for whom we had rented a room, at full price, for a week—to use that toilet as well, though it was wintertime and quite cold. Separate facilities like these cannot enforce racial segregation by themselves, but *combined with deeply ingrained habits and norms,* they helped it to persist.

Toilet Wars

In 2009, Cape Town erected modern porcelain flush toilets in Makhaza, an informal settlement in the larger Khayelitsha suburb that houses some 400,000 mostly black South Africans (primarily of the Xhosa ethnicity). Prior to that, residents of Makhaza had employed the so-called flying toilet or bucket system: defecating or urinating into plastic bags or buckets, then hurling the waste into a nearby wetland. The flush toilets were a huge improvement, except for one thing: some fifty of them remained completely unenclosed, sitting on concrete pads right out in the open.

The backstory of this bizarre situation is complicated. In Makhaza, the Cape Town government had installed one toilet per family, an upgrade from the national standard of one toilet for every five families in informal settlements. In return, the council expected residents to build their own enclosures for these toilets, in a kind of cost-sharing arrangement. Most agreed, and residents did in fact build enclosures for 1,265 of the 1,316 toilets installed. However, some citizens of Makhaza claimed they could not afford to pay for the enclosures. A long, complex, mostly local political battle ensued, widely known as the "Cape Town toilet wars." Its details need not concern us here; the upshot was that for several years, Makhaza had about fifty modern flush toilets without enclosures. To maintain some shred of dignity, residents covered themselves with blankets while sitting on the exposed toilets.

Here, my point is simply to emphasize how much infrastructure incorporates and depends on habits and norms. As Steve Robins has pointed out[12], published photos of the "anti-dignity toilets" in Makhaza struck a nerve, outraging many residents—*despite the fact that for many years previously, open defecation and urination had been the habit and norm in exactly the same area.* The stark imagery of the exposed white porcelain toilet beside a residential street, in a crowded neighborhood with people walking by, had an almost pornographic character. Literally stripped of its normal enclosure, the naked toilet effectively revealed the norm of open defecation, forcing residents to do it even more publicly than before. This transformed the norm from invisible necessity to visible obscenity, insulting the dignity of people who understood that flush toilets and sewers are not merely waste-disposal technology, but part of a socio-technical package *that includes more stringent norms of privacy.*

In the South African context, the naked toilet stood as a symbol of ongoing inequality and incomplete infrastructure: graffiti posted nearby read: "Give us houses, not toilets." Robins and others interpret this to mean that residents wanted houses with their own indoor toilets, rather than out-houses, even ones with flush toilets.

Fig. 4: Children from the Sweet Home informal settlement drag a portable toilet onto Lansdowne Road before setting fire to it in protest against their ward councillor who they say has done nothing to improve their living conditions.

It may also have conjured up, for some, images of the outdoor apartheid toilets in white-owned houses, as described above (though in many cases, even those offered more privacy than the ones in Makhaza).

Conclusion

The infrastructures built under apartheid persist, in part, because people keep on doing what they have always done. Of course, this is not particular to South Africa; it's everywhere. Having lived for long periods of time in foreign countries with customs very different from what I am used to, I've seen new habits entrench themselves in my own life. Watching this process closely has helped me understand (among other things) why and how racial segregation can persist *de facto* when it is no longer *de jure*.

We conceal infrastructure physically when we can, but it becomes invisible in other ways as well. One of those is through the acquisition of habits, skills, and social norms. These should be seen as vital components of infrastructure—they help explain how infrastructures work and why they endure. And habits, as we all know, die hard.

1. Paul N. Edwards, Steven J. Jackson, Geoffrey C. Bowker, and Cory P. Knobel, *Understanding Infrastructure: Dynamics, Tensions, and Design* (Ann Arbor, MI: Deep Blue, 2007).
2. Gary Toth, "Where the Sidewalk Doesn't End: What Shared Space Has to Share," *Project for Public Spaces*, 2009, http://www.pps.org/reference/shared-space/.
3. Matt Richtel and Connor Dougherty, "Google's Driverless Cars Run into Problem: Cars with Drivers," *New York Times*, September 2, 2015.
4. Anthony Giddens, *The Constitution of Society* (Washington, DC: Spectrum Educational Enterprises, 1984).
5. K. Nelson and R. R. Nelson, "On the Nature and Evolution of Human Know-How," *Research Policy* 31 (2002): 719–33.
6. Hubert Dreyfus, Stuart E. Dreyfus, and Tom Athanasiou, *Mind over Machine: The Power of Human Intuition and Expertise in the Era of the Computer* (New York: Free Press, 2000); Stuart E. Dreyfus, and Hubert L. Dreyfus, *A Five-Stage Model of the Mental Activities Involved in Directed Skill Acquisition* (Berkeley: Operations Research Center, University of California, 1980).
7. Richard R. Nelson and Sidney G. Winter, *An Evolutionary Theory of Economic Change* (Cambridge, MA: Harvard University Press, 1982).
8. Paul N. Edwards and Gabrielle Hecht, "History and the Technopolitics of Identity: The Case of Apartheid South Africa," *Journal of Southern African Studies* 36, no. 3 (2010): 619–39.
9. Gabrielle Hecht, *The Radiance of France: Nuclear Power and National Identity after World War II* (Cambridge, MA: MIT Press, 1998).
10. Stewart Joy, "The Kombi-Taxi in South African Cities," *Fourth International Conference on Competition and Ownership in Land Passenger Transport* (1995): 268–76.
11. Consultancy African Intelligence, "The Minibus Taxi Industry in South Africa: A Servant for the Urban Poor?," *Polity.org.za*, 2013, http://www.polity.org.za/article/the-minibus-taxi-industry-in-south-africa-a-servant-for-the-urban-poor-2013-05-06
12. Steven Robins, "The 2011 Toilet Wars in South Africa: Justice and Transition between the Exceptional and the Everyday after Apartheid," *Development and Change* 45, no. 3 (2014): 479–501.

Transformative Capacity of Resilience: Learning from Rebuild by Design

Henk Ovink

In 2012, Rebuild by Design was inaugurated as a new kind of design competition, aiming to combine public-private collaboration whilst setting a new standard for resilient development. Its developer, Henk Ovink, explains the approach behind the initiative, part of President Obama's Hurricane Sandy Rebuilding Task Force, and identifies six key lessons that can be learnt from the project.

Contemporary Context

The annual Global Risks Perception Survey released by the World Economic Forum (WEF) repeatedly proves the increase in frequency and impact of environmental risks such as climate change, water crises, biodiversity loss, ecosystem collapse, extreme weather events, and natural and man-made catastrophes. At the same time, these risks demonstrate a clear and strong interdependency on the regional and metropolitan scale. While this larger scale may multiply these risks' complexity and impact, this is also the scale at which we humans can best adapt to and mitigate these risks. This is the scale at which we can—and must—act.

The 2015 WEF report, presented in Davos in January 2016, put the impact of water crises as the number-one global risk facing humanity over the next decade. Water is global connector: Two billion people will be devastated by 2050[1]—four billion in 2080[2]—if we continue with our current practices of water mismanagement on all scales, over-extraction and pollution. Of all the disasters that occur worldwide, 90 percent are water related.[3] Added to this is the fact that 50 percent of the earth's aquifers—nature's own groundwater storage capacity—are now beyond the tipping point, meaning that a natural recovery has become impossible. Global urbanization may provide us with growth, prosperity, emancipation, and development opportunities, but climate change, rising sea levels, and the increasing impact these risks carry puts huge pressure on our cities, societies, and citizens. If we don't act, the economic, social, and environmental system this all hinges upon will collapse, leaving us as victims of our own failure to seize a last window of opportunity.

Water is at the heart of this uncertain future. It is through water that we feel the impact of climate change most forcefully.[4] Water is essential for our economy and our social and cultural well-being. Water quality defines our economic prosperity and, in turn, water provision determines the level of vulnerability for our societies: it is key for agriculture, food, and energy production, as well as for facilitating the much-needed transition to cleaner energy. Water is also an urban matter—an asset if managed right, a severe risk if not. With 75 percent of the global population set to live in urban environments in 2050, lives and assets in cities will be most in danger if not developed in accordance with a sustainable and resilient approach. The combined value of the assets of the ten places deemed to be most at risk in 2050 already totals more than $1.7 trillion; Miami, Florida, tops the list, with a total of $278 billion worth of assets at risk.[5]

While urbanization has an emancipatory capacity—facilitating gender equality and education—the collective water challenge puts these urbanizing places at higher risk. Water connects economy and ecology. We can best adapt and mitigate the risks associated with water at the regional scale, thus strengthening our cities and communities worldwide. But this means that we have to not only change our approach, we must also increase our approach's comprehensive resilience capacity.

Hurricane Sandy

In the fall of 2012, Hurricane Sandy made landfall in the northeast of the United States, the nation's biggest metropolitan region and a great global economic force. The storm claimed more than 150 lives and destroyed or damaged more than 650,000 homes, along with hundreds of thousands of businesses, across 24 states. More than 8.5 million people lost power and heat, some for months, and many lost their jobs as well.

Fig. 1: Hurricane Sandy made landfall in the northeast of the United States in October, 2012.

Overall, Hurricane Sandy cost an estimated $65.7 billion in damages and economic loss. Moreover, it revealed the physical and social vulnerabilities of coastal cities, which all face the threat of extreme weather events that continue to be exacerbated by climate change. Sandy also showed how physical challenges are interwoven with social and cultural needs. The socially vulnerable live in the most at-risk places, and, as a result, were the hardest hit by the storm's devastation, and fully dependent on others to get back on their feet. Sandy exposed the man-made social and environmental disaster we are actively provoking. For the Obama administration, it was clear from the outset that just repairing the damage was not the way to go; to prepare the region for future uncertainties, all of its vulnerabilities needed addressing, using the impact of the hurricane to leapfrog toward a state of resilience. On this premise, I developed Rebuild by Design, an inclusive and collaborative process for President Obama's Hurricane Sandy Rebuilding Task Force. Rebuild by Design encompassed all levels of government, stakeholders, and residents working together in a scheme that was one part policy process, one part rebuilding program, and one part design competition. Its goal was to ignite innovation for a new standard of regional resilience in design and development, both for building and rebuilding, while positioned to respond to issues of climate change, rising sea levels, and other future economic, environmental, and cultural demands.

Fig. 2: One of the Rebuild by Design community workshops, hosted by the BIG Team.

Rebuild by Design

With Rebuild by Design, a large and inspired coalition of stakeholders was formed with the aim of setting a new standard for resilient development. The competition challenged interdisciplinary design teams to create innovative, implementable solutions for regional resilience. The process was unlike any design competition seen before. Ten teams of architects, urbanists, engineers, scientists, and activists from all over the world were selected from a total of 148 submissions. The teams engaged with more than 500 community organizations, held dozens of public workshops, toured hundreds of cities and neighborhoods, and met with almost 200 government agencies. The federal government examined 41 potential design opportunities and ten final proposals, and awarded $930 million to state and local governments for the implementation of the six winning designs.

This process of interaction, research by design, and regional collaboration across disciplines delivered the first true understanding of the region's complexity in terms of its vulnerabilities and interdependencies. It provided insights in the region's capabilities and future opportunities for viable responses. Global expertise was matched with regional and local expertise through innovative funding and a process that started with questions and research that would then lead to solutions. Supported by cross-governmental coalitions, partners like New York University's Institute for Public Knowledge, the Regional Plan Association, the Van Alen Institute, and the Municipal Art Society of New York, as well as a group of dedicated funders such as the Rockefeller Foundation and the JPB Foundation, Rebuild by Design became more than a program: it evolved into a movement for resilience, dedicated to changing the prevailing cultural currents.

Learning from Rebuild by Design

The Organisation for Economic Co-operation and Development (OECD) embraced Rebuild by Design as an inspiration for public-private partnership, while the United Nations presented it as an exemplifying "institutional arrangements for national adaptation planning and implementation in the context of climate change." Yet Rebuild by Design is by no means a blueprint for a global approach, it is rather an inspiration for a shared global ambition for resilience. In encountering future risks and their impacts and uncertainties, we must learn about their interdependencies and the opportunities worldwide to mitigate and adapt to these risks. In this way, vulnerable regions are provided for, together with global sustainable development as a whole. Six interconnected and interdependent aspects of Rebuild by Design stand out:

1. Long-term planning coupled with short-term innovative projects

We have to take the time to better understand the risks and uncertainties of our future challenges along with our strengths in responding to them. Comprehensive regional research is necessary to understand the complexity of the issues at stake, their interdependencies, and the risks on the ground. Long-term planning is vital for defining the right response and ways forward to deal with this level of complexity. But long-term strategies need to be coupled with short-term

innovative interventions. These are the kind of projects that will produce a ripple effect, inspiring responses and follow-ups. It is through replication and up-scaling that their values are spread and have an impact across the world. This connection between planning and projects is critical to engender a strong and resilient approach; without one, the other fails. Plans are left on the shelf, while projects are rendered as mere incidents.

2. Public-private funding

Public-private partnerships, built on trust and mutual gains, need to be embedded in a process of transparency and accountability. Only then we can get to new ways of financing, matching public and private sources of funding. For this we need better benefit-cost analyses (BCAs), and improved processes for monitoring and evaluation. The necessary comprehensive, long-term approaches must be addressed through evaluations and analyses in such a way to promote transparency and attract donors—both public and private. At present, BCAs lack the capacity to capture comprehensive long-term integrated resilience approaches. Monitoring ensures that all partners can guide the process and their own contributions, stepping in when needed. Evaluations, if done right and positioned to effect political change, enable the loop-back to existing structures, resolving institutional mismatches and increasing capacity as well as bringing improvements that pave the way for resilience.

3. Coalition building and inclusive collaboration

Rebuild by Design was grounded in the understanding that real change is *cultural* change, the kind of change that begins in the "hearts and minds" of the people of the region. For this reason, Rebuild by Design began the outreach process by matching global expertise with expertise at the local level. This resulted in a cross-cutting collaborative process engaging over 500 organizations across the region, plus thousands of people from government, academia, business, and communities; investors, activists, and more. Aiming to bring about cultural change in an innovative manner, the process was an open one built on trust, inclusiveness, and participation.

Fig. 3: The BIG U: a project proposal by the BIG Team, combines protection and social infrastructure for 10 miles of coastline that encompasses the waterfront of lower Manhattan.

4. Building institutional capacity

A comprehensive approach like that taken by Rebuild by Design demands a critical level of institutional capacity, establishing a coalition among public and private stakeholders that ensures accountability and transparency. This approach has to be sustainable. Building this up from the start is key for successful development and transformation at both the local and regional levels. At the same time, strengthened institutional capacity is the inevitable result of such a process. Rebuild by Design built this capacity across all layers of government as well as within community organizations, support groups, and institutions like the Regional Plan Association, NYU, and the Municipal Art Society.

Fig. 4: New Meadowlands, a project proposal by MIT ZUS Urbanisten, a large nature reserve that doubles as flood protection infrastructure.

5. Programmatic approach

The initiative's programmatic approach acts as an engine that ensures a lasting connection between short- or medium-term interventions and the wider, comprehensive, and long-term regional strategy. The engine joins the kind of decision-making that transcends political cycles with the implementation of the projects. In the process, it facilities accountability and transparency with clear BCAs, plus instruments for monitoring and evaluation that create, again, an enabling environment for (new) public-private partnerships to emerge. This programmatic approach demands and assembles a critical level of institutional capacity.

6. Design

Finally, design brings ambition, quality, and the complexity of thinking required for this approach. Design has the power to identify opportunities and transform them into innovative examples. Design can connect regional interdependencies with local needs, connecting people and places, making visions tactile, making ambitions practical. Design is key for showing clearly and comprehensively the added value of investments across sectors and scales and over a period of time. Design is essential for collaborative and inclusive processes, building the alliances needed for critical change. It accomplishes this not through a trade-off of interests, but by bridging gaps, such as those between quality and safety, between local needs and political capacity, between regional interdependencies and community assets, between economy, society, and the environment. Design in that sense is both the "cultural" process as well as the "economic" outcome.

Context and Conditions

Rebuild by Design is a great example of how it all came together: long-term planning and short-term projects, public-private funding, and capacity building among all partners in an inclusive collaboration. But we should not forget the context and conditions that made this possible. Hurricane Sandy, as any disaster, was like a magnifying glass: it brought to the surface and enhanced the region's vulnerabilities and interdependencies as well as its physical, social, and political strengths. In its aftermath, President Obama installed the Hurricane Sandy Rebuilding Task Force, which consisted of the heads of more than twenty federal departments, agencies, and offices, and was spearheaded by then Secretary of Housing and Urban Development Shaun Donovan. The agencies would not only work closely together with each other, but also with regional, local, and tribal governments, the private sector, communities, and businesses. And although Rebuild by Design would not have been possible without the context of Sandy, it was only recognized as a catalyst for change by the task force *after* coalitions were formed, *after* private philanthropy had stepped in, *after* the first hurdles had been overcome. Rebuild by Design had to define and then guard its position on the edges of government, philanthropy, and the inhabitants of the region. This balancing act was exactly what was needed to build trust among stakeholders while ensuring independence and ambition played a part in catalyzing transformative approaches.

Fig. 5: A project proposal by the SCAPE Team, Living Breakwaters is a piece of living infrastructure in which a necklace of breakwaters serve as protective buffers for coastal neighborhoods while providing a more biodiverse habitat for the region's water-based wildlife.

This was the particular political and institutional context in which Rebuild by Design was devised. Since such contexts always differ, Rebuild by Design cannot be replicated as a direct blueprint. However, its model can be regarded as an inspiration for other situations across the world, demonstrating that one always needs to know and understand the context to develop the right approach, and in doing so embed the process in the local culture and politics.

Conclusion

Rebuild by Design revealed that successful impact is all about process, one that allows global expertise to be connected with what is already present, locally, at the places at risk.

Regional and comprehensive research for better understanding is a necessity when it comes to defining these kinds of responses. This understanding can only be developed by a strong coalition of committed partners, which encompasses actors from a range of backgrounds with the best professional skills as well as specific regional ties and personal convictions. Instead of looking for immediate answers to local problems, it is about looking for the right *questions* as they apply to the region.

The protracted effects of climate change have in turn prompted a slow approach in responding to the challenges it presents. Furthermore, this approach has been focused on response, as opposed to preparedness. But here we have a choice to make: either to proceed according to slowness and incrementalism or to leapfrog into taking transformative action. We have to acknowledge that complexity needs to be embraced, which leads to an appreciation of the fact that design, research, and collaboration go hand in hand with politics, policy development, and investment strategies. This enables an approach with the capacity to impact and transform, where better science, research, and data will find solid ground. This is an approach where innovation and implementation go hand in hand with collaborations across all sectors, all layers of government, all stakeholders, from activists and vulnerable communities to private and public institutions. What is necessitated is a cultural change when it comes to governance, or, in other words, inclusive and innovative collaboration. Too good to be true? No, this can be done—as Rebuild by Design ably demonstrates, we've already begun to make this a reality.

1. World Water Assessment Programme, *The United Nations World Water Development Report 4: Managing Water under Uncertainty and Risk* (Paris: UNESCO, 2012).
2. United Nations Development Programme, *Human Development Report 2007/2008* (New York: Palgrave Macmillan, 2007), http://hdr.undp.org/sites/default/files/reports/268/hdr_20072008_en_complete.pdf
3. World Water Assessment Programme, *The United Nations World Water Development Report 4: Managing Water under Uncertainty and Risk.* (Paris: UNESCO, 2012).
4. Ibid.
5. Stephane Hallegatte, Colin Green, Robert J. Nicholls, and Jan Corfee-Morlotm "Future flood losses in major coastal cities," *Nature Climate Change* 3 (Nature Publishing Group: 2013).
6. Adaptation Committee, *Institutional Arrangements for National Adaptation Planning and Implementation* (UNFCCC, 2015), https://unfccc.int/files/adaptation/application/pdf/ adaption_commitee_publication_-_web_high.pdf

Designing the Coast in the Moment of Rain

Anuradha Mathur and Dilip da Cunha

What are the implications for infrastructure if "the coast" is considered not as a fixed point on a map but rather—as it is in reality— as something movable, ever shifting and changing? What if designers cast anchor in another moment of the water cycle, such as precipitation? Anuradha Mathur and Dilip da Cunha explore such an approach, with reference to the Bengal Delta of South Asia and Chesapeake Bay, Virginia.

Challenging the Moment of Flows

A delta and an estuary are two ways by which rivers meet the sea. In deltas, rivers dominate the sea, depositing sediment and, in the process, extending land. The conditions are such that upon meeting the sea, the river slows down, dropping its load of sediment, dividing and spreading, and in the process constructing ground in the form of the Greek letter Δ. The layers of silt upon silt conceal a past, which makes it not surprising that some have attributed the term delta to Herodotus, the "father of history." This keen observer of the ancient world writes about seeing the Nile's sediment over "a day's journey" at sea, an observation that led him to conclude that Egypt was once a gulf and that the river, over thousands of years, made it land. Egypt, he famously writes, is the gift of the river.

An estuary, in contrast, does not layer as dramatic a history as the delta, perhaps because it allows the sea, with its affinity for erasure, to have more of a say. Indeed, some choose to define an estuary as a body of water through which rivers enter the sea, in comparison to a delta, a landmass of alluvium made by a roving, dividing, and extending river. Certainly, estuaries allow the sea to come inland, its tides operating a scale of salinity that varies diurnally, at times exceptionally, with storms and sea surges on one side and the river on the other. A number of beings reside in this dynamic transition, adapted to or perhaps naturally tuned to accommodating its variabilities, or at least a range of them.

This difference between a delta and an estuary, however, is articulated in a particular moment when a river, defined as "flowing water in a channel with defined banks," can be assumed to exist.[1] What if the chosen moment is in rain when water is everywhere rather than somewhere, when the banks of channels are blurred, even erased, when there is no clear directionality of water by which to call out a flow? Here, rain does more than challenge a difference in the way rivers meet the sea; it says that rivers are products of choice in the extended presence of water, popularly known as the hydrologic, or water, cycle. This cycle, which some call an "infinite river" because its water keeps circulating, is described in distinct moments.[2] The artist Paul Klee called out four—precipitation from clouds to earth, flow formation from earth to sea, evaporation from sea to air, and cloud formation from sea to land.

days; but in others it can take months, years, millennia, even millions of years to go the course."[4] The diagram of the water cycle that they draw is consequently more complex, with cycles within cycles.

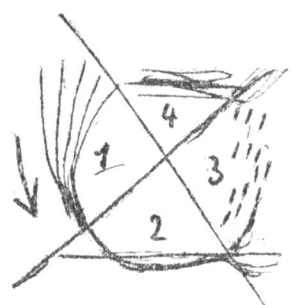

Fig. 1: Paul Klee, "The Water Cycle" (source: Wittenborn Inc., 1964).

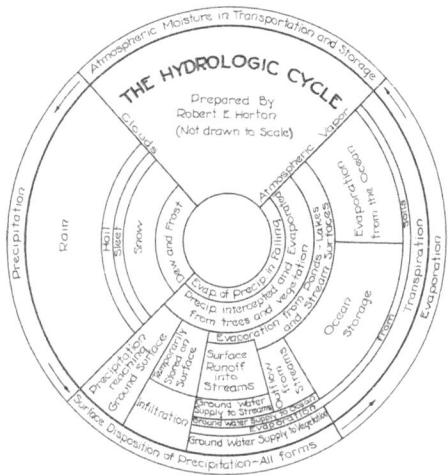

Fig. 2: Robert E. Horton, "The Hydrologic Cycle" (source: Horton, 1931).

Hydrologists, of course, count many more. The water cycle, writes Robert Horton, can begin anywhere, anytime, in an "isolated tree, even a single leaf or twig of a growing plant, the roof of a building, the drainage-basin of a river-system or any of its tributaries, an undrained glacial depression, a swamp, a glacier, a polar ice-cap, a group of sand dunes, a desert playa, a lake, an ocean, or the Earth as a whole."[3] It can also flow in many ways. "We speak of the water cycle as if there were only one," notes Robert Kandel, "but in fact there are many: some circuits are completed in a few

Irrespective of its complexities, however, drawings of the water cycle show rivers as a presence in one moment of the cycle. In Klee's drawing, this moment is the second quadrant, when water can be assumed to have a place on the earth's surface and *not* when it is precipitating, evaporating, soaking the earth with moisture and wetness, saturating the air with mist, clouds, and humidity, circulating in living beings, generally being in unseen places and taking forms that cannot be easily demarcated. Indeed rivers, together with other "water bodies" such as seas and lakes, not only come with a particular choice of moment; they also come with a line that is granted the ability to separate water from land and keep water in place. In the case of rivers, the line is granted the added ability to calibrate a flow of water from a point source to a destination, or at least from an earlier place to a later place. On the ground, this line takes the form of a riverbank; on maps, it is familiar as a geometric line.

not only is water kept to a certain place and maps drawn, but properties are de-marcated, histories are written, places are described, and the future is envisioned. Arguably, this moment has inspired the very ideas of property, history, and place. In other words, the world has cast anchor in the moment of flow formation, making it the time of reality while turning other moments of the water cycle into moments of ephemerality. Thus, rain, mist, snow, etc., are visitors in places where the river is resident. It is not surprising, then, that rivers are taken to be natural entities. Ecologists see them gathering a unique ecosystem. They even see their floods as natural events, floods that are nothing but water crossing a line that has been drawn in a moment of choice. Geographers, too, see rivers as natural features on the earth's surface, tasked to drain water off landmasses, while geologists see them shaping the earth, eroding

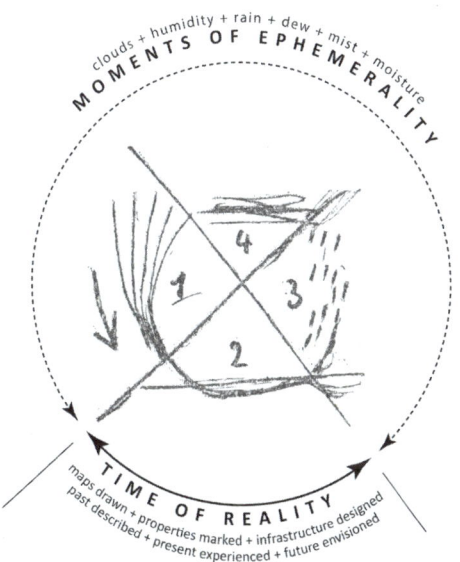

Fig. 3: Rivers are products of anchoring in a particular moment of the water cycle. With this moment chosen to be the time of reality, other moments become moments of ephemerality. Thus, rain, mist, and clouds are visitors in a place where rivers reside.

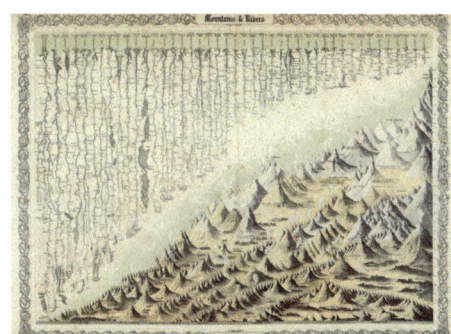

Fig. 4: G. W. Colton, "Mountains & Rivers" (Source: Colton, 1856)

The choice of the moment of flow formation is significant. In this moment,

ground and building alluvial plains. Historians and archaeologists certainly do not hesitate to place the existence of rivers beyond culture. With rivers serving critical infrastructural needs for water supply, irrigation, drainage, transportation, and power, and with an edifice of powerful ideas built upon its banks, including the city and civilization, we would be hard-pressed to find anybody today who would want to challenge the choice of anchoring time in the moment of flow formation.

Yet the moment of flow formation cannot be assumed to be everyone's choice. We suspect that there are people who have chosen other moments of the hydrologic cycle in which to anchor their existence, their language, and the things they see constituting nature. As such, what archaeologist Brian Fagan calls the "clash of cultures" that followed the European discoveries in the fifteenth to eighteenth centuries, which he saw as "a progressive confrontation between [...] societies living in totally incompatible worlds," could well be a clash of lives anchored in different moments of the water cycle. These are places where efforts were made by erstwhile colonial governments to impose, through education, maps, technologies, and a "development" agenda, the separation of land from water; and to cultivate people to appreciate the economic, ecological, aesthetic, and hydraulic possibilities that result from this separation. Their efforts continue today in the hands of independent governments. These are also places where infrastructures, ways of life, and imagination grounded in rain and other moments of water continue to be reduced to the informal, the uncer-

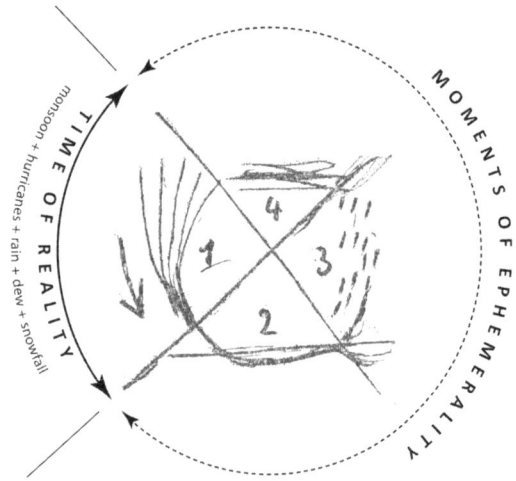

Fig. 5: People could choose to anchor in the moment of precipitation. It will be the ground of another time and another place.

tain, the ephemeral, the relative, the nomadic, the primitive, the exotic, and, not surprisingly, the unmappable.

We see here a more fundamental starting point of design; one that constructs possibilities that stem from asking, what if we drop anchor in another moment of the water cycle? What if India, a country that continues to be ridden with the "informal," is seen as a rain terrain rather than a river landscape, a place where the monsoon is resident rather than an annual visitor that stays for a season? What about the East Coast of the United States, where hurricanes—carriers of rain for a shorter and less predictable time than the monsoon—have been made terrifying and unwanted visitors to a coast firmly anchored in the moment of flow formation of the hydrologic cycle? Does this moment afford another approach to designing the coast?

The Case of the Bengal Delta: Mouth of the Ganges River

Despite the overwhelming presence of monsoons in India, rain is presented in school textbooks, government gazetteers, and scientific treatises as a visitor in a land where rivers have been granted residency. Indeed, rivers here are not only an intrinsic part of the subcontinent's infrastructure, they are also considered sacred, particularly the Ganges. Millions venerate this river as a goddess, Ganga. Her "real" abode, they say, is in "the highest heaven."[5] The story of her descent to earth is told in a number of ancient Sanskrit texts as being initiated by King Bhagiratha. Only the celestial waters of this goddess, he was told, could reconstitute the 60,000 sons of his ancestor, King Sagara. They had been reduced to ashes by Sage Kapila, whose meditation they had interrupted when they found him in possession of their father's sacrificial horse that had been sent out by the king to roam the world. If someone possessed this horse it meant a call to war. After others before him failed to persuade Ganga to come down from her abode in the sky, it was left to Bhagiratha. His asceticism impressed the gods, and they convinced Ganga to descend; but they worried that the earth would shatter under her fall. Shiva offered to mediate by taking her fall on his head. Ganga, it is said, then flowed down his hair and, led by Bhagiratha, reached the netherworld, where she reconstituted Sagara's sons.

Millions of people read this story as portraying a river descending by the "locks" of Shiva's hair. They see this river beginning at the end of the Gangotri glacier in the Himalayas and extending 1,569 miles to meet the sea via the Bengal Delta. Here, writes Amitav Ghosh in *The Hungry Tide*, "the braid comes undone," dividing "into hundreds, maybe thousands, of tangled strands," channels which form "an immense archipelago of islands."[6]

Mapmakers have long tried to capture these strands on paper, beginning with the geographer Ptolemy in the second century, who, with information from sailors, drew five channels fanning out from a point.

Fig. 6: Detail of Ptolemy's, "Tabula Asia X", in La geografia di Claudio Tolomeo Alessandrino (source: Ptolemy, 1564).

The number varies in later maps, particularly those drawn following the arrival of the Portuguese in the early 1500s, and then again following the arrival in the 1600s and 1700s of a number of European trading companies who set up "factories" in the delta. When the English East India Company turned from merchant to ruler and acquired the delta in the second half of the 1700s, they sought to map it with precision. James Rennell was assigned the task. He pursued it with as much creativity as diligence, and in a place where he saw water rise and fall as much as fifteen feet, "tracts of land [...] swept away in the course of one season as would astonish those who have not been eye witnesses to the magnitude and force of the mighty streams occasioned by the periodical rains of the tropical regions," and where vast swaths of ground become "inland seas" and "swampy morasses" for a time, he separated land from water, forming a ground of clear

Fig. 7: James Rennell, "The Delta of the Ganges with the Adjacent Countries on the East: Comprehending the southern inland Navigation," A Bengal Atlas, 1781. Rennell counted eight mouths of the Ganges: "In tracing the sea coast of the delta, we find no less than eight openings; each of which, without hesitation, one pronounces to have been in its time, the principal mouth of the Ganges."

and distinct islands and channels, at least on paper.

His language of islands and channels became the official language of government. W. W. Hunter, a pioneer of the government gazetteer that informs officials about their region and locality, describes the delta as a multiplicity of islands gradually falling in height from an apex toward the sea, where they become "a sort of drowned land, covered with jungle, smitten by malaria, and infested by wild beasts; broken up by swamps, intersected by a thousand river channels and maritime backwaters." Those to the north were relatively fixed, "locked into their channels," while the islands in the south were "in an unfinished state." But many of these unfinished islands were settled following Rennell's survey, a feat that required clearing the jungle and raising the surveyor's line into an embankment to keep water out, often after extending and filling earth in an act known as "reclamation." For much of the time these islands are below the level of the sea, their vulnerability exacerbated by heavy rains and their mud embankments in constant need of vigilance.

The few islands left unsettled, but still foraged by settlers on adjacent islands, are protected as a UNESCO World Heritage site for the "ecological processes" of "island formation" that they display and for their jungles, which, far from being smitten by malaria and infested by wild beasts, are seen to be populated by a diversity of mangrove species that are believed to be exceptional and of great value. Be-

sides, they provide a barrier against a surging sea—a "coastal defense" that absorbs the force of storms.

Janapadas in Ganga

There is much to suggest that the mouth of the Ganges is an estuary rather than a delta. For one thing, the tide extends far inland. A number of maps from the fifteenth and sixteenth centuries show a meeting ground of river and sea that is more bay-like than delta-like. Charles Lyell, author of the influential text *Principles of Geology*, which ran into twelve editions between 1830 and 1875, describes the sea reaching to the "heads of the delta" over 200 miles inland on a regular basis when rivers ran low in the non-rainy season. He singled out two heads for attention, one on the Ganges and the other on the Brahmaputra, but the bay, which is still discernible, receives numerous other rivers that have long defied the single apex of a delta. They introduce a complexity and variation from across the diverse terrain of northern India, the Himalayas, Tibet, and the eastern ranges. Here, one can imagine a moment when runoff consumes the entirety of the bay with rain, and another time when a surging sea consumes it just as entirely.

However, even though an estuary accommodates more fluidity and complexity than a delta, it still anchors the moment of flow formation when water seems containable with lines. This is a moment that is increasingly defied not merely by exceptional

events such as hurricanes and ts-
unamis, but by tides and monsoon
downpours on a regular basis. Is it
possible to anchor Bengal in a moment of precipitation? In this moment
the story of the descent of Ganga will
be heard differently, with another eye
and imagination. Shiva here would let
the goddess down not the locks of
his hair, but down each of his infinite
hairs. Her descent then will not picture a river as much as rain. Here,
Ganga does not flow as the Ganges
does, in a course to the sea; she is
rather held in soils, aquifers, glaciers,
living things, snowfields, agricultural
fields, tanks, terraces, wells, cisterns,
even the air, all for a multiplicity of
durations that range from minutes
and days to centuries and eons.
She soaks, saturates, and fills these
places before overflowing in a multiplicity of ways only to be held again.
Bhagiratha's task of leading her to a
netherworld is much more challenging, much more mysterious, much
more befitting of the infinite capacity
of the gods. Unlike the Ganges, her
source is not in a point or points, but
in clouds. Also unlike the Ganges, her
course cannot be drawn in a map, her
'routes' being too complex, emergent,
and changing, besides occurring
across a vast cross section extending
from the sky deep into the earth. The
only anchor she offers people is the
time of her descent. It is celebrated
each year at the coming of the monsoon with the Ganga Dasahara festival.

Here, Ganges and Ganga, names
that scholars use interchangeably in
the belief that they refer to the same

thing—namely, a river—in fact refer to
two different things. Ganges refers to
a river, a linear flow of water draining
land to the sea or some lower ground.
Ganga, on the other hand, refers to a
rain terrain, a nonlinear field of hol-
dings of rain driven to saturation and
then overflow, only to be held again
and again. Everything participates
in holding rain when it arrives on the
winds of the monsoon. As one author
put it, "With the monsoon the tempo
of life and death increases. Almost
overnight grass begins to grow and
leafless trees turn green. Snakes,
centipedes, and scorpions are born
out of nothing. At night, myriads of
moths flutter around the lamps. [...]
Inside rooms, the hum of mosquitoes
is maddening."[8] A world such as this
is not divided between land and water; instead, there is an appreciation
for gradients of wetness, a depth of
material across air, water, and earth.

Settlement in a rain terrain such
as the Ganga does not occur on
land across a line from water (or
exotically, on water). It rather occurs
on the slopes of *janapadas*, a word
that translates as "footholds." These
raised grounds, many of them built
up with earth, anchor in a rain terrain
with infrastructure that facilitates
practices on a slope, practices
that respond to the rise and fall of
wetness. Importantly, *janapadas*
are called out not by area but by
trajectories that intersect upon
them and extend toward open
horizons. These trajectories, which
are activated by movements, anchor
janapadas in a network; in turn,

janapadas anchor networks. Raised grounds like the *janapada* were noted in other places, such as in Egypt and Mesopotamia by Herodotus, and in India by Alexander's men. Of the monsoon that arrived in Egypt from the Ethiopian highlands around the summer solstice, Herodotus writes: "The whole country is converted into a sea, and the towns, which alone remain above water, look like the islands in the Aegean. At these times water transport is used all over the country, instead of merely along the course of the river."[9] It is said that he believed that "the size of the Nile at its swelling is its natural one."[10] If this is true, he saw the equivalent of *janapadas in* the Nile as a rain terrain, rather than *on* the banks of a river. As he put it, mounds operated in a field that reached "all over the country, instead of merely along the course of the river."[11]

Today, *janapadas* in rain terrains have lost out to settlements on riverbanks. Operations on their slopes that once held the rains of the monsoon and worked their overflow by means of tanks, fields, and jungles have given way to leveled grounds protected from the high waters in rivers by mud embankments while being fed by canals, pipes, drains, and other extensions of a river system. In a time when these embankments are being considered to be built in concrete amid disasters blamed on rain and a rising sea, reinstituting the *janapada*, its gradients, and its open network offers a more resilient alternative.

The Case of the Chesapeake Bay: The Coastline of the Tidewater Region

The Chesapeake Bay is, without a doubt, an estuary: a number of rivers meet the sea through it. Its edge is complex and its varying salinity does not just reach up rivers, it reaches into the creeks that run into the rivers, and the rills that run into the creeks. The bay forms an intricate coast that harbors unique ecologies and species, many of which move between freshwater and saltwater.

Fig. 8: European settlers to America brought with them the idea of land separated from the sea with a clear and distinct line. Among the earliest map of this line in Virginia is John White's *La Virginea Pars*, 1585.

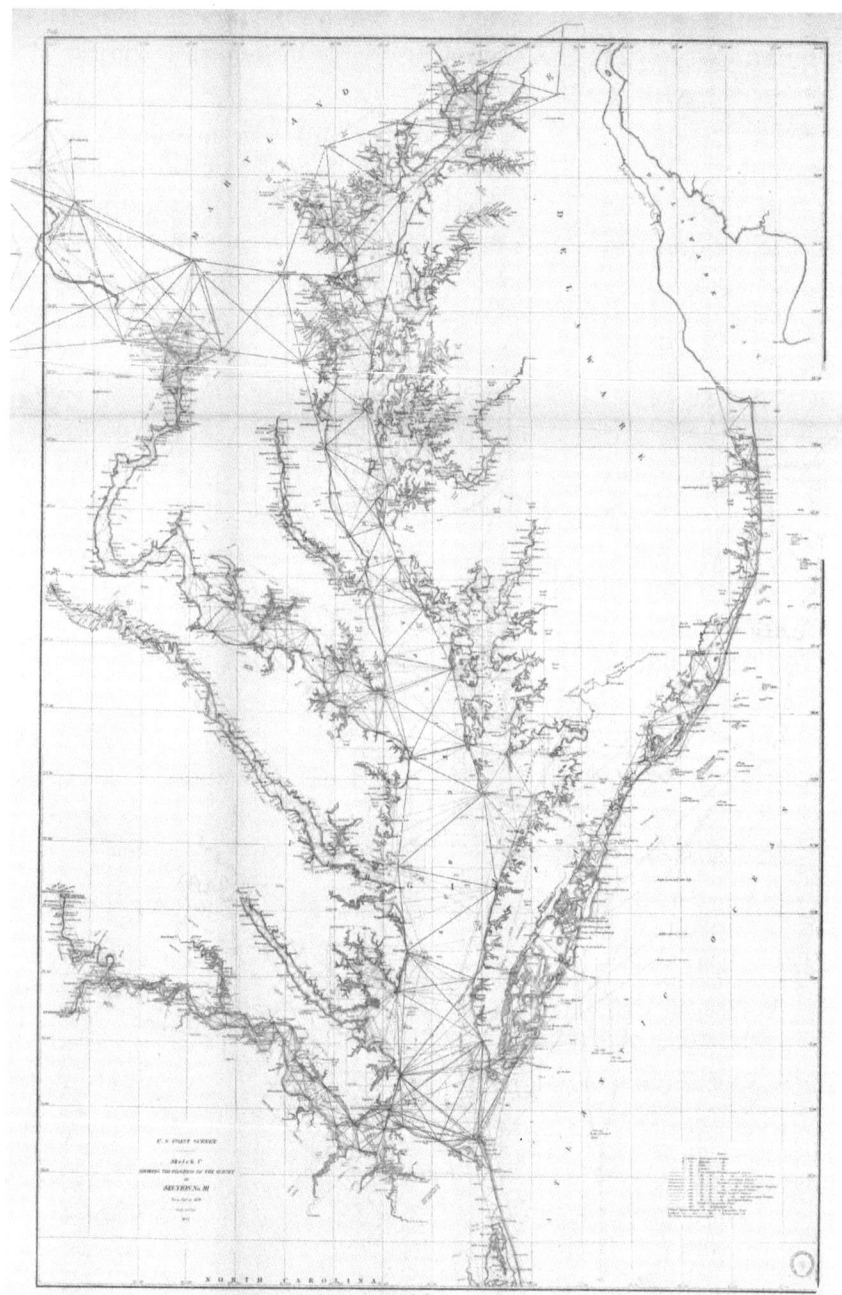

Fig. 9: The coast drawn by White
would be affirmed by trigonometrical
surveyors in the 1800s, as in this
map of the Chesapeake Bay. E. &
G.W. Blunt, Map of Part of Virginia,
Maryland and Delaware, 1861.

354

When Europeans arrived on this coast with ambitions for settlement, they brought with them the coastline. One of the earliest drawings of this line was by the artist John White in 1585, *La Virginea Pars*.

In 1587 White returned at the behest of Sir Walter Raleigh as leader of a group of over 100 colonists. But the colony that he was instructed to begin, called Virginia, on Roanoke Island, did not take root. However, two decades later the English set a firm foot on land that they separated from water with a clear and distinct line, a line respected not just for the separation it made, but also the property that it marked. It was the making of place famously at odds with the "native peoples" encountered by Europeans post-1492. These people were seen to lack the concept of possession (and civilization), a lack that would inspire the legal concept of *terra nullius*, meaning land not belonging to anyone. The concept was used to justify European occupation in Australia, Africa, and the Americas until 1973, when the International Court of Justice ruled it indefensible and recognized the peoples of these places as "first inhabitants." But does the concept of *terra nullius* really stem from the idea of possession, or does it stem from a preferred moment of the water cycle when Europeans could claim possession, most effectively by means of the map? This is a moment probably as unfamiliar to the natives as maps were, or perhaps it was ephemeral to them because they chose to anchor their time in the moment of precipitation, a moment exemplified by the hurricane

that prevented John White from looking for his famous "lost colony."

A month after setting up his colony on Roanoke, White had to return to England to get supplies for a colony unable to live off the land (and water). He could not come back for three years, and when he did, the colony was no more. He was not able to search for survivors; a hurricane was bearing down on them and his captain refused to stay. White never returned but others would; in 1607, the settlement of Jamestown was founded. These settlers drew the coast with a firmer line, doing so when it was not raining.

Fig. 10: Hurricane Sandy caused much damage to the East Coast of the United States in October 2012, doing much to erase the coastline plotted so meticulously in maps, but it also situated recovery efforts in the context of rising sea levels.

This line has been threatened and often erased by hurricanes, and each time, after some debate, dissent, and marginal change, it has been redrawn. Hurricane Sandy in 2012 is the most recent hurricane to erase the coastline not merely in Virginia, but up and down the East Coast. Its destruction was tremendous. The debate that it has instigated is seen in a different light than previous hurricanes. It is framed by climate change, which is discernible in global warming and sea-level rise with consequences expected in the increasing frequency of hurricanes and larger amounts of rain.

The Lower Chesapeake has already experienced a rise of fifteen inches in the last eight decades. One option being discussed is to defend the coastline against an advancing sea with seawalls and gates, including one across the entrance to the Chesapeake Bay. This option is not just difficult to implement because of the intricate nature of the coastline; it also forces a reliance on pumps, besides being detrimental to species that live and move between freshwater and saltwater. A second option being considered is to retreat from the coastline, allowing it to be erased and replaced by a "higher" line. In the face of these two alternatives, we ask: What if we see rain and hurricanes not as outsiders but as events that make us re-evaluate the very idea of a coastline? What if we see the coast in a moment of rain?

"Fingers of High Ground" in a Rain Terrain

There is another reading of the coast in the tidewater region of Virginia. It is not divided between land and water but structured by fingers of high ground. These grounds grow from higher fingers and extend into lower ones. Their fall is complemented by the rise of the webs between them, webs that in a moment of flow formation have been characterized hierarchically as rills flowing into creeks, creeks flowing into rivers, and rivers flowing into the bay. However, in a moment of precipitation, fingers and webs are merely two different "directions" of the same ground that operates by a dynamic gradient of wetness—high to low, low to high.

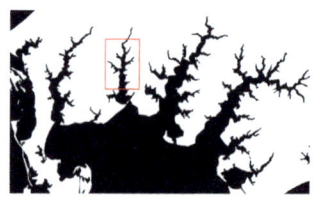

Fig. 11: Fingers structure the relative high ground of the Lower Chesapeake, falling from larger ones to smaller ones. The same ground can be read the other way, as webs that structure the relative low ground, rising from larger ones to smaller ones.

Fingers and webs are not just another reading of "nature's ground"; they are also another reading of existing settlements with an eye and an imagination driven to appropriate and make gradients of wetness. Design here is necessarily opportunistic, seeking out places that allow a meaningful

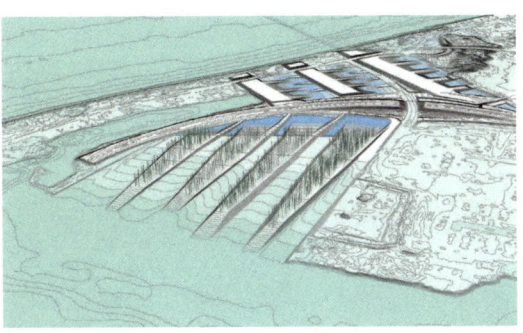
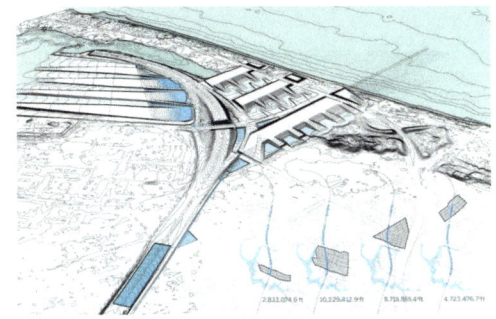

<u>Fig. 12 and 13:</u> We choose two sites in Norfolk to demonstrate how gradients for fingers of high ground can be opportunistically discerned and developed. Each site presents unique topographical challenges and has inherent infrastructural, ecological, productive, and "emergency" value: Lambert's Point, where rail lines and shipping piers meet on the Elizabeth River; and Willoughby Spit on the Chesapeake Bay.

Lambert's Point is home to a coal-exporting facility and a wastewater treatment plant. The rail lines that meet this facility extend inland on a ridge flanked by warehouses that are currently transitioning to postindustrial uses. It is an opportune site to initiate a finger of high ground. This finger begins with a number of smaller fingers on the Elizabeth River, one of which is a "living barge/raft pier" in association with the waste-treatment plant, and gathers into a single high ground that continues inland as an infrastructural corridor along the rail track. This spine, upon which we propose a public walk/bike way, reaches down along slopes designed with emergency facilities, public amenities, biotic cleansing of waste, fields, parks, forests, and housing to rain-holding systems that gather webs of low ground.

Created by a hurricane in the mid-1700s, Willoughby Spit is a sandbar with settlement comprised primarily of beach houses, a school, and a fishing pier that extends far into the Chesapeake Bay. Route 64, a US highway and a primary evacuation route in an emergency, is an opportune high ground in association with the low-lying housing. The finger here is organized along a constructed raised ground that begins in a "living research pier" in the bay and continues inland as a new ground for an elementary school and shelter in place. It connects to Route 64, modified to accommodate a rainwater holding and overflow system. Over time we see other fingers developing off this spine and off the high ground afforded by the highway. They "turn" the settlement from confronting the bay to meeting it at points, while accommodating various wetland and temporal uses in the web of low grounds that gather between them.

357

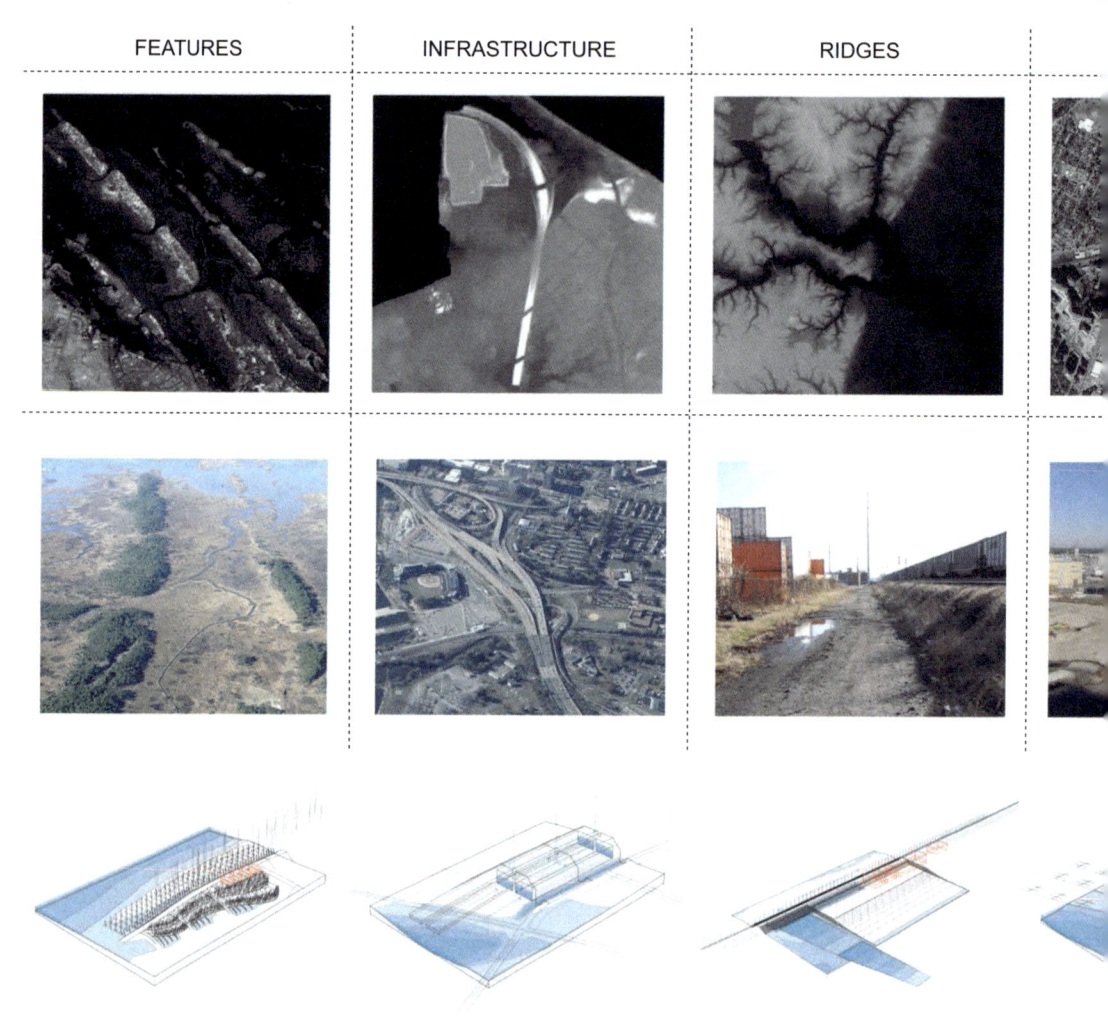

| FEATURES | INFRASTRUCTURE | RIDGES |

LOBLOLLY PINE HUMMOCKS   HIGHWAY RESERVOIRS   DEVELOPMENT SPINES

Fig. 14: There are a number of places in the natural and built environment of the Lower Chesapeake that can be read with an imagination toward developing fingers of high ground, places where there can be a meaningful gradient between falling rain and rising tide. They include the loblolly pine hummocks, which can be raised for communities endangered by rising seas; elevated highways that can be modified and extended to hold rain; ridges that can be thickened to provide critical services and shelter-in-place opportunities; parking lots and retail stores that can again be designed to hold rain; and piers that can be widened to harbor and nurture a range of ecologies besides attenuating waves.

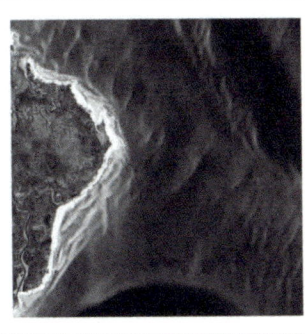

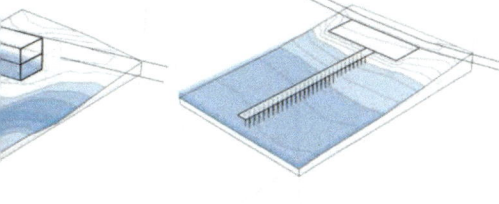

LOTS   LIVING PIERS

complementarity of falling rain and rising tide. Unlike a ground enclosed by seawalls and gates that requires "completion" in order to be effective, fingers and webs enjoy an autonomy that allows their conception and construction to be open to time, growth, and replication with a sense of experiment, adaptability, learning, and strategy. They protect by accommodating rising and falling tides rather than confronting the sea, avoiding the catastrophes that can result from the failures of walls, gates, and pumps.

The design of fingers of high ground drives us to rework the way we understand "land use," which is typically seen in terms of exclusive areas of the earth surface. In the moment of rain, land use can be infused with an appreciation of section, direction, and time, such that occupancies on high ground can extend opportunistically and temporally to low ground; and those on low ground can extend in the same way to high ground. Here, humans are not the only beneficiaries; organisms that occupy gradients of salinity stand to gain as well, particularly in the face of rising seas, when entire ecological gradients are shifting up. Add to this the possibility that fingers of high ground can be an emergent process both in their construction and in their accommodation of risk, and design can become a powerful means of turning the coast from a continuous line to one of cumulative gradients.

Over four decades ago, architect Kevin Lynch asked, "what time is this place?" The evidence of time, he writes, "is embodied in the physical world." And the image of time "is crucial for individual well-being and also for our success in managing environmental change, and that the external physical environment plays a role in building and supporting that image of time." We have suggested that this image of time, exemplified in features such as the coastline and the riverbank, is conceived and constructed in a particular moment of the hydrologic cycle when it can be believed that we have the capacity to keep land and water apart. This choice has made events such as the monsoon and the hurricane outsiders. The possibility of anchoring in another moment of water and, as such, conceiving and constructing "another time and another place" where the monsoon and hurricane are insiders, opens new horizons for designing the coast. Both the *janapada* and finger of high ground exemplify this possibility. The more we study them, the more their infrastructure potential, stemming as it does from accommodating rather than confronting water, makes sense in the face of rising seas. At the very least, they expand the conversation on coastal resilience.

1. *Encyclopaedia Britannica*, 15th ed., s.v. "river."
2. Biologist William Amos writes that this cycle is an "infinite river," flowing from sea to sky to earth and back to the sea, where it is "born again as it had been and would be, every moment of earthly time." William Amos, *The Infinite River: A Biologist's Vision of the World of Water* (New York: Random House, 1971), 244.
3. Robert E. Horton, "The Field, Scope, and Status of the Science of Hydrology," in *Transactions of the Geophysical Union* 12 (1931): 192.
4. Robert Kandel, *Water from Heaven: The Story of Water from the Bing Bang to the Rise of Civilization, and Beyond* (New York: Columbia University Press, 2003), 6–7.
5. Diana L. Eck, *India: A Sacred Geography* (New York: Harmony Books, 2012), 131.
6. Amitav Ghosh, *The Hungry Tide* (New Delhi: HarperCollins Publishers, 2004), 6–7.
7. W. W. Hunter, *A Statistical Account of Bengal: District of the 24 Parganas and Sundarbans*, vol. 1 (London: Trubner & Co., 1875), xiii–xiv.
8. Khushwant Singh, "The Indian Monsoon in Literature," in *Monsoons*, ed. Jay S. Fein and Pamela L. Stephens (New York: John Wiley & Sons, 1987), 37.
9. Herodotus, *The Histories,* bk. 2, 97, trans. Aubrey de Sélincourt (London: Penguin Books, 2003).
10. *Diodorus of Sicily*, trans. C. H. Oldfather, vol. 1, bk. 1 (New York: G. P. Putnam's Sons, 1933), 135.
11. Herodotus, *The Histories*, bk. 2, 97.
12. Kevin Lynch, *What Time Is this Place?* (Cambridge, MA: MIT Press, 1972), 1.

Image Sources:

Paul Klee, *The Thinking Eye* (New York: George Wittenborn Inc., 1964).

Robert E. Horton, "The Hydrologic Cycle," in *Transactions of the Geophysical Union*, vol 12, 1931.

J. H. Colton and Company, 1856, David Rumsey Historical Map Collection.

Ptolemy, *La geografia di Claudio Tolomeo Alessandrino* (Venetia: Appresso Giordano Ziletti, 1564; Kislak Center, University of Pennsylvania).

Geography and Oil:
The Territory of Externalities

Design Earth (Rania Ghosn and El Hadi Jazairy)

Urban analyses have a tendency to focus upon the realm of the cityscape, speaking of that which lies beyond only with reference to its effect upon the city. But taking a view that encompasses and makes visible territorial infrastructures—such as that of oil—can articulate design's environmental agency, suggest Design Earth's Rania Ghosn and El Hadi Jazairy.

In his 1997 book *Homo Geographicus*, Robert Sack notes, "We humans are geographical beings transforming the earth and making it into a home." He adds that the consequences of our geographical agency are more pressing because we are now "geographical leviathans."[1] Such a large transformation of the earth differentiates between economic value attributed to extracted resources and unproductive or environmental costs or by-products, such as pollution, public health, and the degradation of shared resources. The term "externality field" commonly refers to such territorial transformations, which are invisible from urban centers, insofar as a substantial portion of the infrastructure of urbanization remains unaccounted for.[2] Although urban infrastructures reach out to geographies beyond the city, the discourse of urbanism often abstracts territorial infrastructures severing and divesting the city from the environmental costs of urbanization. Many urban analyses leaves out how infrastructures—for example, those of fossil fuel in the twentieth century—have shaped geographies. Such "designed" abstractions are powerful tools to contain and essentialize (hence depoliticize) infrastructure in the planning for present and future energy territories.

If a city-centered worldview has served to abstract the political and spatial dimensions of territorial infrastructures, could the representation of territorial infrastructure expand the scale of the urban to account for the earth and involve it in public and disciplinary controversies? Design Earth has developed an approach that drafts geographic portraits of infrastructure as both a political and aesthetic project, to make such resource territories into matters of concern.[3] The drawings engage infrastructure as a grand question of design: a concern, site, scale, and aesthetics. They make visible the unaccounted-for spaces of "technological externalities"—of energy, trash, space debris—to subsequently channel such matters of the earth into speculative scenarios.

Figs. 1–3: "Das Island, Das Crude," *After Oil*, 2016.

Fig. 2

Fig. 3

From Resource Metabolism to Resource Territories

The extraction of resources requires the de-territorialization and re-territorialization of matter—from the extraction pit to world market—or what has been conceptualized as a metabolism. Promulgated by discoveries regarding the vascular system, the "ideology of circulation" draws on physiological analogies to conceptualize the geographic footprint of urbanism. Urbanization is typically represented as a circulatory system, the veins and arteries of which extend across the land and are to be freed from all possible sources of blockage.[4] While all very significant, such conceptualization does not sufficiently emphasize the infrastructural relations that underpin the harvesting of the earth's materials and the formation of urban settlements.[5] The natural sciences, Donna Haraway reminds us, "are stories with a particular aesthetic, realism, and a particular politics, commitment to progress."[6] They instrumentalize an image of the objectivity of science, in particular as they naturalize the infrastructures of circulation and accumulation, blurring the relations between the political economy of circulation and the emergent forms of territorialities. By favoring homeostasis or balance, these worldviews also overlook blockage, friction, and violence, all the inevitable corollaries of circulation.

Rather than metabolism, territory might better conceptualize the spatial condition of the circulation of resources.[7] Historically, the management of natural resources has been mediated and enabled by the consolidation of power over nature in the form of the concession territory, a right granted by a central political authority to extract value. Territory is "a rendering of space as a political category: owned, distributed, mapped, calculated, bordered, and controlled,"[8] and as such is *reformed* with every claim over space. "The relation to the earth as property," as Marx claims in *Grundrisse*, is hence "always mediated through occupation of the land and soil, peacefully or violently."[9] In *Terror and Territory*, Stuart Elden draws on two etymologies of territory: *terra*, "piece of earth," a terrain that sustains and nourishes the people; and *terrere*, "to frighten," a place from which people are warned off, and which is closely associated with the maintenance and survival of the state over its territory. The linkage between "terror" and "territory," Stuart Elden insinuates, "is more than merely coincidental. [...] To occupy territory is to receive sustenance and to exercise violence."[10] In rentier economies, which derive all or a substantial portion of their national revenues from renting out resources, the management of resource metabolism is entrusted to the sovereign state. Territory thus intertwines the control of economic resources with the governance of population and the settlement and security of the nation-state. It is reordered by resource infrastructures rather than eroded by metabolic flows.

Portrait of Oil Infrastructure

The largest single item in international trade both in value and weight, oil requires a large infrastructure for extraction, transportation, and distribution. The exploitation of oil is grounded in multiple forms of territories. It is enabled by the political authority of the sovereign state to legitimatize extraction rights and demarcate zones of operation. Often deployed in peripheral areas, oil infrastructure "develops" the region by deploying roads, ancillary services, and security posts. Fixating itself in space, infrastructure materializes a territory—simultaneously epistemological and geographical—that harnesses its own geography of places and relations. In this framework, the resource system is a "technical zone," a set of coordinated but widely dispersed regulations, calculative arrangements, infrastructures, and technical procedures that render certain objects or flows governable.[11] "Closely following the oil," as Timothy Mitchell suggests, means "tracing the connections that were made between pipelines and pumping stations, refineries and shipping routes, road systems and automobile cultures, dollar flows and economic knowledge, weapons experts and militarism," all of which do not respect the boundaries between the material and the ideal, the political and the cultural, the natural and the social.[12]

Riding the wave of neo-Malthusian scarcity claims, a growing body of design projects has proposed to reconcile the imperatives of energy, economy, and ecology.[13] They define the energy issue to be tackled as an inherent "problem of the environment" or "problem of carbon," the responses to which are further environmental fixes that resole the "trash crisis," manage "energy security," or reverse "dry futures." Drawing on the imagery of objectivity—on a myriad of tables, diagrams, charts, and graphs—these projects serve to tame uncertain futures and contain political disagreement on how to organize the world and its resources. Under the heavy weight of scientific data-scapes and the crippling guilt of the environmental age, the representational approach of these projects invites the public "to switch off our aesthetic vigilance" when it comes to political ecology.[14] Their response to the context of crisis does not question the socio-spatial infrastructures of the present environment or their associated environmental externalities. By reproducing infrastructural fixes and geographic abstractions, these projects are likely to yield (uneven) future worlds similar to those that underpin the current crisis.

At a time when the energy-economy-environment triad is at the forefront of design concerns, it is important to avoid a "green" or "clean" urbanism that perpetuates the separation of urban infrastructure from the more expansive territory it occupies and produces. Counteracting the violence of abstraction, the representation of infrastructures within an geographic field upholds the political

Figs. 4–6: "Strait of Hormuz
Grand Chessboard," *After Oil*,

significance of spatializing technological systems and their processes, sites, objects, and externalities. This approach responds to a condition of designers increasingly being compelled to address and transform larger contexts that had previously been confined to the domains of engineering, ecology, or regional planning. This has prompted designers to reexamine their tools and play the synthesizing role that geography had aspired to play between the physical, the economic, and the representational, opening up the formal repertoire and political project of architecture. In this geographic worldview, landscapes of energy, waste, and water are not framed in isolation as things in themselves, but are drawn in relation to other attributes of the territory, such as topography, political lines, species population, mythologies, and cultural associations. Such political ecology of the earth shifts the agency of the drawing from the consensus of matters of fact toward the controversies of matters of concern. "A matter of concern," Bruno Latour explains, "is what happens to a matter of fact when you add to it its whole scenography, much like you would do by shifting your attention from the stage to the whole machinery of a theatre."[15] He goes on to list the attributes of matters of fact that "begin to render a different sound, they start to move in all directions, they overflow their boundaries, they include a complete set of new actors, they reveal the fragile envelopes in which they are housed." They accept contingency;

in fact, they are political *because* they are open to multiple contradictory interests. Matters of concern are populated and disputable. They demystify a picture-perfect image of progress and a singular politics of improvement in favor of the perpetual construction of contested uncertainties.

What are the aesthetics of such portraits of infrastructure? Echoing Donna Haraway in the practice of "speculative fabulation," we are reminded that it "matters what matters we use to think other things with; it matters what stories we tell to tell other stories with,"[16] and we might add that it matters what drawings we etch the earth with. Rather than the mapping view from above, which favors the space of logistics and flows, the sectional drawing that cuts through the layers of the earth becomes the privileged way of seeing territory. Nauseated by the environmentalist shade of "bright green," these drawings explore the possibilities of an ecological aesthetics, which builds on surrealism, to make explicit unexplicated cultural relations. "Dark ecology," as Timothy Morton refers to it, "puts hesitation, uncertainty, irony, and thoughtfulness back into ecological thinking."[17] The resultant portraits of infrastructure highlight the political and ethical implications of our impermanent Earth, all while imagining fantastic survival and adaptation strategies that invite us to make sense of the world and reenvision it in ways that generate inquisitive, delightful, and potentially subversive responses.

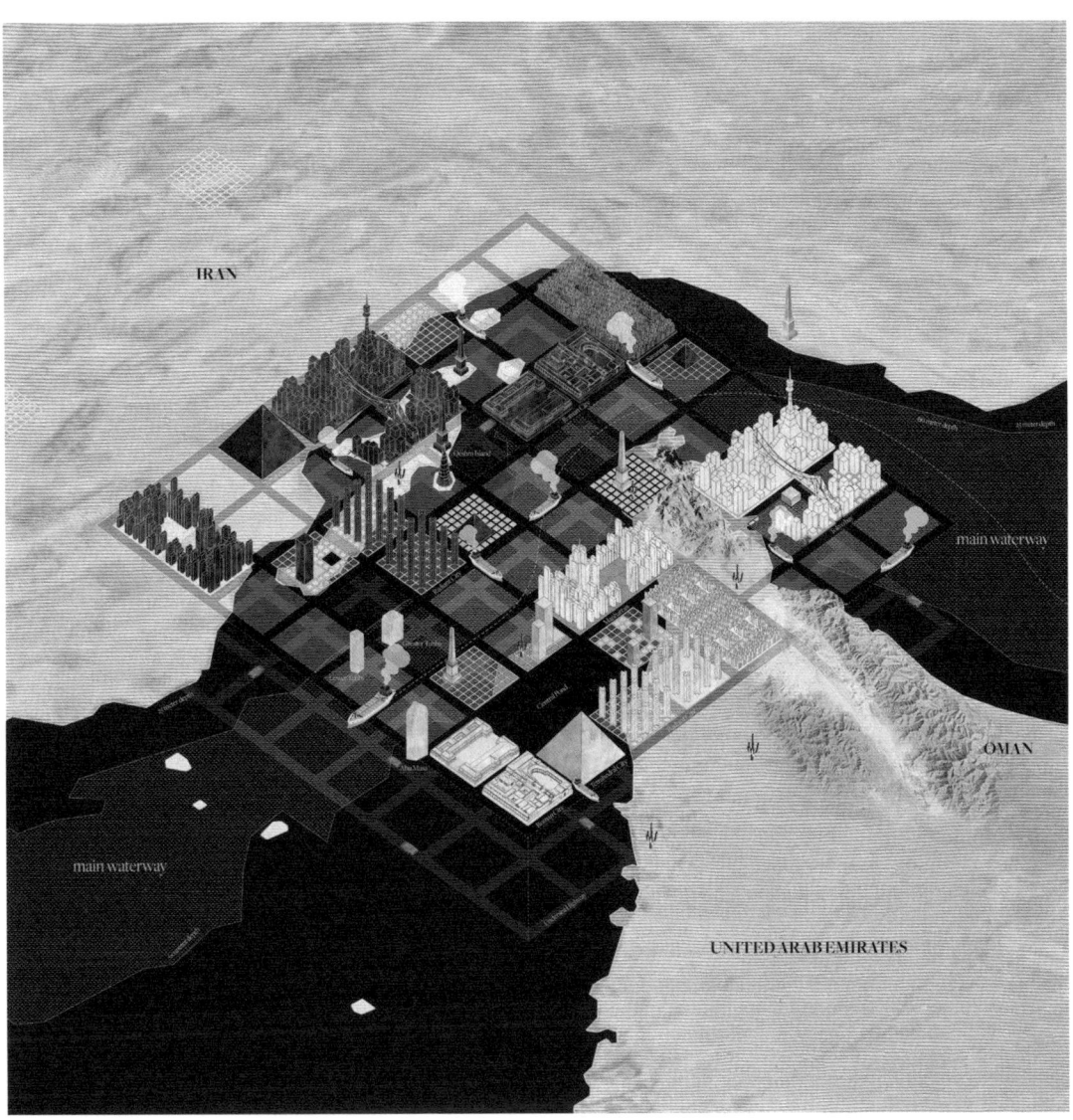

Fig. 5

369

Fig. 6

After Oil

What is the agency of architecture in making visible and speculative the geographic transformations associated with the deployment of infrastructure in resource territories? *After Oil* deploys the agency of architectural representation in three speculative tales that are staged in a future when the Persian Gulf and the world will transition away from fossil fuel forms of energy. These stories are a reflection on the present condition: they stage and extrapolate critical issues of today's oil landscape to reveal the energy systems on which modern life is dependent, and the long-term consequences of the current fossil-fuel regime. Through speculative drawings of the post-oil future, *After Oil* critically engages the future and present geographies of oil in the Gulf region. The projects chart matters of concern for sites of extraction (Das Island), transit logistics (Strait of Hormuz), and the slow violence of climate change (Bubiyan Island). *After Oil* renders visible the embeddedness of the oil system in the region and invites us to imagine the long-ranging effects of such a crude relationship with the earth.

1. Das Island, *Das Crude* (Figs. 1–3)

Das Island is a major Emirati offshore oil and gas industrial facility. Since the first expeditions in 1953, the island has fueled the urbanization of Dubai and Abu Dhabi, with many of the country's iconic buildings being built from oil wealth. "Das Crude"

makes visible such displacement of value in oil urbanism by imagining the island in relation to a subsurface field of depleted oil reservoirs. The United Arab Emirates' architectural landmarks are indexed in relation to the geological depths and times of extraction. The volume of excavated soil and stone is assembled into an artificial mountain, a landform monument to the age of oil.

2. *Strait of Hormuz Grand Chessboard* (Figs. 4–6)

The Strait of Hormuz is a critical oil-transit chokepoint, with twenty percent of world oil trade moving through its 34-mile-wide passage. The strait was never actually shut down in spite of a persistent geopolitical anxiety over territorial disputes, notably the disagreement between the UAE and Iran over the three islands of Abu Musa, Greater Tunb Island, and Lesser Tunb Island. The "Grand Chessboard" repurposes the strait into a real estate territorial game that is financed by the oil futures of the traditional adversaries across the Gulf. The board game absorbs the three islands among the chess pieces of iconic speculative urban projects.

3. Bubiyan Island, *There Once Was an Island* (Figs. 7–9)

The end of the Persian Gulf War in 1991 was accompanied with what is considered the world's largest oil spill, which drastically affected Kuwait's costal environment. Beyond

Figs. 7–9: "Bubiyan Island, There Once Was an Island," *After Oil*, 2016.

Fig. 8

Fig. 9

9. Karl Marx, *Grundrisse: Foundations of the Critique of Political Economy*, trans. Martin Nicolaus (New York: Vintage Books, 1973), 485.

10. Stuart Elden, *Terror and Territory: The Spatial Extent of Sovereignty* (Minneapolis: University of Minnesota Press, 2009), xxviii–xxix.

11. Andrew Barry, "Technological Zones," *European Journal of Social Theory* 9, no.

the apocalyptic intensity of such a geo-traumatic event, the everyday business-as-usual oil industry, with its increasing rates of carbon emissions, subjects the world to a slower violence in the form of anthropogenic climate change. The flat and low-land Bubiyan Island is one vulnerable to sea-level rise. "There Once Was an Island" gives forms to such invisible threats. It redraws the island's shrinking shoreline, as its highest sixteen elevation mounds are stabilized into an archipelago of edenic islands.

Conclusion

By making visible these infrastructures, the *After Oil* projects articulate design's environmental agency and its appropriate scales of intervention. They show the urgency to question the politics of all proposed (new) contracts with the planet. The drawings furnish the designer with an affection for the whole, to relocate urban existence and action to a planetary scale. A geographic sensibility prompts us to think further about the design of such things as scale and territory. But above all, it elicits an intervention within the workings of power and its representations, in ways that make a difference. The challenge of a geographic imagination is thus not simply to represent these systems and their futures, but to intervene in such representations so as to render visible the inequality between the promises of technological fixes and the distribution of geographic externalities.

375

Endnotes

The Design Earth After Oil project team is Rania Ghosn + El Hadi Jazairy, with Jia Weng, Rawan Al-Saffar, Kartiki Sharma, Hsin-Han Lee, Namjoo Kim, and Sihao Xiong.

1. Robert Sack, *Homo Geographicus* (Baltimore: Johns Hopkins University Press, 1997), 1.
2. David Harvey, *Social Justice and the City* (Oxford: Blackwell, 1973), 57–60.
3. See Rania Ghosn and El Hadi Jazairy, "A Geographic Stroll around the Horizon," MONU, no. 20 (2014): 12–17; and Rania Ghosn and El Hadi Jazairy, "Hassi Messaoud Oil Urbanism," in *Grounding Metabolism: New Geographies #6*, ed. Daniel Ibañez and Nikos Katsikis (Cambridge, MA: Harvard University Press, 2014), 144–53.
4. Erik Swyngedouw, "Circulations and Metabolisms: (Hybrid) Natures and (Cyborg) Cities," *Science as Culture* 15, no. 2 (2006): 105–21; Erik Swyngedouw and Maria Kaika, "Fetishizing the Modern City," *International Journal of Urban and Regional Research* 24, no. 2 (2000): 120–38.
5. Erik Swyngedouw, "The City as a Hybrid: On Nature, Society and Cyborg Urbanization," *Capitalism, Nature, Socialism* 7 (1997): 65–80; Swyngedouw, "Circulations and Metabolisms"; Matthew Gandy, "Rethinking Urban Metabolism: Water, Space and the Modern City," *City* 8, no. 3 (2004): 363–79.
6. Donna Haraway, *Primate Visions: Gender, Race, and Nature in the World of Modern Science* (New York: Routledge, 1989), 4.
7. David Harvey, *Spaces of Capital: Towards a Critical Geography* (Edinburgh: Edinburgh University Press, 2001), 328.
8. Stuart Elden, "Governmentality, Calculation, Territory," *Environment and Planning D: Society and Space* 25, no. 3 (2007): 562–80.

9. Karl Marx, *Grundrisse: Foundations of the Critique of Political Economy,* trans. Martin Nicolaus (New York: Vintage Books, 1973), 485.

10. Stuart Elden, *Terror and Territory: The Spatial Extent of Sovereignty* (Minneapolis: University of Minnesota Press, 2009), xxviii–xxix.

11. Andrew Barry, "Technological Zones," *European Journal of Social Theory* 9, no. 2 (2006): 23–53; Gavin Bridge, "Global Production Networks and the Extractive Sector: Governing Resource-Based Development," *Journal of Economic Geography* 8, no. 3 (2008): 389–419.

12. Timothy Mitchell, "Carbon Democracy," *Economy and Society* 38, no. 3 (2009): 422.

13. For a more detailed overview on such practices, and in particular the work of OMA in this respect, refer to Rania Ghosn, "Energy Regions: Production without Representation," *Journal of Architectural Education* 68, no. 2 (2014): 224–28.

14. Timothy Morton, *Ecology without Nature: Rethinking Environmental Aesthetics* (Cambridge, MA: Harvard University Press, 2007), 35.

15. Bruno Latour, *What Is the Style of Matters of Concern?* (Spinoza lectures, April–May 2005, Department of Philosophy, University of Amsterdam), 39; http://bruno-latour.fr/sites/default/files/97-SPINOZA-GB.pdf.

16. Donna Haraway, *SF: Science Fiction, Speculative Fabulation, String Figures, 100 Notes—100 Thoughts*, no. 33 (Ostfildern: Hatje Cantz, 2012).

17. Timothy Morton, *The Ecological Thought* (Cambridge, MA: Harvard University Press, 2010), 16.

Document:

The following is a theoretical exposé by Georges Teyssot, architect, scholar, and professor at the School of Architecture of Laval University in Quebec, as well as author of numerous publications, including *A Topology of Everyday Constellations* (MIT Press, 2013). Challenging the prevalent division between architecture and infrastructure, Teyssot draws upon the work of French philosophers Gilbert Simondon and Gilles Deleuze to argue that synergetic alliances between the discipline of architecture and the realm of infrastructural constructions must be sought, allowing the technical object to acquire its aesthetic capabilities when placed in the world—a plaidoyer for an understanding of infrastructure as techno-aesthetic project.

For a Techno-Aesthetic: Infrastructures and Metastable Systems

Georges Teyssot

Infrastructures bring comfort to living spaces. It is urgent to challenge the division (and the divide) between architecture and infrastructure. In order to dissect the notion of infrastructure, one could introduce some of Gilbert Simondon's concepts, such as "key points," listing, among them, antennas and telephone exchanges. These objects—in Simondon's view, both technical and aesthetic, organize the territory. They create key points embedded in the landscape. In a synergetic alliance of technical patterns and natural powers, the new grid establishes privileged places in the world, generating a novel form of *genius loci*. For Simondon, the technical object acquires its aesthetic capabilities against the background of a vaster reality. Types of energy-crossing nodes, these key points confer aesthetic meaning to topography. In building a network, such points are placed in the middle, between things; they form a *milieu*.

I

While examining the question in a geographical (and a topo-graphical)context, one has to redraw a map between design, technology, and landscape.

Techno-Science

Heidegger's anti-scientism is well established.[1] In his essay on the "essence of technology," Heidegger announces that, under the influence of the *Ge-stell* (frame, shelf; by extension: device, apparatus), beings are reported in advance to a stock (*Bestand*) where they wait to be supported by a device, like an article in a warehouse.[2] This understanding of Western technology leads to an "enframing" of all nature as a standing reserve, ready for human purposes.[3] It is not a minor paradox that Heidegger's technophobia has found fertile ground in "leftist" thinkers such as Jacques Derrida, Philippe Lacoue-Labarthe, Giorgio Agamben, and Bernard Stiegler, who (to excessively oversimplify their work) partly based their criticism of technology on Heidegger.

Moreover, an amalgamation occurs, in which science, technology, and capitalism are combined in an arbitrary manner. In a single gesture, the conflation of these three terms criticizes technology as a reductive process; science as a representative project serving the technical, thus mingling with technology; and capitalism operating toward the same result, expanding global commodity trade.

Fig. 1: 47° 42' 10.4" N 70° 06' 44.0" W 2015-19-02

II

Through its simplicity, such a homogenization of political criticism feeds a kind of obsessive catastrophism, seductive to many discourses.[4]

Conversely, it seems urgent and necessary to think of capitalism, science, and technology separately, to the extent that, in their history as in their practice, these three fields may both converge and diverge.[5] Moreover, such "criticism" does not take into account changes since the time of Heidegger. For half a century, the thought about devices—their shapes and rhythms—has undergone fundamental changes, especially since the introduction of finer and cleaner computerized techniques.[6] These open up a world possibly spared the immense devastation of the first industrialization, without (or with less) damage and with fewer disruptions.

An antidote to Heidegger's doom comes from the French philosopher Gilbert Simondon, whose deep understanding of technical objects offers a remarkable return from the bilious and dyspeptic pessimism of the German philosopher. For Simondon, the technical object moves toward a state of organicity, in an intermediate stage between the biological object and the physical object.[7] Simondon's original philosophy overcomes most of metaphysics' historical oppositions (subject/object, form/matter, concrete/abstract, figure/ground, material/immaterial). He develops a thought of the environment (*milieu*) that questions the genesis of individuals and their interaction with the environment, and has developed a thinking about creation and production where the distance between animate and inanimate wanes, as much as that between individual and collective.

Contemporary dominant trends in the history of technology and theory of science are associated with Bruno Latour's books *Science in Action* (1987) and *Pandora's Hope* (1999).[8] These exemplary works are in continuation with the so-called social constructivism program, for which science is first and primarily a social construction. Such a trend confers the status of social actors to technical objects, which is a positive hypothesis. However, social constructivism imposes a relativistic position. The question to ask, as the Canadian philosopher Ian Hacking ultimately wonders, is: A social construction of what? Of ev-

45. Simondon, *Du mode d'existence des objets techniques*, 155–56.
46. Ibid.
48. Didier Debaise, "Qu'est-ce une pensee relationnelle?," *Multitudes*, no. 18 (2004), 5;8.
49. Gilbert Simondon, *L'individuation à la lumière des notions de forme et d'information*, 225.
50. Victor Petit, "L'individuation du vivant. Sur une intuition simondonienne restée ignorée," *Cahiers Simondon* 1 (2009), 57.
51. Gilles Deleuze, *The Logic of Sense*, trans. Mark Lester and Charles Stivale (New York: Columbia University Press, 1990), 103–4.
52. Paul Valéry, "L'idée fixe," in *Œuvres*, vol. 2 (Paris : Gallimard/La Pléiade, 1960), 215.
53. Gilbert Simondon, *L'individu et sa genèse physico biologique* (Paris: PUF, 1964), 260–64; cited in Gilles Deleuze, *The Logic of Sense*, 104: "The entire content of internal space is topologically in contact with the content of external space at the limits of the living; there is, in fact, no distance in topology; the entire mass of living matter contained in the internal space is actively present to the external world at the limit of the living. [...] *To belong to interiority does not mean only 'to be inside', but to be on the 'in-side' of the limit.* [...] At the level of the polarized membrane, internal past and external future face one another."
54. Gilbert Simondon, *L'individuation à la lumière des notions de forme et d'information*, 24–25; Barthélémy, *Simondon ou l'Encyclopédisme génétique*, 41.
55. Anne Sauvagnargues, *Deleuze, l'empirisme transcendental* (Paris: PUF, 2009), 244.
56. Gilbert Simondon, *L'Individuation à la lumière des notions de forme et d'information*, op. cit., 45.
57. Ibid., 228.
58. *Matrix: machine philosophique*, Alain Badiou, Thomas Bénatouïl, Elie During, ..., et al., new ed., (Paris : Ellipses, 2013), p. 11., l'empirisme transcendental (Paris: PUF, 2009), 244.
59. *Matrix*, op. cit., 139.
60. Barthélémy, *Simondon*, 2014, 212–214.
61. "Allagmatic": The Greek word "allagma" can mean change or vicissitude, but it can also mean that which can be given or taken in exchange, which more genuinely captures the idea of energy exchange in Simondon's usage. https://fractalontology.wordpress.com/2007/11/28/a-short-list-of-gilbert-simondons-vocabulary/]
62. Matrix, op. cit., 141.

A Visual Atlas

Part 4

Compiled by Something Fantastic

Fig. 119: Mauvoisin Dam in Valais,
Switzerland

Fig. 121: The Turkestan-Siberia railroad
under construction in Aika Bulka, Russia

Fig. 120: Concrete highway
bridge in the Swabian Alps, Germany

Fig. 122: Marina City in Chicago, USA
The lower floors of the corn-cob shaped, twin residential
towers, designed in 1964 by Bertrand Goldberg,
serve as one big spiral parking ramp.

Fig. 123: Salvanei Bridge near Mesocco, Switzerland

Fig. 124: Nanpu bridge interchange in
Shanghai, China

Fig. 125: John Hancock Center parking garage
in Chicago, USA The spiral ramp was designed in
1969 by Skidmore, Owings and Merrill (SOM).

Fig. 126: Grate in Berlin, Germany

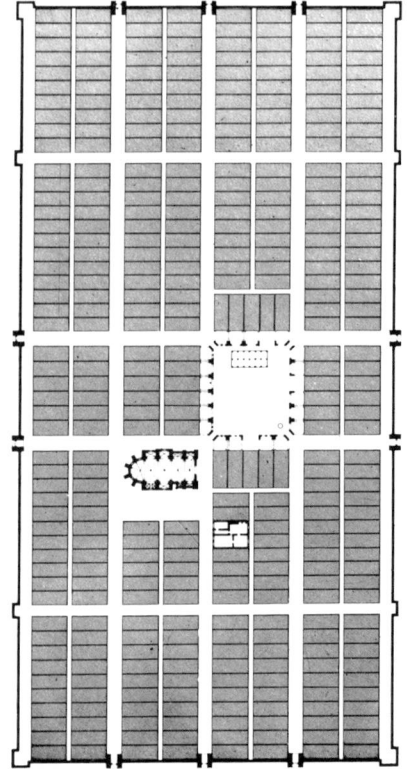

Fig. 127: Gridded street plan of Monpazier, France
Fortified towns like this one, which was planned in 1284,
are known as *bastides* and are numerous
in the south of France.

Fig. 128: Façade of the Ministry of Education
and Health in Rio de Janeiro, Brazil
Sun louvers shade the building designed by
a group of architects that included Lucio Costa and
Le Corbusier in 1936.

Fig. 131: Cadyl horizontal silo
in Young, Uruguay
Eladio Dieste designed
these continuous double
curvature vaults in 1978.

Fig. 132: Free-form wall surrounding the
Royal Court of Lealui, Zambia

Fig. 133: Tent-like roof of King Abdulaziz
International Airport in Jeddah, Saudi Arabia

Fig. 134: Drone Port test structure, Venice, 2006
The drone port project explores the potential of an infrastructural leap,
using drones as an alternative means of transport to remote regions.

Fig. 135: Roman aqueduct
in Segovia, Spain

Fig. 136: Grand Central Terminal
in New York City, USA

Fig. 137: Ponte Vecchio in Florence, Italy
The oldest bridge across the Arno River
houses shops to this day.

Fig. 138: Combined car park and
baseball pitch in Tokyo, Japan

Fig. 139: Museum park in Rotterdam, the Netherlands The parks in Rotterdam are lower than the city itself, doubling as retention basins in case of flooding.

Fig. 140: Doma room of a traditional farm house
on the island of Honshū, Japan
The ground-floor entrance, cooking and storage room is part
of the typical Japanese Nōka farm house typology.

394

Fig. 141: Rua Gonçalo de Carvalho in Porto Alegre, Brazil
Trees on both sides of the residential street form a closed
roof and create the impression of a linear urban forest.

Fig. 142: Breakwater at the Amalfi Coast, Italy

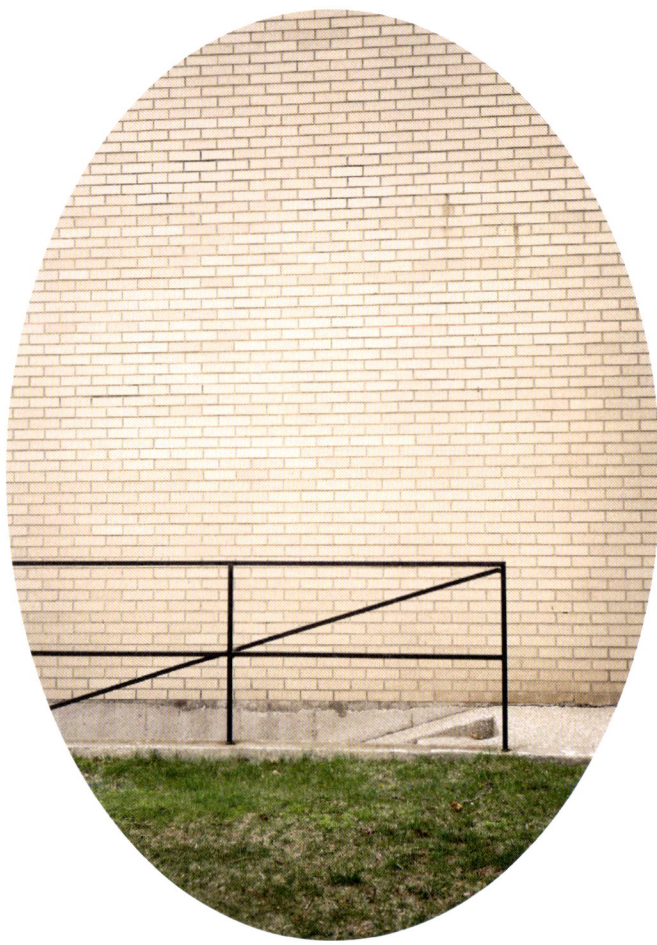

Fig. 143: Handrail at Lafayette Park in Detroit, USA
This housing complex was designed by
Ludwig Mies van der Rohe in 1958.

Fig. 144: Water outlet and utilities in Kyoto, Japan

Fig. 145: Lightweight fishing station off the coast of Vieste, Italy

Fig. 146: Tensile bridge
in Chitral, Pakistan

Fig. 147: Carport in Cairo, Egypt

Fig. 148: New Jersey Turnpike and Bayway Refinery near Newark, USA
This toll road is used by more than 200 million vehicles a year.

Fig. 149: Hangar entrance at the
Offutt Air Force Base in Nebraska, USA

Fig. 150: Alley in Rio das Pedras,
Rio de Janeiro, Brazil

Fig. 151: Awning of a car repair shop in Canaa, Brazil

Fig. 152: Sun cover over a market stand in Cairo, Egypt

406

Fig. 153: Covered sidewalk
in Milan, Italy

Fig. 154: Airship hangar in
Brand-Briesen, Germany
The largest self-supporting hall structure
in the world, originally built as an airship
hangar but never used as such, was
transformed into a theme park in 2003.

Biographies

Marc Angélil is a professor of architecture and design at the Department of Architecture of ETH Zurich and founding partner of agps architecture with studios in Zurich and Los Angeles. His research at the Network City and Landscape (NSL) focuses on social and spatial developments of large metropolitan regions worldwide, with a particular focus on the political economy of territory. He is currently co-authoring a book with Cary Siress entitled *Mirroring Effects: Tales of Territorial Production*, due to be published in late 2017. He is a member of both the Board and the Academic Committee of the LafargeHolcim Foundation for Sustainable Construction.

Tom Avermaete is a professor of architecture at Delft University of Technology. With the chair of Methods and Analysis he focuses on the changing roles, approaches and tools of architects. He is the author of *Another Modern: the Post-War Architecture and Urbanism of Candilis-Josic-Woods* (2005) and co-editor of *Architectural Positions* (2009), *Colonial Modern* (2010), and *Architecture of the Welfare State* (2014). He is an editor of the *OASE Journal for Architecture* and curator of exhibitions such as "Casablanca Chandigarh" (Montreal, 2015) and "Lived-In. The Modern City as Performative Infrastructure" (Antwerp, 2016).

Claudia Bode is a graduate of the Master of Architecture Program at MIT where she also worked in the Urban Risk Lab for several years. She has worked in architecture offices in the US, Germany, and the Netherlands, and taught at Northeastern University as well as the Boston Architectural College. She founded the Kujenga Collaborative and is currently in rural Tanzania working with The Olive Branch for Children, a non-profit organization, on the design and construction of their new buildings.

Neil Brenner is a professor of urban theory at the Harvard Graduate School of Design, where he writes and teaches on critical urban theory, urbanization and geopolitical economy. His books include *Critique of Urbanization* (2016), *New State Spaces: Urban Governance and the Rescaling of Statehood* (2004), and the edited volume *Implosions/ Explosions: Towards a Study of Planetary Urbanization* (2013).

Ricky Burdett is a professor of urban studies at the London School of Economics & Political Science (LSE), and Director of LSE Cities and the Urban Age Programme. He was Chief Adviser on Architecture and Urbanism for the London 2012 Olympics, and architectural adviser to the Mayor of London from 2001 to 2006. He has been a member of the UK's Urban Task Force, a judge in the Rockefeller Foundation's 100 Resilient Cities initiative, and a member of the Hurricane Sandy Regional Planning and Design Competition jury organized by the US Secretary of Housing and Urban Development (HUD). He is editor of

The Endless City (2008), *Living in the Endless City* (2011) and *Innovation in Europe's Cities: A report by LSE Cities on Bloomberg Philanthropies' 2014 Mayors Challenge* (2015).

François Charbonnet is co-founder along with Patrick Heiz of the architecture studio Made in, based in Geneva, Switzerland. After graduating from the ETH Zurich with a thesis supervised by Prof. Hans Kollhoff, he collaborated with Herzog & de Meuron and OMA, before setting up his own office in 2003. In addition to his work in practice, he lecturs frequently and was visiting professor at EPF Lausanne between 2010 and 2001, ETH Zurich between 2011 to 2013 and the Accademia di Archittetura, Mendrisio from 2014 to 2015.

Nancy Couling is an architect. In 2016 she completed a PhD at laboratoire bâle (laba), an architecture and urban design studio of the Swiss Federal Institute of Technology (EPFL), based in Basel. She researched and coordinated the Barents Sea project in 2011 before beginning her doctoral studies on "The Role of Ocean Space in Contemporary Urbanization". In 1995 she formed the interdisciplinary partnership cet-0 in Berlin with S. Schnorbusch & K. Overmeyer, (from 2005, cet-01), focusing on urban design, and taught in the Department of Urban Design at TU Berlin. She is the co-editor of *Barents Lessons: Teaching and Research in Architecture* with Harry Gugger and Aurelie Blanchard (2012).

Salmaan Craig is a lecturer in environmental technology at the Graduate School of Design (GSD), Harvard University, and a Research Associate in the Harvard Center for Green Buildings & Cities where he specializes in materials design and building physics. He previously worked for Buro Happold consulting engineers as a façade engineer, specializing in the design of material systems in extreme climates, such as the perforated, multilayer dome of the Louvre Abu Dhabi. Other projects include the Apple Campus and Bloomberg HQ. He has consulted for Timberland, Abalos & Sentiwtitz and Empressa de Desarollo Urbano, Medellín. From 2010 to 2013 he was part of the specialist modelling group at Foster + Partners.

Dilip da Cunha is an adjunct professor in the School of Design (PennDesign) at the University of Pennsylvania. He is currently completing a book provisionally entitled *The Invention of Rivers: Alexander's Eye and Ganga's Descent* that stems from questioning the natural status given to rivers and the imaging and imagining that this assumption has inspired. He is author with Anuradha Mathur of *Mississippi Floods: Designing a Shifting Landscape* (2001), *Deccan Traverses: The Making of Bangalore's Terrain* (2006). *Soak: Mumbai in an Estuary* (2009), and *Design in the Terrain of Water* (2014).

Carlotta Darò is an assistant professor at the Ecole nationale supérieure d'architecture Paris Malaquais (ENSAPM), where she is also a member of Laboratoire Infrastructure, Architecture, Territoire (LIAT). She is an art historian whose work explores the impact of sound technologies, telecommunications, infrastructures, and media on modern architectural and urban theories. She has published *Sound avant-garde in architecture* (2013) and *Les Murs du Son* (2015), and organized the international conference on *The Architectural Acoustics: Theories, Practices, Cultures* at the Centre Pompidou, Paris, in October 2016.

Michael Dear is an Emeritus Professor in the College of Environmental Design at the University of California, Berkeley. His research focuses on the intersection of cultural geography and the humanities, with a focus on the US-Mexico borderlands. He is the author of *Why Walls Don't Work: Repairing the US-Mexico Divide* (2013), which was awarded the Globe Prize from the Association of American Geographers in 2014. He was co-editor of *Geohumanities: Art, History, Text at the Edge of Place* (2011), has been a Guggenheim Fellowship holder, a Fellow at the Center for Advanced Study in the Behavioral Sciences at Stanford, and in 2014 was elected Fellow of the Learned Society of Wales.

Keller Easterling is a professor of architecture at Yale University, and is an architect, urbanist, and writer. Her books include *Extrastatecraft: The Power of Infrastructure Space* (2014); *Enduring Innocence: Global Architecture and Its Political Masquerades* (2005); and *Organization Space: Landscapes, Highways and Houses in America* (2001). She has also completed two research installations online: *Wildcards: A Game of Orgman* (2000) and *Highline: Plotting NYC* (2002). Her work has been

published in journals such as *Grey Room*, *Volume*, *Cabinet*, *Assemblage*, *Log*, *Praxis*, and *Harvard Design Magazine*. She has exhibited at the 2014 Venice Biennale as well as at Storefront for Art and Architecture in New York, the Rotterdam Biennale, and the Architectural League in New York.

Paul N. Edwards is a professor in the School of Information and the Department of History at the University of Michigan. His research explores the history, politics, and cultural aspects of computers, information infrastructures, and global climate science, including knowledge infrastructures for the anthropocene. He has taught at Sciences Po (Institut d'Études Politiques de Paris), the Oslo Summer School in Comparative Social Sciences, and Eindhoven University of Technology. His publications include *A Vast Machine: Computer Models, Climate Data, and the Politics of Global Warming* (2010) and *Changing the Atmosphere: Expert Knowledge and Environmental Governance*, edited with Clark Miller (2001).

Ross Exo Adams is an assistant professor of Architecture & Urban Theory at the College of Design, at Iowa State University. His research looks at the historical and political intersection between circulation and urbanization and he has published widely on the inherent relations between architectural practice and geography, political and legal theory, political ecology, and philosophy. He has taught at the Bartlett School of Architecture at University College London, the Architectural Association, the Berlage

Institute in Rotterdam, and the University of Brighton. His work has been exhibited at the Venice Biennale, Storefront for Art and Architecture in New York, the Centre of Contemporary Architecture in Moscow, and the Netherlands Architecture Institute in Rotterdam. He is author of *Circulation and Urbanization*, forthcoming from Sage in the Society & Space series edited by Stuart Elden (2017).

Rania Ghosn is an assistant professor at the Massachusetts Institute of Technology School of Architecture & Planning. She is partner of Design Earth, a research-based practice engaged in the relationships between design and geography. Her current research examines the urban condition at the scale of the territory through the lens of technological systems such as those of energy, trash, and agriculture. Her work has been widely published and recognized with several awards, including the Young Architects Prize from the Architectural League of New York and an ACSA Faculty Design Award. She is editor of *New Geographies 2: Landscapes of Energy* (2010), and co-author of *Geographies of Trash* (2015) and *Two Cosmograms* (2016).

El Hadi Jazairy is an assistant professor at the University of Michigan Taubman College of Architecture & Urban Planning. He is an architect and partner of Design Earth, a research-based practice engaged in the relationships between design and geography. His research addresses the agency of design in re-qualifying the urban question at a territorial scale. His work has been recognized with several awards, including the Young Architects

Prize from the Architectural League of New York, Europan 6, and the Regle d'Or de l'Urbanisme. He is editor of *New Geographies 4: Scales of the Earth* (2011), and co-author of *Geographies of Trash* (2015) and *Two Cosmograms* (2016).

Julia King is an architectural designer, creative practitioner, and urban researcher at LSE Cities, London School of Economics & Political Science (LSE). Her research is concerned with housing, sanitation, infrastructure, inclusive development, urban planning, and participatory design processes. She has won numerous awards including a Holcim Award (2011), SEED Award for 'Excellence in Public Interest Design' (2014), and Emerging Woman Architect of the Year (2014). She has taught at the Bartlett School of Architecture, the Architectural Association and the CASS, Faculty of Art, Architecture and Design, where she completed a PhD-by-practice entitled *Incremental Cities: Discovering the Sweet Spot for making town-within-a-city*.

Jesse LeCavalier is an assistant professor in the College of Architecture & Design at the New Jersey Institute of Technology. An architect interested in logistics and urbanism, his current work investigates the spatial consequences of Walmart's logistics operations. He has published in design journals such as *Cabinet*, *Public Culture*, and *AD*. He is co-author, with John Harwood and Guillaume Mojon, of *This Will _ This* (2009), and has contributed to the collections *Infrastructure as Architecture* (2010), *Cities of Change:*

Addis Ababa (2009), and *Deviations: Designing Architecture* (2008).

Carlos Lopes is Executive Secretary of the Economic Commission for Africa (ECA) at the level of United Nations (UN) Under-Secretary-General. His research and writing on development issues specializes in strategic planning. He was a member of the United Nations Development Programme executive team and serves on the advisory boards of the Kofi Annan Foundation, World Economic Forum African Council, ISCTE Lisbon University Institute, Instituto Ethos, Geneva Graduate Institute of International & Development Studies, and journals such as *Géopolitique Africaine, African Sociological Review, African Identities and Strategic Review for Southern Africa.* He has authored and edited numerous books, and taught at universities and academic institutions in Lisbon, Coimbra, Zurich, Uppsala, Mexico City, São Paulo and Rio de Janeiro.

Charlotte Malterre-Barthes is an architect and urban designer. Involved with the chair of Prof. Dr. Marc Angélil since 2011, she directed the MAS in Urban Design at ETH Zurich from 2014 to 2016, investigating the urban dynamics of Cairo and is currently completing a PhD on food and territories, with Egypt as case study. She co-founded the urban research and design office OMNIBUS and co-edited *The Book, The School, The Town* (2013) and *Housing Cairo-The Informal Response* (2016).

Anuradha Mathur is a professor in the Landscape Architecture Department, at the University of Pennsylvania School of Design (PennDesign). She is an architect and landscape architect, and in collaboration with her partner, Dilip da Cunha, has focused her artistic and design expertise on the cultural and ecological issues of contentious landscapes. She is co-author with Dilip da Cunha of *Mississippi Floods: Designing a Shifting Landscape* (2001), *Deccan Traverses: The Making of Bangalore's Terrain* (2006), *Soak: Mumbai in an Estuary* (2009), and *Design in the Terrain of Water* (2014).

Miho Mazereeuw is an assistant professor and founding director of the Urban Risk Lab in the School of Architecture & Planning at the Massachusetts Institute of Technology (MIT). She is known for her work in disaster resilience, working on a large, territorial scale, and with an interest in public spaces and the urban experience. She has taught at the Graduate School of Design (GSD) at Harvard University and the University of Toronto, Canada. As an Arthur W Wheelwright Fellow, she is completing her forthcoming book entitled *Preemptive Design: Disaster and Urban Development along the Pacific Ring of Fire.*

Rahul Mehrotra is principal of RMA Architects in Mumbai and a professor of urban design & planning in the Department of Urban Planning & Design at the Harvard University Graduate School of Design (GSD). He is co-author of *Bombay: The Cities Within* (1995), *Banganga: Sacred Tank* (1996), *Anchoring a City Line* (2000), *Bombay to Mumbai: Changing Perspectives* (1997),

413

and *Architecture in India since 1990* (2010). He also co-authored *Conserving an Image Center: The Fort Precinct in Bombay* (1994), a study that lead to the historic Fort area being declared a conservation precinct in 1995.

Sarah Nichols is a doctoral fellow at the Institute for History and Theory of Architecture (GTA) at the Swiss Federal Institute of Technology (ETH) in Zurich. On behalf of the academic committee of the LafargeHolcim Foundation for Sustainable Construction, she acted as scientific coordinator of the 2016 Forum in Detroit and the 2015 Roundtable in Einsiedeln. She is the editor, together with Marc Angélil, of the book *Reform! Essays on the Political Economy of Urban Form* (2015).

Henk Ovink is the first Special Envoy for International Water Affairs for the Kingdom of The Netherlands and Sherpa to the UN/World Bank High Level Panel on Water. He is also Principal for Rebuild by Design, the resilience innovation competition he developed and led for President Obama's Hurricane Sandy Rebuilding Task Force. He served as Director General for Planning and Water Affairs and Director for National Spatial Planning in The Netherlands. Ovink curated the 5th International Architecture Biennale Rotterdam 2012 "Making City". He initiated the Design as Politics research program at Delft University of Technology and is chief editor of the Design as Politics series published by nai010.

Ilka & Andreas Ruby trained as an architect and an architectural historian respectively. They publish, curate, teach,

and consult on issues around architecture, cities, and communication. Their publications include *Urban Transformation* (2008), *Of People and Houses* (2008/9), *EM2N: Both-And* (2009), *Re-Inventing Construction* (2010), *Sadar + Vuga: A Review* (2012), and *MVRDV Buildings* (2013). They have organized several international symposia and exhibitions on architecture and design, such as the "Min to Max" symposium on affordable housing and the traveling exhibition "Druot, Lacaton & Vassal—Tour Bois le Prêtre." They are the founders of the German architecture debate platform www.bkult.de and of the award-winning architecture publishing house Ruby Press. As of 2016, Andreas Ruby is director of the Swiss Architecture Museum S AM in Basel.

Christian Schmid is a professor of sociology at the Department of Architecture at ETH Zurich. He is a geographer, sociologist and urban researcher who has written and edited numerous publications on Henri Lefebvre and on urban and spatial theory. In 1999 he became the scholarly director of the project Switzerland: An Urban Portrait at ETH Studio Basel, publishing a book of the same name in 2006 which he co-authored with Roger Diener, Jacques Herzog, Marcel Meili, and Pierre de Meuron. He currently works with Neil Brenner on the theorization and investigation of emergent formations of planetary urbanization.

Fiona Shipwright is a writer and editor in Berlin who focuses on architecture, urbanism and culture. A founding member of the &beyond collective, from 2014 to 2016 she was an editor for uncube, the digital magazine for architecture and beyond. Between 2009 and 2014 she worked for the visual arts publisher Phaidon Press in London, first as an editor on titles such as *Art & Place: Site-specific Art of the Americas* (2013), 20th Century Architecture: The Phaidon Atlas (2012) and *Dieter Rams: As Little Design As Possible* (2011), and later on the publisher's emerging digital list. She was the English language editor for the inaugural edition of Make City architecture and urbanism festival in 2014. Her writing has also appeared in *Rhizome, super/collider* and elsewhere.

Cary Siress is an architect and researcher in urban studies at ETH Zurich. He was formerly a professor at the University of Edinburgh and senior researcher in territorial organization at the Future Cities Laboratory in Singapore (FCL). His research pertains to global urbanization processes and how human and material realms become entangled under various political-economic agendas. He is currently co-authoring a book with Marc Angélil entitled *Mirroring Effects: Tales of Territorial Production*, due to be published in late 2017.

Something Fantastic is a design practice founded by three architects, Leonard Streich, Julian Schubert, and Elena Schütz. Since 2016 they direct the Master of Advanced Studies in Urban Design at the chair of Marc Angélil at the Swiss Federal Institute of Technology (ETH Zurich) with a focus on informal and rapidly developing urban contexts. Other research and educational projects include

collaborations with Harvard University and Yokohama GSA. They designed the German Pavilion at the 15th International Architecture Biennale in Venice (2016), have been nominated for the Iakov Chernikhov Prize, and won numerous awards for their design work. Forthcoming publications in 2017 include *Desert Cities* and *The Index for Those Who Want to Reinvent Construction.*

Laurent Stalder is a professor in the Institute for the History & Theory of Architecture (GTA), Department of Architecture (D-ARCH), at the Swiss Federal Institute of Technology (ETH Zurich). The main focus of his research is the intersection between the history of technology and the history and theory of architecture from the nineteenth to the twenty-first centuries. His publications include *Hermann Muthesius, 1861-1927: das Landhaus als kulturgeschichtlicher Entwurf* (2008), *Valerio Olgiati* (2008), *Der Schwellenatlas: von Abfallzerkleinerer bis Zeitmaschine* (2009), and *Fritz Haller: Architekt und Forscher* (2014). His articles have been published in journals, including *AA Files, Arch+, Greyroom, Journal of Architecture, Werk, Bauen & Wohnen,* and *Zeitschrift für Kunstgeschichte.*

Sven Stremke is an assistant professor of landscape architecture at Wageningen University. His research focuses on sustainable landscapes with special attention to renewable energy. He is founding director of the NRGlab, a laboratory devoted to research on energy transition, and Principal Investigator for energy at the Amsterdam Institute for Advanced Metropolitan Solutions. Together with Andy van den Dobbelsteen he edited the book *Sustainable Energy Landscapes: Designing, Planning and Development* (2012), and publishes extensively in leading scientific journals.

Georges Teyssot is a professor in the School of Architecture at Laval University in Quebec City. He has taught architecture at Princeton University, Istituto Universitario di Architettura in Venice, and the Swiss Federal Institute of Technology (ETH Zurich). His publications have been translated into twelve languages and include *Interior Landscape* (1988), *Die Krankheit des Domizils* (1989), *The History of Garden Design* (1991, 2000), *The American Lawn* (1999), *Walter Benjamin: Les maisons oniriques* (2013), and *A Topology of Everyday Constellations* (2013), of which he has edited the French version: *Une topologie du quotidien* (2016).

Geoffrey Thün and Kathy Velikov are associate professors at Taubman College of Architecture and Urban Planning at the University of Michigan, where Thün is also Associate Dean for Research and Creative Practice. They are founding principals of the award-winning design-research practice RVTR. Their work and writing explores the agency of architecture and urban design within the context of dynamic ecological systems, infrastructures, energies, materially and technologically mediated environments, and emerging social organizations. Their work on urban systems and infrastructure has been published in the *OASE Journal*,

Volume, *MONU*, *New Geographies*, and in the book *Sustainable Energy Landscapes* (2012). Thün and Velikov co-authored *Infra Eco Logi Urbanism: A Project for the Great Lakes Megaregion* (2015), and were collaborators on EXTRACTION, the Canadian Pavilion exhibition at the 2016 Venice Architecture Biennale. Their work in composite material systems that operate as thick, sensing, kinetic skins has been published in *Leonardo*, *IJAC*, *JAE*, *eVolo*, *[bracket] Goes Soft*, and featured in the books *Hypernatural: Architecture's New Relationship with Nature* (2015), *Paradigms in Computing* (2014), *Performative Materials in Architecture and Design* (2013), and *Design and Construction of High Performance Homes* (2012). Most recently, their research project "Infundibuliforms: Kinetic Tensile Surface Environments" received a 2016 R+D Awards honorable mention from *Architect Magazine*.

Milica Topalović is an assistant professor of architecture and territorial planning in the Department of Architecture (D-ARCH) at the Swiss Federal Institute of Technology (ETH Zurich), Switzerland. Her research and teaching focus on territorial urbanization, particularly on the relations between cities and their hinterlands. She has worked on projects in different spatial scales and visual media since 2000, and has collaborated on urban design and urban planning competitions and studies with offices in the Netherlands, Belgium and Switzerland. She is author/editor of *Belgrade—Formal/Informal: A Study on Urban Transformation* (2012), *Architecture of Territory—Hinterland: Singapore,*

Johor, Riau (2013), and *The Inevitable Specificity of Cities* (2014).

Simon Upton is director of the Environment Directorate at the Organisation for Economic Co-operation and Development (OECD). In 1981, he was elected to the New Zealand Parliament and became one of the country's youngest Cabinet Ministers holding a wide variety of portfolios, including Environment, Biosecurity, Science and Technology, as well as Health and State Services. He chaired the 7th Session of the UN Commission on Sustainable Development in 1998 and was OECD chair of the Round Table on Sustainable Development from 2001 to 2005. He has been a member of the Board of the LafargeHolcim Foundation for Sustainable Construction since its inception in 2004.

Diane Van Buren is President of Zachary & Associates based in Detroit. Her work integrates urban redevelopment with historic preservation and sustainable development principles to maximize community resources and the energy efficiency of the built environment. In practice for more than 25 years, she has made the redevelopment of Detroit a primary focus of Zachary & Associates. She was Rebuild Michigan Detroit Director at the WARM Training Center between 2007 and 2009, Nonprofit Facilities Center Director at the Nonprofit Financial Fund from 2001 to 2007, and has served on the National American Institute of Architects (AIA) board and the Visitors Board for Wayne State University Honors College.

Felipe Vera is an associate professor in landscape and urbanism and co-director of the Center for Ecology, Landscape & Urbanism at DesignLab UAI. He is also a consultant at the Emergent and Sustainable Cities Initiative at the Inter American Development Bank (IADB). He is curator of the forthcoming Chile Biennale and of Ephemeral Urbanism: Cities in Constant Flux at the Venice Biennale (2016) and Radical Temporalities at the Shenzhen Biennale of Architecture and Urbanism (2015) in collaboration with Rahul Mehrotra. His books include *Kumbh Mela: Mapping The Ephemeral Mega City* (2014), *Andrea Branzi: Ten Recommendations for a New Athens Charter* (2015), *Rahul Mehrotra: Dissolving Thresholds* (2015), and *Ephemeral Urbanism Cities in Constant Flux* (2016).

Jason Young is a professor at and director of the School of Architecture at the University of Tennessee. His academic research explores contemporary conditions of American urbanism in a post-city, digitally organized culture and he has taught at the University of Michigan and the University of California, Berkeley. He was a contributing co-editor for *Stalking Detroit* (2001), an anthology of essays, projects, and photographs concerning Detroit during the 1990s. Recently, he has lectured and published work from a forthcoming book entitled, *Skirmishes with the MacroPhenomenal*. A licensed builder, he has worked in a design and build capacity since 1998, complementing his interests in vivid urban formations in and outside of the city.

417

Image Credits

pp. 356–58, Figs. 11–14 © Anuradha Mathur / Dilip da Cunha
pp. 362–64, 367, 369–70, 372–74, Figs. 1–9 © DESIGN EARTH

Documents

For a Techno-Aesthetic: Infrastructures and Metastable Systems
Figs. 1–3 © Bertrand Rougier

Shades of Gray and a Green Thumb with Out-of-the-Blue Couplings
Figs. 1–3 © Made in

The Planet's Infrastructure
Figs. 1–3 © Simon Upton / OECD

Windowscape
All images © Yoshiharu Tsukamoto

A Visual Atlas

p. 42, Fig. 1 © Edward Schwarz
p. 45, Fig. 7 © Frank Schultze
p. 48, Fig. 11 © David P. Billigton
p. 50, Fig. 12 © Livia Corona
p. 50, Fig. 13 © Len Combrinck
p. 52, Fig. 17 © Christian Kerez
p. 56, Fig. 21 © Guillaume Habert
p. 57, Fig. 23 © Qyd
p. 59, Fig. 27 © UMA Press, Inc. / Alamy
p. 61, Fig. 29 © dbimages / Alamy
p. 67, Fig. 37 © Adrien Fainsilber
p. 72, Fig. 43 © Leo Bruhns
p. 163, Fig. 45 © M. Wolgensinger
p. 166, Fig. 51 © Hugo Schmölz
p. 168, Fig. 53 © Erich Mayer
p. 178, Fig. 53 © Giorgio Vasari
p. 187, Fig. 77 © Fritz Leonhardt

p. 278, Fig. 89 © Fritz Leonhardt
p. 282, Fig. 93 © Fritz Leonhardt
p. 283, Fig. 95 © Library of Congress
p. 284, Fig. 96 © Tom Jeffs
p. 285, Fig. 97 © Silvio Maraini
p. 286, Fig. 98 © Oscar Savio
p. 302, Fig. 115 © Christopher Herwig
p. 379, Fig. 120 © Fritz Leonhardt
p. 390, Fig. 135 © Georg Gerster
p. 396, Fig. 141 © Ricardo Stricher
p. 400, Fig. 141 © Albert Herrlich
p. 404, Fig. 95 © Library of Congress

Fig. 2, 3, 4, 18, 30, 38, 42, 47, 50, 54, 56–58, 60–63, 65–67, 71–73, 79–81, 83, 84, 86, 90, 91, 100, 101, 103, 105, 107, 111, 117, 118, 126, 128, 138, 139, 142–44, 147, 148, 150–53 © Something Fantastic

Donor Acknowledgement

LafargeHolcimFoundation

LafargeHolcim is the global leader in providing building materials and solutions. The Group is a pioneer in seeking and promoting intensive collaboration across all facets of the construction industry to help the world to build better. This includes new developments, such as innovative materials, to be adopted rapidly in the sector and beyond. LafargeHolcim aims to increase the sustainability of construction in social, environmental, and economic terms. In this way, the Group is meeting its responsibilities for the future of the planet and of the global community. A key pillar in this endeavor is the LafargeHolcim Foundation for Sustainable Construction, sponsored by LafargeHolcim and its operational companies in 90 countries.

Since 2003, the Foundation expands and enriches its network of leading experts and technical universities that promote and develop sustainable construction at national, regional, and global levels. It acts as a link between the LafargeHolcim Group and other players along the value chain of the construction industry, including architects, engineers, urban planners, contractors, NGOs, and authorities.

The Foundation has established itself as a globally significant information hub for sustainable construction through its key activities: organizing symposiums for expert discussions, producing technical publications, providing an online knowledge platform and conducting the LafargeHolcim Awards – the world's most prestigious competition for sustainable design.

Together with its affiliated universities on all continents, the Foundation advances the academic discourse of sustainable construction through the LafargeHolcim Forum for Sustainable Construction every three years. The 5th International Forum was dedicated to the topic of "Infrastructure Space" and created an interdisciplinary platform for exchanging ideas and information for 300 architects, engineers, building professionals and experts from all generations and geographic locations. This publication is based on the presentations and findings of this Forum held in Detroit, USA, in April 2016. The LafargeHolcim Foundation wishes to thank everyone involved in editing, designing and publishing this book.

For more information about the LafargeHolcim Foundation and its activities, please visit

www.lafargeholcim-foundation.org.

To find out more about the USD 2 million LafargeHolcim Awards for Sustainable Construction see

www.lafargeholcim-awards.org.

Colophon

Editors: Ilka & Andreas Ruby
Project Editor: Fiona Shipwright,
Sarah Nichols
Design: Something Fantastic (Elena
Schütz, Julian Schubert, Leonard Streich
with Charlotte Schönberger, Sarah
Scherzer and Elsa Lherm Delorme)
Copyediting: Max Bach, Fiona Shipwright
Proofreading: Diana Ibáñez López

A CIP catalogue record for this book is
available from the Library of Congress,
Washington, DC, USA.

Bibliographic information published by
Die Deutsche Bibliothek. Die Deutsche
Bibliothek lists this publication in the
Deutsche Nationalbibliographie; detailed
bibliographic data is available online at
http://dnb.ddb.de

for Sustainable Construction, Zurich
© The contributors for their texts
and images

Font: Azidenz-Grotesk Pro, Regular
Paper: Gardamatt 135g, Munken Print
White 1.5 100g, Circle Offset 70g

Printed in Germany
ISBN 978-3-944074-18-4

http://www.ruby-press.com
https://www.lafargeholcim-foundation.org